Mastering Adobe Captivate 7

Create interactive SCORM-compliant demonstrations, simulations, and quizzes with Captivate 7

Damien Bruyndonckx

PUBLISHING

BIRMINGHAM - MUMBAI

Mastering Adobe Captivate 7

Copyright © 2014 Packt Publishing

All rights reserved. No part of this book may be reproduced, stored in a retrieval system, or transmitted in any form or by any means, without the prior written permission of the publisher, except in the case of brief quotations embedded in critical articles or reviews.

Every effort has been made in the preparation of this book to ensure the accuracy of the information presented. However, the information contained in this book is sold without warranty, either express or implied. Neither the author, nor Packt Publishing, and its dealers and distributors will be held liable for any damages caused or alleged to be caused directly or indirectly by this book.

Packt Publishing has endeavored to provide trademark information about all of the companies and products mentioned in this book by the appropriate use of capitals. However, Packt Publishing cannot guarantee the accuracy of this information.

First published: August 2012

Second edition: February 2014

Production Reference: 1140214

Published by Packt Publishing Ltd.
Livery Place
35 Livery Street
Birmingham B3 2PB, U.K.

ISBN 978-1-78355-988-6

www.packtpub.com

Cover Image by Céline Frère

Credits

Author
Damien Bruyndonckx

Reviewers
Joe Ganci
Anita S. Horsley
James Lang
Jack Massa
Chris Petrizzo

Acquisition Editors
Harsha Bharwani
Kunal Parikh

Content Development Editor
Ruchita Bhansali

Technical Editors
Kapil Hemnani
Edwin Moses

Copy Editors
Alisha Aranha
Sarang Chari
Gladson Monteiro

Project Coordinator
Priyanka Goel

Proofreaders
Simran Bhogal
Maria Gould
Paul Hindle

Indexer
Mehreen Deshmukh

Production Coordinator
Nilesh R. Mohite

Cover Work
Nilesh R. Mohite

Foreword

People have a thirst, an unrelenting thirst for knowledge, learning, and understanding; from the mundane how-tos of life, like changing the washer of a leaking faucet, to learning about the possibility of life on habitable exoplanets millions of light-years away. Computers, e-books, tablets, and smartphones with their access to the Internet have all changed the way we learn in incredible, simply amazing ways; here's a personal example of what I'm talking about.

I recently moved from sunny Ventura, California, to sub-zero degrees Myersville, Maryland, in the U.S. In Ventura, I rented a house with a fireplace I never used; however, in freezing cold Maryland, where I purchased my first home, the fireplace has become a huge deal to keep my family and me warm during extremely cold days and nights.

Renters know when something goes wrong with your rental, it's usually a matter of picking up the phone, calling your property manager who sends out a plumber, electrician, and so on to take care of the problem. This is not so when you're the home owner! As a home owner (if you're lucky enough to be handy), you start wearing dozens of tradesperson hats to fix stuff and perform maintenance on your home. And if you're anything like me, the do-it-yourself (DIY) type on a budget, you rush out and buy a bunch of DIY home repair books with a chapter titled, for example, *How to Unstop a Toilet in Three Easy Steps*, in order to save money.

However, what if your many DIY books don't cover some home maintenance you need insight on? Case in point, fireplaces and how to determine if I need to sweep out the build-up of explosive creosote (wood tar) after burning up cords of wood in the fireplace? So where did I turn to learn about fireplace maintenance? Did I make my way to another bookstore and hope for the best in finding another DIY guide that might cover fireplace maintenance? You know where I'm going with this. The Internet of course! Where thousands of websites, blogs, and videos abound, including wonderful YouTube how-to videos (many made with Adobe Captivate, which publishes directly to YouTube with a few mouse clicks), which provided me with the answers I was seeking in a matter of seconds; all viewable on my phone while sipping my beloved grande extra hot-whipped mocha at my local Starbucks!

I *love* books. Don't get me wrong, books are incredible (I purchase dozens and dozens each year). But in our short attention span and "blurry-eyed-glued-to-multiple-devices era," printed books must extend their reach from the printed page (such as e-book readers) to the Internet or suffer obsolescence in the future.

Thankfully, you hold in your hands a book that accomplishes this! A book that successfully bridges the gap of the printed page wonderfully to the exciting world — the futuristic world of eLearning and mLearning on the Internet and back to the printed page for all of your answers about the incredible world of eLearning and mLearning creation with Adobe's award winning Captivate 7!

As an eLearning solutions consultant for Adobe, I've seen countless incredible examples of what Captivate authors and developers have done with Adobe Captivate 7. From people working in our state, local, and federal government agencies, to K12 through higher education institutions, nonprofits, healthcare, finance, the military, and commercial enterprises worldwide, I'm always knocked out by the fantastic Captivate projects they share with me. And hands down, I've heard countless times a resounding, "I wanted a powerful solution to create my eLearning and mLearning projects, but I also needed the solution to be easy-to-use — both of which Captivate delivered to me."

I'm excited as heck to re-read this book cover to cover since Damien has jam-packed it with so many best practices, tips, and tricks, which even I don't know and it's *my job* to know! Don't delay, start your reading today, and jump into the wonderful world of the eLearning and mLearning authoring tool of choice used by your peers the world over.

Sitting by a safe cozy fire,

Richard John Jenkins

eLearning Solutions Consultant

Adobe Systems

About the Author

Damien Bruyndonckx is a trained elementary school teacher and began his career teaching French as a foreign language in two elementary public schools of Louisiana, USA. In 2001, he returned to his home country, Belgium, and began working as an IT trainer. He soon acquired the title of Adobe Certified Instructor on Dreamweaver, Coldfusion, Acrobat, and Captivate, which allowed him to work for various Adobe-authorized training centers in Europe and participate in many web- and eLearning-related projects for countless customers. In 2009, he went back to teaching in a school. He now works at IHECS, a higher education school of communications, based in Brussels, where he teaches Multimedia and serves as the eLearning Coordinator of the school. Thanks to his work at IHECS, Damien became an Adobe Education Leader in November 2011. Damien also owns a company that provides Adobe Training and eLearning consultancy. He authored *Mastering Adobe Captivate 6* and *Adobe Captivate 7 for Mobile learning*, published in August 2012 and August 2013, respectively, by Packt Publishing. He lives in Thuin (Belgium) with his fiancée and his two children. Damien is a big music lover and occasionally works as a sound and light technician in the entertainment industry. You can follow him on Twitter at `@damienbkx` and contact him by visiting his website at `http://www.dbr-training.eu`.

Acknowledgments

With the release of *Mastering Adobe Captivate 7*, a new adventure comes to an end. This one was a very smooth adventure thanks to the awesome team that has worked with me to make this book a reality.

The first people I would like to thank are the readers of *Mastering Adobe Captivate 6*. Thank you for the extraordinary feedback you gave me through your e-mails, tweets, and comments on my blog. I tried to incorporate your great comments and suggestions in this book and I think it makes it much stronger.

A special mention of the reviewers that have worked on this title with me: Anita, Joe, Chris, James, and Jack, I feel blessed that I could work with you on this project. You are among the best **Captivaters** out there. Your comments and suggestions have made this book much stronger than what it was after the first draft.

I also want to thank the Captivate team in India for putting together such an awesome eLearning application. Special thanks to Allen, Pooja, Vish, and Richard, the extraordinary team of Adobe Captivate evangelists I had a chance to meet and/or work with.

Also, special thanks to the Packt Publishing team that has trusted me once again and allowed me to be a published author for the third time! Big thanks to Priyanka, Harsha, Edwin, Kapil, and their respective teams for this smooth project.

Finally, the one thing that makes this book very special to me is the cover picture. It was taken by my sweet Céline three years ago when we were on holiday in Florida. Céline and I got engaged during that trip, just the day before the picture was taken. I'm so glad that the Packt Publishing team has accepted to use it as the cover of this book.

As you can see, there is a lot of hard work, passion, and love that has gone into this title. I hope you will enjoy reading it as much as I enjoyed writing it for you.

About the Reviewers

Joe Ganci is an eLearning consultant with a long track record. Joe's design approaches and innovative use of tools, such as Adobe Captivate, Presenter, and Acrobat, have caused many to rethink how they design and develop their eLearning and to implement new and better methods. Joe's personal and hands-on style of consulting has kept his services constantly in demand, and he is privileged to have been visited by many clients from all over the world.

He is the President of eLearning Joe, LLC, a custom training and learning company located in Ashburn, VA, right outside Washington D.C. Since 1983, he has been involved in every aspect of learning development. Joe holds a degree in Computer Science and is a published author, having written several books and many articles about eLearning. He is widely considered a guru for his expertise in eLearning development and conducts classes and seminars at commercial companies, government facilities, leading universities, and at many industry conferences. He is on a mission to improve the quality of eLearning with practical approaches that work.

His company, eLearning Joe, LLC, covers all aspects of eLearning analysis, design and development, and evaluation. They help organizations get started in implementing cost savings and higher retention in eLearning using the best combination of design approaches and development tools. They are experts in various tools, including Captivate, Storyline, Raptivity, Roleplay, and ZebraZapps, among others.

Anita S. Horsley is passionate about all forms of teaching and education. She has been conducting instructor-led and train-the-trainer courses since 1998. As a firefighter, she was a State- and National-level Instructor III and as a personal trainer, she received national and international train-the-trainer fitness certifications. As the Training and Development Specialist for the Oregon State Fire Marshal, she implemented, since inception in 2009, the eLearning track and designed and developed eLearning courses for adult learners. She has a Master's degree in Education and is an Adobe Certified Expert in Captivate.

She is the founder and President of CALEX Learning Consultants, LLC. CALEX Learning Consultants, LLC, provides technology-based training solutions to business and local, state, and federal agencies. They provide creative eLearning project design, course/curriculum development, and management of education efforts that are focused on customers' direct goals. Additionally, they train customers on how to build eLearning through the use of Adobe Captivate by offering on line instruction and instructor-led training. Moreover, they provide consultation and project planning and deployment. Their key focus is to develop exceptional engaging and interactive adult educational programs that positively affect agency goals and objectives.

She authored *Fast Track to Adobe Captivate 6, Packt Publishing*, a tutorial course with 40 3 to 5 minute videos that teach you the fundamentals of using Adobe Captivate.

She writes a blog, *Crazy About Captivate*, that provides written and video tutorials on Adobe Captivate. She also provides webinars for ASTD and Adobe and presents at conferences. She is a technical reviewer for Packt Publishing and Adobe. She works with the Charleston Animal Society to teach elementary schools kids about the humane treatment of animals. So also volunteers at Charleston Area Therapeutic Riding to work with kids who have various disabilities riding horses.

James Lang has been an educator for over 15 years, initially as a classroom teacher and now working in corporate education. Currently, James works as a training specialist, developing and delivering a wide variety of training programs including instructor-led and synchronous and asynchronous eLearning for a proprietary software program. He has always had a passion for helping others learn and improve their performance. You can learn more about him on his blog or contact him through his website, `jwlang.com`.

> I would like to thank those who have come before me and lifted me to where I am today.

Jack Massa is the Principal of Guidance Communications, Inc. (www.guidancecommunications.com), where his mission is to make complex information clear. He has designed, developed, and delivered training and eLearning solutions for organizations such as Unisys, Equifax, The Home Depot, InterCall, Digital Insight/Intuit, and many others.

He has a Master's degree in Creative Writing and certificates in Learning Design and Computer Programming. He is an associate fellow at the Society for Technical Communication and was the Vice President of Technology at Greater Atlanta ASTD.

Chris Petrizzo is the Founder of CLIQ Instructional and Performance Solutions, which helps organizations leverage their people by developing and delivering creative, logical, integrated, quality training, both online and in the classroom.

He has developed and facilitated training on personal effectiveness, project management, mind mapping, thinking skills, train-the-trainer courses, communication skills, customer service, management, leadership, and a wide gamut of custom and off-the-shelf software applications. He has worked in sectors including information technology, nonprofit, finance, retail, education, and government.

He holds a Bachelor's degree in Interpersonal Communication and a Master's in Instructional and Performance Technology. He is an Adobe Certified Expert in Captivate and has been using it to develop engaging eLearning for almost 15 years.

He lives in Broomfield, Colorado, which provides him with easy access to the cultural opportunities of Denver, the spiritual richness of Boulder, and the wildness of the Rocky Mountains.

You can contact him through his website, www.cliq.biz.

> I would like to thank my wife Joni for providing that perfect balance of support and pushiness, and knowing when I need to hear I'm doing great and when I need to hear the opposite. There's nobody else I'd rather journey with.

www.PacktPub.com

Support files, eBooks, discount offers and more

You might want to visit `www.PacktPub.com` for support files and downloads related to your book.

Did you know that Packt offers eBook versions of every book published, with PDF and ePub files available? You can upgrade to the eBook version at `www.PacktPub.com` and as a print book customer, you are entitled to a discount on the eBook copy. Get in touch with us at `service@packtpub.com` for more details.

At `www.PacktPub.com`, you can also read a collection of free technical articles, sign up for a range of free newsletters and receive exclusive discounts and offers on Packt books and eBooks.

`http://PacktLib.PacktPub.com`

Do you need instant solutions to your IT questions? PacktLib is Packt's online digital book library. Here, you can access, read and search across Packt's entire library of books.

Why Subscribe?

- Fully searchable across every book published by Packt
- Copy and paste, print and bookmark content
- On demand and accessible via web browser

Free Access for Packt account holders

If you have an account with Packt at `www.PacktPub.com`, you can use this to access PacktLib today and view nine entirely free books. Simply use your login credentials for immediate access.

Table of Contents

Preface	**1**
Chapter 1: Getting Started with Captivate	**7**
Obtaining Captivate	**8**
A glance at the Captivate production process	**10**
Step zero – the preproduction phase	10
Step one – capturing the slides	10
Step two – the editing phase	11
Step three – the publishing phase	11
Touring the Captivate interface	**12**
The first look at the Captivate interface	12
Working with panels	17
Adding and removing panels	20
Moving panels around	22
Creating a custom workspace	23
Renaming and deleting custom workspaces	25
Exploring the sample applications	**26**
Experiencing the Encoder demonstration	26
Experiencing the Encoder simulation	28
Experiencing the Driving In Belgium sample application	30
Experiencing the Encoder Video Demo	31
Discussing the sample apps scenario	**34**
Summary	**34**
Meet the community	**35**
Pooja Jaisingh	35
Bio	35
Contact details	35

Chapter 2: Capturing the Slides — 37
Choosing the right resolution for the project — 38
- What exactly is the problem? — 38
- Resizing the project after the initial shooting — 39
- Downsizing the application during shooting — 39
- Using the panning feature of Captivate — 40
- Using the Scalable HTML Content feature — 40
- Conclusion — 41

Shooting your first movie — 42
- Preparing the application to shoot — 42
- Rehearsing the scenario — 43
  - Resetting the application — 44
- Shooting the movie — 45
  - Enabling access to assistive devices (Mac users only) — 45
  - Preparing Captivate to shoot the movie — 45
  - And... Action! — 47
- Previewing the rushes — 48

The inner working of the Captivate capture engine — 48
- The Full Motion Recording mode — 50

Controlling Captivate during the shooting session — 52
Exploring the preferences — 54
- The automatic recording modes — 54
- Exploring the recording settings — 57
- The Video Demo preferences — 57

Shooting the other versions of the project — 58
- Previewing the second rushes — 60

Shooting with System Audio — 62
The Video Demo recording mode — 64
Automatic and manual panning — 67
Rescaling a project — 69
Summary — 70
Meet the community — 72
- Anita Horsley — 72
- Contact details — 72

Chapter 3: Working with Standard Objects — 73
Preparing your work — 74
Working with the Properties panel — 75
Exploring the objects of Captivate — 77
- The Text Caption object — 77
  - Modifying the content of a Text Caption — 78
  - Creating new Text Captions — 80
  - Formatting a Text Caption — 82

The Highlight Box object	88
Working with the mouse	92
Understanding the mouse movements	92
Formatting the Mouse object	94
Editing a full motion recording	96
Working with images	98
Inserting a slide from another project	98
Inserting an image into a slide	99
Using the image editing tools	101
Inserting a picture slide	101
Extra credit – working with Characters	102
Working with Smart Shapes	104
Formatting a Smart Shape	106
Adding text inside Smart Shapes	109
Working with Text Animations	111
Duplicating slides	113
Converting a Typing object into a Text Animation	114
Extra credit – creating the introductory and ending slides of another project	116
Inserting external animations in the project	117
Inserting a Video file	119
The Equation Editor	122
Using the Align toolbar	**124**
Selecting multiple objects	126
Extra credit – aligning and distributing the remaining objects	128
Working with the Timeline panel	**129**
Using the Timeline panel to select objects	129
Hiding and locking objects with Timeline	130
Using Timeline to change the stacking order of the objects	131
Using Timeline to set the timing of the objects	132
Extra credit – adjusting the timing of the other slides	134
Adding effects to objects	**136**
Combining effects	137
Extra credit – adding effects to images	138
Finishing touches	139
Working with the Library panel	**140**
Reusing Library items	142
Importing objects from another Library	143
Deleting unused assets from the Library panel	144
Summary	**145**
Meet the community	**146**
Lieve Weymeis	146
Contact details	146

Chapter 4: Working with Styles, Master Slides, Themes, and Templates — 147
Working with Styles — 148
Managing Styles with the Properties panel — 148
- Resetting a style — 149
- Creating new styles — 150
- Applying styles — 150
- Modifying a style — 151
- Applying styles automatically — 151

Working with the Object Style manager — 155
- Exporting a style — 155
- Importing a style — 157
- Creating a style in the Object Style Manager — 158

Working with the Themes — 161
The elements of a Theme — 162
- The Master Slides — 162
- The Styles — 165

Creating a Theme — 167
Customizing the Master Slides of the Theme — 167
- Customizing the Main Master Slide — 168
- Adding a Master Slide to the Theme — 169
- Adding Placeholders to the Master Slides — 170
- Applying the Master Slides to the slides of the project — 171
- Modifying a Master Slide — 172

Adding Styles to the Theme — 174
- Styling the titles — 175
- Working with the Swatches panel — 176
- Styling the Smart Shapes using the Swatches panel — 179

Saving the Styles in the Theme — 181

Working with Templates — 181
- Creating a Template — 182
- Adding Placeholder Slides — 183
- Adding the last slides — 184
- Saving the Template — 184
- Creating a new Captivate project from a Template — 185

Summary — 187
Meet the community — 188
- Jim Leichliter — 188
- Contact details — 188

Chapter 5: Adding Interactivity to the Project — 189
Preparing your work — 190
Working with Buttons — 190
- Formatting Buttons — 192
- Using Smart Shapes as Buttons — 195

Branching with Buttons	197
Discovering Rollover objects	**199**
Working with Rollover Captions	200
Working with Rollover Smart Shapes	201
Working with Rollover Images	204
Working with Rollover Slidelets	206
Inserting and formatting a Rollover Slidelet	206
Inserting objects in a Rollover Slidelet	208
Creating a simulation	**211**
Hiding the Mouse object	211
Using Find and Replace	213
Working with Click Boxes	215
Extra Credit – adding the remaining Click Boxes	218
Working with Text Entry Boxes	219
Finishing touches	222
Working with the Drag and Drop Interaction	**223**
Using the Drag and Drop Interaction wizard	224
Using the Drag and Drop panel	226
Using the Drag and Drop Interaction for branching and navigation	228
Objects and Animations in Video Demo projects	**232**
Interactivity in Video Demo projects	232
Standard objects in Video Demo projects	232
Animations in Video Demo projects	233
Using Pan and Zoom	233
Adding Transitions in Video Demos	235
Summary	**236**
Meet the community	**237**
Rod Ward	237
Tristan Ward	237
Contact details	238
Chapter 6: Working with Audio	**239**
Preparing your work	**240**
Adding audio to objects	**240**
Extra credit – adding sound effects to objects	242
Adding background music to the entire project	**243**
Adding audio to slides	**247**
Recording narration with Captivate	247
Setting up the sound system	248
Recording the narration	250
Importing an external sound clip	252
Using the library to import the remaining audio files	253
Editing a sound clip in Captivate	256

Extra credit – synchronizing the audio clips	259
Using Text-to-Speech to generate narration	**260**
Installing the Captivate speech agents	260
Working with the Slide Notes panel	260
Converting text to speech	262
Using the Speech Management window	264
Using the Advanced Audio Management window	**266**
Adding Closed Captions to the slides	**267**
Viewing Closed Captions	270
Closed Captioning a video file	271
Extra credit – adding Closed Captions	273
Summary	**274**
Meet the community	**274**
Allen Partridge	275
Contact details	275
Chapter 7: Working with Quizzes	**277**
Preparing your work	**278**
Introducing the quiz	**278**
Creating Question Slides	**279**
Inserting the first Question Slide	280
Using the Multiple Choice question	283
Understanding the basic question properties	284
Working with Partial Scoring	285
Branching with Question Slides	286
Finalizing the Question Slide	287
Importing Question Slides from a GIFT file	288
Working with the Matching question	289
Working with the Short Answer question	291
Working with the True/False question	293
Adding the remaining Question Slides	294
Working with the Fill-In-The-Blank question	295
Working with the Hotspot question	297
Working with the Sequence question	298
Creating surveys with Likert questions	299
Previewing the quiz	**301**
Creating a Pretest	**301**
The Quiz Preferences	**304**
Setting the passing score of a quiz	306
Working with Question Pools	**309**
Creating a Question Pool	309
Inserting questions in a Question Pool	311

Inserting random Question Slides into the main project	312
Styling the elements of the Question Slides	**314**
Styling the quiz buttons	316
Extra credit – styling the elements of the Question Slides	318
Reporting scores to an LMS	**319**
Understanding SCORM, AICC, and Tin Can	320
Enabling reporting in Captivate	321
Reporting options at the interaction level	321
Setting up project-level reporting options	328
Creating a SCORM manifest file	331
Using Acrobat.com as an alternate reporting method	**332**
Configuring the Captivate project for Acrobat.com reporting	333
Uploading files to Acrobat.com	335
Taking the Quiz	335
Using the Adobe Captivate Quiz Results Analyzer	336
Summary	**339**
Meet the community	**339**
Kevin Siegel	339
Contact details	340
Chapter 8: Finishing Touches and Publishing	**341**
Preparing your work	**342**
Finishing touches	**342**
Checking spelling	342
Exploring the Start and End preferences	346
Discussing the project metadata and accessibility	348
Exploring other project preferences	352
Exporting project preferences	353
Working with the Skin Editor panel	355
Customizing the Playback Controls bar	355
Working with Borders	359
Adding a Table of Contents	361
Applying the same Skin to other projects	366
Publishing a Captivate project	**368**
Publishing a Video Demo project	369
Publishing to Flash	371
Using the Scalable HTML content option	374
Publishing to HTML5	375
Using the HTML5 Tracker panel	375
Publishing the project in HTML5	377
Publishing an eLearning-enabled project	379
Working with the MultiSco packager	382
Publishing to PDF	388

Publishing as a standalone application	390
Publishing as a .mp4 video file	391
Publishing to YouTube	392
Publishing to Microsoft Word	393
Extra credit – publishing to Word	395
Other publishing options	395
Summary	**397**
Meet the community	**397**
Joe Ganci	398
Contact details	398
Chapter 9: Using Captivate 7 with Other Applications	**399**
Preparing your work	**400**
Integrating Captivate with PowerPoint	**400**
Converting an existing presentation to Captivate	401
Viewing the presentation in PowerPoint	401
Creating a Captivate project from a PowerPoint presentation	402
Round Tripping between Captivate and PowerPoint	406
Updating a linked PowerPoint presentation	409
Inserting a PowerPoint slide in a Captivate project	412
Localizing a Captivate project using Microsoft Word	**415**
Exporting the project to XML	**418**
Importing a Photoshop file into Captivate	**419**
Round Tripping between Captivate and Photoshop	422
Exporting to Flash Professional	**424**
Summary	**427**
Meet the community	**427**
Richard Jenkins	428
Contact details	428
Chapter 10: Reviewing a Captivate Project	**429**
Preparing your work	**430**
The review process at a glance	**430**
Distributing the project	**431**
Commenting a Captivate project	**433**
Installing the Adobe Captivate Reviewer application	434
Using the Captivate Reviewer to create new comments	434
Exporting comments	437
Collecting and addressing comments	**437**
Addressing comments in Captivate	439
Using Acrobat.com in the review process	441
Ending a review	441
Summary	**442**

Meet the community	442
Michael Lund	443
Contact details	443

Chapter 11: Variables, Advanced Actions, and Widgets — 445

Preparing your work	446
Working with Variables	**447**
System and user-defined Variables	447
Exploring System Variables	448
Generating text dynamically	449
Extra credit – generating a Quiz Results slide for the Pretest	451
Using user-defined Variables	451
Creating a User Variable	452
Capturing values with Text Entry Boxes	452
Using user-defined variables to dynamically generate text	454
Working with Advanced Actions	**455**
Using Standard Action	456
Automatically turning on Closed Captions with Advanced Actions	456
Extra credit – turning Closed Captions off	459
Using Conditional Actions	459
Creating the necessary variables	460
Assigning a score to each possible answer	462
Giving names to objects	463
Conditionally showing and hiding objects	465
Using a Conditional Action to implement branching with the Pretest	471
Discussing Shared Actions	474
Understanding and using Widgets	**476**
Locating Widgets	477
Understanding the three types of Widgets	478
Using Static Widgets	480
Finding Widgets	482
Adobe Captivate Exchange	482
Blogs and websites	483
Working with Smart Learning interactions	**483**
Working with the Accordion interaction	484
Working with the YouTube Interaction	487
Working with the Web Object interaction	490
Extra credit – working with the Award of Excellence interaction	492
Summary	**493**
Meet the Community	**494**
Josh Cavalier	494
Contact details	494

Index — 495

Preface

Adobe Captivate is the industry-leading solution for authoring highly interactive eLearning content. With Adobe Captivate, one can capture the on-screen action; enhance eLearning projects; insert SCORM, AICC, and Tin Can-compliant quizzes; and publish work in various formats (including Adobe Flash and HTML5) for easy deployment on virtually any desktop and mobile device.

Mastering Adobe Captivate 7 is a comprehensive, step-by-step learning guide to creating SCORM-compliant demonstrations, simulations, and quizzes with Adobe Captivate. The sample projects demonstrate virtually every feature of Adobe Captivate, giving you the expertise you need to create and deploy your own professional-quality eLearning courses.

Mastering Adobe Captivate 7 will guide you through the creation of full-featured eLearning projects including a demonstration, simulation, video demo, and SCORM-compliant quiz.

What this book covers

Chapter 1, *Getting Started with Adobe Captivate*, introduces Captivate as an eLearning solution. It takes you through the tool icons and panels of the Captivate interface. At the end of this chapter, you will be walked through the finished sample applications that you will build during the course of the book.

Chapter 2, *Capturing the Slides*, shows you how to use the screen capture engine of Captivate to capture the slides of your projects. You will also learn how to choose the right size for the projects you have to make.

Chapter 3, *Working with Standard Objects*, explains how to use the standard objects of Captivate to enhance the slides captured in the previous chapter. The standard objects discussed in this chapter include the Text Captions, the Highlight Boxes, the Images, and the Mouse movements.

Preface

Chapter 4, *Working with Styles, Master Slides, Themes, and Templates*, focuses on the cosmetic part of the project. You will learn about themes; create styles and master slides, save them into themes, and create and use templates. This will ensure visual consistency both within a given project and across projects.

Chapter 5, *Adding Interactivity to the Project*, introduces the objects that bring interactivity into the project. These objects include the Rollover objects, the new Drag and Drop Interaction, the Click Box, the Text Entry Box, and the Button. These objects will be used to convert a demonstration into a simulation and to discuss branching.

Chapter 6, *Working with Audio*, explains how to add sound effects on objects, voice-over narration on slides, and background music to the entire project. You will use the text-to-speech engine of Captivate to generate some of the needed audio clips and you will add Closed Captions for enhanced accessibility.

Chapter 7, *Working with Quizzes*, discusses the powerful quizzing engine of Captivate. You will import questions into your Captivate project using various techniques, review each and every question type of Captivate one by one, and integrate them into question pools to generate random quizzes. In the second part of this chapter, you will see how these interactions can be reported to a SCORM, AICC, or Tin Can-compliant LMS for easy tracking of your student's performance.

Chapter 8, *Finishing Touches and Publishing*, in the first part, shows you how to ready your projects for publishing by modifying project-level options and preferences. One of these options is the Skin Editor that will let you customize the playback controls and the table of contents of your projects. In the second part of this chapter, you will make your projects available to the outside world by publishing them in various formats including Adobe Flash, HTML5, video, and PDF.

Chapter 9, *Using Captivate 7 with Other Applications*, will explore the relationship between Captivate and other Adobe and third-party applications. First, you will convert a PowerPoint presentation into a Captivate project. You will then export some Captivate data to Microsoft Word in order to localize a Captivate project. You will also import an Adobe Photoshop file and export the project to Adobe Flash.

Chapter 10, *Reviewing a Captivate Project*, discusses the distribution of the project to a team of reviewers. The reviewers will use the Adobe Captivate Reviewer to comment on your work. Finally, you will import the reviewers' comments into Captivate and address them one by one.

Chapter 11, *Variables, Advanced Actions, and Widgets*, discusses how you can unleash the true power of Captivate. It explains the variables, the advanced actions, the widgets, and the smart learning interactions. These features will help you design and develop highly interactive eLearning content that proposes a unique experience to each and every learner.

What you need for this book

- Adobe Captivate 7 (available as a free 30-day trial on the Adobe website).
- Some exercises require the free Captivate 7.0.1 update patch available on the Adobe website.
- Adobe Media Encoder CS6 or CC (AME CS6 is part of the Captivate 7 download).
- The Adobe Captivate Reviewer and the Adobe Captivate Quiz Result Analyzer, both of which are included in the standard Captivate download. These applications require the AIR runtime to be installed on your system to work. The AIR runtime is available as a free download on the Adobe website.
- A modern web browser with the latest version of Flash Player installed.
- Microsoft PowerPoint 2003 or higher (optional).
- Microsoft Word 2003 or higher (optional).
- Adobe Photoshop CS3 or higher (optional).
- Adobe Flash CS6 or CC (optional).

Who this book is for

If you fit any of the following profiles/criteria, this book is for you:

- A teacher wanting to produce highly interactive eLearning content for your students
- An instructional designer, eLearning developer, or human resources manager working in a training department wanting to implement eLearning in your company
- You use a SCORM, AICC, or Tin Can-compliant LMS and want to produce eLearning content and track the performances of your students
- A webmaster in need of a fun and interactive way to produce an FAQ or a support site
- Interested in eLearning

A basic knowledge of your operating system (Mac or Windows) is all it takes to author the next generation of eLearning content.

Conventions

In this book, you will find a number of styles of text that distinguish between different kinds of information. Here are some examples of these styles, and an explanation of their meaning.

Code words in text, database table names, folder names, filenames, file extensions, pathnames, dummy URLs, user input, and Twitter handles are shown as follows: "Delete all the .flv files present in the videos/MOV folder of the exercise."

New terms and **important words** are shown in bold. Words that you see on the screen, in menus or dialog boxes for example, appear in the text like this: "In the **Click Boxes** section, tick the **Add Click Boxes on Mouse Click** option. Also, tick the **Failure Caption** and **Hint Caption** boxes."

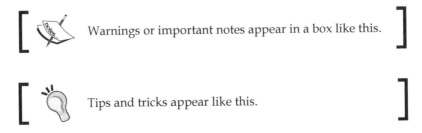

> Warnings or important notes appear in a box like this.

> Tips and tricks appear like this.

Reader feedback

Feedback from our readers is always welcome. Let us know what you think about this book—what you liked or may have disliked. Reader feedback is important for us to develop titles that you really get the most out of.

To send us general feedback, simply send an e-mail to feedback@packtpub.com, and mention the book title via the subject of your message.

If there is a topic that you have expertise in and you are interested in either writing or contributing to a book, see our author guide on www.packtpub.com/authors.

Customer support

Now that you are the proud owner of a Packt book, we have a number of things to help you to get the most from your purchase.

Downloading the example code

You can download the example code files for all Packt books you have purchased from your account at http://www.packtpub.com. If you purchased this book elsewhere, you can visit http://www.packtpub.com/support and register to have the files e-mailed directly to you.

Errata

Although we have taken every care to ensure the accuracy of our content, mistakes do happen. If you find a mistake in one of our books — maybe a mistake in the text or the code — we would be grateful if you would report this to us. By doing so, you can save other readers from frustration and help us improve subsequent versions of this book. If you find any errata, please report them by visiting http://www.packtpub.com/submit-errata, selecting your book, clicking on the **errata submission form** link, and entering the details of your errata. Once your errata are verified, your submission will be accepted and the errata will be uploaded on our website, or added to any list of existing errata, under the Errata section of that title. Any existing errata can be viewed by selecting your title from http://www.packtpub.com/support.

Piracy

Piracy of copyright material on the Internet is an ongoing problem across all media. At Packt, we take the protection of our copyright and licenses very seriously. If you come across any illegal copies of our works, in any form, on the Internet, please provide us with the location address or website name immediately so that we can pursue a remedy.

Please contact us at copyright@packtpub.com with a link to the suspected pirated material.

We appreciate your help in protecting our authors, and our ability to bring you valuable content.

Questions

You can contact us at questions@packtpub.com if you are having a problem with any aspect of the book, and we will do our best to address it.

1
Getting Started with Captivate

Since its introduction in 2004, Captivate has always been the industry-leading solution for authoring eLearning content. In the beginning, it was a very simple screen-capture utility called FlashCam. In 2002, a company named eHelp acquired FlashCam and turned it into an eLearning authoring tool called RoboDemo. In 2004, another company called Macromedia acquired eHelp, changed the name of the product once again, and **Macromedia Captivate** was born. A few months later, Adobe acquired Macromedia and, consequently, Macromedia Captivate became **Adobe Captivate**.

As the years passed, Adobe released Captivate 2, Captivate 3, and Captivate 4, adding tools, objects, and features along the way. One of the most significant events in the Captivate history took place in July 2010, when Adobe released Captivate 5. For the release of Captivate 5, Adobe engineers rewrote the code of the entire application from the ground up. As a result, Captivate 5 was the first version to be available on both Mac OS and Windows. Captivate 5 was also equipped with a brand new user interface similar to that of other Adobe applications, not mentioning an impressive array of new and enhanced tools.

Version 6 was another milestone for Captivate as it was the first version to propose an HTML5 publishing mechanism. Prior to Captivate 6, the main publishing option was Adobe Flash.

As of today, the latest version of Captivate is Version 7. Captivate 7 comes with improved HTML5 support, an enhanced interactions library, good drag-and-drop interaction, the ability to record system audio, and tons of other (not so) small enhancements. With all this power sitting one click away, it is easy to overcharge your projects with lots of complicated audiovisual effects and sophisticated interactions that can ultimately drive the user away from the primary objective of every Captivate project: teaching.

Getting Started with Captivate

While working with Captivate, one should never forget that Captivate is an eLearning authoring tool. At the most basic level, it simply means that you, the developer of the project, and your audience are united by a very special kind of relationship: a student-teacher relationship. Therefore, from now on, and for the rest of the book, you, the reader of these pages, will not be called "the developer" or "the programmer," but "the teacher." And, the ones who will view your finished applications will not be the "users" or the "visitors," but will be called "the learners" or "the students." You will see that this changes everything...

In this chapter, we shall:

- Discuss the available options to obtain Captivate
- Discuss the general steps of the Captivate production process
- Tour the Captivate interface
- Work with panels and workspaces
- View the finished sample applications

Obtaining Captivate

There are three ways to obtain Captivate:

- **The Captivate perpetual license**: This is the old-fashioned way of obtaining the software. You buy Captivate and get a serial number to activate your installation. Once activated, Captivate will be permanently available on your computer, even when you won't need it. With this option, you get all the core functionalities of Captivate and you can start working on your eLearning projects right away! This book works flawlessly with the Captivate perpetual license.

[See the Captivate page on the Adobe website at `http://www.adobe.com/ap/products/captivate.html`.]

You can download and use this version of Captivate free of charge for 30 days. It should be more than enough to go through the exercises of this book. Be aware though that once the trial expires, you will not have access to Captivate unless you convert your trial to a licensed version. This can be a perpetual or a subscription license.

[Download your Captivate 30-day trial from `http://www.adobe.com/downloads/`.]

- **The Captivate subscription**: With this new licensing model, you subscribe to Captivate on a monthly basis. This means that you pay a certain amount of money each month to keep using Captivate.

    The main benefit of the subscription model is that you automatically get all the updates as they are released. The subscription model is the best way to ensure that you always have the latest version of Captivate installed on your system. Subscribed customers also have early access to great new features. Note that the subscription is just another licensing model. With the exception of the subscription-only exclusive updates, the software is identical to the perpetual licensing model.

    > More information on the Captivate subscription model can be found at http://www.adobe.com/products/captivate/buying-guide-subscriptions.html.

    Although the Captivate subscription model is very similar to the way Adobe Creative Cloud works, Captivate is, at the time of this writing, not part of the Creative Cloud.

    > **Captivate and the Creative Cloud**
    >
    > If you already have a Creative Cloud subscription, you'll need another separate subscription for Captivate.

- **Captivate in the Technical Communication suite**: The **Technical Communication Suite (TCS)** is yet another bundle of applications from Adobe. It is designed to create technical content such as help files and user guides. The Technical Communication Suite includes applications such as Adobe RoboHelp, Adobe FrameMaker, Adobe Acrobat Professional, and of course, Adobe Captivate.

    > For more information on the Technical Communication Suite, visit http://www.adobe.com/products/technicalcommunicationsuite.html.

A glance at the Captivate production process

Producing content with Captivate is a three-step process, or to be exact, a four-step process. But only three of the four steps take place in Captivate. That's why I like to refer to the first step as "Step zero"!

Step zero – the preproduction phase

This is the only step of the process that does not involve working with the Captivate application. Depending on the project you are planning, it can last from a few minutes to a few months. Step zero is probably the most important of the entire process as it is where you actually create the scenarios and the storyboards of your teaching project. This is where you develop the pedagogical approach that will drive the entire project. What will you teach the students? In what order will you introduce the topics? How and when will you assess the students' knowledge? These are some of the very important questions you should answer before opening Captivate for the first time. Step zero is where the teacher's skills fully express themselves.

> **Blog post – Scenario-based training**
>
> Make sure you read this series of posts on the official Adobe Captivate Blog. Dr Pooja Jaisingh shares her experience in creating scenario-based training. These posts clearly stress the importance of *Step zero* and give you the first high-level approach to the Captivate production process. The first post of the series can be found at http://blogs.adobe.com/captivate/2012/03/my-experience-with-creating-a-scenario-based-course-part-1.html.

Step one – capturing the slides

When you know exactly where and how you will lead your students, it is time to open Captivate. During this first phase, you will use one of the most popular Captivate features: the ability to record any action you perform on-screen. You will simply use your mouse to perform actions on your computer. Behind the scenes, Captivate will be watching and recording any action you do using a sophisticated screen capture engine based on screenshots. This first step can be compared to shooting a movie. The goal is to acquire the needed images, actions, and sequences. In the movie industry, the raw material that comes out of the shooting is called *rushes*. It is not uncommon for a movie director to discard lots of rushes along the way so that only the very best sequences are part of the final release.

Step two – the editing phase

This phase is the most time-consuming phase of the process. This is where your project will slowly take shape. In this step, you will arrange the final sequence of actions, record narrations, add objects to the slides (such as Text Captions and Buttons), arrange those objects in the Timeline, add title and ending slides, develop advanced interactions, and so on. At the end of this phase, the project should be ready for publication.

Sometimes, the Captivate project you will be working on will not be based on screenshots. In such a case, you will create the slides entirely in Captivate or import them from Microsoft PowerPoint. Importing PowerPoint slides in Captivate will be covered in *Chapter 9, Using Captivate 7 with Other Applications*.

Step three – the publishing phase

This is where you make your project available to the learners, and this is where Captivate really is awesome! Captivate lets you publish your project in the popular Adobe Flash format. This is great since it makes the deployment of your eLearning courses very easy – only the Flash player is needed. The very same Flash player that is used to read flash-enabled websites or YouTube videos is enough to read your published Captivate projects.

Captivate can also publish the project as standalone applications (`.exe` on Windows and `.app` on Macintosh) or as video files that can be easily uploaded to YouTube and viewed on a tablet or smartphone.

When Captivate 6 was released, one of the most significant new features was the ability to publish projects in HTML5. By publishing in HTML5 format, you make your eLearning content available to mobile devices that do not support the Flash technology. The door is open for the next revolution of our industry: Mobile Learning (or mLearning).

> **Blog post**
>
> Make sure you read this wonderful blog post by Allen Partrige, *The How & Why of iPads, HTML5 & Mobile Devices in eLearning, Training & Education* at `http://blogs.adobe.com/captivate/2011/11/the-how-why-of-ipads-html5-mobile-devices-in-elearning-training-education.html`.

Touring the Captivate interface

In this book, we shall cover the three steps of the process requiring the use of Captivate. You will discover that Captivate has specific tools to handle each of the three steps. Actually, each step requires so many options, tools, and features that Captivate has a very large numbers of icons, panels, dialog boxes, and controls available. Therefore, when developing Captivate, Adobe's designers were confronted with a very significant issue—how to display all those tools, features, boxes, and controls on a single computer screen.

To address the issue, the designers at Adobe decided that:

- Depending on the production step you are working on, you do not need the same set of tools at all times
- Some tools relevant for a given project are useless in another
- Each teacher has different working habits, so each teacher should be able to display the tools of Captivate as he/she sees fit
- While some Captivate users have large screens, others have much smaller display areas

These simple considerations helped the Adobe design team create a very flexible user interface.

If you already use other Adobe applications, you'll be on known ground, as the Captivate user interface works the same way as the user interface of the most popular Adobe applications.

The first look at the Captivate interface

When you open the application for the first time, you'll have a default set of tools available. Let's check them out using the following steps:

1. Open Captivate.
2. On the left-hand side of the Welcome screen, click on the open icon.
3. Navigate to the `final/drivingInBe.cptx` file situated in the exercise folder.

>
> **Downloading the example code**
>
> You can download the example code files for all Packt books you have purchased from your account at http://www.packtpub.com. If you purchased this book elsewhere, you can visit http://www.packtpub.com/support and register to have the files e-mailed directly to you.

4. Your screen should look similar to what is seen in the following screenshot:

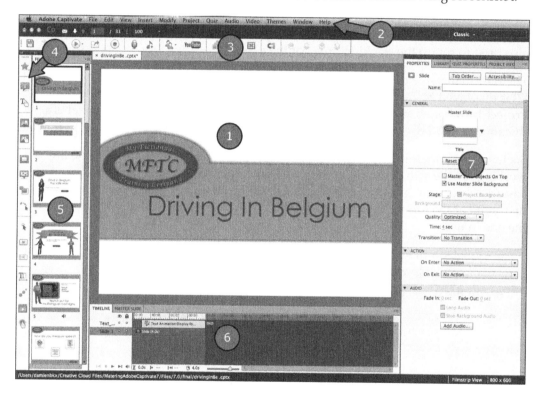

The Captivate user interface is composed of panels laid out around the **stage (1)**. The stage is the main area of the screen. It is where you will lay out the objects that make up each slide of the project.

At the very top of the screen is the menu bar **(2)**. The menu bar gives you access to every single feature of Captivate.

Right below the menu bar is the main options toolbar **(3)**. Each icon of the main options toolbar is a shortcut to a feature that also exists in the menu bar.

Getting Started with Captivate

A special toolbar spans across the left-hand side of the screen from the top down. This is the object toolbar **(4)**. The object toolbar lets you insert new objects on your Captivate slides. This is one of the most important toolbars of Captivate, and one you will use a lot during the course of this book.

The next panel is called the **Filmstrip (5)**. It shows the sequence of slides that makes up your Captivate project. The primary use of the **Filmstrip** is to enable navigation between the slides of the project, but it can also be used to perform basic operations on the slides such as reordering or deleting slides.

At the bottom of the screen is another important panel: the **Timeline (6)**. As its name implies, this panel is used to arrange the objects of the slide as per time. This panel is also used to set up the stacking order of the objects.

The right-hand side of the screen shows a group of five panels. The **Properties** panel **(7)** is displayed by default, while the **Library** panel, the **Quiz Properties** panel, the **Project Info** panel, and the **Swatches** panel are hidden. The **Properties** panel is a dynamic panel. This means that its content depends on the currently selected item.

Such a set of panels is known as a **workspace**. Depending on the project you are working on, the size of your computer screen, your working habits, and so on, this basic workspace might fit your need…or not. The name of the workspace in use is displayed at the top-right corner of the screen. Currently, the **Classic** workspace is the one in use.

5. Click on the word **Classic** in the top-right corner of the screen to reveal a list of available workspaces.
6. In the workspace switcher, choose the **Quizzing** workspace.

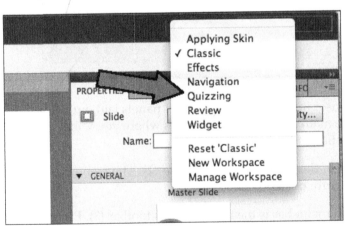

When done, take a close look at the screen. The set of available panels is not exactly the same as before. First of all, the **Filmstrip** panel is displayed at the bottom of the screen, where the **Timeline** panel used to be. The **Timeline** panel is still there but hidden by default, while two new panels (**Master Slide** and **Question Pool**) are shown between the **Filmstrip** and the **Timeline** panels. The left-hand side of the screen has also changed. Right where the **Filmstrip** panel used to be, a big empty panel called **Quiz Properties** is now displayed.

This example clearly shows what a workspace is: a set of panels arranged in a specific layout. While the **Classic** workspace you explored earlier was perfect to perform some basic tasks, the **Quizzing** workspace currently in use is perfect when developing a Captivate Quiz.

7. At the bottom of the screen, click on the **Question Pool** tab to open the **Question Pool** panel.
8. The **Question Pool** panel displays six question slides. Click on each question slide one by one while taking a look at the **Quiz Properties** panel on the left-hand side of the screen.

As you go through each of the question slides listed in the **Question Pool** panel, the **Quiz Properties** panel displays the properties relevant to the currently selected question slide. Note that at the very top of the **Quiz Properties** panel is the type of the active question slide (**Matching**—as shown in the next screenshot—Sequence, Hot spot, and so on).

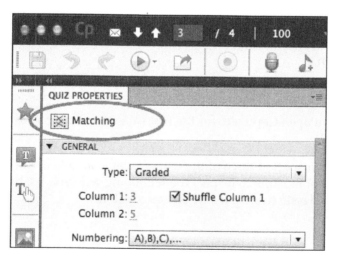

This demonstrates what a dynamic panel is. The **Quiz Properties** panel displays information relevant to the current selection. As the selected item changes, so does the content of the **Quiz Properties** panel. Many panels of Captivate (including the **Properties** panel) work the same way.

9. Reopen the Workspace switcher at the top-right corner of the screen.
10. In the list of available workspaces, choose **Navigation**.

The **Navigation** workspace is applied and, again, the panels are rearranged. This time, the **Branching** panel pops up and covers most of the available screen area. The **Branching** panel is known as a floating panel, because it floats freely on the screen and is not attached (docked) anywhere.

Branching is an important concept in Captivate. When you ask the students to perform an action, they might do either the right or the wrong action. The teacher can make Captivate perform one action when the student does the right thing and another action when the student does the wrong thing. As a result, students experience the Captivate application differently (in other words, take different branches) based on their actions and answers. The branching panel offers a visual representation of this concept.

11. At the top-right corner of the screen, reopen the Workspace switcher.
12. Choose the **Classic** workspace to reapply the original default workspace.

Thanks to these little experiments, you have been exposed to some important basic concepts about the Captivate interface. Before moving on, let's summarize what you have learned so far:

- The Captivate interface is composed of panels laid out around the main editing area called the stage.
- A workspace is a selection of panels in a specific arrangement. No workspace shows every available panel, so there are always tools that are not shown on the screen.
- Captivate ships with seven different workspaces. These workspaces are available in the Workspace switcher in the top-right corner of the screen.
- When you open Captivate for the first time, the **Classic** workspace is applied by default.

You have rapidly inspected three of the workspaces available in Captivate. It is a good idea to take some time to inspect the remaining workspaces. Just make sure you reapply the **Classic** workspace when you are done.

Working with panels

Captivate has a very flexible user interface. You can move the panels around, open more panels, or close the ones you don't need. You can enlarge and reduce the panels or even turn them into icons to gain some space on your screen:

1. Double-click on the **Filmstrip** tab at the top of the **Filmstrip** panel. This collapses the **Filmstrip** panel.
2. Double-click on the **Filmstrip** tab again to expand the panel.

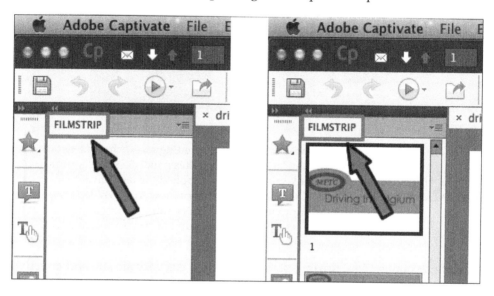

3. Do the same experiment with the other panels of the screen including the **Timeline** (at the bottom) and the **Properties** panel (on the right-hand side).
4. When you are done, reset the **Classic** workspace to its original state by navigating to **Window | Workspace | Reset Classic**.

Collapsing and expanding panels is very simple, and is the first tool at your disposal to customize the Captivate interface. The second tool you will experiment with is the very small double-arrow icon that is displayed on top of every panel or groups of panels. For the **Properties**, **Library**, **Quiz Properties**, **Project Info**, and **Swatches** panel group, this very small icon is located at the far right side of the interface.

5. Click on this double arrow to turn the **Properties**, **Library**, **Quiz Properties**, **Project Info**, and **Swatches** panel group into a set of five icons (see the following screenshot).
6. Click on the **Properties** icon to reveal the **Properties** panel. Click on the same icon again to hide the **Properties** panel.

7. Reveal and hide the **Library**, **Quiz Properties**, **Project Info**, and **Swatches** panels by clicking on their respective icons.
8. Click on the double arrow to toggle the panel group back to its original state.

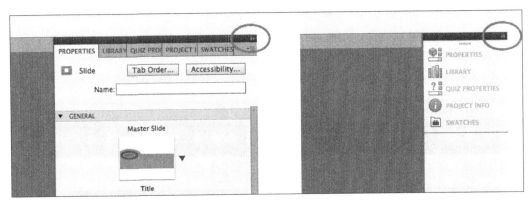

 The **Swatches** panel shown in the preceding screenshot is a new feature of Captivate 7.0.1. If the **Swatches** panel does not appear on your screen, make sure you have applied the latest available update patch for Captivate. More info on how to download and install the latest Captivate updates can be found at http://www.adobe.com/support/captivate/downloads.html.

If you have a small screen, turning panels into icons is a very simple and effective way to optimize your screen real estate. Note that a similar double-arrow is available at the top of the objects toolbar. Clicking on that one toggles the objects toolbar between a two-column and a single-column display.

Another way to customize the interface and optimize the screen real estate is to change the size of the panels present on the screen. This is particularly interesting when working with the **Filmstrip** panel.

9. Place your mouse above the vertical line that separates the **Filmstrip** panel from the stage until the mouse pointer turns to a double arrow.

10. Click-and-drag the vertical separator to the right until the **Filmstrip** panel covers more or less half of the screen, as shown in the next screenshot:

The layout shown in the preceding screenshot helps you see the big picture more efficiently. It can be compared to the Slide Sorter view of Microsoft PowerPoint.

Of course, the other panels can be resized the same way. Take **Timeline** for instance. Resizing **Timeline** might be very interesting if you have a large number of objects on a given slide.

11. Open the **Window** menu and navigate to **Workspace | Reset Classic**. This resets the current workspace to its default state.
12. In the **Filmstrip** panel, select slide **16**.

Slide 16 contains a large number of objects. If you take a look at the **Timeline** panel, you'll note that it is not high enough to display all objects present on the slide. A vertical scrollbar appears on the right-hand side of the **Timeline** panel. In order to have a clearer view of the objects that compose this slide and of their timing, you will now enlarge the **Timeline** panel.

Getting Started with Captivate

13. Place your mouse above the horizontal separator that spans between the **Timeline** panel and the stage until the mouse pointer turns into a double arrow.
14. Click-and-drag the horizontal separator toward the top of the screen until the **Timeline** panel is high enough to display all the objects of the slide.

You now have a much clearer view of the stack of objects present on slide 16.

Adding and removing panels

So far, the panels that you have manipulated were already displayed in the **Classic** workspace. You will now use the **Window** menu to add new panels on the screen:

1. Open the **Window** menu.

The **Window** menu is a list of all the panels that exist in Captivate. When a checkmark is displayed in front of a panel name, it means that the corresponding panel is already displayed on the screen.

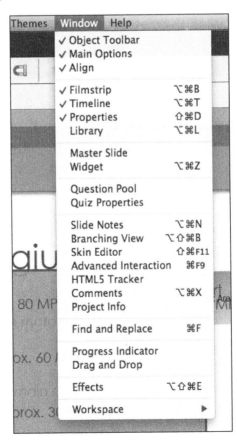

2. Click on **Slide Notes** to add the **Slide Notes** panel to the workspace. It should appear at the bottom of the interface, right next to the **Timeline** panel.

This is the first time you see this panel. This illustrates the fact that some panels are simply hidden from the default workspace unless you explicitly ask Captivate to display them. If you are looking for a tool that you cannot find on the screen, there is a good chance that the tool you are looking for is available in a panel that is currently hidden. In such a case, simply open the **Window** menu and tick the panel you want to see.

Of course, the same is true when you want to hide a panel.

3. Open the **Window** menu again.
4. Click on the **Filmstrip** menu item to hide the **Filmstrip** panel from the screen.

The **Filmstrip** panel is now completely gone. To reopen it, the only solution is to go back to the **Window** menu and turn the **Filmstrip** entry back on.

Another way to close a panel (or even an entire panel group) is to use the small menu associated with every group of panels.

5. Click on the small icon associated with the **Properties**, **Library**, **Quiz Properties**, **Project Info**, and **Swatches** panel group (see the following screenshot).
6. Choose **Close Group** from the available options.

This operation removes the whole group (five panels) from the interface.

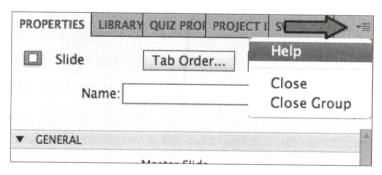

7. Navigate to **Window** | **Properties** to turn the **Properties** panel back on.

Note that this operation restores the entire panel group (five panels).

Moving panels around

The last thing to learn about panels is how you can move them around. The **Slide Notes** panel is currently displayed at the bottom of the screen. In the **Classic** workspace, this is its default-predefined location:

1. Place your mouse on the **Slide Notes** tab located at the top of the **Slide Notes** panel.
2. Click-and-drag the **Slide Notes** panel away from its current location.
3. Release the mouse when the panel floats in the middle of the screen.

Your screen should look similar to what is shown in the following screenshot:

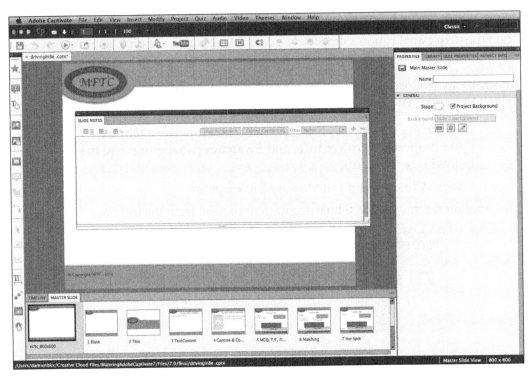

Unlike the other panels that are docked, the **Slide Notes** panel now floats in the middle of the screen. This is known as a floating panel. Captivate allows panels to be either docked or floating.

4. Place your mouse on the **Slide Notes** tab again.
5. Click-and-drag the **Slide Notes** panel toward the left-hand side of the screen until you see a blue line spanning across the entire height of the window.
6. When the blue line appears, release the mouse.

7. The **Slide Notes** panel should now be docked to the left-hand side of the screen, where the **Filmstrip** panel used to be.

Feel free to move other panels around before proceeding to the next topic. For example, take the **Properties** panel at the right-hand side of the screen and make it float. Then, try to dock it at the bottom of the screen before moving it back to its original location. When a panel is moved above a possible docking location, a blue bar appears on the screen. Releasing the mouse at that moment docks the panel at the location highlighted by the blue bar.

8. When you are done, reset the **Classic** workspace to its original state by navigating to **Window** | **Workspace** | **Reset Classic**.

This concludes your exploration of the Captivate panels. Let's look at a quick summary of what has been covered in this section:

- Double-click on the panel tab to open, expand, or collapse it.
- Use the small double-arrow icon to turn a panel (or a set of panels) to icons. This helps in optimizing the screen real estate if you have a smaller screen at your disposal.
- The **Window** menu shows a list of all the available panels. Use it to display a panel that is not present on the screen or to completely remove a panel from the interface.
- The panels can either be docked or floating.
- To dock a panel, move the panel around with the mouse and release the mouse button when a blue line appears.
- If your screen becomes messy, navigate to **Window** | **Workspace** | **Reset XXX** to change the current workspace back to its original state.

Creating a custom workspace

By hiding, showing, and moving panels on the interface, you actually create new workspaces. Captivate allows you to save these new workspaces, so when you come up with a workspace you like, save it, give it a name, and reapply it later.

Make sure you have reset the **Classic** workspace to its original state before doing this exercise:

1. Open the **Window** menu and click on **Slide Notes** to display the **Slide Notes** panel at the bottom of the screen next to the **Timeline** panel.
2. Click on the **Timeline** tab to make it the active panel of the bottom panel group.

Getting Started with Captivate

3. Double-click on the same **Timeline** tab to collapse the **Timeline** panel.
4. Click on the small double arrow associated with the **Properties** panel to turn the **Properties**, **Library**, **Quiz Properties**, **Project Info**, and **Swatches** panels to icons.

When done, your screen should look similar to what is shown in the following screenshot:

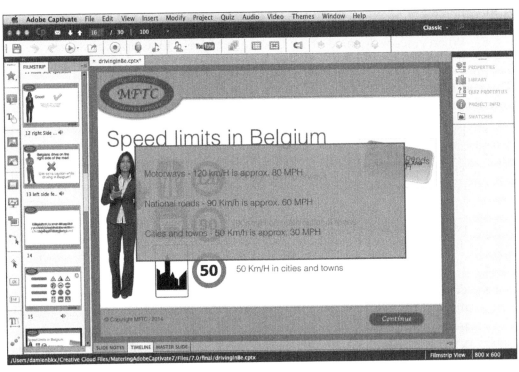

Let's pretend that this new panel layout makes you so happy that you want to save it as a new workspace.

5. Navigate to **Window** | **Workspaces** | **New Workspace**.
6. In the box that pops up, give the workspace your first name and click on **OK**.

When done, take a look at the Workspace switcher at the top-right corner of your screen. Your name should appear there, indicating that the workspace currently in use…is your very own customized workspace!

7. Click on the Workspace switcher to reveal the list of available workspaces.
8. In the list, choose any workspace but the one that bears your name. The chosen workspace is applied and the screen is rearranged.
9. Open the Workspace switcher again.
10. Click on your name to reapply your custom workspace!

Awesome! You now have a way to create custom workspaces and have Captivate look exactly the way you want.

Renaming and deleting custom workspaces

If you need to rename or delete a custom workspace, execute the following steps:

1. Navigate to **Window** | **Workspace** | **Manage Workspace**.
2. In the box, choose the workspace to delete/rename.
3. Click on the **Rename** or **Delete** button. In this example, click on the **OK** button to close the box without any changes.
4. Open the Workspace switcher one last time to reapply the **Classic** workspace before moving on to the next topic.

> There is no menu item to update an existing workspace. If you want to update an existing workspace, use the **New Workspace** command and give the new workspace the name of the existing workspace you want to update.

Also, note that you cannot delete or rename the default workspaces of Captivate.

Before moving on to the next topic, these are the key points to keep in mind when creating custom workspaces:

- When you make changes to your interface, you actually create new workspaces
- Navigate to **Window** | **Workspace** | **New Workspace** to save the current panel layout as a new workspace
- Navigate to **Window** | **Workspace** | **Manage Workspace** to rename or delete your custom workspaces
- To update an existing workspace, use the **New Workspace** command and give the new workspace the same name as the workspace you want to update
- The default workspaces of Captivate cannot be deleted or renamed

Exploring the sample applications

Now that you know a bit more about the Captivate interface, take a look at the sample applications you will build during the course of this book. These applications have been designed to showcase almost every single feature of Captivate. Use them as a reference if there is something unclear during one of the exercises.

Experiencing the Encoder demonstration

The first application that you will explore is a typical Captivate project. It uses the screen capture engine of Captivate to create a screenshots-based movie:

1. Navigate to **File** | **Open** to open the encoderDemo_800.cptx file in the final folder, situated in the exercise folder you downloaded from the Web.
2. The file opens as a separate tab in the Captivate interface.
3. In the main options toolbar, right next to the slide navigator, click on the Preview icon.
4. In the drop-down list, choose the **Project** item to preview the entire project.

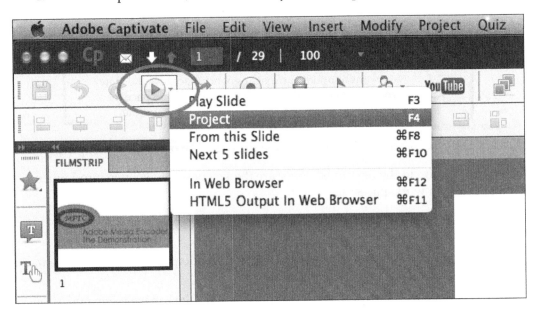

Take a closer look at the Preview icon (see the preceding screenshot). It will be one of the icons you'll use the most during the course of this book. It has six options to control which part of the project you want to preview and how you want to preview it. Note that each of these options is associated with a keyboard shortcut that depends on the system you work on (Mac or Windows).

Let's look at the Preview icons in detail:

- **Play Slide**: This option plays the current slide in the Captivate interface. It is the only preview option that does not open a floating preview pane. Consequently, this preview option is not able to render all the features of Captivate. Previewing a single slide is a good option to quickly test the timings of the objects.
- **Project**: When choosing this option, Captivate generates a temporary flash file and plays the entire project in the **Preview** pane.
- **From this Slide**: Captivate opens the **Preview** pane and plays the project from the currently selected slide to the end. This option generates a temporary Flash file, so every single feature of Captivate is supported in this preview mode.
- **Next 5 Slides**: Captivate opens the **Preview** pane to play a temporary flash file containing five slides, starting from the currently selected slide. It is a great option to quickly test a specific sequence of the project.
- **In Web Browser**: Captivate generates a temporary flash file as well as a temporary HTML file. It then plays the entire project in the default browser. Using this preview option, you will the project in a context very close to the one that will be used by your learners.
- **HTML5 Output in Web Browser**: When using this option, the project is published in HTML5, JavaScript, CSS, and images. It is then played in the default web browser. Note that some features and objects of Captivate are not supported in the HTML5 output. If you plan on publishing your project in HTML5, make sure you use this preview option to ensure that the features, animations, and objects you used in your project are supported in HTML5.

> **Floating and Modal panels**
>
> In Captivate, a panel can be floating or docked. When a panel floats, the tools and switches situated on other panels are still active. But when the **Preview** panel is open, only the buttons of that panel are active, while the tools of the other panels are not active anymore. The **Preview** pane is said to be a **Modal** floating panel because it disables every tool situated on other panels. Also, note that the **Preview** panel cannot be docked.

In this case, you clicked on the **Preview** project option. Captivate generates a temporary flash file and opens it in the floating **Preview** pane. Follow the on-screen instructions to go through the project. This puts you in the same situation as a learner viewing the eLearning course for the first time.

Getting Started with Captivate

This project begins with a short welcome video followed by a pretest of three questions. The pretest is made to check if the student really needs to take this particular training. Students that fail the pretest must take the course, while those who pass can skip the course if they want to. To fully understand this feature, it is necessary to take the course twice. Try to answer the questions of the pretest correctly the first time and incorrectly the second time to see how you experience the project in both situations.

The second part of this first sample application (after the pretest) is known as a demonstration. As the name suggests, a demonstration is used to demonstrate something to the learner. Consequently, the learner is passive and simply watches whatever is going on in the Captivate movie. In a demonstration, the mouse object is shown. It moves and clicks automatically.

This particular demonstration features some of the most popular Captivate tools such as Text Captions and Highlight Boxes. You have experienced sound in the Captivate demonstration as well as in the close-captioned sound-enabled slides.

Experiencing the Encoder simulation

You will now open another sample application. Actually, it is not a real "other" application, but another version of the Encoder demonstration you experienced in the previous topic:

1. Navigate to **File | Open** to open the `encoderSim_800.cptx` file in the `final` folder, situated in your exercise folder.
2. Once the file is open, click on the Preview icon in the main toolbar and choose to preview the entire project.
3. The **Preview** pane opens and the Encoder simulation starts to play.

> Slide 4 contains a YouTube video. This video will not work in the default **Preview** pane of Captivate. If you want to see this slide playing correctly, you must ensure that the following two conditions are met. First, you need to be connected to the Internet. Second, navigate to **Preview | In Web Browser** instead of **Preview | Project**.

When the animation reaches slide 5, the playhead stops moving and waits for you to interact with the movie. This is the main difference between a demonstration and a simulation.

In Captivate, a simulation is a project in which the learner is active. In a simulation, the mouse object is hidden as learners will use their own mouse to click around the screen in order to progress toward the end of the movie. The very fact that the students are active implies a whole new level of complexity as the learners can perform either the right or the wrong action. In each case, the application must react accordingly. This concept is known as branching, that is, each student experiences the application based on his/her actions.

4. Follow the on-screen instructions and try to perform the right actions. The application has been set up to give you two chances to perform each action correctly.
5. When you are through, close the **Preview** pane.

In order to experience the branching concept hands on, preview the entire movie again, but this time, give yourself a break and perform the wrong actions at each and every step of the simulation (don't worry, it is not graded!). You will see that the application reacts differently and shows you things that were not shown when the right actions were performed! That's branching in action!

This particular simulation features pretty much the same Captivate objects as the demonstration you experienced earlier, only the mouse had to be replaced by interactive objects. Three of those interactive objects have the ability to stop the playhead and wait for the learner to interact with the movie. All these interactive objects can implement the branching concept. Using these interactive objects will be covered in *Chapter 5, Adding Interactivity to the Project*.

Both the Encoder demonstration and simulation are based on screenshots. To create these sample applications, the first two steps of the production process described earlier have been used:

- In step one (the capture phase), the actions have been actually performed in the real Adobe Media Encoder; they were recorded by Captivate behind the scenes.
- In step two (the post-production phase), the movie has been edited in Captivate. Sound and closed captions were added, video was imported, the title and ending slides were created, the timing was adjusted, and so on. We even imported a slide created in Microsoft PowerPoint!
- Step three (the publishing phase) has not (yet) been performed on these files.

Experiencing the Driving In Belgium sample application

You will now preview the third sample application. Normally, it should already be open in Captivate as a tab in the main area. Click on the `drivingInBe.cptx` tab to make it the active file.

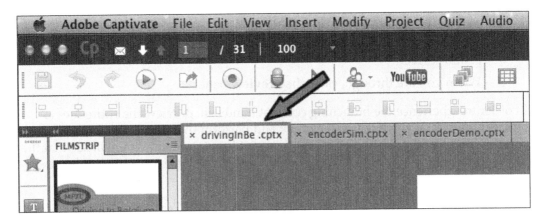

 If the file is not open, navigate to **File** | **Open** to open the `drivingInBe.cptx` file in the `final` folder, situated in your exercise folder you downloaded from the Web.

When the file is open and active, use the Preview icon to preview the entire project. Follow the on-screen instructions as a student would. When done, close the **Preview** pane, then use the Preview icon again to preview the entire project a second time. Answer the question differently from the first time. You will have yet another experience of the branching concept.

 Slide 19 of this project will not work as intended if you are not connected to the Internet while viewing the application.

This third sample application is very different from the previous projects you have experienced so far. It is not really a demonstration, nor a simulation. It is none of it and a bit of both at the same time. As you can see, the borderline between a demonstration and a simulation is sometimes very difficult to spot!

When it comes to sound, this movie makes use of the text-to-speech engine of Captivate. Text-to-speech is a great alternative to quickly create the sound clips you need, but the quality of the speech is not as good as when a real human being speaks in front of a good old microphone!

This application is not based on screenshots and does not teach software-related skills. Instead, each slide has been created one by one in Captivate or imported from an existing PowerPoint presentation.

This application is also much more sophisticated than the Encoder applications. Advanced Actions and Variables are used throughout the project to power dynamic features such as the name of the student appearing in a Text Caption. It also features the certificate interaction on the last slide (only if you pass the quiz!) and uses the built-in collection of Characters to spice up the training with a human touch! But the most impressive feature of this particular project is probably the **Quiz**, one of the biggest and most appreciated tools of Captivate.

The project contains eight Question Slides. Six of these are stored in the **Question Pool** panel. Each time the project is viewed, one question is asked to the student and a second one is randomly chosen from the question pool. That's why the second time you previewed the application, you did not experience the exact same Quiz as the first time.

Experiencing the Encoder Video Demo

The **Video Demo** mode is a special recording mode of Captivate that is used to produce `.mp4` video files. These files can easily be uploaded to online services such as YouTube, Vimeo, or Daily Motion for playback on any device (including iPad, iPhone, and other Internet-enabled mobile devices):

1. Navigate to **File** | **Open** to open the `encoderVideo.cpvc` file in the `final` folder, situated in your exercise folder.

First, note that a Video Demo project does not use the same `.cptx` file extension as a regular Captivate project. It uses the `.cpvc` file extension instead. This is the first indication that this project is not going to behave like the other ones you have experienced so far. In addition to a specific file extension, Video Demo projects also have their own Captivate interface as shown in the following screenshot:

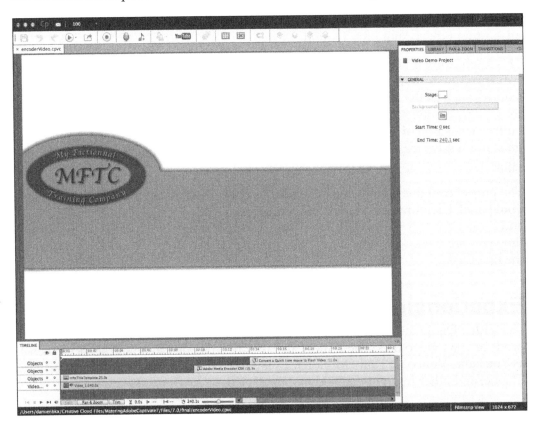

In the preceding screenshot, note the absence of the **Filmstrip** panel. A Video Demo project is not based on slides. Actually, it is a single big video file, so the **Filmstrip** panel makes no sense in a Video Demo project.

In a video file, interactions are not possible. The file can only be experienced from start to finish in the order defined by the teacher. To use proper words, it is said that a video file proposes a linear experience to the learner while branch-aware interactive projects propose a non-linear experience. Therefore, interactive objects as well as quizzes and branching are not available in a Video Demo project.

2. Take some time to inspect the rest of the interface. Try to spot the other differences between the regular Captivate interface and the interface used for Video Demos.

3. When you are ready, click on the Preview icon.

Surprise! Only two options are available in the Preview icon!

4. In the **Preview** dropdown, choose the **Full Screen** option.
5. Watch the whole movie as if you were viewing it on YouTube!
6. When the movie is finished, click on the **Edit** button at the bottom-right corner of the screen to return to the Video Demo editing interface.
7. Navigate to **File | Close All** to close every open file. If prompted to save the changes, make sure you do NOT save the changes to these files.

After viewing these four sample applications, you should have a pretty good idea of the tools and general capabilities of Captivate. Before moving on, let's summarize what we have learned from these movies:

- Captivate is able to capture the actions you do on your computer and turn them into slides using a sophisticated capture engine based on screenshots.
- A **Demonstration** is a project in which the learner is passive and simply watches the on-screen action.
- A **Simulation** is a project in which the user is active.
- PowerPoint slides can be imported into Captivate and converted to Captivate slides.
- Sound and video can be imported in Captivate. The application also features a text-to-speech engine and closed captioning.
- Question Slides can be created in Captivate. These Question Slides can be stored in Question Pools to create random quizzes.
- Other objects that can be included in a Captivate project include Text Captions, Highlight Boxes, and so on.
- Captivate contains interactive objects. Three of these interactive objects are able to stop the playhead and wait for the user to interact with the movie.
- A Video Demo is not based on screenshots, but is a big video file instead.
- Video Demo projects use the `.cpvc` file extension and have a specific user interface.

Discussing the sample apps scenario

In the exercise folder you downloaded from the Web, you'll find the scenarios of these sample apps in PDF format in the scenarios folder. Take some time to read those documents and to compare them to the finished applications.

When working with Captivate, the scenario is a very important document. Its goal is to guide you during the whole production process. Thanks to the scenario, you'll always have the big picture of the entire project in mind. The scenario will also help you stay within the scope of your project.

That being said, the scenario can, and probably will, evolve during the production process. And this is a good thing! Every teacher knows that his/her own understanding of a given topic increases and changes while teaching it. What is true in a classroom is also true in a Captivate project. After all, working in Captivate is all about teaching and consequently, your scenario is nothing more than a guide.

Summary

In this chapter, you have been introduced to the four (3 + 1) steps of a typical Captivate production process. You toured the application's interface and learned how to customize it to fit your needs. Thanks to the workspace feature, you have been able to save your customized interface as a new workspace in order to reapply your custom panel layout anytime you want to. Best of all, the Captivate interface works the same way as the interface of other Adobe applications. So, if you plan on learning Photoshop, Illustrator, InDesign, Dreamweaver, and so on, you already know how the interface of these applications works!

Finally, you have been walked through the sample applications used in this book, which gave you your first high-level overview of Captivate's rich set of features.

In the next chapter, you will concentrate on the first step of the Captivate production process: the capture step. You will learn various techniques used to capture the slides and you will discover the inner working of Captivate's capture engine. You will also learn about tips and tricks that will help you take the first critical decision—choosing the right size for your project.

 To see and experience more Captivate applications, visit http://www.adobe.com/products/captivate/showcase.html.

Meet the community

The title of the book you are reading is *Mastering Adobe Captivate 7*. In order to truly "master" a piece of software, I'm convinced that one must be introduced to the community that supports it.

At the end of each chapter is a *Meet the community* section that will introduce you to a key member of the community. By the end of the book, you'll have know the names, blog addresses, twitter handles, and so on of some of the most influential members of the Captivate and eLearning community. I hope these resources will jump start your own Captivate career and, who knows, your own involvement in the community.

Pooja Jaisingh

In this first *Meet the community* section, I'd like to introduce you to Pooja Jaisingh. Pooja is one of the Adobe eLearning evangelists. In particular, she is one of the main contributors to the official Adobe Captivate blog and to the Captivate page on Facebook. Pooja also organizes free Captivate trainings and webinars. See the schedule of these free trainings at http://www.adobe.com/cfusion/event/index.cfm?event=list&loc=en_us&type=&product=Captivate.

Bio

Pooja Jaisingh has worked for more than 12 years as a teacher trainer, eLearning instructional designer, and, currently, is an eLearning evangelist with Adobe Systems. Pooja's core strengths are communication and innovation. In all her roles, she has promoted eLearning as a mode of delivery and has created a host of eLearning courses. In her current role, she conducts numerous seminars and workshops, educating training folks on the features of Adobe Systems' eLearning products. She regularly blogs, initiating creative discussions on multiple opportunities in eLearning. She holds a Master's degree in Education and Economics and a Doctorate in Educational Technology.

Contact details

- **Blog**: http://blogs.adobe.com/captivate
- **Twitter**: @poojajaisingh
- **Facebook**: http://www.facebook.com/adobecaptivate

2
Capturing the Slides

Now that you have a better understanding of the features offered by Captivate, it is time to discover the first step of the production process: capturing the slides.

This step can be compared to the filming of a movie. When filming a movie, the director wants to capture all the images, sequences, and shots he needs. In the movie industry, this raw material is called the **rushes**. When the filming is complete, the director goes back to the studio to start the post-production process. It is during the post-production step of the process that the final movie takes shape. Only the best rushes will make their way to the movie theatre while the others will be discarded along the way. That being said, the post-production phase can only be successful if the filming provides enough good-quality material to create a great movie.

The same basic idea applies to Captivate. When capturing the slide, one should always keep in mind the fact that the post-production phase will follow. Therefore, the goal of the capture phase is to create enough quality slides to ensure the success of the next phase of the process.

At the end of this chapter, you will be far from the final result you want to achieve, but you will have enough slides to start editing your projects.

In this chapter, we will be:

- Discussing how to choose the right size/resolution for the project
- Discussing the recording preferences and the recording modes
- Recording Demonstrations and Simulations
- Recording System Audio
- Discussing and using Full Motion Recording
- Discussing and experiencing the Video Demo recording mode
- Using manual panning
- Resizing a project

If you are ready, it's almost time to turn the camera on and start the real action!

Choosing the right resolution for the project

Choosing the right resolution for capturing the slides is the first critical decision you have to make. And you have to make it right because the size of the captured slides will play a critical role in the quality of the final movie.

What exactly is the problem?

A typical Captivate project, such as the Encoder Demonstration you experienced in *Chapter 1, Getting Started with Captivate*, involves taking screenshots of an actual piece of software. At the end of the process, the project will typically be published in Flash or HTML5 and placed on a web page (or **Learning Management System** (**LMS**)). Most of the time, that web page displays many other page elements (for example, logos, headers, footers, navigation bars, and so on) in addition to incorporating your Captivate movie. This can lead to a very delicate situation as illustrated by the following image.

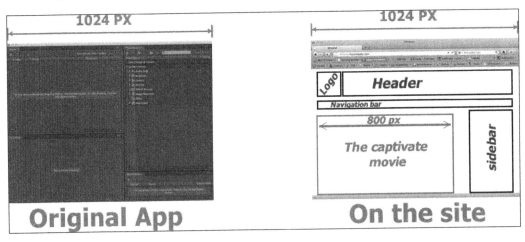

The preceding image shows the application you need to capture on the left. Let's pretend this application requires a minimal width of 1024 pixels to be displayed without horizontal scrollbars. On the right-hand side of the image is the wireframe of the web page you must put your finished movie on. The page has been designed to fit a 1024-pixel-wide screen and has to display lots of elements in addition to the Captivate movie. To cope with the design requirements of the web page, your project should not be wider than 800 pixels.

So, here is your problem: you have to find a way to fit 1024 pixels in 800 pixels!

Several approaches are available to address this problem. Each of these approaches has its pros and cons. Following is a brief review of each.

Resizing the project after the initial shooting

The first approach is a two-step process. The first step is to shoot the movie in 1024-pixel size, and the second step is to use the **Rescale Project** feature of Captivate to downsize the project to 800 pixels.

By shooting with a screen size of 1024 pixels, the application will be captured in its intended size, matching the student's experience of the application!

The main disadvantage of this approach is that it requires resizing the Captivate project. In Captivate, the resize operation is a one-way destructive operation. It always has a cost in terms of image quality. Surprisingly, the resize operation can result in a larger file size, even if the new resolution is smaller than the original one. Also, in case the new resolution is smaller, the screenshots will be smaller as well, and the information they contain might become very difficult to read.

The following are a few tips to keep in mind when resizing a project:

- It is always better to downsize a project than to make it bigger.
- Always keep a backup copy of the project in its original resolution. Remember that the resize operation is a one-way destructive operation. Your backup copy is the only way to rollback the resize operation in case something goes wrong!

Downsizing the application during shooting

The second approach is to downsize the application to shoot during the capture in order to fit the requirements of the project. In this example, this means the application would be 800 pixels wide instead of 1024 pixels during the capture.

As far as Captivate is concerned, this is the easiest solution, as no destructive or complex resize operation is needed. But for the application that is being captured, this situation is quite uncomfortable.

Remember that the application you capture requires a minimal width of 1024 pixels, so by downsizing it to a width of 800 pixels, it does not have enough room to display all its components and generates horizontal scrollbars. These scrollbars and their associated scrolling actions (if any) will be captured and will appear in the resulting Captivate movie. Also, scrollbars sometimes hide important information from the screen, and therefore, from your students.

Using the panning feature of Captivate

In the movie industry, panning refers to moving the camera while filming. In Captivate, it means that you can move the recording area while capturing the slides.

This approach tries to cope with both the requirements of the application to shoot and the requirements of the movie to be produced.

The idea is to leave the application to its intended width of 1024 pixels, and at the same time, define a capture area that is 800 pixels in width. During the shooting, the smaller capture area can be moved over the bigger application as illustrated by the following image:

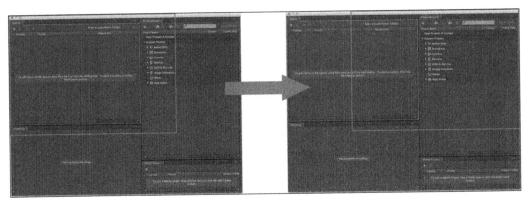

In the preceding illustration, the capture area is the red rectangle. In other words, Captivate only captures what is *inside* the red rectangle. As you can see, the capture area does not always cover the same part of the application during the shooting.

This approach is a good compromise, but it has two major disadvantages. First, moving the recording area while filming increases the file size of your final movie. But more importantly, using this approach, your learner never sees the application entirely, which could compromise the quality of the learning process.

Using the Scalable HTML Content feature

Captivate 6 introduced a new way to deal with the size problem. The **Scalable HTML Content** feature makes the published movie fluid, so it fits the screen it is viewed on (even as the screen is resized).

For example, say you shoot and publish your movie at a size of 1024 pixels, but the movie is viewed on a website where the maximal resolution can only be 800 pixels. In such a case, the **Scalable HTML Content** feature scales the movie down to 800 pixels so it fits in the available space.

The main advantage of this approach is that it makes your Captivate content ready for mobile transition. When viewed on a tablet or a smartphone, the content will be resized.

The major disadvantage though is that you lose control over how your content will be actually experienced. Only a small percentage of your students (those who have the exact same screen as yours) will see the course as you designed it. The other students will see the course either bigger (which means possibly pixelized) or smaller (which may mean too small to be comfortable).

This option will be covered in *Chapter 8, Finishing Touches and Publishing*.

Conclusion

None of these approaches is perfect, but you'll have to choose one anyway. The best approach depends on the project, your learners, and your personal taste. Here are some general guidelines to help you make the best choice:

- The size of the capture area must match the size of the application to capture whenever possible.
- If you need to resize the project, take a bigger project and make it smaller to help maintain the best possible image quality. Also, make sure you keep a backup copy of the project at its original size.
- Use panning only if you really need it.
- When using panning, move the camera (the red capture area) only when necessary, and move it slowly enough to help the students build a mental picture of the entire application.
- If you use the **Scalable HTML Content** feature, make sure you test your work on an array of different screens and devices to ensure the best possible student experience in the majority of scenarios.

Finally, never forget that you are teaching. Your students don't care about your sizing concerns; they just want to learn something. If the chosen approach compromises the quality of the learning process, then it is the wrong approach.

> **About screen sizes**
>
> For more information about the screen sizes in use today, visit the great website `http://www.websitedimensions.com/`.

Shooting your first movie

It is time to have your first hands-on experience of an actual recording session. Shooting a movie is a four-step process:

1. Preparing the application to shoot.
2. Rehearsing the scenario.
3. Shooting the movie.
4. Previewing the rushes.

Let's review these four steps one by one.

Preparing the application to shoot

For this exercise, the application you will use is **Adobe Media Encoder CS6**. This application is used to convert virtually any type of video files to Flash video and HTML5 video. **Adobe Media Encoder (AME)** is part of the standard Captivate package. So, if you have Captivate (even the trial version), you also have AME.

You will now reset the Captivate workspace and open AME by performing the following steps:

1. Open Captivate. If Captivate is already open, close all the open files.
2. Make sure the default **Classic** workspace is applied.
3. Open AME. On a Mac, it is situated in the `/Applications/Adobe Media Encoder CS6` folder. On Windows, a shortcut to AME should be available in the Start menu.

When AME opens, make sure it looks like the following screenshot:

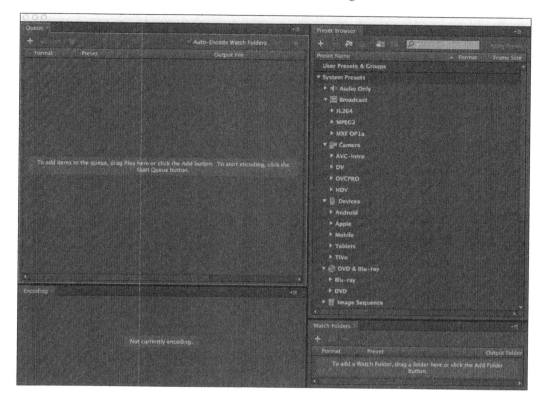

 This exercise also works with Adobe Media Encoder CC.

Rehearsing the scenario

The goal of this Captivate project is to teach students how to use AME to convert a QuickTime movie (with a .mov extension) to Flash video (with a .flv extension). This scenario follows the exact same steps as those used in the Encoder Demonstration and Simulation of the previous chapter. Make sure the audio system of your computer is turned on before rehearsing the following scenario. Here are the steps:

1. Go to the **Adobe Media Encoder** application.
2. In the top-left corner of the application, click on the **+** icon.
3. Browse to the videos/MOV folder of the exercise files and load the demo_en.mov QuickTime movie into AME.

Capturing the Slides

4. Open the **Format** drop-down list and choose the `.flv` format.
5. Open the **Preset** drop-down list and apply the last **4 x 3** preset (the one before the last in the list).
6. Click on the preset name to open the **Export Settings** dialog.
7. In the lower right-hand side area of the **Export Settings** dialog, open the **Video** tab (if needed).
8. Scroll down the **Video** tab until you see the **Resize Video** section.
9. Make sure the **Maintain Aspect Ratio** icon (the chain icon) is active and change the **Width** value of the video to `400` pixels. Normally, the new **Height** value of the video is automatically set to **300** pixels.
10. Click on the **OK** button to validate the new **Export Settings**.
11. Click on the Start Queue button (the green Play icon) to start the actual encoding.

The encoding process begins. In the **Encoding** panel at the bottom of the screen, a yellowish bar shows the progression of this operation. When the operation is complete, the system plays a brief *chime* sound effect.

Make sure you master these steps, and make sure AME behaves as expected before continuing. If you need more practice, feel free to rehearse this scenario a few more times before the recording. After all, on a real movie set, even the most famous actors rehearse their scenes many times before the director finally decides to turn the camera on.

Resetting the application

When you are ready to shoot the scene, don't forget to reset AME to its original state. The best way to do this is to perform the following steps:

1. Close AME.
2. When the application is closed, reopen it.
3. When the application reopens, make sure it looks like the previous image again.

Also, delete the `.flv` file(s) you generated during the rehearsal(s) by performing the following steps:

4. Open the Finder (Mac) or the Windows Explorer (Windows) and browse to the `videos/MOV` folder of the exercise files.
5. Delete every `.flv` file present in this folder.

On a real movie set, this is the job of the script girl!

Shooting the movie

You know the scenario, and now the application is ready to be captured. Let's head back to Captivate and start the actual shooting process.

Enabling access to assistive devices (Mac users only)

If you work on a Mac, there is one preliminary step to be taken before Captivate can record the movie. The exact procedure depends on the version of Mac OS X you are using. If you are using Version 10.8 (Mountain Lion) or below, the procedure goes as follows:

1. Open the **System Preferences** application.
2. In the **Personal** section of **System Preferences**, click on the **Universal Access** icon.
3. At the bottom of the **Universal Access** preference pane, select the **Enable access for assistive devices** checkbox.
4. Close the **System Preferences** application and return to Captivate.

If you are using Mac OS X 10.9 (Mavericks), the following is the procedure:

1. The first time you create a new software simulation with Captivate 7, a dialog box will appear on the screen asking you if you want to let Captivate access the assistive devices.
2. Click on **Open System Preferences** to open the **System Preferences** application.
3. If needed, click on the lock icon in the bottom-left corner of the **System Preference** application and authenticate as an administrator.
4. Tick the **Captivate** option to grant Captivate access to the assistive devices.

Without the preceding step, Mac OS does not broadcast the events that Captivate uses to capture user interactivity (clicking on a button, typing into a text entry, and so on).

Preparing Captivate to shoot the movie

For this first practice recording, you will use the default options of Captivate to shoot the movie as follows:

1. Close every open file so that the Captivate welcome screen is displayed.
2. In the right-hand side column of the welcome screen, click on the **Create New | Software Simulation** link. You can also use the **File | Record new Software Simulation** menu item to achieve the same result.

Capturing the Slides

The Captivate interface disappears and a red rectangle is displayed on the screen. This red rectangle is the recording area:

3. In the recording window, choose **Application** to record an application.
4. In the **Select the window to record** drop-down list, choose to record the **Adobe Media Encoder CS6** application.

The **Adobe Media Encoder** application opens, and the red recording area snaps to the application window:

5. In the **Snap to** section of the box, choose to record at **Custom Size**.
6. Choose the **1024 x 768** size in the drop-down list. The red recording area and AME are both resized to the chosen size.
7. Leave the remaining options at their default settings.
8. The recording window should look like the following screenshot:

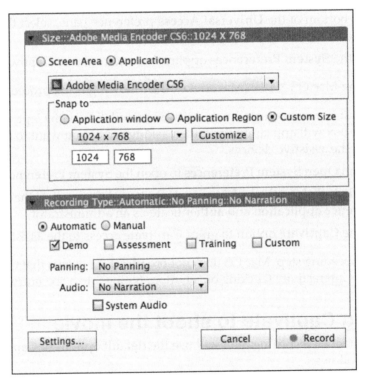

 Mac users, the **System Audio** checkbox might be unavailable on your system. This problem will be addressed later in this chapter.

In the preceding screenshot, notice the **Demo** checkbox in the lower part of the window. Make sure this checkbox is the only one selected.

The stage is set, and the actors are in place. Everyone is waiting for the director's signal to get started!

And... Action!

The signal is the red **Record** button at the bottom of the recording window. Once you click on it, all your actions are recorded by Captivate until you stop the capture:

 If you have a problem while doing this exercise, refer to the Chapter02/final/encoderDemo_1_1024.cptx file of your exercises folder.

1. Click on the red **Record** button at the bottom of the recording window. After a short countdown, you'll be in the recording mode.
2. In the **Adobe Media Encoder** window, perform the actions as written in the scenario you rehearsed earlier in this chapter.

During the recording, pay close attention to the following things:

- Each time you click, you should hear a camera shutter sound
- When you type in the **Width** field, you should hear keystrokes
- After clicking on the Start Queue button, AME displays a yellowish progression bar in the bottom-left panel

Also, make sure you perform the actions slowly to allow Captivate enough time to capture all the needed images and actions:

3. After completing all the steps, hit the *End* key (Windows), or do the *cmd* + *enter* shortcut (Mac), to stop the recording and have Captivate generate the slides.

 On some Mac models, it is the *cmd* + *fn* + *enter* shortcut that is needed to stop the recording.

4. When the project has finished loading in Captivate, save it as Chapter02/encoderDemo_1_1024.cptx.
5. Close the **Adobe Media Encoder** application.

The shooting phase of the movie is now finished. If you don't get it right the first time, don't worry; you can simply discard your sequence and start over. On a real movie set, even the most famous actors are granted many chances to do it right.

Previewing the rushes

The project should be open in Captivate. To launch the preview, you will use the same icon as in *Chapter 1, Getting Started with Captivate*:

1. On the Main Options toolbar, click on the Preview icon. In the drop-down list, choose **Project** to preview the entire project (you can also use the *F4* shortcut key to do the same thing).
2. Captivate generates the slides in a temporary Flash file and opens the **Preview** pane.

Captivate has already generated lots of objects on the slides. Remember that in the recording window, the **Demo** mode was selected by default. The **Demo** mode automatically adds Text Captions, Highlight Boxes, and Mouse movements to the slides.

Of course, some of the content of the Text Captions must be corrected the size and position of the Highlight Boxes must be fine-tuned and the overall rhythm of the project is probably too fast, but this is an acceptable starting point.

The main problem with these rushes is how the movie ends. While previewing the project, you probably noticed that the yellowish encoding progression bar has not been captured by Captivate.

In order to understand why Captivate did not capture the yellowish progression bar at the end of the movie, it is necessary to further dive into the inner working of the Captivate capture engine.

3. Close the **Preview** pane when done.

The inner working of the Captivate capture engine

The Captivate capture engine is based on screenshots. Going back to the Adobe Media Encoder project, let's review what exactly happened when you clicked on your mouse during the capture using the following steps:

1. Return to the `Chapter02/encoderDemo_1_1024.cptx` file.
2. Make sure that the first slide is selected in the **Filmstrip** panel.

The first slide shows the initial state of the application. When filming, you used your mouse to click on the **Add Source** icon of AME. When you clicked on this icon, Captivate launched a sequence of actions behind the scenes:

- Captivate recorded the position of the mouse at the time of the click (using X, Y coordinates)
- Adobe Media Encoder executed the action
- When Adobe Media Encoder completed its action, Captivate took a static screenshot of the new state of the application (the second slide)

You then used your mouse a second time to double-click on the `demo_en.mov` file. When this second click occurred, Captivate launched the same sequence of actions and took a third screenshot to generate slide 3.

When the movie plays, the static screenshot of the first slide (a `.bmp` image) is displayed. When the mouse has to move, Captivate recreates a movement from the top-left corner of the slide to the position of the click as recorded during the filming. Just after the click, Captivate displays the static (`.bmp`) screenshot of slide 2.

When it is time to move the mouse slide 2, Captivate recreates a movement from where the click occurred on slide 1 to the location of the click slide 2 as recorded during the filming. Right after the second click, Captivate displays the third static screenshot. This process repeats itself till the end of the movie.

It may sound very simple and logical, but the way this process works has lots of implications, as mentioned in the following list:

- Only the starting points and the ending points of the mouse movements are recorded by Captivate. During the playback, a movement is recreated between these points.
- Every mouse movement made during the filming between two clicks is therefore not recorded.
- The animations displayed by the Captured application (in this case, the progression of the yellowish bar during encoding) are not captured.
- The **Timeline** of the generated movie is independent of the time that has passed during filming.

This system creates a very lightweight animation. A bunch of images and a few coordinates are enough to reproduce an entire movie.

However, this system is limited. Some mouse actions, such as drag-and-drop and scrolling actions, cannot be reproduced that way. These actions require an actual frame-by-frame video recording to be played back correctly. Such a frame-by-frame animation is known as **Full Motion Recording (FMR)**.

The Full Motion Recording mode

To make sure you understand this concept, let's take a look at some of the preferences of Captivate:

1. In Captivate, navigate to the **Edit | Preferences** (Windows) or **Adobe Captivate | Preferences** (Mac) menu item to open the **Preferences** window.
2. Once the **Preferences** window opens, click on the **Settings** category in the **Recording** group as illustrated in the following screenshot:

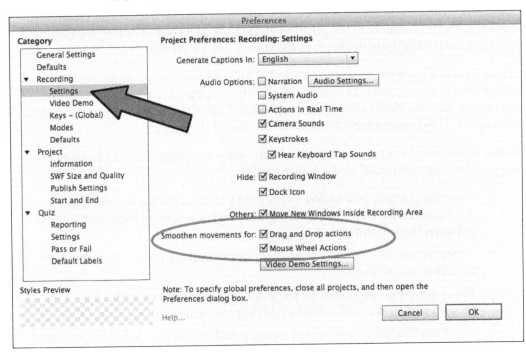

Notice at the end of the **Preferences** window two options that help you control the Full Motion Recording behavior of Captivate: **Smoothen movements for Drag and Drop actions** and **Smoothen movements for Mouse Wheel Actions**.

Chapter 2

These two options are selected by default, and you should not tamper with them unless you have a good reason to. Thanks to those two boxes, Captivate automatically switches to the Full Motion Recording mode when a drag-and-drop or a mouse wheel action is detected during the filming:

3. Close the **Preferences** window.
4. Take a close look at the icons situated in the bottom-right corner of each slide's thumbnail in the **Filmstrip** window.

While most of the slides display the icon of a mouse, one slide should display the icon of a video camera. This is shown in the following screenshot:

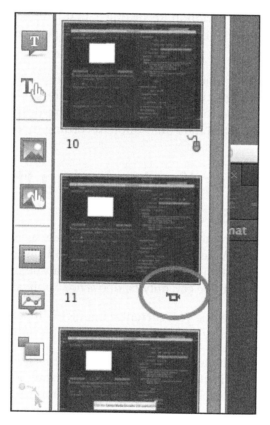

The preceding screenshot is the slide where the scrolling movement on the **Video** tab of AME occurs.

 The actual slide number may vary depending on how the shooting session went.

Thanks to the **Smoothen movements for Drag and Drop actions** and **Smoothen movements for Mouse Wheel Actions** options being turned on, Captivate has detected this scrolling movement and has automatically switched to the Full Motion Recoding mode when capturing that particular slide.

One of the limitations of Full Motion Recording is that it does not allow any kind of interaction. During the playback, the student cannot perform such scrolling movement, themselves.

The Full Motion Recording mode will also help you to capture the progression of the yellowish bar at the end of the project. The only thing is that the yellowish progression bar is not linked to any scrolling or drag-and-drop action. Fortunately, there is another way to control the Full Motion Recording mode.

Controlling Captivate during the shooting session

Controlling Captivate during the shooting session is quite a challenge for your operating system (Mac or Windows). Even though both Windows and Mac OS are multitask operating systems (this means they can handle multiple applications running at the same time), there can only be one *active* application at any given time.

The active application is the one you currently interact with, and therefore, is the one that currently listens to the keyboard, the mouse, and other input devices.

When recording with Captivate, there are two active applications: the application you capture and Captivate itself. You should be able to interact with both these applications, so both these applications share the same mouse and the same keyboard at the same time. That is a very unusual situation to deal with for an operating system.

Chapter 2

By default, the mouse and the keyboard send their data to the application you record, except for a few keys and shortcuts that are wired to Captivate:

1. Open the **Preferences** window of Captivate by navigating to the **Adobe Captivate | Preferences** (Mac) or **Edit | Preferences** (Windows) menu.
2. In the left-hand side column of the **Preferences** window, open the **Keys - (Global)** category.

This part of the **Preferences** dialog lists all the keys and shortcuts that allow you to interact with Captivate during the recording, as shown in the following screenshot:

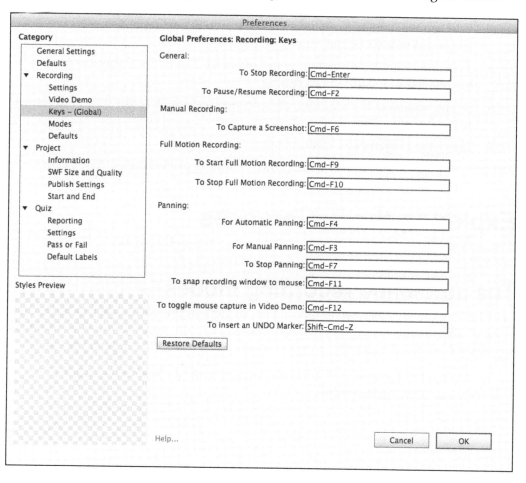

Remember that all the other keys as well as the mouse are wired to the application you capture:

3. Take some time to review the available keys and shortcuts.

Of special interest are the keyboard shortcuts used to manually start and stop a Full Motion Recording. Also, notice that you can use a keyboard shortcut (*Print Screen* on Windows or *cmd + F6* on Mac) to manually take extra screenshots if needed. Finally, the *End* (Windows) or *cmd + enter* (Mac) shortcut is used to stop the recording.

In some situations, you may need to change these recording keys:

4. Click on the field where the key used to stop recording is defined (*End* on Windows or *cmd + enter* on Mac).
5. Type the *Ctrl + E* shortcut on your keyboard. The *Ctrl + E* shortcut is now the one to use to stop the recording.
6. At the bottom of the window, click on the **Restore Defaults** button to return to the default settings.
7. Leave the **Preferences** window open.

You will now take some time to inspect the remaining preferences of Captivate.

Exploring the preferences

First, let's explore the four automatic recording modes of Captivate.

The automatic recording modes

Your first shooting experience was based on the default preferences of Captivate. In order to take full control on the situation, you will explore and fine-tune the automatic recording modes before having a second try by performing the following steps:

1. On the left-hand side of the **Preferences** window, click on the **Modes** category in the **Recording** section.

Chapter 2

2. At the top of the **Preferences** window, make sure the **Mode** drop-down list is set to **Demonstration**. This is shown in the following screenshot:

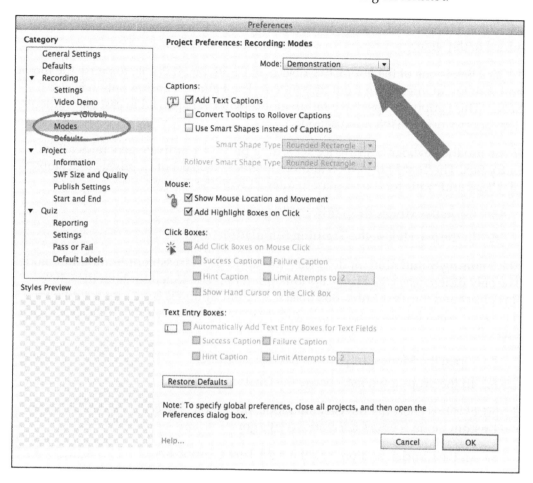

The **Preferences** window currently displays the settings of the **Demonstration** recording mode you used during your first capture session. As expected, this recording mode adds Text Captions to the slides. It also features the Mouse and adds a Highlight Box each time the mouse is clicked during the capture. These settings reflect what you saw when previewing the rushes of the first movie:

3. At the top of the **Preferences** window, open the **Modes** drop-down list.
4. Choose the **Assessment Simulation** option.

Capturing the Slides

The **Assessment Simulation** mode is the second automatic recording mode of Captivate. As discussed earlier, a Simulation is a project in which the user is *active*, so the **Show Mouse Location and Movement** option is, logically, not ticked. Instead, each time a mouse click occurs during the filming, a **Click Box** is automatically added to the slide.

A Click Box is one of the interactive objects of Captivate. It is able to pause the movie and wait for an interaction from the student. The **Failure Caption** option is also ticked. This simply means that a failure notice will be displayed in case the student does not perform the intended action.

If you use the keyboard during the recording process, Captivate generates a **Text Entry Box.** The Text Entry Box is another interactive object of Captivate that stops the playhead and waits for the student to interact with the course:

5. Open the **Modes** drop-down list again.
6. In the list, choose the **Training Simulation** mode.

The **Training Simulation** mode is very similar to the **Assessment Simulation** mode. The only difference is the **Hint Caption** option that is selected for both the **Click Box** object and the **Text Entry Box** object. A Hint Caption is a piece of text that is displayed when the student rolls the mouse over the hit area of the Click Box / Text Entry Box:

7. Open the **Modes** drop-down list one last time.
8. In the drop-down list, choose the **Custom** mode.

Surprise! When choosing the **Custom** mode, no option is selected by default. In fact, the **Custom** mode is yours to create, so let's go:

9. In the **Caption** section, tick the **Add Text Captions** box.
10. In the **Click Boxes** section, tick the **Add Click Boxes on Mouse Click** option. Also, tick the **Failure Caption** and **Hint Caption** boxes.
11. Finally, in the **Text Entry Boxes** section, tick the **Automatically Add Text Entry Boxes for Text Fields** option with a **Failure Caption** box and a **Hint Caption** box.

Depending on the recording mode, Text Captions, Failure Captions, and/or Hint Captions will be added to the slides.

Exploring the recording settings

Let's now focus on the **Recording Settings** category of the **Preferences** window:

1. Open the **Recording Settings** category by clicking on **Settings** in the left-hand side column of the **Preferences** window.

The first available option at the top of the recording settings preference pane is the **Generate Captions In** drop-down list. Use it to choose the language used by Captivate to generate the various types of captions.

Other options available on this pane include the following:

- The **Camera Sounds** checkbox is used to turn the camera shutter sound on or off during shooting. Make sure this option is ticked.
- The **Keystrokes** and **Hear Keyboard Tap Sounds** options are responsible for recording the keystrokes and for the keystrokes sound during the filming. It is best to leave these options selected.
- The **Move New Windows Inside Recording Area** option is used during the capture when the application you record opens a new window or a dialog box. It prevents the new window from opening outside or even partially outside of the recording area. This option should be ticked at all times.
- (Windows only) The **Hide System Tray Icon** and **Hide Task Icon** checkboxes are great when you record full-screen. When turned on, they hide the Captivate button from the taskbar and the Captivate icon from the notification area.
- (Mac only) The **Hide Dock Icon** checkbox is used to remove the Captivate icon from Dock during the filming. This option is very useful when shooting fullscreen.

The Video Demo preferences

To finish off with the **Recording** preferences, you will now explore one last **Preferences** pane:

1. Click on the **Video Demo** category to open the **Video Demo** preferences pane.

The **Video Demo** preferences pane shows options to optimize the conversion of a Full Motion Recording into a Flash or HTML5 video. Normally, the default options should work fine in almost every situation, so there is no need to change anything on this page right now:

2. Click on **OK** to close the **Preferences** window and save the changes.

Capturing the Slides

Now that you have a better idea of the available preferences, it is time to have a second try at recording your project.

Shooting the other versions of the project

For this second recording session, you will pursue the following objectives:

- You will generate both the Demonstration and Simulation versions of the project in a single shooting session
- At the end of the project, you will capture the yellowish bar showing the progression of the encoding process using a Full Motion Recording

Your first concern is to reset the stage by preforming the following steps:

1. Reopen AME. When the application appears, make sure it looks like the screenshot in the *Preparing the application to shoot* section.
2. Delete all the .flv files situated in the videos/MOV folder of the exercise files you downloaded from the Internet.
3. Return to Captivate and close every open file, if needed.
4. Navigate to the **File | Record new Software Simulation** menu item to create a new project. The main Captivate interface disappears and the red recording area is displayed.
5. In the recording window, choose **Application** to record **Adobe Media Encoder**. The red recording area snaps to the **Adobe Media Encoder** window.
6. Use a **Custom Size** value of **1024 x 768** pixels to shoot your application.
7. In the recording modes section of the recording window, select all four recording modes (**Demo**, **Assessment**, **Training**, and **Custom**).
8. Leave the other options at their current value.

Chapter 2

9. Make sure your recording window looks like the following screenshot:

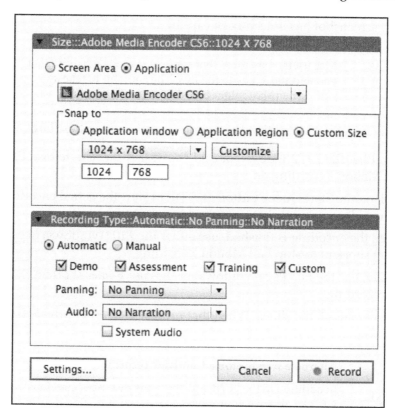

10. When you are ready, click on the red **Record** button. After a short countdown, you'll be back in the recording mode.
11. In **Adobe Media Encoder**, perform the actions as rehearsed earlier in this chapter. Behind the scenes, Captivate is recording!

You should hear a camera shutter sound each time you click and a keystroke sound each time you use the keyboard. Notice that even though two applications are currently active, the mouse and the keyboard are interacting with AME, not with Captivate:

12. Just before clicking on the Start Queue button (the Play icon), click on either the *Print Screen* (Windows) or *cmd + F6* (Mac) buttons to take an extra screenshot manually.

Capturing the Slides

This extra screenshot is necessary to correctly capture the progression of the yellowish bar with a Full Motion Recording. A camera shutter sound lets you know that an extra screenshot has indeed been captured.

> Mac users, remember that some Mac models require that you add the *fn* key to the mix: The shortcut to take an extra screenshot might therefore be *cmd + fn + F6*.

You will now turn the Full Motion Recording on and click on the Start Queue button:

13. Use either the *F9* (Windows) or *cmd + F9* (Mac) shortcut to turn the Full Motion Recording on.
14. Click on the Start Queue button of AME to start the actual encoding of the video.
15. When the encoding is finished, use either the *F10* (Windows) or *cmd + F10* (Mac) shortcut to stop Full Motion Recording.
16. Finally, use the *End* key (Windows) or the *cmd + enter* shortcut (Mac) to stop the recording.

Captivate generates all the slides. When that process is over, Captivate has a nice surprise for you!

> **Alternate way to stop a Captivate recording**
>
> In addition to the keyboard shortcuts discussed previously, you can also use your mouse to stop a Captivate recording. On Windows, click on the Captivate icon situated in the taskbar at the bottom of the screen. On Mac, the same icon is situated in the notification area in the top-right corner of the screen.

Previewing the second rushes

The nice surprise is that Captivate has generated four versions of the same project. This is due to the four checkboxes that you selected at the end of the recording window just before pressing the Record button:

- **untitled_demo1.cptx** was generated based on the **Demo** mode. Save it in your exercises folder as `Chapter02/encoderDemo_1024.cptx`.
- **untiteld_assessment1.cptx** was generated based on the **Assessment Simulation** mode. Save it in your exercises folder as `Chapter02/encoderAssessment_1024.cptx`.

- **untiteld_training1.cptx** was generated based on the **Training Simulation** mode. Save it in your exercises folder as `Chapter02/encoderTraining_1024.cptx`.
- **untiteld_custom.cptx** was generated with the settings of your very own **Custom** mode. Save it in your exercises folder as `Chapter02/encoderCustom_1024.cptx`.

Once these files are saved, you will preview them one by one:

1. Select the `Chapter02/encoderDemo_1024.cptx` file.
2. Use the Preview icon to preview the entire project.

Captivate generates the slides and opens the **Preview** pane.

> If you did not succeed in producing great recordings, you can use the files situated in the `Chapter02/final` folder of the exercises.

The **Demo** mode version of the project is very similar to the one you shot earlier in this chapter. The only major difference is the progression of the yellowish bar that has been correctly captured by Full Motion Recording:

3. When the preview is finished, close the **Preview** pane.
4. Select the `Chapter02/encoderAssessment_1024.cptx` file.
5. Use the Preview icon to preview the entire project.

As described in the **Assessment Simulation** recording mode, the mouse pointer and the Text Captions are not added. After a short while, the project pauses. If you don't do anything, nothing happens, as Captivate is waiting for you to click on the right spot. If you click on the right icon, the project moves on to the next slide and pauses again waiting for your second action. If you do not perform the right action, a red Failure Caption is displayed:

6. When you complete the entire project, close the **Preview** pane.
7. Return to the `Chapter02/encoderTraining_1024.cptx` file.
8. Once again, use the Preview icon to preview the entire project.

As expected, this version of the project is very similar to the previous one. The only difference is the orange Hint Caption that is displayed when the mouse rolls over the hit area of the Click Boxes or Text Entry Boxes. This Hint Caption provides some useful information on the action to be performed by the student:

9. When you are through with the entire project, close the **Preview** pane.

10. Go to the `Chapter02/encoderCustom_1024.cptx` file.
11. Use the Preview icon one more time to preview the entire project.

Your **Custom** recording mode has added Text Captions, Click Boxes, and Text Entry Boxes to the slides, effectively providing an entirely new customized experience.

Of course, none of these four versions of the project are final in any way. There is a lot of work to be done before these projects can be published. That being said, the automatic recording modes of Captivate have successfully provided enough raw material of good quality to get you started. Remember, this is exactly what you should expect from the shooting step of the process.

Shooting with System Audio

New to Captivate 7 is the ability to capture **System Audio** during the recording of a project. System Audio is the sound effects that originate from the application you capture or from your operating system. In the AME example, it is the *chimes* sound effect that is played when the encoding is finished. In this exercise, you will once again capture the sequence of actions described in the scenario, but this time, Captivate will record the System Audio in addition to screenshots and mouse movements.

First, you should reset your applications to their original state:

1. Close AME if it is still open.
2. Reopen AME.

By closing and reopening AME, you effectively reset the application to its default state:

3. Delete every `.flv` file that is situated in the `video/MOV` folder of the exercises.

The second step is to get Captivate ready for the capture session:

4. Return to Captivate and navigate to the **File** | **Close All** menu item to close all open files (if any).
5. Navigate to the **File** | **Record New Software Simulation** menu item to start a new project.
6. In the recording window, choose **Application** to record the **Adobe Media Encoder** application. The red recording area snaps to the AME window.
7. Use a **Custom Size** value of **1024 x 768** pixels to shoot your application.

8. In the recording modes section of the recording window, make sure the **Demo** mode is the only one selected.
9. Also, select the **System Audio** checkbox.

>
> **System Audio on Mac**
>
> If you are on a Mac, the **System Audio** checkbox is not available. Actually, you have to install the **Soundflower system extension** and configure your audio system accordingly before being able to use the new System Audio feature of Captivate 7. The procedure is explained in the knowledge base article at `http://helpx.adobe.com/captivate/kb/system-audio-disabled.html`.

On Windows, System Audio should work right out of the box!

> System Audio requires at least Windows Vista to work. In other words, it does not work on Windows XP!

Once the System Audio has been correctly set up, the recording window should look like the following screenshot:

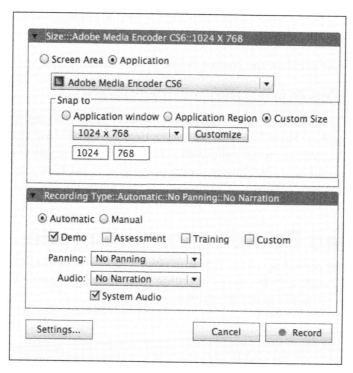

[63]

Capturing the Slides

10. When you are ready, click on the red **Record** button. After a short countdown, you'll be back in the recording mode.
11. In **Adobe Media Encoder**, perform the actions as rehearsed earlier in this chapter. Behind the scenes, Captivate is recording!

Notice that you do not hear the camera shutter sounds and the keystrokes sounds anymore. When System Audio is activated, these sounds are automatically disabled, because, obviously, they don't need to be recorded:

12. Just before clicking on the **Start Queue** button (the Play icon), press the *Print Screen* (Windows) or *cmd + F6* (Mac) shortcut to take an extra screenshot manually.
13. Use the *F9* (Windows) or *cmd + F9* (Mac) shortcut to turn Full Motion Recording on.
14. Click on the Start Queue button of AME to start encoding the video.
15. When the encoding is finished, use the *F10* (Windows) or *cmd + F10* (Mac) shortcut to stop the Full Motion Recording.
16. Finally, use the *End* key (Windows) or the *cmd + Enter* shortcut (Mac) to stop the recording.
17. When Captivate has finished generating all the slides, save this file in the exercises folder as `Chapter02/encoderDemo_sysAudio_1024.cptx`.

As usual, let's now preview the rushes of this new recording session:

18. Use the Preview icon to preview the entire project.

This version of Encoder Demonstration is, again, very similar to the demonstrations you have seen earlier. However, you should notice one significant difference. At the end of the project, when the yellowish progression bar animation is completely finished, you should hear the chimes sound of AME that has been captured thanks to the new System Audio feature of Captivate 7!

The Video Demo recording mode

The **Video Demo** recording mode was introduced as a new feature of Captivate 6. It allows you to create a video file by shooting the onscreen actions. A Video Demo recording project actually is a big Full Motion Recording.

A Video Demo project is very different from the other projects you have worked on so far. Because it is a video file, no interactive objects are possible in such a project. In other words, a Video Demo can only be a demonstration. Because a Video Demo project is based on a single big video file, there are no Slides and no Filmstrip in a Video Demo project.

When it comes to publishing, a Video Demo project can only be published as a .mp4 video file. This makes Video Demo projects particularly suitable for upload to an online video hosting service such as YouTube, Vimeo, or Daily Motion.

In the next exercise, you will create a Video Demo version of Encoder Demonstration. The first operation to do is to reset your system:

 If you have a problem while doing this exercise, refer to the Chapter02/final/encoderVideo.cpvc file of your exercises folder.

1. If the **Adobe Media Encoder** application is still open, close it.
2. Reopen the **Adobe Media Encoder** application.
3. Delete all the .flv files present in the videos/MOV folder of the exercise files.

Now that your system is ready, let's create a Video Demo project:

4. Navigate to the **File | Record new Video Demo** menu item to start a new Video Demo project.

A link to this option is also available on the welcome screen of Captivate when no file is open:

5. In the drop-down list at the top of the recording window, choose to record the **Adobe Media Encoder** application.
6. In the **Snap to** section, choose to record at a **Custom Size** value of **1024 x 768** pixels.

Most of the time, a narration is added to such a project. If you have a microphone available, you'll record your voice in addition to the onscreen action. If you don't have a microphone available, just read through these steps. Audio can also be added later in the process if needed:

7. If a microphone is available, open the **Audio** drop-down list and choose your microphone in the list of entries. The actual content of the list depends on the configuration of your system. In my case, I chose **Built-in Microphone** to use the built-in mike of my laptop.

Capturing the Slides

8. Make sure the other options are at their default settings. The recording window should now look like the following screenshot:

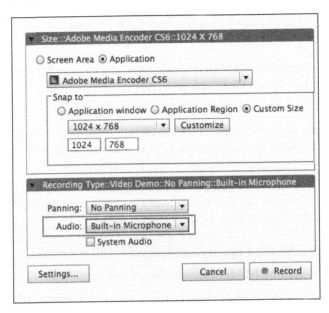

9. Click on the red **Record** button to start the recording.

If this is the first time you are recording sound with your Captivate installation, you'll have to calibrate the sensitivity of your microphone:

10. [Optional] In the **Calibrate Audio Input** dialog, click on the **Auto Calibrate** button. Speak normally in the microphone until the **Input level OK** message appears on the screen. Click on **OK** to validate the sensitivity settings and to discard the box.
11. [Everyone] After a short countdown, the recording begins.
12. [Everyone] In **Adobe Media Encoder**, perform the actions as rehearsed earlier in this chapter. If you have a microphone, speak as you go through the steps of the scenario.
13. When done, hit the *End* key (Windows) or the *cmd + enter* shortcut (Mac).

Captivate finalizes the video capture. When the finalization process is finished, your entire video is played back. Enjoy the show:

14. When the video has finished playing, click on the **Edit** button in the lower right-hand side of the screen.

By clicking on the **Edit** button, you leave the preview mode of the Video Demo project and enter the editing mode. Note how the interface of a Video Demo project is different from the interface of a standard Captivate project:

15. Save your file as Chapter02/encoderVideo.cpvc.

Notice that a Video Demo project does not use the standard .cptx file extension, but uses the .cpvc file extension instead.

Automatic and manual panning

In the movie industry, panning refers to moving the camera during filming. In Captivate, the camera is the red recording area. When panning is turned on in Captivate, it simply means that the red recording area can be moved during the shooting. This enables you to shoot a bigger application with a smaller recording area.

Earlier in this chapter, we had a discussion on how to solve the project-sizing problem. Panning was one of the possible approaches. Let's take a closer look at it:

> If you have a problem while doing this exercise, refer to the Chapter02/final/encoderDemo_panning.cptx file of your exercises folder.

1. Close and reopen AME to reset the user interface.
2. Delete all the .flv files present in the videos/MOV folder of the exercise.
3. Return to Captivate and navigate to the **File | Record New Software Simulation** menu item. The Captivate interface disappears and the red recording area shows up.
4. In the recording window, choose to record a **Screen Area** (and not an **Application** as before). Give the area a **Custom Size** value of **800 x 600** pixels.

Normally, the size of the **Adobe Media Encoder** application should still be **1024 x 768** pixels from the previous filming sessions:

5. Move the red recording area such that its top-left corner corresponds to the top-left corner of the **Adobe Media Encoder** application window.

In this configuration, the size of AME does not match the size of the red recording area. The recording area should be smaller than the AME:

6. In the bottom part of the recording window, make sure the **Demo** mode is the only one selected.
7. In the **Panning** drop-down list, choose **Manual Panning**.

Capturing the Slides

8. If necessary, set the **Audio** drop-down option to **No Narration**.

Your computer screen should look like the following screenshot:

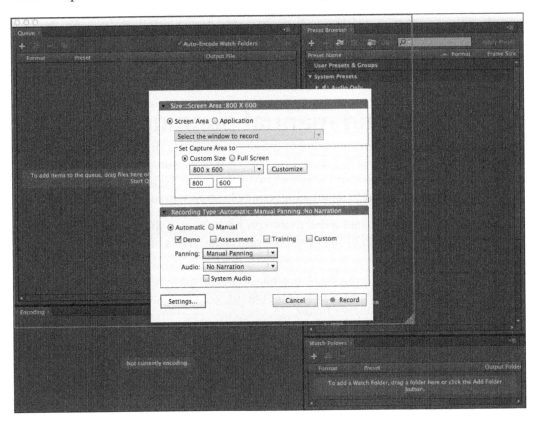

9. When ready, click on the red **Record** button to switch to the recording mode.
10. After the countdown, perform the first few steps of the scenario in the **Adobe Media Encoder** application.
11. When the **Export Settings** window opens, place your mouse above the red line of the recording area until the mouse turns into a grabbing hand. Then, slowly move the red recording area until it covers more or less the lower right-hand part of the **Export Settings** window.
12. In AME, modify the size of the video as defined in the scenario.
13. When the **Export Settings** dialog closes after you clicked on the **OK** button, move the red recording area back to its original position.
14. Click on the Start Queue button (the green Play icon) as defined in the scenario.
15. When done, hit *End* (Windows) or *cmd + enter* (Mac) to return to Captivate.

16. When the project loads in Captivate, use the Preview icon to preview the entire project. Can you see the panning movements in the **Preview** pane?
17. When the movie is finished, close the **Preview** pane and save the file as `Chapter02/encoderDemo_panning.cptx`.

Back in Captivate, take a look at the **Filmstrip** panel. Beneath some of the slides thumbnails, you should see the Camera icon indicating that there are some Full Motion Recording slides in the project. Full Motion Recording is used to reproduce the panning movements made during the capture.

In this example, you have used manual panning. When using automatic panning, Captivate places the mouse at the center of the red recording area. During filming, the red recording area automatically follows any mouse movement. Automatic panning produces a lot of unnecessary movements, and, consequently, a lot of extra Full Motion Recording slides.

Rescaling a project

This chapter opened with a discussion on choosing the right size for the project. This discussion led to four possible approaches to manage the size difference between the application to capture and the movie to produce.

The first approach was to shoot big and then downsize. The first step of this approach was done when you used a resolution of 1024 x 768 pixels to shoot your very first movie. You will now take care of the second step: resizing the movie to 800 x 600 pixels.

Remember that resizing a project is a one-way operation that always results in data and quality loss. If another solution that does not require resizing the project is available, go for it! If a resize operation cannot be avoided, always keep a backup copy of your project at its original size.

1. In Captivate, open the `chapter02/encoderDemo_1024.cptx` file.

If you did not successfully save this file earlier in this chapter, you can use the one saved in the `chapter02/final` folder.

If you have a problem while doing this exercise, refer to the `Chapter02/final/encoderDemo_800.cptx` file of your exercises folder.

2. Navigate to the **File | Save As** menu item to save the file as `Chapter02/encoderDemo_800.cptx`.

Capturing the Slides

3. When the project is saved, navigate to the **Modify | Rescale Project** menu item.

The **Rescale Project** window opens. This window is divided into three parts. The top part allows you to define the new size of the project. It is the only part available at the moment:

4. Make sure the **Maintain Aspect Ration** box is selected.
5. Reduce the **Width** value of the project from **1024** to **800** pixels. The new **Height** value of **600** pixels should be calculated automatically.

As the new size is smaller than the original size, the lower right-hand part of the box becomes available. It is titled: **If new size is smaller**. The lower left-hand part of the box is still inactive. It would activate if the new size of the project were larger than the original size:

6. Take some time to review the available options, but leave the default unchanged. When ready, click on **Finish**.
7. A dialog box informs you that resizing a project cannot be undone. Click on **OK** to confirm you want to resize the project anyway.
8. Captivate resizes each slide, one by one.
9. Save the file when the resize process is complete.

Although Captivate does a great job resizing all the objects on the slides, I still recommend going though each slide to ensure the size conversion was successful for every object on every slide.

Summary

In this chapter, you have completed the first step of the Captivate production process: capturing the slides. Throughout this chapter, your main concern was to manage the size of the project as compared to the size of the application to capture.

Several approaches are possible to address this size issue. While experiencing each of these approaches, you uncovered two important features of Captivate: Full Motion Recording and panning.

Shooting a Captivate recording is a four-step process. First, you have to prepare the application to shoot and reset your system to default. Then, you rehearse the script as many times as needed to fully master all the actions. The third step is to shoot the movie, and the last step is to preview the rushes. If you decide that the rushes are not good enough, just start over until you get it right. Remember that the success of the editing phase that follows depends on the quality of the shooting.

You also discovered that Captivate has four automatic recording modes that are **Demonstration**, **Assessment Simulation**, **Training Simulation**, and a **Custom** mode that is yours to create. Each of these automatic recording modes adds Text Captions and other objects to the slides.

The Video Demo recording mode is entirely dedicated to producing linear, non-interactive .mp4 video files. These can be easily uploaded to online video hosting services such as YouTube, Vimeo, and DailyMotion.

Finally, Captivate 7 introduces the System Audio feature that allows you to capture sound effects originating from the applications or from the system in addition to the screenshots and the onscreen action.

Of course, the recordings made in this chapter are by no means final products, but that was not your goal anyway. These projects now have to go through the editing phase to reach their final aspect.

To wrap up this chapter, these are some additional tips and tricks for successful recordings:

- Use the automatic recording modes whenever possible.
- If you have to shoot full-screen, reset your desktop to its default appearance, that is, remove your custom wallpaper and turn off any custom color scheme or mouse pointer sets. Your computer should look like any computer.
- Turn off your screensaver.
- Turn on the sound so that you can hear the camera shutter and the keystrokes. This will help you have better control over the recording process. Remember, however, that if you turn on **System Audio**, these sound effects are automatically disabled.
- If you are not sure whether or not Captivate took a given screenshot, don't hesitate to take one manually using the *Print Screen* key (Windows) or the *cmd + F6* shortcut (Mac). During the editing phase that follows, it is much easier to delete an extra slide than to generate a missing slide.
- Perform the actions slowly, especially the text typing actions and the actions that require Full Motion Recording. You'll be able to set up the timing of each slide with great precision during the editing phase.
- Rehearse your scripts before shooting.

With these tips and tricks and a bit of practice, you'll soon be producing high-quality eLearning content!

In the next chapter, you begin the editing phase of your work. The editing phase is the most time-consuming phase of the entire process. There are so many options and tools to discover that one chapter will not be enough to cover it all. Consequently, the editing phase will span the next few chapters.

Meet the community

In this section, I'd like to introduce you to Anita Horsley, one of the most active members of the Captivate community and an awesome Captivate Certified Instructor. She authored

the *Fast Track to Adobe Captivate 6* video series by *Packt Publishing* (see `http://www.packtpub.com/fast-track-to-adobe-captivate-6/video`). She has also been a reviewer for two of my Captivate books (including this one!). So if you like this book, part of the credit goes to her. (Thanks Anita! I owe you one!)

Anita Horsley

During Anita Horsley's tenure as a firefighter, she initiated, developed, and managed the health and safety program. At the Oregon State Fire Marshal, she founded the eLearning track as well as implemented and coordinated the eLearning team and internal training. She managed the learning management system and chaired the Oregon State Captivate User Group. She is the founder and President of CALEX Learning Consultants, LLC, and an independent consultant. In addition, she is an Adobe Captivate instructor and eLearning developer. She presents webinars for Adobe and ASTD and at conferences nationally. She authored the video tutorial series *Fast Track To Adobe Captivate 6* by *Packt Publishing*. She also has a blog named *Crazy About Captivate* that provides tips and tricks on Adobe Captivate. She holds a Master's in Education and is an Adobe Certified Expert in Captivate.

Contact details

- **Web**: `http://calex-llc.com`
- **Blog**: `http://captivatecrazy.blogspot.com`
- **Twitter**: `@captivatecrazy`
- **LinkedIn**: `http://www.linkedin.com/in/anitahorsley`
- **Google +**: `https://plus.google.com/u/0/+CALEXLearningConsultantsLLCCharleston/posts`
- **Facebook**: `https://www.facebook.com/CALEXLearningConsultantsLLC`

3
Working with Standard Objects

Once filming is complete, the director takes the rushes and heads toward the post-production studio to begin the most time-consuming phase of the project. While in the studio, the director arranges the sequences that were shot during the filming in the correct order, adds sound effects, arranges transitions, fine-tunes visual and special effects, adds subtitles, and re-records narration, among other actions. When the director leaves the post-production studio, the motion picture is complete and ready for publishing.

The same basic principle applies to your Captivate projects. During the post-production phase, you will revisit each slide one by one to arrange, reorder, synchronize, add, modify, align, delete, and so on. To help you turn your rushes into a great eLearning experience, Captivate provides an extensive array of tools, features, and objects. In the next few chapters, you will take a closer look at each of them.

The first thing you can do to enhance your projects is to add objects on top of the slides. This particular chapter focuses on nine of those objects and on various tools to effectively manage them once in place.

In this chapter, you will be doing the following:

- Learning how to use the **Properties** panel
- Taking an in-depth look at nine objects of Captivate
- Adding basic formatting to these objects
- Creating custom animations with the **Effects** panel
- Using the alignment tools of Captivate to arrange objects on the slide
- Using the **Timeline** to organize the sequence of events
- Working with the **Library** panel

Working with Standard Objects

Preparing your work

Before getting started, you will prepare Captivate by opening the required files and by resetting the **Classic** workspace to its default appearance as follows:

1. Open Captivate.
2. Navigate to **File** | **Open** to open the `encoderDemo_800.cptx` file in the `Chapter03` folder in your exercise folder.
3. Also, open the `drivingInBe.cptx` file in the `Chapter03` folder of your exercise folder.
4. When both files are open, make sure the **Classic** workspace is applied.
5. Navigate to **Window** | **Workspace** | **Reset 'Classic'** to reset the **Classic** workspace to its default look.

Resetting the **Classic** workspace to its default appearance ensures that your computer screen will look exactly like the screenshots of this book.

To ensure maximum accuracy between the files you work with and the exercises described in this book, make sure you use the files of the `Chapter03` folder and not the ones you created in the previous chapter. During the exercises, feel free to experiment with the files. You'll have a fresh set of files to work with at the beginning of each chapter.

Each of the open files has its own window in the Captivate interface. When doing the exercises of this chapter, make sure you are using the right file.

The `final` folder in `Chapter03` contains the completed projects as they are supposed to be at the end of this chapter. If you get confused with any of the exercises, use these projects as references.

Chapter 3

Working with the Properties panel

For this section, use the `encoderDemo_800.cptx` file **(1)**.

As shown in the following screenshot, in the **Classic** workspace, the **Properties** panel is situated on the right-hand side of the interface **(2)**. It is one of the most important and useful panels of Captivate.

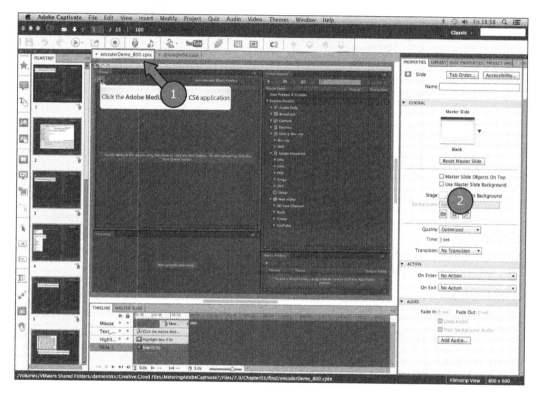

The **Properties** panel **(2)** is a dynamic panel. It means that the content of this panel changes depending on the selected object. Let's experiment with this, hands-on.

1. In the **Filmstrip** panel, click on the first slide to make it the active slide.

You should be able to read the word **Slide** at the very top of the **Properties** panel. This tells you that the selected object is of type **Slide**. The selected object's properties are displayed in the **Properties** panel.

2. Take some time to examine the available properties in the **Properties** panel.

The selected slide contains three objects: a Text Caption, the Mouse object, and a blue **Highlight Box** next to the mouse pointer. These three objects have been automatically generated by the **Demo** recording mode used during the capture.

[75]

Working with Standard Objects

3. Click on the Text Caption object of slide 1 to make it the active object.

At the very top of the **Properties** panel, you should now read **Text Caption** because the selected object is of that type. Consequently, the panel now shows the properties relevant to an object of type Text Caption.

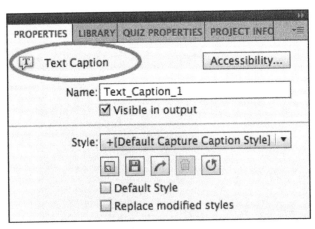

In the panel, the properties of the Text Caption are divided into sections. These sections can be expanded and collapsed by clicking on their respective title bars. For an object of type Text Caption, there should be eight sections available in the **Properties** panel (**General, Characters, Format**, and so on).

4. Click on the word **Character** to collapse the **Character** section of the **Properties** panel.
5. Click on the **Character** word again to expand the section.

Before moving on, take a look at the other sections of the **Properties** panel, but leave all the options at their current settings.

6. While still on slide 1, select the blue **Highlight Box** next to the mouse pointer.

 Because all three objects share the same area of the slide, selecting the **Highlight Box** might be tricky. To make the selection easier, you can select the blue **Highlight Box** from the **Timeline** panel (at the bottom of the screen) as well.

7. The word **Highlight Box** is now written at the very top of the **Properties** panel, which displays the properties relevant to an object of type Highlight Box.

With the **Highlight Box** selected, take a close look at the sections of the **Properties** panel. Most of the sections available for an object of type Highlight Box are the same as those available for an object of type Text Caption.

Usually, the sections situated at the top of the stack (here, the **Fill & Stroke** section) are specific to the selected type of object. The sections at the bottom of the stack (such as the **Timing** or the **Transition** sections) contain *shared* properties relevant to many types of objects.

To work with the **Properties** panel, remember the following:

- In the default **Classic** workspace, the **Properties** panel is displayed on the right-hand side of the screen.
- The **Properties** panel is a dynamic panel. It means it shows the properties relevant to the active object. Consequently, selecting another object updates the content of the **Properties** panel.
- The **Properties** panel is divided into sections that can be expanded and collapsed at will.
- Some of these sections are specific to a certain type of object.
- Other sections are shared by many types of objects.

Now that you know how the **Properties** panel works, you will learn about the basic objects of Captivate.

Exploring the objects of Captivate

Captivate offers more than a dozen objects. In this chapter, you will learn about nine of those objects. These nine objects are the standard non-interactive objects of Captivate. In *Chapter 5, Adding Interactivity to the Project*, you will learn about the more complex interactive objects. The first one you will focus on is the Text Caption object.

The Text Caption object

The Text Caption object is the most basic object in Captivate. It is typically used when there is a need to display text to the learners. In its most basic form, the Text Caption is a text item that appears and disappears from the screen according to its position on the **Timeline** panel.

The Demonstration auto-recording mode you used during the filming already added many Text Captions on your slides. Some of these might be just right, but most of them, if not all of them, will need some extra work.

Working with Standard Objects

Modifying the content of a Text Caption

There are two editing modes available when working with Text Captions:

- First, you can consider the Text Caption as an object. In this case, eight white squares appear around the text caption **(1)**. These white squares are the handles used to resize the Text Caption. This is the non-editing mode. You can move the Text Caption around and resize it, but you cannot edit the text inside the Text Caption.
- To edit the text, you must be in the editing mode. In the text-editing mode, the eight white handles disappear and a blinking cursor **(2)** appears in the Text Caption.

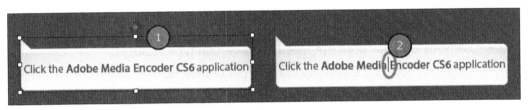

In the next exercise, you will modify the content of the Text Captions:

1. In the `encoderDemo_800.cptx` file, click on the Text Caption of slide 1 to make it the active object.
2. Double-click on the Text Caption object or press the *F2* shortcut key.

The eight white handles disappear and a blinking cursor appears in the Text Caption **(2)**.

By double-clicking on the Text Caption object, you switch to text-editing mode, where you can easily modify the content of a Text Caption.

3. Triple-click inside the Text Caption to select all of its current content.
4. In the Text Caption, type `The Mouse will now click on the Add files` icon.
5. Hit the *Esc* key to toggle the Text Caption back to the non-editing mode.

Now, take some time to practice that by updating the content of the remaining Text Captions of the project according to the following table. You may need to resize the Text Captions appropriately.

Slide number	Content of Text Caption
Slide 2	The Mouse will now double-click on the demo_en.mov video file.
Slide 3	The Mouse will now click on the Format drop-down menu.
Slide 4	The Mouse will now click on the FLV menu item.
Slide 5	The Mouse will now click on the Preset drop-down menu.
Slide 6	The Mouse will now click on the WEB - 640x480, 4x3... preset.
Slide 7	The Mouse will now click on the preset's name to open the Export Settings dialog.
Slide 10	The Mouse will now click the current Width of the video.
Slide 11	Enter the desired Width (in this case 400 pixels) and hit the Enter key.
Slide 12	The Mouse will now click on the OK button to validate the changes and close the Export Settings dialog.

These simple edits already make the project much easier to understand for learners.

6. Save the file (*Ctrl + S* for Windows or *command + S* for Mac).
7. Use the Preview icon to test the entire project.

Of course, you still have to fine-tune the formatting and the timing of the objects, but the content of the Text Captions should be correct.

8. Close the **Preview** pane when finished.

Next, you will learn how to add new Text Captions to the project.

Creating new Text Captions

So far, you have modified the Text Captions that were automatically generated during the filming. You will now create and modify brand new Text Captions.

1. Use the **Filmstrip** panel to return to slide 1.

Slide 1 already contains one Text Caption. You will now add a second one.

2. Navigate to **Insert | Standard Object | Text Caption** to create a new Text Caption.

By default, a new Text Caption appears in the middle of the slide in text editing mode.

3. Type `Welcome to the Adobe Media Encoder` in the new Text Caption.
4. Hit the *Esc* key to leave the text editing mode. The new Text Caption should still be selected.

In this particular project, the default formatting of a new Text Caption does not allow for comfortable reading.

5. With the Text Caption still selected, look at the **Properties** panel. Under the **General** section, note that the **Caption** drop-down list is set to **Transparent**.
6. Open the **Caption** drop-down and choose **Halo Blue** in the list of available Caption types.

There is another Text Caption to add to slide 4.

7. Use the **Filmstrip** panel to select slide 4.
8. Use the second icon, down from the top of the objects toolbar, to insert a new Text Caption.
9. Double-click inside the Text Caption and type `The H.264 options generate a .mp4 video file [Press Enter] The MP3 option is for sound only!`.
10. Hit the *Esc* key to leave the text editing mode while keeping the Text Caption selected.
11. In the **Properties** panel under the **General** section, apply the **Halo Blue** caption type to the new Text Caption.
12. Use the **Filmstrip** panel to go to slide 5.
13. Use the *Ctrl + Shift + C* (Windows) or the *command + shift + C* (Mac) shortcut to add a second Text Caption to the slide.
14. Enter `The conversion settings will be different depending on the intended purpose of your video file` in the Text Caption.
15. Apply the **Halo Blue** caption type to the new Text Caption.

The preceding exercise shows you three different ways of inserting a new Text Caption into the project:

- Navigate to **Insert** | **Standard Object** | **Text Caption**.
- Use the second icon of the objects toolbar. Remember that the objects toolbar is the set of icons that is on the left edge of the screen.
- Use the *Ctrl + Shift + C* (Windows) or *command + shift + C* (Mac) shortcut key.

Extra credit – adding Text Captions

Add the remaining Text Captions in the project according to the following table. Make sure you apply the **Halo Blue** caption type to each new Text Caption.

Slide	Text Caption	Final amount of Text Captions on the slide
Slide 1	Welcome to the Adobe Media encoder.	2
Slide 5	The Adobe Media Encoder contains a list of presets to help you make the right choice.	3
Slide 7	The chosen preset needs some adjustments to perfectly match your needs.	2
Slide 8	The chosen preset already adjusted most of these options correctly. Only the size of the generated video must be changed.	3
Slide 12	Notice that AME has automatically calculated the new height of the video. This is because the Maintain aspect ratio icon is currently selected.	3
Slide 13	By modifying an existing preset, you actually created a new one. The mouse will now click on the Process Queue icon.	2
Slide 14	The encoding panel contains information about how the conversion is progressing.	1
Slide 15	All done!	1

Formatting a Text Caption

Captivate offers many tools and features to format a Text Caption object. Most of them are available in the various sections of the **Properties** panel.

Resizing and moving Text Captions

In Captivate, resizing and moving objects is very easy and can be done in two different ways: using the white handles or using the **Transform** section in the **Properties** panel.

1. While still in the `encoderDemo_800.cptx` file, use the **Filmstrip** panel to select slide 1.
2. Click on the **Welcome to the Adobe Media Encoder** Text Caption to make it the active object.
3. At the end of the **Properties** panel, expand the **Transform** section.

In the **Transform** section, take a look at the size of the selected Text Caption. **W** indicates the width of the object, while **H** stands for the height. Both dimensions are expressed in pixels. (Actual values may differ from the following screenshot):

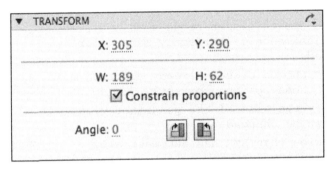

4. On the stage, use the white handles to make the Text Caption a bit bigger.
5. Take another look at the **Properties** panel. The height and width fields of the **Transform** section should reflect the new size of the object.

If you want to give your objects a specific size, you can enter the height and the width in the **Properties** panel directly. If the **Constrain proportions** checkbox is selected, Captivate automatically calculates the new height of the object when you modify the width (and vice versa) so that the height/width ratio of the object does not change.

6. With the Text Caption still selected, take look at the **X** and **Y** values in the **Transform** section.
7. Use your mouse to move the Text Caption around the slide.

See how the **X** and **Y** values of the **Transform** section change as you move the Text Caption. The **X** coordinate is the distance (in pixels) between the left edge of the selected object and the left edge of the slide. The **Y** coordinate is the distance (in pixels) between the top edge of the selected object and the top of the slide. You can manually enter the **X** and **Y** coordinates in the **Transform** panel to give the selected object a pixel-precise location on the slide.

Changing the Callout and the Caption type

You probably noted that a Text Caption has the shape of a callout. Captivate proposes five **Callout** types for each Text Caption.

1. Use the **Filmstrip** panel to go to slide 5 of the encoderDemo_800.cptx file.
2. Select the Text Caption that starts with **The Adobe Media Encoder contains**....
3. Resize this Text Caption so the entire text fits well on two lines.
4. Take a look at the **General** section of the **Properties** panel.
5. In the **Callout** section, choose the second **Callout** type as shown in the following screenshot:

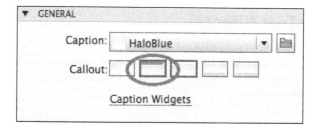

Captivate applies the new callout to the Text Caption.

6. In the **General** section of the **Properties** panel, open the **Caption** drop-down list.
7. In the list, choose the **Business Yellow** Caption Type.

The **Business Yellow** caption type is applied to the object.

Formatting characters and paragraphs

To finalize the formatting of this Text Caption, use the options under the **Character** and **Format** sections of the **Properties** panel.

1. Still on slide 5, make sure the Text Caption (**The Adobe Media Encoder contains**...) is still selected.

2. In the **Character** section of the **Properties** panel, change the font **Family** to **Verdana**.
3. Also change the font **Size** to 19 points.
4. In the **Format** section, align the text as **Center** and **Middle**.
5. Make sure the Text Caption looks similar to what is shown in the following screenshot before moving on.

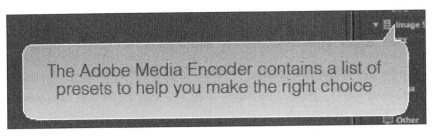

6. Save the file when done.

In the next chapter, you will learn how to use the Styles and the Master Slides to quickly apply this formatting to the other Text Captions of the project.

Working with Text Effects

The Text Effects feature was introduced in Captivate 6. It lets you create and apply some sophisticated visual effects to Text Captions. If you use Photoshop, you'll be in known territory as Captivate's Text Effects feature shares most of its functionalities with the effects of Photoshop.

To experiment with Text Effects, switch to the Driving in Belgium project.

1. Open the `drivingInBe.cptx` file in the `Chapter03` folder from your exercises folder. If the project is already open, just switch to the right tab in Captivate.
2. Use the **Filmstrip** panel to go to slide 5 of this project.

Slide 5 should contain two Text Captions.

3. Select the Text Caption that reads **Good** to make it the active object.
4. In the **General** section of the **Properties** panel, change the **Caption** type to **Transparent**.
5. In the **Character** section, change the font **Family** to **Verdana** and the font **Size** to 49.

Chapter 3

6. Still in the **Character** section of the **Properties** panel, click on the Text Effects icon (identified as **(1)** in the following screenshot).

The Text Effects menu opens. In the topmost area of the menu, eight predefined effects are ready to use **(2)**. The last four effects are yours to create **(3)**.

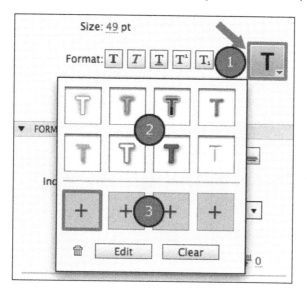

7. Click on the first empty effect.

The **Text Effects** window opens. The left-hand side of the window contains nine effects. You can easily turn these effects on and off by clicking on their respective checkbox. The right-hand side of the window displays the options of the effect selected on the left. At this moment, no effect is applied.

8. In the left column of the **Text Effects** window, select the **Drop Shadow** checkbox.

A Drop Shadow effect is added to the selected Text Caption. For this example, you will accept the default settings of the Drop Shadow effect.

9. In the left column of the **Text Effects** window, select the **Outer Glow** checkbox.

The **Outer Glow** effect is also applied to the Text Caption, and the options of the **Outer Glow** effect are displayed on the right-hand side of the **Text Effects** window. To make your effect more attractive and visible, modify the color of the Outer Glow effect.

10. On the right-hand side of the **Text Effects** window, click on the **Color** option of the **Outer Glow** effect.

Working with Standard Objects

11. In the color picker on the right-hand side of the window, choose any bright green color. After this procedure, the **Text Effects** window should look similar to what is shown in the following screenshot:

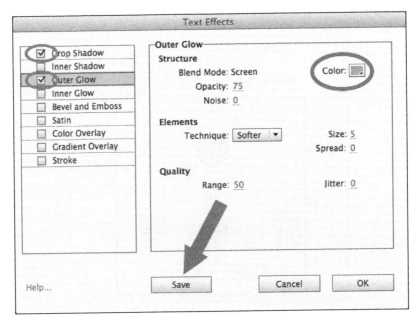

Hey! It looks like you just came up with a very nice effect. Let's save it for future use.

12. At the bottom of the **Text Effects** window, click on the **Save** button (see the arrow in the preceding screenshot).

The **Text Effects** window closes and your effect is applied to the selected Text Caption. Because you have saved your nice effect, it will be very easy to apply it to another Text Caption of the project.

13. While in the `drivingInBe.cptx` file, use the **Filmstrip** panel to go to slide 10.
14. Once on slide 10, select the Text Caption that reads **Good**.
15. In the **General** section of the **Properties** panel, change the **Caption** type to **Transparent**.
16. In the **Character** section, change the font **Family** to **Verdana** and the font **Size** to 49.
17. While in the **Character** section of the **Properties** panel, open the **Text Effects** menu.

Surprise! A ninth effect is now available in the Text Effects icon! It is the effect that you just saved a few lines ago.

18. Click on this new effect to apply it to the selected Text Caption.

Great! You can now create some sophisticated visual effects and easily apply them to the Text Captions of your movie.

19. While in the `drivingInBe.cptx` file, use the **Filmstrip** panel to go to slide 6.
20. Once on slide 6, select the Text Caption that begins with **Belgians use…**.
21. In the **General** section, change the **Caption** type to **Transparent**.
22. In the **Character** section, change the font **Family** to **Verdana** and the font **Size** to 49. Resize the Text Caption if necessary.
23. While in the **Character** section of the **Properties** panel, open the Text Effect icon one more time.
24. Apply your new effect to the selected Text Caption.

Your new effect is applied to the **Belgian use…** Text Caption. You will now modify the color of the Outer Glow effect. By doing so, you will come up with a new Text Effect that you will save and apply to another Text Caption of the project.

25. Make sure the Text Effects icon is still open in the **Character** section of the **Properties** panel.
26. Click on the **Edit** button.

The Text Effects window will re-open.

27. On the left-hand side of the **Text Effects** window, click on the **Outer Glow** effect (make sure you click on the name of the effect, not on the checkbox).
28. On the right-hand side of the window, open the **Color** option of the **Outer Glow** effect.
29. In the color picker, choose any bright red color. The new **Outer Glow** color is automatically applied to the selected Text Caption.
30. At the bottom of the **Text Effect** window, click on the **Save** button to save this as a new effect.

Make sure the Text Caption looks like the following picture:

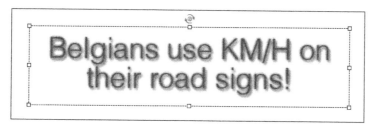

Working with Standard Objects

Finally, you will apply this second effect to another Text Caption of the project.

31. Use the **Filmstrip** panel to go to slide 11.
32. Once on slide 11, select the Text Caption that begins with **Belgians drive...**.
33. In the **General** section, change the **Caption** type to **Transparent**. In the **Character** section, change the font **Family** to **Verdana** and the font **Size** to 49. Resize the Text Caption if necessary.
34. While still being in the **Character** section of the **Properties** panel, open the Text Effects icon.
35. Apply your new red effect to the selected Text Caption.
36. Save the `drivingInBe.cptx` file when done.

 Such a Text Effect must be applied to the entire Text Caption. It is not possible to select a portion of the text and apply the effect to the selected portion only.

This exercise concludes your first exploration of the Text Caption object. Before moving on to the next object, let's summarize what you have learned about Text Captions.

- The Text Caption object is used to display text to the learner.
- The Demo recording mode automatically adds Text Captions to the slides.
- Changing the size or the position of an object with the mouse also changes the corresponding values in the **Transform** section of the **Properties** panel and vice versa.
- Apply a Caption Type to the object to quickly format it.
- Captivate provides five **Callout** types for each Caption Type.
- Text Effects let you create and apply sophisticated visual effect on your Text Captions. They can be saved and reapplied to other Text Captions easily.

There still is some work to be done on the other Text captions of your projects, which you'll complete later in this book. For now, let's explore another object.

The Highlight Box object

The second object you will focus on is the Highlight Box. As its name implies, a Highlight Box is used to highlight a specific area of the screen. It is a rectangle that appears and disappears from the screen according to its position on the **Timeline** panel.

When using the default Demo recording mode during the capture, Captivate adds one Highlight Box for each mouse click.

1. Return to the `EncoderDemo_800.cptx` project in the `Chapter03` folder.
2. In the **Filmstrip** panel, click on slide 1.

Slide 1 should contain four objects: two Text Captions, a Mouse object, and a small blue Highlight Box below the mouse pointer. This Highlight Box has been automatically added by Captivate during filming.

3. Click on the Highlight Box to make it the active object.

Selecting the Highlight Box

Because the Highlight Box is so close to the Mouse object, you may end up selecting the Mouse object instead of the Highlight Box. Remember that you can use the **Timeline** panel to select the desired object.

Selecting the Highlight Box updates the **Properties** panel. At the top of the **Properties** panel, the **Fill & Stroke** section is the only one that is specific to this type of object. It provides the main formatting options of the selected Highlight Box.

- The first option is the **Fill** property. The **Fill** is the inside of the object.
- Next to the **Fill** property is the Alpha parameter. It is used to control the opacity of the Highlight Box. When the Alpha is set to 0 percent, the object is completely transparent. When the Alpha is set to 100 percent, the object is completely opaque.
- The third setting is the **Stroke** property. The **Stroke** is the border around the object. The **Stroke** option lets you change the color of the border.
- The last option is the **Width** property. This option lets you choose the Width of the stroke. Setting this option to 0 removes the stroke from the object.

Now that you have a better idea of the available options, you will change the formatting of the selected Highlight Box.

4. In the **Fill & Stroke** section of the **Properties** panel, click on **Fill**.
5. In the Color picker, choose a dark orange as the fill color.
6. Leave the Alpha value at **20 %**.
7. Click on **Stroke**.

Working with Standard Objects

8. In the color picker, choose the same orange color as the one you chose for the fill. Note that the recently selected colors are available at the end of the color swatch.

9. In the **Width** section, choose a stroke width of 2 pixels.

Make sure your **Fill & Stroke** section looks similar to what is shown in the following screenshot:

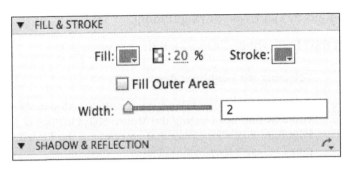

Finally, you will use the **Transform** section of the **Properties** panel to modify the size and position of the Highlight Box.

10. While still on slide 1 of the `encoderDemo_800.cptx` file, make sure the Highlight Box is the selected object.

11. In the **Properties** panel, open the **Transform** section.

12. For the size, change the Width field to 24 pixels and Height field to 19 pixels (to be able to modify the height independently from the width, make sure the **Constrain proportions** checkbox is deselected).

13. For the position, give the Highlight Box an **X** coordinate of 4 pixels and a **Y** coordinate of 32 pixels.

The Highlight Box should precisely cover the Add Files (**+**) icon.

14. Use the Preview icon to preview the next five slides.

Captivate generates the slides and opens the Preview pane. Take a close look at the Highlight box of slide 1. The timing and formatting of the objects are of no importance at this time.

When the preview is finished, close the **Preview** pane to return to Captivate. There is one last option to experiment with.

15. Return to slide 1 of the `encoderDemo_800.cptx` file and select the orange Highlight Box.

16. Make the Alpha % field to 70 percent transparency.

[90]

17. In the **Fill & Stroke** section of the **Properties** panel, select the **Fill Outer Area** checkbox.

With this option enabled, the fill color of the Highlight Box will be applied to the area outside of the object. The only part of the slide that will not be covered by the fill color will be the inside of the Highlight Box. It is necessary to see the project in Preview mode to see the Fill Outer Area option in action!

18. Still on slide 1 of the `encoderDemo_800.cptx` files, click on the Preview icon and choose **Next 5 Slides**.

When the project starts playing in the Preview pane, pay close attention to the way the Highlight Box behaves.

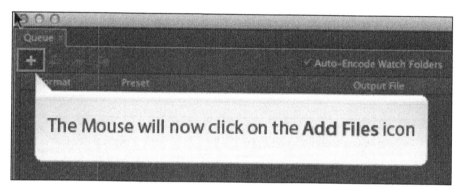

19. Return to slide 1 of the `encoderDemo_800.cptx` file and select the orange Highlight Box one last time.

20. In this particular case, you want the Highlight Box to behave normally, so, in the **Fill & Stroke** section of the **Properties** panel, deselect the **Fill Outer Area** checkbox.

21. Save the file when done.

This last experiment concludes this discussion on Highlight Boxes. Here is a summary of what you have learned.

- A Highlight Box is a rectangle used to highlight a particular spot on the slide.
- The fill is the inside of the Highlight Box object. The **Fill & Stroke** section of the **Properties** panel lets you choose the color and opacity of the fill.
- The Stroke is the border around the Highlight Box object. You can choose the color and width of the stroke in the **Properties** panel.
- Select the **Fill Outer Area** option to apply the fill color to the outside of the Highlight Box rather than to the inside.

Working with the mouse

The third object to study is the Mouse. Remember that during filming, only the coordinates of the mouse clicks were recorded and the mouse movements are recreated during playback.

Understanding the mouse movements

You will start your study of the Mouse object by discovering how Captivate manages the mouse movements.

1. Return to slide 1 of the `encoderDemo_800.cptx` file.

On this slide, you should see four red dots in the top-left corner of the slide. These four dots mark the starting point of the mouse.

2. Use your mouse to move the four red dots anywhere on the slide.

By moving the four red dots, you change the starting point of the mouse on slide 1.

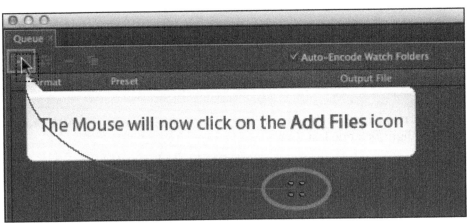

From the chosen spot, Captivate generates a curved blue line that represents the mouse movement. This curved line ends with the mouse pointer.

3. Click on the mouse pointer at the end of the curved blue line to select the Mouse object. The **Properties** panel will be updated.
4. In the **Options** section of the **Properties** panel, tick the **Straight Pointer Path** box.

By clicking on this box, Captivate generates a straight line between the start and end points of the mouse movement.

5. In the **Options** section of the **Properties** panel, deselect the **Straight Pointer Path** checkbox.
6. Use the **Filmstrip** panel to select slide 2.

On the second slide, the four red dots that were visible on slide 1 are not visible. It means that you cannot move the starting point of the mouse on slide 2. This is because the starting point of the mouse on slide 2 corresponds to the end point of the mouse on slide 1.

7. Use the **Filmstrip** panel to browse the remaining slides of the project.

When browsing the slides of the project, note that the first slide is the only one where the starting point of the mouse movement can be moved. No other slides display the four red dots at the beginning of the curved blue line.

8. When done, return to slide 1.
9. Take the mouse pointer and move it to a random location.
10. Use the **Filmstrip** panel to select slide 2.

On slide 2, note that the starting point of the curved blue line has changed and corresponds to the random location you chose on slide 1.

11. On the **Filmstrip** panel, click on slide 1 to make it the active slide.
12. Move the mouse pointer back to its original location.
13. Use the **Filmstrip** panel to go to the last slide of the project (slide 15).

On slide 15, the mouse makes a long movement. As slide 15 is the last one of the project, this movement is unnecessary. What you want to do is completely remove the Mouse object from this slide.

14. On slide 15, right-click the mouse pointer at the end of the blue line.
15. In the contextual menu, deselect the **Show Mouse** item. You can also navigate to **Modify | Mouse | Show Mouse** to achieve the same result.

Note that the coordinates of the Mouse object recorded during the filming are still saved with the slide should you change your mind about the Mouse object being hidden on slide 15.

16. Use the **Filmstrip** panel to go to slide 11 of the `encoderDemo_800.cptx` file.

This is the slide where you typed `400` in the Width field of AME. The next slide (slide 12) is where the Mouse object moves to click on the **OK** button of the **Export Settings** dialog. For this particular sequence, you want to have a single action per slide. So, slide 11 should only show the typing in the Width field with no mouse movement. Slide 12 should show the entire Mouse movement.

17. Still on slide 11, right-click on the mouse pointer to select the Mouse object.
18. In the contextual menu, click on the **Align to Previous Slide** item.

By clicking on the **Align to Previous Slide** item, the mouse pointer on slide 11 is aligned to the mouse pointer on slide 10. Consequently, the start and end points of the Mouse object on slide 11 have the same coordinates and the Mouse object no longer moves on slide 11. Another consequence is that the starting point of the Mouse object on slide 12 has changed to match the location of the Mouse object on slide 11, effectively transporting the entire mouse movement to slide 12.

19. Use the Preview icon to preview the entire movie.
20. In the **Preview** pane, pay close attention to the mouse movements. Make sure each click occurs at the right place.

Note that there is a small problem in the Mouse object's continuity between slides 13 and 14. Because slide 14 is a Full Motion Recording that captured the mouse movement frame by frame, you cannot use the same technique to modify the mouse movement. You will address this problem in the next section.

21. When the preview is complete, close the **Preview** pane.
22. If needed, adjust the position of the Mouse object on the slides where the click is not well positioned.
23. Save the file when done.

Formatting the Mouse object

During the preview, you probably noticed a blue circle and a click sound on most mouse clicks. These two options, and a few others, can be managed in the **Properties** panel.

1. Use the **Filmstrip** panel to return to slide 1.
2. Once on slide 1, select the Mouse pointer to make it the active object.

3. Take some time to inspect the properties available in the **Properties** panel as shown in the following screenshot:

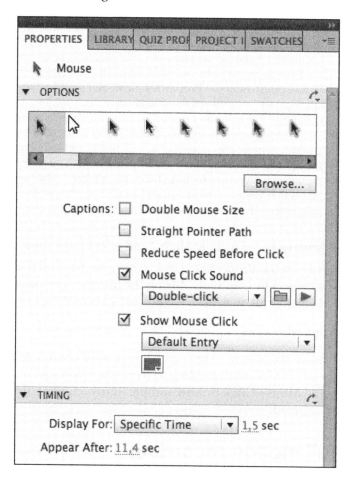

Note the two drop-down lists that let you choose the click sound (single-click or double-click) and the shape of the visual click. You can also change the color of the visual click if needed.

The topmost part of the **Options** section lets you choose the most appropriate mouse pointer. In this example, the default pointer is perfect, so you will not change it in this project.

Working with Standard Objects

>
> **Choosing the right mouse pointer**
>
> My very first big eLearning project was to build an online course on SAP for a huge multinational company. SAP uses custom mouse pointers that I wanted to reproduce in Captivate. A mouse pointer is a .cur file, so I clicked on the **Browse** button situated right below the collection of mouse pointers in the **Properties** panel and searched for the appropriate .cur file in the Program files folder of C: in Windows. I eventually found the .cur file I was looking for and I could import it into Captivate. If you work on a Mac, you can inspect the content of a .app file by right-clicking on the file and choosing **Show Package Content**. You might find the .cur file you are looking for in the package. The bottom line is that your Captivate project should reproduce the behavior of the actual application as closely as possible.

4. Use the **Filmstrip** panel to go to slide 2 and select the Mouse object.

In the **Options** section of the **Properties** panel, note how the double-click sound has been automatically chosen by Captivate during the filming. You can change it to a single-click if needed; after all, it is just a sound, not an actual click!

5. Use the **Filmstrip** panel to go to slide 8 and select the Mouse object.

Slide 8 is used to move the Mouse to the scroll bar of the **Export Settings** window before slide 9 uses a Full Motion Recording to show the scrolling movement. In the **Properties** panel, the **Mouse Click Sound** and the **Show Mouse Click** checkboxes are, therefore, not selected.

Editing a full motion recording

The last detail to address in order to make the mouse path in your project continuous is the transition between slides 13 and 14. Remember that during filming, you used the *Print Screen* (Windows) or the *command + F6* (Mac) shortcut to manually capture slide 13. This was necessary to have a slide available to display the needed Text Captions. After that, you used the *F9* (Windows) or the *command + F9* (Mac) shortcut to start a Full Motion Recording and clicked on the **Start Queue** icon. The consequence is that the Mouse object clicks on the **Start Cue** icon once on slide 13 and a second time on slide 14.

In this section, you will modify the Full Motion Recording of slide 14 so it begins right after the click on the **Start Cue** icon.

1. Use the **Filmstrip** panel to go to slide 14 of the encoderDemo_800.cptx project.

2. Scroll down to the bottom of the **Properties** panel until you see the **FMR Edit Options** section.

This section of the **Properties** panel is only available on Full Motion Recording slides.

3. Open the drop-down list and select the **Trim** option.
4. Leave the **Trim From** option at **0 sec** but set the **Trim To** option to 1,7 **sec**.

This action is reflected on the **Timeline** panel, where two vertical black bars mark the **Trim From** and the **Trim To** points, respectively. Note that you can also adjust the position of these markers by moving them on the **Timeline** panel directly.

As illustrated in the following screenshot, these two markers select a portion of 1.7 seconds at the very beginning of your Full Motion Recording. This portion is the one you want to remove.

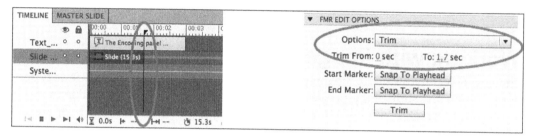

5. Click on the **Trim** button situated in the **FMR Edit** section of the **Properties** panel.

This last action removes the portion of the FMR identified by the **Trim From** and **Trim To** markers. The Full Motion Recording now begins exactly when the mouse clicks on the **Start Queue** icon, providing a smooth transition between the mouse movement on slide 13 and the Full Motion Recording of slide 14.

 Editing the Full Motion Recording does not edit the corresponding sound clip. The Chimes sound effect captured with the new System Audio feature is, therefore, currently out of sync. You will address that issue in *Chapter 6, Working with Audio*.

This concludes the exploration of the Mouse object of Captivate. Let's quickly summarize what you learned in this section:

- During the capture, only the position of the mouse at each click is recorded. A mouse movement is recreated between these positions at runtime.
- By default, the mouse movement uses a curved line, but you can make it a straight line in the **Options** section of the **Properties** panel.

- The first slide of the project is the only slide where you can move both the starting and ending points of the mouse movement.
- To prevent the mouse from moving on a given slide, right-click on the mouse pointer and choose **Align to Previous Slide** in the contextual menu.
- Removing the Mouse object from a slide does not remove its coordinates. This makes it easy to turn the Mouse object back on should you change your mind.
- Moving the mouse pointer on a slide also moves the origin of the mouse movement on the next slide.
- You can add a visual click as well as a click sound in the **Options** section of the **Properties** panel.
- It is possible to edit a Full Motion Recording animation with the tools provided in the **FMR Edit** section of the **Properties** panel. This section is only available when on an FMR slide.

Working with images

The next object to discuss is the image object. Captivate lets you insert various types of images on any slide of the project. Once an image is inserted, you are able to modify and format the image using the image editing tools of Captivate. Keep in mind though that Captivate is not an image editing application. To guarantee the best possible results, you should always prepare your images in a real image editing application (such as Adobe Photoshop or Adobe Fireworks) before inserting the image in Captivate. However, if you don't have access to these types of software applications, you can do some great image editing right in Captivate.

Inserting a slide from another project

Before moving on to inserting images you will first insert one extra slide in the **Filmstrip** panel.

1. Open the `videoInCaptivate.cptx` file in the `Chapter03` folder from your exercises folder.

This project is a one-slide Captivate movie. That single slide contains four Text Captions. In order to accelerate your work, you will simply copy and paste this slide in the `encoderDemo.cptx` file.

2. While in the `videoInCaptivate.cptx` file, right-click on the slide thumbnail in **Filmstrip**.
3. In the contextual menu, select the **Copy** item.
4. Return to the `encoderDemo_800.cptx` file.

5. In the **Filmstrip** panel, right-click on the first slide and select the **Paste** menu item.

When inserting a new slide in a Captivate project, it is inserted after the selected slide. There is no way to insert a new slide as the first slide directly, but the **Filmstrip** panel lets you easily reorder the slides by simply dragging the slides up and down.

6. Use the **Filmstrip** panel to drag the new slide up so it becomes the first slide of the project.

Inserting an image into a slide

Now that the stage is set, let's move on to what is really the subject of this particular section—inserting pictures.

About image types

Captivate lets you insert many different image types in your projects including .jpg, .gif, and .png images. If you want to know more about these image formats, here is a great blog post to do so: http://www.sitepoint.com/gif-jpg-png-whats-difference/.

1. Make sure you are still on the first slide of the encoderDemo_800.cptx file.
2. Navigate to **Insert** | **Image**.
3. Browse to the AMELogo.png file under images stored in your exercise folder.
4. Click on **Open** to insert the picture.

The image is inserted in the middle of the slide. Obviously, it is way too big for this slide. Your next operation will be to resize and position this image so it is well integrated with the other elements of the slide.

5. Make sure the image is selected on your slide.
6. Use your mouse to change the size of the image. This will most likely distort the image.

You can avoid distortion by pressing and holding the *Shift* key on your keyboard while using a corner handle to resize (scale) the image.

7. In the **Image** section of the **Properties** panel, click on the **Reset To Original Size** button for the image to restore to its original aspect.

Working with Standard Objects

You will now use the **Transform** section of the **Properties** panel to resize this picture.

8. If needed, expand the **Transform** section of the **Properties** panel.
9. Make sure the **Constraint Proportions** checkbox is selected and change the width of the picture to 180 pixels. Captivate calculates the new height of the image (176 pixels) so that its height/width ratio does not change.
10. Move the image to the lower-left area of the slide next to the Text Captions.

Your slide should now look like the following screenshot:

> **The blinking dashed green lines**
>
> While moving the image into place, you probably noted some dashed green lines appearing and disappearing automatically on the screen. This is a brand new feature of Captivate 7 called **Smart Guides**. Smart Guides help you align objects together. If you want to turn them on or off, you can navigate to **View | Show Drawing | Smart Guides**.

Using the image editing tools

Inserting an image in Captivate is that easy! You will now explore some of the image editing tools available in Captivate.

1. Make sure the newly imported image is selected and take a look at the **Properties** panel.

It shows properties pertaining to the selected image. The first two sections (**Image** and **Image Edit**) should be expanded. The remaining sections are, more or less, the same as those for the Text Caption and Highlight box objects and should be collapsed by default.

2. Move the sliders of the **Image Edit** section to see how each affects the selected image.
3. When done, click on the **Reset All** button to return all sliders to their original position.

For the finishing touch, you will use the options of the **Shadow & Reflection** section of the **Properties** panel.

4. Make sure the image is still selected.
5. In the **Properties** panel, expand the **Shadow & Reflection** section.
6. Select the **Reflection** checkbox and choose the preset you like the most.

Great! This little effect adds a whole new dimension and impact to your picture. Your students will certainly enjoy this level of detail in their visual experience.

Inserting a picture slide

Inserting images on an existing slide is one of the many possibilities offered by Captivate. Another nice feature is the ability to create a brand new slide based on an image. The chosen image is used as the background picture of the new slide. You will now examine that workflow, hands-on.

1. Make sure you are still on the first slide of the `encoderDemo_800.cptx` file.
2. Navigate to **Insert | Image Slide**.
3. Browse to the `mftcTitleTemplate.jpg` file under `images` stored in your exercise folder.
4. Click on the **Open** button.

The new picture is inserted as a new slide. Note that the picture has a width of 800 pixels and a height of 600 pixels, which is the exact same size as the project itself. It is not a coincidence. Remember that the images must be prepared before being inserted in Captivate. In this case, preparing the image was making sure it was the right size.

5. In the **Filmstrip** panel, drag the new slide up so it is the first slide of the project.

6. Save the file when done.

Extra credit – working with Characters

Characters are a collection of images that can be inserted in your Captivate projects. These images represent male and female characters in various postures. Inserting such pictures in your eLearning projects brings in a human and humoristic touch.

> **Downloading the eLearning assets**
>
> These characters are part of the eLearning assets available with Captivate 7. These eLearning assets are not part of the main Captivate installation package. A separate package must be downloaded and installed to take advantage of the Characters. You can find these extra installers at http://www.adobe.com/go/Cp7_win_assets_installer (Windows) or http://www.adobe.com/go/Cp7_mac_assets_installer (Mac). This Extra credit - working with Characters section assumes that the eLearning assets have been installed on your system.

In this section, you will work on the drivingInBe.cptx file and insert characters on top of your slides. These characters are actually .png images that can be manipulated in Captivate just like any other images. The general steps to do so are as follows:

- Switch to or open the drivingInBe.cptx file.

- Navigate to **Insert** | **Characters** to open the **Characters** dialog (see the following screenshot).

- Note the four categories in the drop-down menu; each category has various types of characters.

- Choose two characters: one male character and one female character. Insert various versions of each character in your project as you see fit.

- Use the tools provided in the **Image Edit** section of the **Properties** panel to edit the imported character(s).

[The Flip image horizontal icon is an easy way to double the number of available postures!]

- Save the `drivingInBe.cptx` file when done.

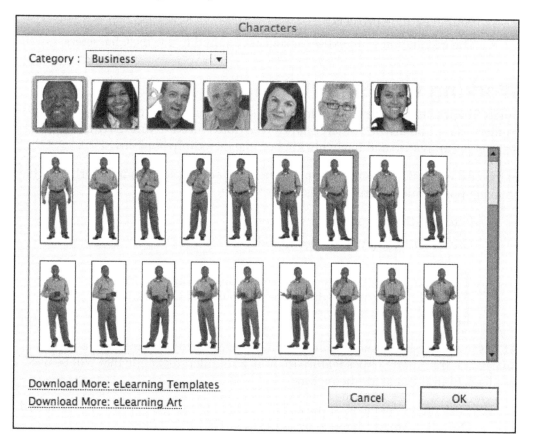

Refer to the `drivingInBe.cptx` file in the `final` folder for inspiration.

This last exercise concludes your first overview of the image object. Here is a summary of what you have learned in this section:

- You can easily insert many types of images in Captivate
- Captivate provides image editing capabilities in the **Properties** panel
- It is best to prepare the image in another image editing application before inserting it in Captivate

- If needed, use the **Reset To Original Size** and the **Reset All** buttons to change the picture back to its original state
- By navigating to **Insert | Image Slide**, you can create new slides that are based on images
- The **Characters** window contains a collection of pictures that you can use in your eLearning projects
- The installation of an extra package is required to use the Characters

Working with Smart Shapes

Smart Shapes are a predefined collection of shapes including rectangles, circles, banners, stars, and arrows. Smart Shapes were introduced in June 2012 as a new feature of Captivate 6 and have quickly become incredibly popular.

In the next exercise, you will draw a Smart Shape and explore a small portion of the amazing possibilities offered by this type of object.

1. Return to the `drivingInBe.cptx` project.
2. Use the **Filmstrip** panel to go to slide 3.

 This exercise does not account for an eventual Character image added during the previous *Extra Credit – working with Character* section.

At this moment, slide 3 should contain three objects: two Text Captions and one image. Use the Smart Shapes feature to draw a rounded rectangle that will be used as a background frame for the picture.

3. Click on the first icon of the objects toolbar or navigate to **Insert | Standard Objects | Smart Shape** to open the **Smart Shapes** panel.

The Smart Shapes panel displays all the available shapes.

4. Click on the rounded rectangle shape situated in the **Basic** section of the **Smart Shape** panel to activate the rounded rectangle tool (shown in the following screenshot).

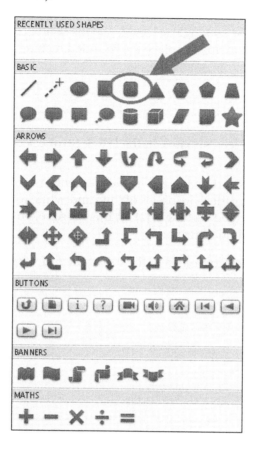

The Smart Shape panel disappears and the mouse pointer turns to a small cross.

5. Click-and-drag your mouse to draw a rounded rectangle shape that entirely covers the image present on slide 3. Don't hesitate to resize and move the shape if needed.

In the top-left area of the shape, you should see a yellow handle in addition to the eight white handles that surround the shape. This yellow handle is one of the features that make a Smart Shape… smart. It is used to modify the shape. In the case of the rounded rectangle, this yellow handle is used to adjust the roundness of the rectangle.

6. Use the yellow handle to adjust the roundness of the rectangle to your taste.

Working with Standard Objects

Formatting a Smart Shape

You've got the Smart Shape in place. Now, let's adjust the look and feel of the shape so it integrates well with the rest of the slide.

1. With the rounded rectangle selected, use the Send Selected Object Behind icon of the main toolbar to place the rounded rectangle behind the image.

2. Click on the **Fill** icon situated in the **Fill & Stroke** section of the **Properties** panel.

By default, the fill of a Smart Shape is a linear gradient. As you can see, this particular gradient uses different shades of blue and white to achieve the current look and feel of the rounded rectangle **(1)**. In this exercise, you want to use a solid color as the fill of the rounded rectangle.

3. Click on the Solid Color icon at the top of the **Fill** window **(2)**.

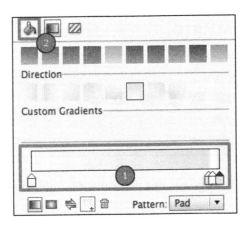

4. Type the color code `#AB8F1D` in the **Fill** window. It is a light brown color.

About the color codes

If you want to know more about the color codes and about what code corresponds to what color, see the following web page: `http://www.w3schools.com/html/html_colors.asp`.

5. While still in the **Fill & Stroke** section, change the Alpha parameter to `100 %` (entirely opaque).
6. Click on the **Stroke** icon and type the color code `#4C421D` as the color of the stroke. It is a dark brown color.
7. Increase the stroke **Width** to 2 pixels.
8. Make sure your **Fill & Stroke** section looks similar to what is shown in the following screenshot:

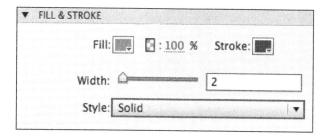

Using Smart Shapes as Highlight Boxes

The Alpha parameter available in the **Fill & Stroke** section of the **Properties** panel for Smart Shapes makes it possible to create transparent and/or semi-transparent Smart Shapes. This allows you to mimic the behavior of a Highlight Box with a Smart Shape. The benefit of this approach is that you have access to a much wider range of shapes compared to the unique rectangle shape of a Highlight Box object.

Using Smart Guides

The rounded rectangle now has the right look, but it is not necessarily in the right place. To perfectly align it with the picture, use the new Smart Guide feature of Captivate 7.

1. Open the **View** menu.
2. Check if the **Show Drawing/Smart Guide** option at the very end of the **View** menu is enabled. If not, enable it now.
3. Move the image slowly on top of the rounded rectangle.

4. Release the mouse when you see both a vertical and a horizontal Smart Guide (shown in the following screenshot).

Grouping objects

Thanks to the new Smart Guide feature of Captivate 7, it has been very easy to perfectly align the picture with its frame. Now that these two objects are correctly positioned relative to one other, you will select both the image and the rounded rectangle and group them as a single entity.

1. Click on the rounded rectangle to make it the active object.
2. Click on the image while holding the *Shift* key down. This adds the image to the current selection. You can also click-and-drag with your mouse to "marquee-select" multiple objects.
3. With both objects selected, navigate to **Edit | Group** to group the rounded rectangle and the image together. Alternatively, you can use the *Ctrl + G* (Windows) or the *command + G* (Mac) shortcut.

Now that the picture and the Smart Shape are grouped as one entity, they can be moved together without breaking their alignment.

4. Arrange the objects on the slide, including the newly created group, so that no object overlaps.

In this exercise, the Smart Guides and their ability to group objects have proven their efficiency by enabling you to quickly and easily align and lay out the objects of this slide.

Adding text inside Smart Shapes

The awesomeness of Smart Shapes does not end with the yellow handles you used in the previous exercise to modify the shape. In this exercise, you will explore another capability of the Smart Shape object by adding text inside a Smart Shape.

1. Use the **Filmstrip** panel to go to slide 2 of the `drivingInBe.cptx` file.
2. Use the first icon of the objects toolbar or navigate to **Insert | Standard Object | Smart Shape** to open the Smart Shape collection.
3. In the **Banners** section of the Smart Shape collection, choose the Curved Up Ribbon banner (the fifth available icon in the **Banners** section).
4. Draw a Curved Up Ribbon in the topmost area of the currently selected slide. Don't worry about the exact size and position of this new shape.

With the newly inserted shape selected, notice that three yellow squares are available for that type of shape (shown in the following screenshot).

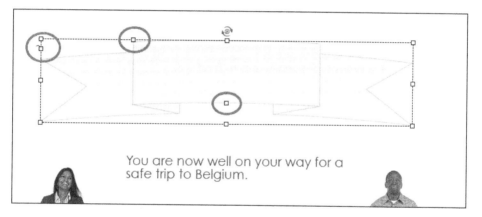

5. Experiment with these three yellow squares to see how each of them affects the Curved Up Ribbon shape.

Try to give this object a shape that suits your needs. When done, it is time to move on to the core part of this exercise by adding some text into the Curved Up Ribbon shape.

6. With the Smart Shape selected, look at the **Properties** panel. You should currently see six collapsible sections.
7. Double-click in the Curved Up Ribbon Smart Shape. This action brings a blinking cursor inside of the shape.
8. Type `Welcome` inside of the Smart Shape. When done, use the *Esc* key to leave the text-editing mode and select the shape as an object.

9. Take a second look at the **Properties** panel. There should now be eight collapsible sections available.

By adding text inside your Smart Shape, the **Properties** panel has automatically revealed the **Character** and the **Format** sections to let you format the text that is inside a Smart Shape. These two sections are usually found on a Text Caption object. It means that you have the exact same text formatting capabilities on a Smart Shape as on a Text Caption.

Smart Shape or Text Caption?

Since the introduction of Smart Shapes in Captivate 6, I very seldom use the Text Caption object anymore. I tend to use Smart Shapes as much as possible. I find Smart Shapes much more flexible than Text Captions and I like the much larger array of possible shapes compared to a standard Text Caption.

Smart Shapes still have some hidden treasures left to be discovered later in the book.

Converting Smart Shapes to freeform

A Smart Shape is a vector object similar to those you can draw with Adobe Fireworks or Adobe Illustrator. To create these shapes, designers use the Pen tool of Illustrator or Fireworks to draw Bezier points and Bezier curves. If you know how to use these points and curves, Captivate offers the possibility to further customize your Smart Shapes. Simply right-click a Smart Shape and choose **Convert to freeform** in the contextual menu. Have fun!

This concludes this section on Smart Shapes. It is time to quickly summarize what has been covered in this section.

- Smart Shapes are a collection of pre-defined shapes that can be manipulated in many ways with the tools of Captivate
- The collection of Smart Shapes includes rounded rectangles, banners, triangles, and callouts, among others
- When a Smart Shape object is selected, special yellow handles allow you to modify the Smart Shape itself
- The formatting capabilities of Smart Shapes are similar to those of a Highlight Box

- It is possible to write text into a Smart Shape. In such a case, the **Properties** panel displays additional properties to let you format the text
- If you know how to use the Bezier points and curves, you can convert your Smart Shapes to freeform for even more amazing possibilities

In *Chapter 5, Adding Interactivity to the Project*, you will discover some more capabilities of this very flexible object of Captivate.

Working with Text Animations

A **Text Animation** is an animated object that can be created and managed entirely from within Captivate.

In the next exercise, you will create the front slide and the final slide of the encoder demo project and add a Text Animation on both these slides.

1. Return to the `encoderDemo_800.cptx` file.
2. Use the **Filmstrip** panel to go to the first slide of the movie.

The first slide of the `encoderDemo_800.cptx` file was created earlier in this chapter. There are currently no objects on this slide. You will now add a Text Animation onto it.

3. Navigate to **Insert | Text Animation** menu item or the corresponding icon of the objects toolbar.
4. In the **Text Animation Properties** box type `Adobe Media Encoder The Demonstration`.
5. Change the **Font** to **Verdana** and the **Size** to 52.
6. Click on the **OK** button. The new object appears on the slide.

With the new Text Animation selected, take some time to inspect the available sections of the **Properties** panel. At the top of the stack, the **General** section contains options that are specific to a Text Animation. The other sections are the same as usual.

The new Text Animation is too wide to fit on the slide. If this situation happens with a regular Text Caption, you would use the white resize handles or the **Transform** section of the **Properties** panel to resize the object.

7. Make sure the Text Animation is the selected item.
8. If needed, expand the **Transform** section of the **Properties** panel.

As usual, the **X** and the **Y** coordinates as well as the rotation **Angle** are available in the **Transform** section. But where are the Width and the Height properties?

Actually, Captivate automatically calculates the size of a Text Animation based on the text content and on the font size. So your only options to modify the size of a Text Animation are to modify its text content and/or its font size. In this case, you will add a line break just before the **The demonstration** part of the content.

9. Make sure the Text Animation is still selected.
10. In the **General** section of the **Properties** panel, click on the **Properties** button. Alternatively, you can also double-click on **Text Animation**.

This action reopens the **Text Animation Properties** box where you can change both the text content and the font size of your Text Animation object.

11. In the upper area of the **Text Animation Properties** box, use your mouse to place the cursor between **Encoder** and **The demonstration**.
12. Hit the *Enter* key to create a line break at the location of the cursor.
13. Click on the **OK** button to confirm the changes.

The **Text Animation Properties** box closes and the Text Animation object is updated.

14. Use your mouse to move the Text Animation in the middle of the brownish area of the slide.
15. In the **General** section of the **Properties** panel, choose an effect in the **Effect** drop-down list.

Use the Preview option at the top of the **Properties** panel to view the chosen effect. In the *final* application of *Chapter 1, Getting Started with Adobe Captivate*, the **Waltz** effect has been used.

16. To test your new Text Animation, use the Preview icon to preview the next five slides.
17. Close the **Preview** pane when done and save the file.

Chapter 3

The first slide of the project should now look similar to what is shown in the following screenshot:

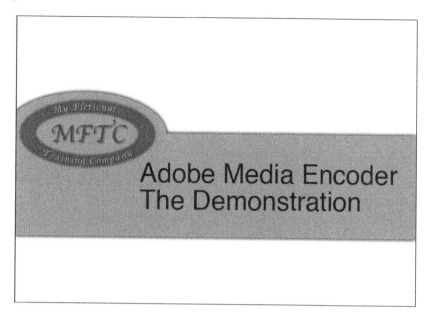

Duplicating slides

Now that the front slide of the project is finished, you will create the closing slide. It will be very similar to the front slide, so instead of repeating the whole procedure a second time, you will simply duplicate the first slide and change the content of the Text Animation.

1. In the **Filmstrip** panel, right-click on the first slide of the project and choose **Duplicate** in the contextual menu. Alternatively, you can use the *Ctrl + D* (Windows) or the *command + D* (Mac) shortcut.

2. In the **Filmstrip** panel, drag slide 2 to the very end of the project.

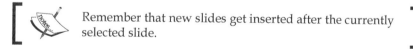

Remember that new slides get inserted after the currently selected slide.

3. Go to the last slide (slide 18) and select the Text Animation.

4. In the **General** section of the **Properties** panel, click on the **Properties** button.

5. In the **Text Animation Properties** dialog, change the Text to `Thank you for viewing this demonstration!`. Leave the other properties unchanged and hit the **OK** button.

[113]

Working with Standard Objects

The Text Animation is updated and… is too large to fit on the slide.

6. Make sure the Text Animation is selected and click on the **Properties** button of the **General** section again.
7. In the **Text Animation Properties** box, place your cursor between **Viewing** and **This** and then press *Enter* to force the text onto two lines.
8. Click on **OK** to close the **Text Animation Properties** dialog.
9. Save the file when done.

To test the new slide, use the **Filmstrip** panel to select the slide just before the last one, and then, navigate to **From this Slide** under the Preview icon.

Use Text Animations with care

The Text Animation object must be used with care. It is a great effect if you use it every once in a while, but if you use it too often, it overcharges your projects, which gives a non-professional impression. Also it is not HTLM5 compatible.

Converting a Typing object into a Text Animation

In Captivate, a Typing object is a very special type of object. It appears only in demonstrations and is created during the initial filming of the project when text is typed in the captured application. During the filming of the Encoder Demo project, you typed some text in the **Width** field of the **Video** tab. Consequently a Typing object has been generated.

1. While still in the `encoderDemo_800.cptx` file, use the **Filmstrip** panel to go to slide 13.

Once on slide 13, take a look at the **Timeline** panel. It contains three layers in addition to the slide itself, indicating that the slide contains three objects. One of these objects is labeled **Typing Text**. It represents the text that is typed in the **Width** field during the filming. This object was automatically generated when the slide was captured back in *Chapter 2, Capturing the Slides*.

2. Click anywhere on slide 14 (but not on an object). Make sure the **Properties** panel displays the properties of the slide.
3. In the **Timeline** panel, click on the **Text Typing** object to select it. Notice that the **Properties** panel is not updated and still shows the properties of the **Slide**.

The **Text Typing** object is the only object of Captivate that does not update the **Properties** panel. This unexpected behavior tells you that this object is very special indeed, and that it has no properties that you can adjust. One of the only available options is to control the typing speed by modifying the object's timing in the **Timeline** panel, but there is no solution to modify the text itself, its font, its font size, or its color.

Luckily, Captivate lets you convert the Text Typing objects into Text Animations. Once converted, the Text Typing object has the same editing capabilities as any other Text Animation. Be aware, however, that a Text Animation cannot be converted back into a Typing object. Converting a Typing object into a Text Animation is a one-way definitive operation.

4. In the **Timeline** panel, right-click on the **Text Typing** object.
5. In the contextual menu, choose **Replace with Text Animation**. Remember that this operation cannot be undone.

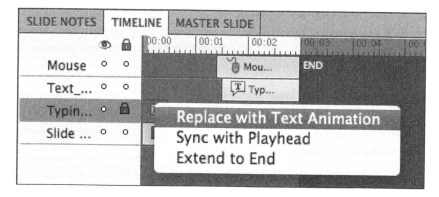

This option can be very handy in many situations, especially when you need to modify the text that was typed during the capture. Note that the effect applied to the converted **Text Typing** object is the **Typing Text With Sound** effect. If needed, you can use another effect, but I strongly recommend you stick to this one as it has been specifically designed to mimic the typing of some text.

The Text Animation object has no Fill property. In other word, it is transparent, which causes a small problem in this case. To solve this problem, I've used a grey Highlight Box with an Alpha set to 100% (to make it completely opaque). I adjusted the size of the Highlight Box so it is exactly the same size as the **Width** field. I then used the **Timeline** panel to send this Highlight Box to the bottom of the stack. Finally, I used the **Timing** section of the **Properties** panel to make the Highlight Box display for the entire duration of the slide and the **Transition** section to remove the default Fade In and Fade Out effect. Look for this Highlight Box on slide 14 of the encoderDemo_800.cptx file in Chapter03/final/. Can you implement it in your file as well?

Extra credit – creating the introductory and ending slides of another project

Now that you have inserted the front slide and the ending slide in the Encoder Demo project, why don't you try to do the same in the *Driving in Belgium* project? The following steps need to be executed:

- Switch to the drivingInBe.cptx file.
- Navigate to **Insert** | **Image Slide** menu to create a new slide based on the mftcTitleTemplate.jpg image in the image folder. Make the new slide the first one of the movie.
- Insert a new Text Animation on the new slide. Type Driving in Belgium and use the **Verdana** font with a size of 52.
- Choose an effect for your Text Animation. In the final version of the application, I used the **Waltz** effect.
- Place your new Text Animation on the slide and adjust its position on the slide. Use the Preview feature to test your changes.
- Once you are satisfied with slide 1, duplicate it and move the copy down the **Filmstrip** panel so it is the last slide of the project.
- Change the text to Thank you for taking this online course!. It might be necessary to insert a line break to make the Text Animation fit on the slide.
- Adjust the position of the updated Text Animation.
- Don't forget to preview your changes along the way and to save the file when done.

This section concludes the discussion on Text Animations. Let's make a quick summary of what you have learned:

- The Text Animation object can be created entirely in Captivate. There is no need for an external application (such as Adobe Flash) to create it!
- The Text Animation object is typically used on the first and on the last slide of the project.
- To resize a Text Animation, change its content, add a line break into the text, or change the font size.
- When text is typed during the capture, a Text Typing object is generated. Convert this object to a Text Animation for enhanced editing capabilities.
- The Text Animation object is not supported in HTML5.

Inserting external animations in the project

The next object type of this chapter is the **Animation**. This object lets you insert an external animation into your Captivate Project. Typically, the external application used to generate these animations is Adobe Flash and the file imported in Captivate is the compiled .swf file, but Captivate can import an animated .gif as well.

The file extensions of Adobe Flash Professional

When saving a file with Adobe Flash professional, the file extension used is .fla. The .fla file contains every object, animation, filter, and so on needed for the flash animation to work properly. Consequently, it can be a very large file. Once the .fla file is finished, it is necessary to export it (the proper word is to compile it) to the .swf format. The .swf file is the compiled version of the .fla file and is the one that can be read by the Flash Player plug in. Converting a .swf file back to .fla (an operation known as reverse engineering) is not possible. (Well actually, it can be done with a specialized software, but you never get back to the original .fla file!)

In the next exercise, you will import a Flash animation in your Encoder Demo project.

1. Return to the encoderDemo_800.cptx file.
2. Use the **Filmstrip** panel to select slide 4.

This is the slide where the Mouse object double-clicks on the demo_en.mov file. You will use an Animation to emphasize the amazing list of file types shown in the **Enable** drop-down menu.

Working with Standard Objects

3. Insert a new rounded corner Smart Shape into the slide. Resize it so it covers the entire **Enable** drop-down menu. The formatting of this object is of no importance right now.
4. Navigate to **Insert | Animation** menu or the corresponding icon of the objects toolbar to insert a new animation on the current slide.

The **Open** dialog box opens to let you locate the animation to insert.

If you do not have Adobe Flash Professional or if you do not know how to use it, don't worry! To get you started, Captivate ships with a gallery containing many objects that you can use in your project. This gallery is situated in:

- `C:\Program Files\Adobe\Captivate 7\Gallery` folder (Windows)
- `Applications/Adobe Captivate 7/Gallery` folder (Mac OS)

The `Gallery` folder itself is divided into several subfolders, containing various types of objects. One of these folders is the `SWF Animations` folder.

5. Browse to the `SWF Animations/Arrows/Orange arrow/down.swf` file of the gallery and click on the **Open** button.

The animation is imported and appears on slide 4. Note that only `.swf` and `.gif` files can be inserted as Animations in Captivate.

6. Use the Smart Guides to place the new object as shown in the following screenshot:

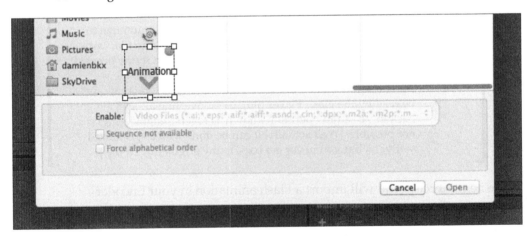

[118]

Inserting animations in the project is that easy! Later in this chapter, you will return to this slide and use the **Library** panel, as well as the alignment toolbar to further enhance the animations, but for now, here is a quick summary of what has been covered in this section:

- Captivate lets you insert external .swf and .gif animations in your projects
- These animations are typically created in Adobe Flash Professional
- These animations are therefore not supported in HTML5
- Captivate ships with an extensive gallery containing various types of objects that you can use in your projects

Inserting a Video file

It's time for the next object of this chapter: the **Video** file. Remember that Captivate was originally designed to create Adobe Flash (.swf) files that can be played back by the Adobe Flash Player plugin. In 2006, Adobe (formerly Macromedia) added video support to Flash. At that time, the Flash Player supported only a specific Flash video format: the .flv format (flv stands for Flash Video). In 2007, some limitations of the .flv format led to the development by Adobe of the .f4v Flash video format. Today, the Flash Player supports both .flv and .f4v video formats. The Adobe Media Encoder is used to convert any kind of video to .flv or .f4v file format.

With the arrival of HTML5, it is now possible for a web browser to play video (or audio) files natively, without the help of an external plugin such as the Flash Player. Unfortunately, the industry has not yet decided what video format/codec should be used for HTML5 video playback. As of today, it looks like two formats are emerging, the .mp4 format and the .webm format. To embrace this futuristic technology, the Adobe Media Encoder supports the .mp4 video format in addition to the .flv and .f4v formats.

 You can visit http://en.wikipedia.org/wiki/Flash_Video for more information on Flash video and http://www.adobe.com/products/mediaencoder.html for more information on the Adobe Media Encoder.

Working with Standard Objects

In the next exercise, you will insert a new slide in the Encoder Demo project and add a video file onto it.

1. Return to the `encoderDemo_800.cptx` file.
2. Use the **Filmstrip** panel to go to slide 1.
3. Navigate to **Insert | New Slide** menu to create a new blank slide.

The new slide is inserted as slide 2. Remember that new slides are always inserted after the active slide. You will now import a video file on this new slide.

4. Navigate to **Video | Insert Video** menu.

The **Insert Video** dialog opens. At the top of the **Insert Video** dialog, you have to choose between **Event Video** or **Multi-Slide Synchronized Video** options. The following table lists some of the differences between these two options:

	Event Video	Multi-Slide Synchronized Video
Sync	Cannot be distributed over several slides.	Can be distributed over several slides.
Timeline	The Timeline of the video is independent from the Timeline of the project.	The video plays in sync with the slide or slides it appears on.
Playback controls	Event Videos can have their own playback controls.	Have no specific playback controls.
Closed Captions	The video cannot be closed captioned.	The video can be closed captioned.
Library	The video is not inserted into the Library.	The video is inserted in the Captivate Library.

In this case, you want the video to be shown on slide 2 only, something that both the Event Video and the Multi-Slide Synchronized Video can do. But in *Chapter 6, Working with Audio*, you will add closed captions to the video, something that only the Multi-Slide Synchronized Video can do.

5. Make sure the **Multi-Slide Synchronized Video** option is the one in use.
6. Click on the **Browse** button, browse to the `videos/flv/demo_en.flv` file of your exercise folder and click on **Open**.
7. In the lower area of the **Insert Video** dialog, select the **Modify slide duration to accommodate video option**.

8. Make sure the **Insert Video** dialog looks similar to what is shown in the following screenshot and click on the **OK** button:

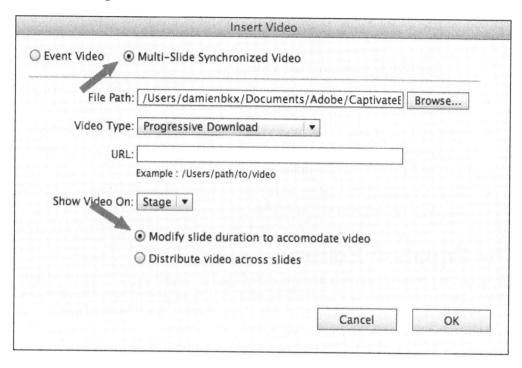

The video is inserted into the slide. Because the first frame of the video is white, it may be necessary to click on the video to reveal its boundaries.

9. Make sure the video is selected and take a look at the **Transform** section of the **Properties** panel.

Notice the message **Proportions are locked**. It means that you cannot change the width of the video independently from its height. This is made to ensure that the proportions of the video are respected when the size is changed. In this case, the size of the video has been set in the Adobe Media Encoder while converting the video from .mov to .flv.

10. For the position, set the **X** and the **Y** coordinates both to 200.

Take a quick look at the **Timeline** panel and notice that the duration of the slide matches the duration of the video file.

Working with Standard Objects

11. Save the file and use the Preview icon to preview the next five slides.
12. When the preview is finished, close the **Preview** pane.

Let's summarize what you just learned about inserting Videos in Captivate:

- There are two options available to insert Videos in Captivate: **Event Video** and **Multi-Slide Synchronized Video**.
- If you want to publish your Captivate movie in Flash format, it is necessary to use the `.flv` or `.f4v` video file format.
- If you want to publish your project in HTML5, use the `.mp4` video format.
- The Adobe Media Encoder is an external application. It is part of Adobe Creative Cloud and of the default Captivate package.
- The **Adobe Media Encoder (AME)** converts any video file to `.flv`, `.f4v`, or `.mp4`, so it can be used in Captivate.

The Equation Editor

The last object of this chapter is a brand new object of Captivate 7. This new feature allows you to create complicated mathematical equations and to insert them in your slides. This feature is powered by an external application called **MathMagic**. A special version of MathMagic is installed along with Captivate. In the next exercise, you will use the Equation Editor to create a simple mathematical equation, teaching your students how to convert kilometer per hour speeds to miles per hour speeds.

1. Return to the `drivingInBe.cptx` file in the `Chapter03` folder and use the **Filmstrip** panel to go to slide 8.
2. Navigate to **Insert** | **Equation** menu item to open the Equation Editor.

The external MathMagic for Captivate application opens and a default equation is added on your slide. You may have to clear a message indicating that you are using a special version of MathMagic meant to be used with Captivate only.

3. Delete the default equation that appears in the main window of the Equation Editor.

MathMagic for Captivate has a lot of tools and icons representing a very large collection of mathematical symbols. In this simple exercise, you will use two of these tools identified in the following screenshot:

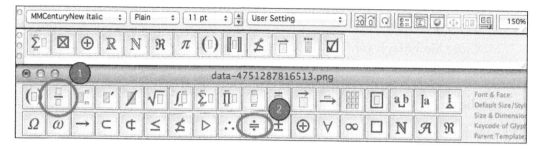

For your information, the speed in miles per hour is approximately two-thirds of the kilometers per hour equivalent. This is what you will represent using an equation.

4. Click on the icon identified as number 1 in the preceding screenshot.
5. Take the very first option proposed by this icon. This inserts a division symbol in the main window of the Equation Editor.
6. Type 60 kph in the top part of the division.
7. Type 3 in the bottom part of the division.
8. Place your cursor on the right side of the division and type * 2.
9. Click on the icon identified as number 2 in the preceding screenshot.
10. Select the third tool in the third row to insert the more or less equal to symbol.
11. Type 40mph on the other side of the symbol.

Make sure your equation looks similar to what is shown in the following screenshot:

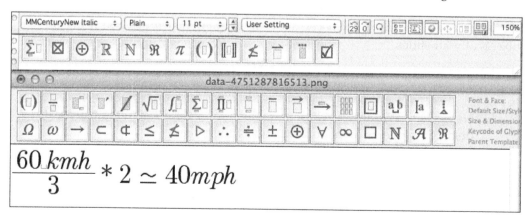

12. Select the entire equation and use the **Font** menu of MathMagic for Captivate to apply the **Verdana** font to the equation.
13. Navigate to **File** | **Save** or the *Ctrl + S* (Windows) or *command + S* (Mac) shortcut to save the equation. This action updates the equation on the Captivate slide.
14. Close MathMagic for Captivate and return to slide 8 of the `drivingInBe.cptx` file.
15. Move and resize the newly inserted equation so that it integrates nicely with the other elements of the slide.

This concludes the exploration of the nine non-interactive objects scheduled for this chapter. Before moving on, let's do a quick summary of what has been discussed in this section.

- One of the new features of Captivate 7 is the Equation Editor.
- This featured is powered by an external application called MathMagic. When Captivate is installed, a special version of MathMagic is installed along with Captivate.
- The Equation Editor can be used to generate complex mathematical equations using specific symbols.
- Once the external MathMagic application has generated an equation, it is inserted as a `.png` image on your Captivate slide.

You will explore some more objects in the coming chapters, but for now, you will focus on some other tools that will help you manage these objects.

Using the Align toolbar

The Align toolbar contains the necessary tools to align, distribute, and resize the objects of your slides.

By default, the Align toolbar is not part of the **Classic** workspace, so your first task is to turn it on.

1. Navigate to **Window** | **Align** menu item to turn the Align toolbar on. By default, it appears in the top-left area of the screen.

As shown in the following image, the Align toolbar contains 14 icons. During the next exercise, you will use many of these 14 icons. To help you with clicking on the right icon, these icons will be numbered from 1 to 14, icon number 1 being the leftmost icon.

By default, none of the icons of the Align toolbar are available. The set of available icons depends on the object that is selected.

2. Go to slide 3 of the `drivingInBe.cptx` file and select the Curved Up Ribbon Smart Shape.

With one object selected on the slide, only the **Center horizontally on the slide** (icon 9) and the **Center vertically on the slide** (icon 10) icons are available.

3. Click on the **Center horizontally on the slide** (icon 9) icon.

The Curved Up Ribbon Smart Shape is now perfectly aligned with the center of the slide!

4. Click on the **Let's go!** button to select it.
5. Hold the *Shift* key down while clicking on the **You are now…** Text Caption to add it to the current selection.

With two objects selected, most of the icons of the Align toolbar are available. Only the **Distribute Horizontally** (icon 7) and the **Distribute Vertically** (icon 8) icons are still disabled.

6. With both the Button and the Text Caption selected, click on the **Center horizontally on the slide** (icon 9) icon.

The selected objects are now perfectly aligned in the middle of the slide.

7. Hold the *Shift* key down while clicking on the Smart Shape to add it to the selection.

With three objects selected, all the icons of the Align toolbar are available.

8. Click on the **Distribute Vertically** icon (icon 8).

Captivate automatically adjusts the position of the selected objects so that the vertical distance between them is the same.

Working with Standard Objects

With the exception of the two character pictures, your slide should now look similar to what is shown in the following screenshot:

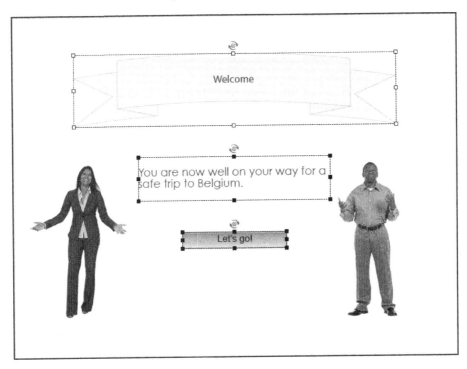

Selecting multiple objects

Most of the tools in the Align toolbar require that at least two objects be selected. Selecting multiple objects is not difficult and it works the same way in Captivate as it does in most other applications. However, Captivate has one important particularity when multiple objects are selected. This is what you will explore in this section.

1. Use the **Filmstrip** panel to go to slide 12 of the `drivingInBe.cptx` file.

Slide 12 contains 12 images and four rounded-rectangle Smart Shapes containing text. That makes a lot of objects! These objects have been quickly placed on the slide in their approximate position. Your next task is to use the tools of the Align toolbar to perfectly align and distribute these objects on the slide.

2. Click once on the topmost rounded rectangle (the one that reads **Warning signs**) to make it the active object.
3. Hold the *Shift* key down and select the three remaining rounded rectangles one by one.

This selects four objects, so all the icons of the Align toolbar should be enabled.

As shown in the following screenshot, the first selected object (the topmost rounded rectangle) is surrounded by white handles while black handles surround the other selected objects.

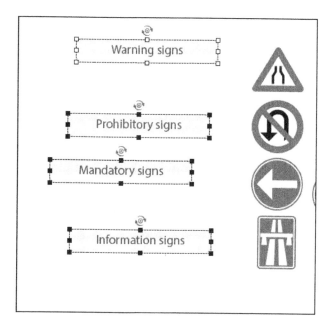

In Captivate, the first selected object is the **master** object of the selection. It means that the tools of the Align toolbar are calibrated based on the size and the position of that object. To make it recognizable, Captivate displays white handles around it and black handles around all the other objects of the selection.

4. Click on the **Align Left** (icon 1) icon of the Align toolbar.

The left edge of the four selected objects are now perfectly aligned to the left edge of the master object.

5. Click on the **Distribute Vertically** icon (icon 8) of the Align toolbar to space the four selected objects equally.

With these operations behind, the four rounded rectangles are now in their final position.

Working with Standard Objects

Extra credit – aligning and distributing the remaining objects

You now have all the knowledge you need to perfectly align the images of this slide. Here is what you need to do:

- Select the objects you want to align, paying close attention to the first one you select. Remember that the tools of the Align toolbar are calibrated based on the first selected object.
- Use the tools of the Align toolbar to move the remaining objects of the slide to their final position.
- Remember that the four rounded rectangles are already in their final position. Use them as reference.

At the end of this section, your slide should look like the following screenshot:

Before moving on to the next topic, let's do a quick summary of what has been covered in this section.

- The Align toolbar is not part of the default **Classic** workspace. It is therefore necessary to explicitly turn it on by navigating to **Window | Align** menu item.

- There are 14 icons on the Align toolbar. The number of icons enabled depends on the number of objects selected.
- It is possible to select multiple objects in Captivate using the same techniques as in most other applications.
- The first selected object of a multiple selection is known as the master object of the selection. The tools of the Align toolbar are calibrated based on that master object.
- Captivate displays white selection handles around the master object and black selection handles around the other objects of the selection.

With a bit of practice, the Align toolbar will soon become one of your best Captivate friends!

Working with the Timeline panel

In the **Classic** workspace, the **Timeline** panel is situated at the bottom of the interface. The primary purpose of the **Timeline** panel is to organize the sequence of events on each slide, but it can be used for other purposes as well.

Using the Timeline panel to select objects

When resizing the Highlight Boxes earlier in this chapter, you probably had a hard time selecting the right object and you ended up moving or resizing the Mouse object or a Text Caption instead of the Highlight Box. Using the **Timeline** panel, you can make sure that the object you select is the one you actually want to select!

1. Return to slide 4 of the `encoderDemo_800.cptx` file.

This slide contains four objects: two Text Captions, one Highlight Box, and the Mouse movement. Each object corresponds to a layer in the **Timeline** panel.

2. In the **Timeline** panel, click on the layer that represents the Highlight Box.

The eight white handles now surround the Highlight Box on the stage. Selecting an object on the **Timeline** panel also selects it on the stage.

Your screen should look similar to what is shown in the following screenshot:

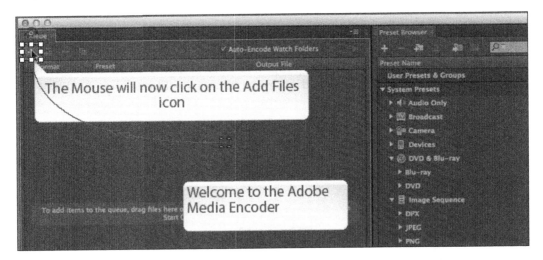

Hiding and locking objects with Timeline

Hiding and locking objects is another feature that can help you make the right selection. It also prevents you from accidentally modifying finished objects.

1. Make sure you are still on slide 4 of the `encoderDemo_800.cptx` file.

On slide 4 the Highlight Box and the mouse pointer share the same area of the slide. If you try to click on one of these two objects on the stage, chances are you'll end up clicking on the other one! For this exercise, imagine that you want to select the orange Highlight Box.

2. In the **Timeline** panel, click on the **lock all objects** icon **(1)**.
3. Click on the **lock** icon situated in front of the **Highlight Box** object **(2)**.

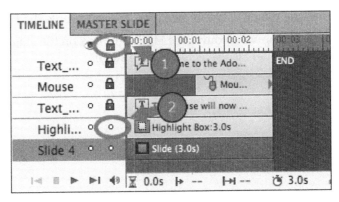

The Highlight Box is now the only object on the slide that is not locked. Consequently, it is the only one that can be selected and modified.

4. On the slide, try to select one of the Text Captions or the mouse pointer. Captivate should not let you do it!
5. However, if you try to select the Highlight Box, the application reacts normally.
6. In the **Timeline** panel, unlock both Text Captions and the Mouse object.

All the objects of the slide should now be unlocked, so you should be back to the original situation.

In the **Timeline** panel, next to the **Lock/Unlock** icons, are the **Show/Hide** icons (the eye icons). You can use them to hide objects on the slide. When the slide holds a large number of objects, it can help you select and work with the right one. Note that hiding an object with this tool hides it from the Captivate interface only, not from the final movie as viewed by the students.

Using Timeline to change the stacking order of the objects

The stacking order decides which object goes in front of or behind the other objects. In the **Timeline** panel, the topmost object is in front of any other objects. It means that in case objects overlap, the topmost object covers the one(s) below it. The slide is always at the very bottom of the stack as it is used as the background on top of which the objects are placed.

1. Make sure you are still on slide 4 of the `encoderDemo_800.cptx` file.
2. If necessary, move one of the two Text Captions so that both objects overlap.

In the **Timeline** panel, notice that the **Welcome to the Adobe Media Encoder** Text Caption is on top of the stack. This should be reflected on the stage in the way the Text Captions overlap.

3. In the **Timeline** panel, take the **Welcome to…**Text Caption and drag it down two levels.

The **Welcome to…** Text Caption is now behind the **The mouse will now…** Text Caption.

4. Right-click on the **Welcome to…** Text Caption.
5. In the contextual menu, navigate to **Arrange | Bring to Front**.

Working with Standard Objects

This brings the **Welcome to...** Text Caption back to the top of the stack, both on the stage and in the **Timeline** panel.

Using Timeline to set the timing of the objects

The primary purpose of the **Timeline** panel is to let you control the timing of the objects on the active slide. For each object, you can choose when it appears on the stage and how long it stays visible. By carefully and precisely arranging the objects on the **Timeline**, you'll be able to achieve great visual effects very easily.

1. Make sure you are still on slide 4 of the `encoderDemo_800.cptx` file.
2. Take a look at the **Timeline** panel and notice how the four objects of the slide are organized.
3. Click on an empty area of the slide to make the entire slide the active item. The **Properties** panel updates and displays the properties of the slide.
4. In the **General** section of the **Properties** panel, change the Display **Time** of the slide property to `10` **sec**. This change is reflected in the **Timeline** panel.
5. In the **Timeline** panel, take the right edge of the slide and drag it to the 15 sec mark. This change is reflected in the Display **Time** property of the **General** section of the **Properties** panel.

The changes made in the **Timeline** panel are reflected in various sections of the **Properties** panel and vice versa. This gives you two methods to organize the timing of your objects.

6. Click on the **Welcome to**...Text Caption to make it the active object. The **Properties** panel updates and shows the properties of the Text Caption.
7. In the **Properties** panel, open the **Timing** section.

The **Timing** section states that the Text Caption appears after 0 seconds and stays visible for a specific time of 3 seconds. The **Timeline** panel is a visual representation of this situation.

> **Adjusting the default timing of the objects**
>
> When a new object is added to the stage, its timing is set to 3 seconds by default. This default timing can be adjusted for each type of object separately. Simply go to **Edit** | **Preferences** | **Defaults** (Windows) or **Adobe Captivate** | **Preferences** | **Defaults** (Mac), choose an object in the **Select** drop-down list and adjust the default timing of the selected object type.

Chapter 3

8. Click on the **The mouse will now**... Text Caption to make it the active object.
9. In the **Timeline** panel, place your mouse in the middle of the selected Text Caption until the mouse pointer turns into a grabbing hand.
10. Move the Text Caption to the right, so it begins at the 7 seconds mark on the **Timeline** panel.
11. While in the **Timeline** panel, place your mouse on the right edge of the selected Text Caption until the mouse pointer turns into a double arrow.
12. Use the mouse to extend the duration of the **The mouse will now**... Text Caption to the 13 seconds mark.
13. In the **Timing** section of the **Properties** panel, confirm that the selected Text Caption is set to **Appear After** 7 **sec** and to **Display For Specific Time** of 6 **sec**.
14. In the **Properties** panel, open the **Transition** section.

In Captivate, it is possible to apply a **Fade In** and/or a **Fade Out** effect on (almost) every object. By default, this **Transition** effect lasts half a second, but you can adjust its timing in the **Transition** section of the **Properties** panel.

15. Change the **Transition Effect** of both Text Captions to **Fade In and Out**.

[Keep these **Transition** effects in mind when setting up the timing of your objects. Imagine a Text Caption set to stay visible for a specific time of 3 seconds with a default Fade In and Fade Out transition applied. The first half a second is used for the Fade In effect and the last half a second is used for the Fade Out effect. It effectively leaves only 2 seconds to the learner to read the text contained in the Text Caption!]

16. Still on slide 4, use the **Timeline** or the **Timing** section of the **Properties** panel to change the timing of the Highlight Box. Make it appear at 8 seconds into the slide and stay visible for a specific time of 6 seconds.
17. Also change the timing of the Mouse movement so it begins at 13 seconds into the slide and lasts 2 seconds.

Working with Standard Objects

The timeline of slide 4 is now correct. Make sure it looks similar to what is shown in the following screenshot:

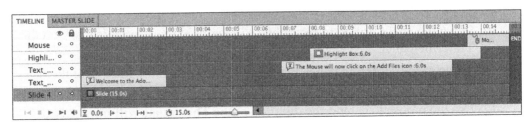

> **The strange red triangle**
>
> When moving objects on the **Timeline** panel, a red triangle might appear on some objects that are at the end of the **Timeline**. Read this great blog post by Kevin Siegel to know more about this mysterious red triangle, http://iconlogic.blogs.com/weblog/2013/07/adobe-captivate-anchors-away.html.

To test the new timing of the objects, use the Preview icon and choose **Next 5 slides**. If you feel that the current timing is not exactly right, don't hesitate to adjust the position of the objects on the **Timeline** panel to your liking. After all, you're the teacher!

Extra credit – adjusting the timing of the other slides

Now that you know the tools and techniques used to set the timing and the stacking order of the objects, browse the other slides of the `encoderDemo_800.cptx` project and adjust the timing of the various objects contained in the project. Navigate to `Chapter03/final/encoderDemo_800.cptx` file of your exercise folders for examples and inspiration. Just a few tips before you get started:

- Use the **Timeline** panel whenever possible. It is the fastest and easiest way to adjust the timing of the objects.
- If you require super-precise timing, then use the **Timing** section of the **Properties** panel.
- Don't hesitate to use the tools of the Align toolbar to resize and re-locate the objects on the slide. The proper size/location combined with precise timing can lead to strong, yet easy to achieve, visual effects.

> **Not too fast and not too slow**
>
>
>
> When creating an online course with Captivate, you'll quickly discover that one of the most difficult aspects is to find the right pace. For the Text Caption object, there is an easy trick. Use the stopwatch function of your cell phone and slowly read the content of the Text Caption aloud, then round up the timing to the upper half a second. For example, if it takes you 5.7 seconds to read a Text Caption aloud, make that Text Caption stay on the stage for a specific time of 6 seconds. If your audience is multi-lingual, add up to 1.5 seconds to the timing so that the students taking the course in a language other than their native language will be allowed some extra time to read and understand your Text Captions. You can also use the **Calculate Caption Timing** preference of Captivate. When this preference is turned on, Captivate automatically calculates the length of the Text Captions based on their content.

This concludes this first overview of the **Timeline** panel. Here is a quick summary of what has been covered in this section:

- The primary purpose of the **Timeline** panel is to arrange the timing of the objects.
- The **Timeline** panel can also be used to select the objects and to modify their stacking order.
- The **Timeline** panel is a visual representation of the **Timing** section of the **Properties** panel.
- Changing the objects on the **Timeline** panel updates the **Timing** section and vice versa.
- It is possible to apply a Fade In and a Fade Out effect on the object using the **Transition** section of the **Properties** panel.
- By default, the Fade In and Fade Out transitions last half a second. You can adjust this default timing in the **Transition** section of the **Properties** panel.

Working with Standard Objects

Adding effects to objects

In the next exercise, you will use the built-in tools of Captivate to add an effect to the Adobe Media encoder logo you inserted on slide 3 of the Encoder Demo project.

1. Return to the `encoderDemo_800.cptx` file in `Chapter03`.
2. Use the **Filmstrip** panel to go to slide 2.
3. Use the Preview icon to preview the next five slides.

When the preview reaches slide 3, pay particular attention to how the Adobe Media Encoder logo enters and leaves the stage. No particular effect should be applied. Close the **Preview** pane when finished.

4. While still in the `encoderDemo_800.cptx` file `Chapter03`, go to slide 3 and select the Adobe Media Encoder logo.
5. Navigate to **Window** | **Effects** menu to open the **Effects** panel.

By default, the **Effects** panel appears at the bottom of the screen next to the **Timeline**.

>
> **The Effects workspace**
>
> One of the workspaces available by default in Captivate is the **Effects** workspace. The advantage of using the **Effects** workspace is that you can see both the **Timeline** and the **Effects** panel at the same time. If your screen is large enough, don't hesitate to switch to the **Effects** workspace for the next exercise.

The **Effects** panel also displays a timeline, but, unlike the **Timeline** panel that displays the timeline of the entire slide, the **Effects** panel displays the timeline of the selected object only. In this case, the **Effects** panel displays the timeline of the Adobe Media Encoder Logo **(1)**.

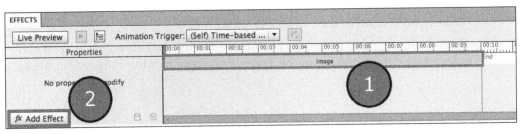

6. Click on the **Add Effect** icon **(2)** situated at the bottom-left corner of the **Effects** panel.

7. In the menu that pops up, navigate to **Emphasis** | **Flip** | **FlipFromCenter**.
8. In the **Effects** panel, reduce the length of the **FlipFromCenter** effect to the first half-second of the Adobe Media Encoder image timeline.
9. Save your file.
10. Open the Preview icon and click on **Next 5 slides**.

Pay particular attention to the way the Adobe Media Encoder logo enters the stage. Thanks to the **Effects** panel, you have applied a cool effect to the image. This adds another great touch of design, professionalism, and dynamism to this eLearning project!

> The duration of an effect is relative to the duration of the object the effect is applied to. In other words, if you change the duration of the object on the main **Timeline** panel, you also change the absolute duration of the effect.

Combining effects

In the next section, you will import an image and animate it using a combination of two effects.

1. Return to the `drivingInBe.cptx` file.
2. Use the **Filmstrip** panel to go to slide 6.

This slide already contains two transparent Text Captions. (It may also contain a Character image.)

3. Navigate to **Insert** | **Image** menu to insert the `check.png` file in the `images` folder, situated in your exercises folder.
4. Use the Smart Guides to position the new image on the right of the Text Caption that reads **Good**.
5. In the **Timeline** panel or in the **Timing** section of the **Properties** panel, make the image **Appear After** `1.5` **sec** and **Display For** the **Rest of Slide**.
6. With the image still selected, open the **Effects** panel at the bottom of the screen.
7. Navigate to **Add Effect** | **Entrance** | **Spiral In** to add the **Spiral In** effect to the picture. Make the effect last for 1.5 sec.
8. Return to slide 5 and navigate to the Preview icon and click on **Next 5 Slides** to preview the next five slides.

Working with Standard Objects

When the preview reaches slide 6, pay close attention to the way the green checkmark image enters the stage. Close the **Preview** pane when the preview is finished.

You will now add a second effect to the same object to make it look even more engaging.

9. Return to slide 6, select the green checkmark image again, and return to the **Effects** panel.
10. Navigate to **Add Effect | Emphasis | Clockwise Rotate** effect to add this effect. Make it last the same 1.5 sec as the **Spiral In** effect you added earlier.
11. Make sure the **Effects** panel looks similar to what is shown in the following screenshot and use the Preview icon to test your sequence. When the preview is complete, close the **Preview** pane.

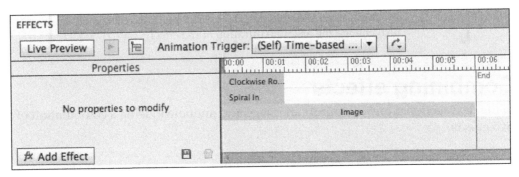

12. Still on slide 6, select the green checkmark image and copy it (*Ctrl* + *C* on Windows or *command* + *C* on Mac).
13. Go to slide 11 and paste (*Ctrl* + *V* on Windows or *command* + *V* on Mac) the image.
14. Save the file when done.

When you copy/paste an object, you also copy/paste the properties of the object including its size, its position, and its effects.

Extra credit – adding effects to images

Now that you have inserted an image and added effects onto it, why don't you try it on your own on another image? The following steps are the general steps to follow:

- You will be working with the `drivingInBe.cptx` file.
- Add the `redCross.png` file of the `images` folder on slide 7.

- Position the red cross image in the middle of the slide, between the two Text Captions.
- On the **Timeline** panel, make the red cross appear after 1 sec and display it for the rest of the slide.
- Use the **Effects** panel to add the **Spiral In** and the **Clockwise Rotate** effects.
- Make both effects last 1.5 sec as you did for the green checkmark.
- Use the Preview icon's **Next 5 slides** feature to test your sequence.
- If everything is fine, copy and paste the red cross image on slide 12.

Finishing touches

To wrap up this section on object effects, you will inspect another slide of the project and see how the **Effects** and the **Timeline** panels can work together to produce a great visual experience.

1. Use the **Filmstrip** panel to go to slide 14 of the `drivingInBe.cptx` file.

This slide contains five Text Captions, six images (without counting the eventual character), and one button.

2. Take a look at the **Timeline** panel to see how the objects of this slide are organized. Notice that some images appear two-tenths of a second from one another.
3. Select any of the road sign images and open the **Effects** panel. The **FlipFromCenter** effect is applied to each and every image.
4. Use the Preview icon's **Next 5 slides** feature to test the slide.
5. If necessary, adjust the timing of the objects as well as the timing of the animations to your liking.
6. Don't forget to save the file when done.

This little experiment concludes your overview of Effects in Captivate. Feel free to experiment further by applying other effects to other objects. The possibilities are endless and this book only shows a few examples of what is possible.

Before moving on to the next topic, this is a list of what you have learned about effects:

- It is possible to add effects to any object of Captivate.
- By default, the **Effects** panel is not a part of the **Classic** workspace. Navigate to **Window | Effects** to turn it on.
- The **Effects** workspace displays both the **Timeline** and **Effects** panel on the same screen.
- At the bottom-left corner of the **Effects** panel, the **Add Effect** icon contains a large collection of effects to choose from.
- Effects can be combined to create sophisticated animations.

Effects in HTML5

When it comes to HTML5 compliance, each effect falls under one of these three categories:

- Some effects are not at all supported in HTML5. In Captivate 7, these effects are identified by a small star (*) by their names.
- A double start (**) identifies the effects that are partially supported in HTML5. These effects will look different in the HTML5 output compared to the Flash (.swf) output.
- The remaining effects are fully supported in both the HTML5 and Flash output. They can be used with no restrictions at all.

Working with the Library panel

When using the **Classic** workspace, the **Library** panel appears as a tab next to the **Properties** panel at the right-hand side of the screen.

1. Return to the `encoderDemo_800.cptx` file.
2. To open the **Library** panel, click on the **Library** tab situated next to the **Properties** panel. Alternatively, navigate to **Window | Library** menu.

Chapter 3

The **Library** panel maintains a list of all the assets of the current file. These assets include the background pictures captured during the filming of the project, all the external files imported into the project (images, video, sounds, and so on) and the Full Motion Recording clips, among others. The following screenshot provides a good picture of the **Library** panel:

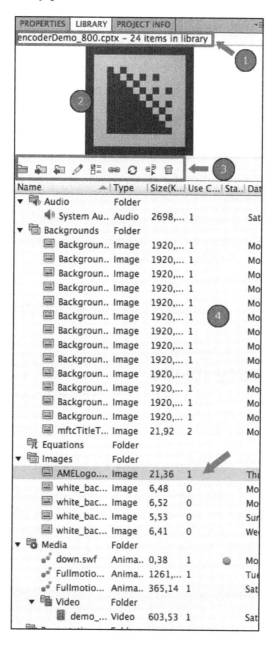

Working with Standard Objects

Let's have a look at the panel in detail:

- At the very top of the **Library** panel is the name of the file the Library belongs to **(1)**.
- The Preview area **(2)** gives a quick preview of the selected item. In the preceding screenshot, the `AMELogo.png` image is selected (see the red arrow) and shows in the Preview area.
- Just below the Preview area, the Library toolbar **(3)** displays a row of icons. These are the tools used to manage the assets present in the Library.
- The main area of the **Library** panel **(4)** lists the assets of the project organized by type.

As depicted in the preceding screenshot, the Library contains one folder for each type of asset.

3. In the **Library** panel, select the `mftcTitleTemplate.jpg` file situated in the `Backgrounds` folder.
4. Click on the *sixth* icon of the Library toolbar. This icon is called **Usage**.
5. A box pops up and informs you that this particular image is used as the background of both slide 1 and slide 19.
6. Click on **OK** to close the **Usage** dialog box.

The only purpose of the **Usage** dialog box is to inform you about where the selected asset is used in the project.

Reusing Library items

When an external file (such as an image or a Flash animation) is inserted in the project, it is automatically added to the project's **Library** panel. That is why the `down.swf` file is listed in the **Media** section of the **Library** panel.

1. While in the `encoderDemo_800.cptx` file, use the **Filmstrip** panel to go to slide 5.

This is the slide where you inserted the orange `down.swf` Flash animation earlier in this chapter. If you want to use the same animation again, there is no need to import it a second time. It can be taken directly from the **Library** panel and reused as many times as needed throughout the entire project. Using many instances of the same file helps in keeping the resulting file size as low as possible.

You will now use the **Library** panel to insert two more instances of this Flash animation on the slide.

2. Drag two more instances of the `down.swf` animation from the **Library** panel to the middle of the slide.

3. Use the Smart Guides to align these two new animations to the one already present on the slide.

4. If necessary, use the tools of the Align toolbar to properly align and distribute these animations.

5. In the **Timeline** panel, all three animations are set to **Appear After** 1 **sec** and **Display For Specific Time** of 6 **sec**.

6. Save the file and use the preview icon to test the sequence.

When done, make sure your slide looks similar to what is shown in the following screenshot:

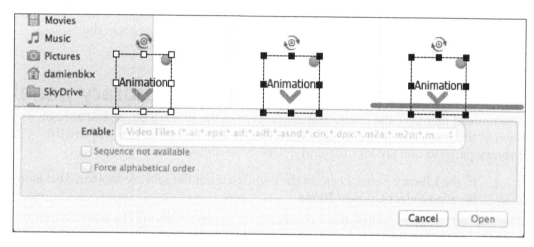

Importing objects from another Library

Another great feature of the **Library** panel is the ability to open the Library of another file. This makes it easy to share assets between different Captivate projects.

In the next exercise, you will open the Library of another Captivate file in order to insert another image in the Encoder Demonstration project.

1. While in the `encoderDemo_800.cptx` file, use the **Filmstrip** panel to go to slide 2.

2. In the **Library** panel, click on the first icon of the Library toolbar and choose Open Library in the drop-down menu.

3. Browse to the exercises folder and open the `library.cptx` file in `Chapter03`. The **Library** panel of this file appears as an extra floating panel.

4. Enlarge the Library of the other file. It contains a single image called `inAmsterdam.jpg`.
5. Drag the `inAmsterdam.jpg` image from the external Library to the middle of slide 2.
6. Close the external Library once done.

Oops, wrong image! Sorry folks, this is an image of me in Amsterdam a few hours before the show of AC/DC during their 2009 Black Ice world tour! Well, even though this is not the intended picture, I've made my point: the **Library** panel can be used to share assets between Captivate files. Notice that the `inAmsterdam.jpg` image is now present in the `Images` folder in the **Library** panel of the `encoderDemo_800.cptx` file.

7. Click on the newly inserted image and delete it.

Take another look at the **Library** panel after you deleted the image. Notice that, even though it is not used in the project anymore, the image still appears in the `Images` folder of the **Library** panel.

Deleting unused assets from the Library panel

The unused items are the assets that are present in the **Library** panel, but are not used in the project. In order to control the size of the `.cptx` file, you will use the **Library** panel to quickly identify and delete these unused items.

1. In the **Library** panel, click on the eighth icon of the Library toolbar. This icon is called **Select Unused Items**.

The unused items, including the `inAmsterdam.jpg` image should be selected in the **Library** panel.

2. Click on the last icon of the Library Toolbar (the trash can icon) to delete the selected assets.
3. Click on **Yes** to confirm the deletion.

That's it! Thanks to the **Library** panel, it has been quick and easy to identify and delete the unused assets. This will help you keep the size of your `.cptx` file as low as possible.

Be careful when deleting background images because you can't get those back if needed! To avoid any problems, I always keep a backup copy of the raw material that comes out of the capture part of the process. This raw file contains every background picture should I need to recover some.

You will discover a few more goodies of the **Library** panel later in the book, but for now, let's make a quick list of what you already know about it:

- The **Library** panel appears on the right-hand side of the screen, next to the **Properties** panel.
- The primary purpose of the **Library** panel is to list the assets present in the active project. These assets include the background pictures and the Full Motion Recordings captured during the filming, the external files imported in the project, and the audio clips recorded with Captivate.
- The **Library** panel provides the necessary tools to let you manage the various assets used in the project.
- You can use the **Library** panel to insert multiple instances of the same asset in your project. This helps in keeping the project size as low as possible.
- It is possible to share assets among various projects by opening the Library of other files and importing the assets they contain in the current project.
- When you delete an asset from a slide, it is not deleted from the **Library** panel. As a result, the **Library** panel may contain many unused items.
- You can easily select and delete the unused items with the tools of the **Library** panel.

Summary

The post-production phase of your projects is now well in progress and you have already come a long way since you entered the studio with your rushes at the beginning of this chapter.

In this chapter, you have learned about nine non-interactive objects that you can use to dramatically enhance the slides of your projects. These objects make the student's experience of your eLearning content much better.

You also learned about various tools and features that help you efficiently manage these objects. The Alignment toolbar and the new Smart Guides make it easy to align and distribute objects on the slides. The **Timeline** panel allows you to decide when the objects appear and disappear from the slide, effectively creating animated sequences that make your eLearning content stand out from the crowd. The **Library** panel helps you control the size of your file by allowing you to reuse assets as many times as needed throughout the project. The tools you learned in this chapter are building your fundamental Captivate skills. In the remaining chapters, you will build on these fundamental skills to create unique interactive eLearning content.

In the next chapter, you will focus on the cosmetic part of the project and take a much deeper look at the formatting properties of the objects you have manipulated in this chapter. Thanks to the Styles, the Master Slides, the Templates, and the Themes, you will be able to quickly apply a highly customized look and feel to your projects. These tools will also help you maintain formatting consistency both within and among your projects.

As you can see, there are lots of exciting materials ahead (and yes, the AC/DC concert in Amsterdam was absolutely awesome!).

See you in *Chapter 4, Working with Styles, Master Slides, Themes, and Templates*!

Meet the community

In this section, I want to introduce you to Lieve Weymeis. Lieve and I share our Belgian nationality, which makes us very close. I first met her in the summer of 2013 in San Jose, California, during an Adobe event. There, she celebrated her 10,000th answer on the Captivate forums with the rest of the Adobe Education team. I was fortunate enough to be part of the celebration and to have my share of the fantastic chocolate cake made for the occasion. Full respect, Lieve!

Lieve Weymeis

Lieve is civil engineer (Ir) and professional musician. After years of teaching/research (project management/eLearning), she is now a freelance consultant/trainer specialized in advanced Adobe Captivate. Her blog (http://blog.lilybiri.com) is a reference for Captivate users worldwide.

In 2009, she was invited to the Advisory Board for Captivate. As an Adobe Certified Expert and Adobe Education Leader, she presented about Captivate and Flipped classes, both online and live (Adobe Summits, DevLearn, Media and Learning, and so on). In the Captivate community (forums) and on social media, she has established herself as a well-known and much appreciated expert.

Contact details

- **Twitter**: @Lilybiri
- **Blog**: http://blog.lilybiri.com
- **LinkedIn**: be.linkedin.com/in/lieveweymeis
- **E-mail**: info@lilybiri.com

4
Working with Styles, Master Slides, Themes, and Templates

In this chapter, you will focus on the cosmetic aspect of the project using Styles, Master Slides, Themes, and Templates. Your primary goal is to reach a high level of consistency in the look and feel of your eLearning content. When developing eLearning material, always keep in mind that your students will most likely experience your content while alone in front of their computer with no one around to guide them. In this chapter, you will discover that a consistent look and feel is an efficient way to get your students on task. The idea is to free them from learning how the eLearning content works and what it looks like so that they can be fully available for the actual topics you want to teach them.

Captivate offers five features to help you achieve this high level of consistency. The first feature that will be discussed in this chapter is the **Object Style Manager** used to create styles. You will then learn about **Master Slides**, the **Swatches panel**, **Templates**, and **Themes**.

The proper use of Master Slides, Templates, Styles, Swatches, and Themes will dramatically speed up the development of your eLearning content.

In this chapter, you will do the following:

- Experiment with Styles and with the Object Styles Manager
- Import and export Styles
- Experiment with the predefined Themes of Captivate
- Create a new Theme from scratch
- Use the all new Swatches panel of Captivate 7.0.1

- Create a full set of Master Slides
- Add Placeholder objects on Master Slides
- Apply these Master Slides to the project slides
- Fine-tune the look and feel of the objects using Styles
- Save the Styles in your Theme
- Create a brand new Template
- Add Placeholder Slides to the Template
- Create a new Captivate project from a Template

There's a lot to cover, so let's dive right into the first discussion of this chapter, Styles.

Working with Styles

When working on an eLearning project, it is very important to precisely format the various objects present in your projects. Never forget that you are actually teaching your students something. In such a situation, most students will try to make sense of every single formatting anomaly. Inconsistent formatting will most likely mislead and confuse them.

Consistent formatting in eLearning

In my first eLearning project with Captivate, I used blue Text Captions to explain things to the learners and black Text Captions when I wanted them to do something. After a short while, the learners knew that when seeing a blue Text Caption, they just had to read through the text, and when seeing a black Text Caption, they made themselves ready to do something. Learners have reported that this formatting consistency helped them structure their learning.

A style enables you to save the formatting properties of an object and to reapply them on other objects of the same type. Captivate comes with predefined styles, but you can of course modify these default styles and even create your own custom styles.

Managing Styles with the Properties panel

For the next exercise, you will return to the encoderDemo_800.cptx project and make sure that the default **Classic** workspace is applied.

1. Run Captivate 7 and open the encoderDemo_800.cptx file under Chapter04.
2. In the top-right corner of the Captivate interface, make sure that the **Classic** workspace is the one currently in use.

3. Navigate to **Window** | **Workspace** | **Reset 'Classic'** to restore the **Classic** workspace to its default state.
4. Use the **Filmstrip** panel to go to slide 8.

Slide 8 contains the Text Caption that you formatted in the previous chapter. In this exercise, you will use the **Properties** panel to save the current formatting of this Text Caption as a style and to apply this style to the other Text Captions of the project.

5. Select the Text Caption that begins with **The Adobe Media Encoder contains a list**....

As depicted in the following screenshot, the **Style** drop-down list (shown as **(1)** in the following screenshot) is situated in the topmost area of the **Properties** panel. It should mention that the style currently applied to the selected Text Caption is the **+[Default Caption Style]** style. Note that there is a **+** sign to the left of the **[Default Caption Style]** style. This **+** sign means that the formatting has been manually changed (there is no way of knowing what the formatting changes are, just that something has changed).

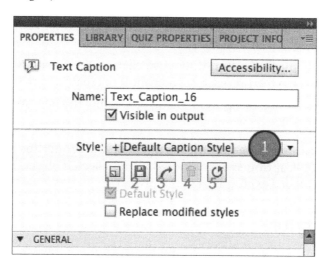

Just below the **Style** drop-down are five icons. For the purpose of this exercise, these icons will be numbered from 1 to 5. These icons are used to create **(1)**, save **(2)**, apply **(3)**, delete **(4)**, and reset **(5)** the styles.

Resetting a style

Resetting a style is one of the operations that can be done using the icons of the **Properties** panel.

1. Below the **Style** drop-down, click on the last icon **(5)** to reset the style.

2. The original **[Default Caption Style]** style is reapplied to the selected caption and the **+** sign disappears from the **Style** drop-down list of the **Properties** panel.
3. Navigate to **Edit** | **Undo** or use the *Ctrl + Z* (Windows) or *Command + Z* (Mac) shortcut to undo the last action.

Resetting a style is very practical when you want to reset the format of the selected object back to the default.

Creating new styles

Creating a new style is another operation that can be done with the icons of the **Properties** panel. In the next exercise, you will save the current formatting of the Text Caption that begins with **The Adobe Media Encoder contains a list**...as a style using the following steps:

1. Click on the Text Caption that begins with **The Adobe Media Encoder contains a list**...to make it the active object.
2. In the **Style** drop-down list of the **Properties** panel, confirm that the applied style is the **+[Default Caption Style]** style.
3. Right below the **Style** drop-down list, click on the **Create New Style** icon (shown as **(1)** in the preceding screenshot) to create a new style.
4. In the **Save New Object Style** dialog box, name the new style `MFTC-Caption` and click on **OK**.

Take another look at the **Style** drop-down menu on the **Properties** panel. It tells you that the new **MFTC-Caption** style is applied to the selected object. This style can now be applied to any other Text Caption in the project.

Applying styles

Applying styles to existing objects is yet another operation that can be done with the **Properties** panel. In the next exercise, you will apply your new **MFTC-Caption** style to another Text Caption of this slide.

1. While still on slide 8 of the `encoderDemo_800.cptx` file under `chapter04`, select the Text Caption that begins with **The conversion settings**....
2. At the top of the **Properties** panel, open the **Style** drop-down list.
3. In the list, select the **MFTC-Caption** style to apply it to the selected object.

Two of the Text Captions of slide 8 should now have the **MFTC-Caption** style applied.

Modifying a style

Modifying a style is the next action that you will perform thanks to the **Properties** panel. In this exercise, you will slightly modify the formatting of one of the Text Captions that has the **MFTC-Caption** style applied. You will then update your custom style to the new formatting and see how the other Text Caption reacts.

1. Make sure that the Text Caption that begins with **The conversion settings**… is still selected.
2. In the **Properties** panel, confirm that the **MFTC-Caption** style is currently applied to the selected object.
3. In the **Characters** section of the **Properties** panel, change the font size to 20.

Because you have made a formatting change, the **+** sign appears in the **Style** drop-down list. Therefore, the style currently applied to the selected Text Caption is **+MFTC-Caption**.

4. In the topmost area of the **Properties** panel, click on the **Save changes to existing style** icon (shown as **(2)** in the preceding screenshot) to save the changes to the existing style.

The **+** sign disappears from the **Styles** drop-down list.

5. Select the Text Caption that begins with **The Adobe Media Encoder contains a list**….
6. In the **Characters** section of the **Properties** panel, confirm that the new font size of 20 is applied to this Text Caption as well.

By updating the **MFTC-Caption** style, you have updated the formatting of every Text Caption of the project this style is applied to.

Applying styles automatically

The style currently applied to the modified Text Captions of slide 8 is the one you want for every Text Caption of the project. You could browse each slide one by one to manually apply the new style to each and every Text Caption, but there is another more automated way.

1. While still on slide 8 of the `encoderDemo_800.cptx` file under `Chapter04`, select the only remaining Text Caption that does not have the **MFTC-Caption** style applied.
2. In the **Style** drop-down menu of the **Properties** panel, confirm that the **[Default Capture Caption Style]** style is applied to the selected object.

What you want to do is apply your custom **MFTC-Caption** style to all the Text Captions of the project that currently use the **[Default Capture Caption Style]** style.

3. Select any of the two Text Captions that currently use your **MFTC-Caption** style.
4. Below the **Style** drop-down menu, click on icon 3, **Apply this style to...**.
5. In the **Apply Object Style** box, select the **[Default Capture Caption Style]** style in the drop-down list and click on **OK**.

This operation applies the **MFTC-Caption** style to every Text Caption of the project that has the **[Default Capture Caption Style]** style. As depicted in the following screenshot, all three Text Captions of slide 8 now have the same **MFTC-Caption** style applied.

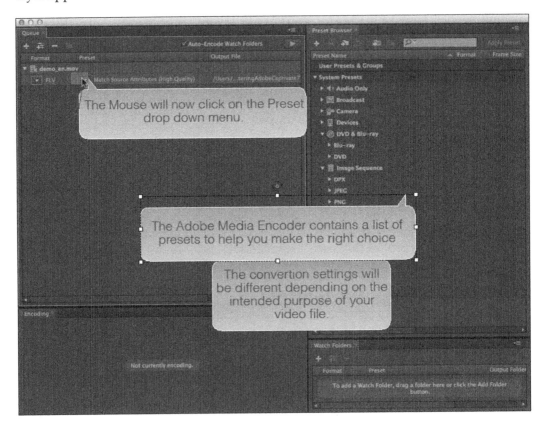

But slide 8 is not the only one that has been affected by this change.

6. Use the **Filmstrip** panel to browse the slides of your project one by one and confirm that all the Text Captions of the project that were using the **[Default Capture Caption Style]** style are now using your custom **MFTC-Caption** style.

While browsing the slides of your project, note that some Text Captions throughout the entire project have been affected by the change, while others still use their default formatting.

7. Use the **Filmstrip** panel to go to slide 4 of the project.

There should be two Text Captions on slide 4. None of them are currently using your custom **MFTC-Caption** style.

8. Select any of the two Text Captions and take a look at the top of the **Properties** panel to see what style is currently applied to the selected object.

The applied style should be the **+[Default Capture Caption Style]** style. This indicates that the current formatting of the selected object is based on the **[Default Capture Caption Style]** style with some manual formatting added on top of it. This Text Caption still uses its default formatting because it did not have the **[Default Caption Style]** style applied.

Extra credit 1– applying Styles automatically

In this section, you will use the same procedure as in the last exercise to apply the **MFTC-Caption** style to every Text Captions currently using the **[Default Caption Style]** style. The general steps are as follow:

- Select any Text Caption of the project that is currently using the **MFTC-Caption** style
- At the top of the **Properties** panel, click on icon 3 under the **Style** drop-down menu
- In the **Apply Object Style** window, select the **[Default Caption Style]** style and click on the **OK** button
- Use the **Filmstrip** panel to browse the slide of the project and confirm that all Text Captions now use the **MFTC-Caption** style

Well, it looks like your last operation didn't work as expected! Some Text Captions still have the same formatting as before. Let's see what's going on!

1. Return to slide 4 and select any of the two Text Captions.
2. In the **Properties** panel, confirm that the selected Text Caption currently uses the **+MFTC-Caption** style.

Actually, the manual edit that you did earlier on this Text Caption (change the **Caption** type to **Adobe Blue**) is still applied and overrides your custom style.

3. In the **Properties** panel, click on the Reset Style icon (shown as (**5**) in the first screenshot) to reset the style to its default look.

4. Repeat the same operation for all the remaining Text Captions starting from slide 3 till the end of the project.

All the Text Captions of the project should now be formatted the same way. Note that the **[Default Caption Style]** style was the style applied by default to the new Text Captions. Now that it has been replaced by your own **MFTC-Caption** style, any new Text Caption you insert in the project will automatically be associated with the **MFTC-Caption** style by default.

> **Replacing all styles**
>
> When the **Replace modified** styles checkbox situated in the topmost section of the **Properties** panel is selected, a new style is applied to the object when the **Apply this Style To** icon is used regardless of the overrides.

Extra credit 2 – creating Styles for another type of object

What is true for the Text Captions also applies to the other type of objects. In this section, you will create a new style for the Highlight Box that you formatted in the previous chapter. You will then apply your new style to all the other Highlight Boxes of the project.

These are the general steps to follow:

- Use the **Filmstrip** panel to return to slide 4 and select the orange Highlight Box you formatted in the previous chapter.
- Save the current formatting of the Text Caption as a new style named **MFTC-HighlightBox**.
- Use the icons of the **Properties** panel to apply the new **MFTC-HighlightBox** style to the remaining Highlight Boxes of the project. (Hint : By default, the Highlight Boxes use the **[Default Blue Highlight Box Style]** style).
- Browse the slides of the project and confirm that all the Highlight Boxes now share the same orange look and feel.
- If needed, move and resize the Highlight Boxes so they are well-integrated into the slides.

This concludes your first explorations of the styles in Captivate. Using the styles, it has been easy and fast to format every Text Caption and every Highlight Box of your project the exact same way. This helps you achieve the high degree of formatting consistency that creates a more professional looking project and assists your students in the learning process.

Before moving on to the next topic, let's summarize what you have learned.

- Styles help you create and maintain consistent formatting throughout the entire project
- In the topmost section of the **Properties** panel, the **Style** drop-down list is used to apply a style to the selected object
- When some additional formatting is applied on an object, a + sign appears in front of the style name
- When you modify a style, you change the formatting of all the objects using that particular style
- The icons situated below the **Styles** dropdown in the **Properties** panel are used to manage the style applied to the selected object

Working with the Object Style manager

So far, you have used the icons of the **Properties** panel to apply and manage styles. These icons give you quick and easy access to the main styling features of Captivate. However, behind the scenes, a much more sophisticated engine is at work!

This engine is the Object Style Manager. The icons of the **Properties** panel are just a remote control to the actual Object Style Manager. Everything these icons made possible is also possible through the Object Style Manager, but the Object Style Manager has much more to offer.

Exporting a style

One of the extra features offered by the Object Style manager is the ability to export styles:

1. Make sure you are still in the `encoderDemo_800.cptx` project.
2. Navigate to **Edit | Object Style Manger** to open the Object Style Manager.

Working with Styles, Master Slides, Themes, and Templates

The Object Style Manager opens as shown in the following screenshot:

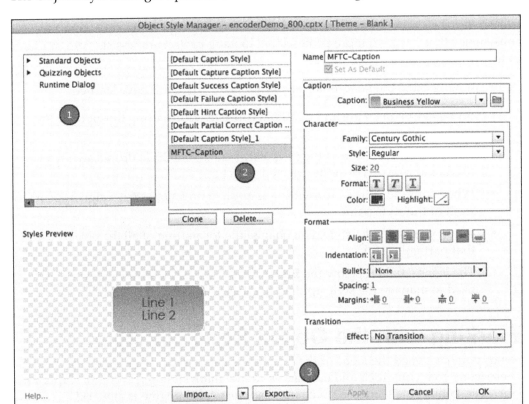

The left-hand side of the Object Style Manager (shown as **(1)** in the preceding screenshot) contains a list of all the objects of Captivate.

3. In the left column of the Object Style Manager, expand the **Standard Objects** section.
4. In the **Standard Objects** section, expand the **Caption** subsection.

The **Caption** subsection shows a list of all the caption types of Captivate.

5. Click on Text Caption.

The middle column (shown as **(2)** in the preceding screenshot) shows a list of the styles that can be applied to the object type selected in the first column. In this case, the styles listed in the middle column can be applied to the Text Caption object. Among them is your custom **MFTC-Caption** style.

6. In the middle column, select the **MFTC-Caption** style.

Chapter 4

7. At the bottom of the **Object Style Manager**, click on the **Export** button (shown as **(3)** in the preceding screenshot).
8. Save the style in your exercises folder as `MFTC-Caption.cps` under `Chapter04`. Acknowledge the successful export by clicking on the **OK** button.
9. Click on **OK** to close the **Object Style Manager**.
10. Save the `encoderDemo_800.cptx` file.

Exporting a style creates a `.cps` file. This file will be used to import the style in another project.

> **Exporting multiple styles**
>
> By clicking on the drop-down arrow situated next to the **Export** button in the Object Style Manager, you will be able to export all the Styles of a specific object type or even of all the objects.

Importing a style

In order to use your custom **MFTC-Caption** style in another project, you will now use the Object Style Manager to import the `.cps` file created in the previous exercise in another Captivate project using the following steps:

1. Open the `drivingInBe.cptx` project under `Chapter04`.
2. Open the Object Style Manger by navigating to **Edit | Object Style Manager**.
3. In the **Object Style Manager** dialog, expand the **Standard Objects** section, then the **Caption** subsection.
4. Select the **Text Caption** object.

In the middle column of the Object Style Manager, note that your **MFTC-Caption** style is not listed. This is because the styles listed in the Object Style Manager are specific to the active file. In Captivate, each project has its own list of styles.

> **Adding styles globally**
>
> If you want to add styles to the Object Style Manager and make them available to every projects of your Captivate installation, close all open files and go to the **Edit | Object Style Manager**. On Windows, make sure you run Captivate as an administrator to access the Object Style Manager when no project is open.

5. At the bottom of the **Object Style Manager** dialog, click on the **Import** button.
6. Browse to the `MFTC-Caption.cps` file under `Chapter04` and click on **Open**.

7. Read the message that pops up and click on **Yes** to discard it.
8. Close the **Object Style Manager** dialog by clicking on the **OK** button.

After this operation, the **MFTC-Caption** style will be transferred to the `drivingInBe.cptx` project and you should be able to apply it to the Text Captions of this project as well.

9. In the **Filmstrip** panel, select slide 14.
10. Select the Text Caption containing the text **Convert Speeds to MPH**.
11. Use the **Style** drop-down list in the topmost area of the **Properties** panel to apply the **MFTC-Caption** style to the selected Text Caption.
12. Follow the same procedure to apply the **MFTC-Caption** style to the following Text Captions beginning with **Pass your mouse on these road signs**... on slide 15 and to the Text Caption beginning with **Pass your mouse on the sentences to**... on slide 16.
13. Return to slide 14 and reselect the caption you applied the style to.
14. In the **Properties** panel, open the **Shadow & Reflection** section and select the **Enable** check box of the **Shadow** option. This applies a drop-shadow effect to the selected Text Caption.
15. In the **Properties** panel, open the **Transform** section, and type `10` in the **Angle** option. This applies a 10 degree rotation to the selected object.
16. Apply the same drop shadow and rotation to the styled Text Caption of slide 15.

Thanks to the Object Style Manager, you have been able to transfer a style from one project to another. This workflow helps you achieve formatting consistency not only within each project but also across different projects.

Creating a style in the Object Style Manager

To create the **MFTC-Caption** style, you used the icons situated in the topmost area of the **Properties** panel. You will now create another style from within the Object Style Manager directly.

1. Make sure you are in the `drivingInBe.cptx` file of `chapter04`.
2. Use the *Shift + F7* shortcut (Windows and Mac) to reopen the Object Style Manager.
3. In the middle column, select the `[Default Caption Style]` style.
4. Right below the middle column, click on the **Clone** button.

Captivate duplicates the **[Default Caption Style]** style and saves the clone as
`[Default Caption Style] 1`.

5. In the rightmost column of the **Object Style Manager** dialog, rename the new style to `transparentTitle`.
6. While still in the rightmost column, change the Caption Type from **Halo Blue** to **transparent**.
7. Change the font's **Family** option to **Verdana**.
8. Change the Character's **Size** option from **20** to `49`.

Make sure the Object Style Manager looks similar to what is shown in the following screenshot:

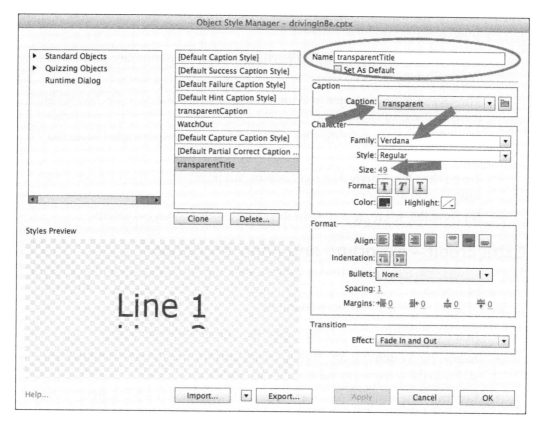

9. Leave the other options at their default settings and click on **OK** to close the Object Style Manager.
10. Use the **Filmstrip** panel to go to slide 1.

11. On slide 1, select the Text Caption containing **Drive in Belgium the safe way**.
12. Use the **Style** drop-down list of the **Properties** panel to apply the new **Transparent Title** style to the selected caption. Resize the Text Caption if needed.
13. With the caption still selected, click on the **Apply this style to**... icon **(1)**.
14. In the box that pops up, apply the **Transparent Title** style to every Text Caption currently using the **[Default Caption Style]** style and click on **OK**.
15. Use the **Filmstrip** panel to browse the slides of your project one by one. There should be no more Text Captions with the default styling.
16. Save the `drivingInBe.cptx` file.

This exercise concludes the overview of the Object Style Manager. Before moving on, let's summarize what you have learned.

- The five styling icons of the **Properties** panel act as a remote control to the Object Style Manager
- The Object Style Manager provides extra tools compared to the five styling icons of the **Properties** panel
- The leftmost column of the Object Style Manager contains a list of all the objects of Captivate
- Using the Object Style Manager, styles can be exported from a project and imported in another
- It is possible to create a style in the Object Style Manager directly

Extra credit – exporting and importing styles

The `drivingInBe.cptx` file contains some interesting styles that are not present in the `encoderDemo_800.cptx` project. Let's make those styles available in all your projects. Here are the general steps to follow:

- In the `drivingInBe.cptx` file, open the Object Style Manager.
- Export the **WatchOut**, the **transparentCaption**, and the **transparentTitle** styles to the `chapter04` folder of your exercises.
- Return to the `encoderDemo_800.cptx` file and use the Object Style Manager to import the three styles in the project.
- Go to slide 3 of the `encoderDemo_800.cptx` file. Use the `transparentTitle` and `transparentCaption` styles to format the Text Captions of this slide.
- Save both files when you're done.

The Styles are the first tool of Captivate that help you achieve a consistent look and feel throughout your project. But it is not the only tool. You will now dive into the Themes, a feature that was introduced in Captivate 6.

Working with the Themes

When Captivate 6 was released in June 2012, a brand new feature called **Themes** was introduced. Captivate ships with a handful of ready-to-use Themes right out of the box. In order to have a better idea of what a Theme is, start with some simple experiments using the predefined Themes.

1. Save and close every open file in Captivate.
2. Navigate to **File** | **New Project** | **Blank Project** to create a new blank project. You can also use the **Blank Project** link on the right-hand side of the Welcome screen.
3. In the **New Blank Project** dialog, use the **Select** drop-down menu to choose a size of **800 x 600** for the project. When you're done, click on the **OK** button.

Captivate creates a new blank project of the chosen size. As shown in the following screenshot, when a new project is created, a single slide is automatically added to the **Filmstrip** panel (shown as **(1)** in the following screenshot). This slide already contains several objects and styles. Note that the Themes panel (shown as **(2)** in the following screenshot) spans across the entire width of the stage.

Where is the Themes panel?

If the Themes panel is not automatically displayed on the screen, navigate to **Themes** | **Show/Hide Themes Panel** to turn it on.

Your new blank project will use the default White theme.

The elements of a Theme

A Captivate Theme is a collection of graphical elements and assets. In the next few pages, you will discover what Themes are made of by manipulating different Themes and exploring how they affect the slides and objects of the project. Let's start with the Master Slides of a Theme.

The Master Slides

The first element that makes up a Captivate Theme is a set of Master Slides. To better understand what these are, your first stop is the **Master Slide** panel.

1. Open the **Master Slide** panel. By default, it is situated at the bottom of the screen, next to the **Timeline** panel.

> Normally, the **Master Slide** panel is part of the default **Classic** workspace. If it is not displayed, navigate to **Window** | **Master Slide** to turn it on.

The White Theme that is currently applied to the project contains an entire set of predefined Master Slides. Each of these Master Slides proposes a predefined layout that you can apply as is to any slides of the project. To ensure visual consistency across the Master Slides of the Theme, the first Master Slide of the panel is known as the **Main Master Slide** (shown as **(1)** in the following screenshot). The Main Master Slide contains the visual elements that are common to most (if not every) slides of the project.

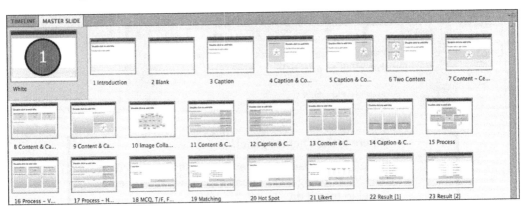

Creating slides based on Master Slides

In Captivate, it is possible to create new slides based on one of the Master Slides of the Theme using the following steps:

1. Select the first slide of the project in the main **Filmstrip** panel.
2. Navigate to **Insert | New Slide From | Caption**.

Captivate creates a new slide based on the **Caption** Master Slide of the Theme. The new slide already contains several Text Captions. Actually, the elements contained on the slides are not actual Text Captions yet. These elements are Text Caption **Placeholders**. They are used to predefine the location, size, and other formatting options of a future Text Caption.

3. Double-click on the **Double click to add title** placeholder.
4. Type some text into the Text Caption and hit the *Esc* key.

Now that some text has been typed into the object, it is not a Placeholder anymore but an actual Text Caption. The size, position, font family, font size, color, and so on of this Text Caption are inherited from the Placeholder, while the content of the Text Caption has just been typed in.

5. Navigate to **Insert | New Slide From | Two Content**.

Captivate inserts yet another slide in the project, but this time, it is based on the **Two Content** Master Slide of the Theme. This slide also contains some placeholders. On the right-hand side of the slide, three Text Caption Placeholders are displayed. On the left-hand side, there are two Content Placeholders.

6. Roll your mouse over the icons of the Content Placeholders. Note that each icon corresponds to a Captivate object.
7. Click on the **Image** icon of the Content Placeholder (see the arrow in the following screenshot).

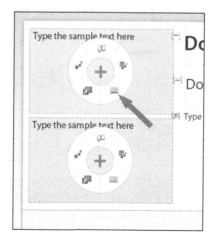

Working with Styles, Master Slides, Themes, and Templates

When clicking on this icon, Captivate immediately opens the **Select Image from Library** dialog. From this dialog, you can choose the image to insert into the Placeholder.

8. Click on **Cancel** to close the dialog without inserting an image.
9. Do the same experiment with the other icons of the Placeholder.

Each of these icons acts as a shortcut that inserts different kinds of content in the Placeholder. This illustrates the basic idea of the Themes and the Placeholders. By providing ready-made slide layouts and shortcut icons in the slides, the Themes and the Placeholders become tremendous time-savers. They enable you to rapidly develop your pieces of eLearning content.

Inserting a blank slide in a themed project

In this section, you will insert a new blank slide in your project and see which Master Slide is applied by default.

1. Navigate to **Insert | Blank Slide** to insert a new blank slide in the project.
2. With the new slide being the active object, take a look at the **General** section of the **Properties** panel.

As depicted in the following screenshot, the **Blank** Master Slide is currently applied to the new blank slide. Also, note that the **Use Master Slide Background** box is deselected. This is what makes this new slide effectively blank.

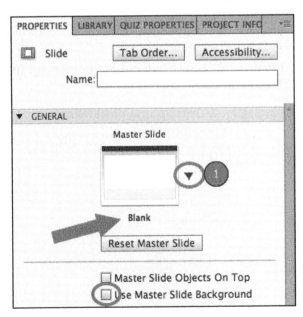

3. Select the **Use Master Slide Background** checkbox.

The background picture of the **Blank** Master Slide is now displayed on the newly inserted slide.

Changing the Master Slide of an existing slide

Sometimes, you may want to change the Master Slide applied to an existing slide. This is precisely what you will learn in this section.

1. Make sure the newly inserted slide is selected.
2. In the **General** section of the **Properties** panel, click on the small arrow next to the Master Slide thumbnail to open the Master Slide picker (shown as **(1)** in the preceding screenshot).
3. Choose any other Master Slide in the Master Slide picker.

The chosen Master Slide is applied to the selected slide, effectively demonstrating that the applied Master Slide can be changed along the way.

This concludes your first exploration of the Master Slides in Captivate.

The Styles

The second element of a Theme is the Styles. You will now experiment with Styles in the Theme using the following steps:

1. Use the **Filmstrip** panel to return to the second slide of this project.
2. Select the Text Caption (actually, a Smart Shape with text) that you created earlier in this exercise.
3. Take some time to inspect the **Properties** panel of the selected object. Note the **Font**, **Color**, **Font Size**, and other formatting properties that are currently in use.

You will now apply another Theme to the project and see how this change affects the slides and the objects.

4. If needed, navigate to **Themes | Show/Hide Themes Panel** to turn the Themes panel back on.

> It is necessary to be on a slide in the **Filmstrip** panel to turn the Themes panel on and off. If a Master Slide is selected in the **Master Slide** panel, the **Show/Hide Themes Panel** menu item is grayed out.

5. Click on the **Timeworn** theme to apply it to the project.
6. Read the warning message and click on **Yes** to continue.

The new Theme is applied to the project.

7. Use the **Filmstrip** panel to go through the slides of the project one by one.

Note how the new Theme affects the look and feel of your project. The most obvious change is the new background picture, but a Theme is far more than that.

8. When on the second slide, select your Smart Shape with text.
9. In the **Properties** panel, note how the formatting properties of the selected object have changed.

This illustrates that, in addition to Master Slides, a Theme contains Object Styles. So, by applying another theme on a project, you also update the styles applied to the objects.

>
> **The third element of a Theme**
>
> In addition to the Master Slides and the Object Styles, a Theme contains a third element called the **Skin**. The Skin of the project will be covered in *Chapter 8, Finishing Touches and Publishing*.

You now have a much better understanding of what a Theme is. In the next section, you will create your own customized Theme and apply it to the *Driving in Belgium* project, but, for the moment, let's quickly summarize what we have covered in this section.

- A Theme is a collection of graphical assets and styles. It is used to quickly define the look and feel of an entire project.
- Captivate is shipped with numerous predefined Themes. These are available in the Themes panel that is displayed across the width of the stage.
- Navigate to **Themes | Show/Hide Themes Panel** to turn the Themes panel on or off.
- A Theme is composed of three basic elements: a collection of Master Slides, the Styles to apply to the objects of the project, and the Skin of the project.
- When inserting a new slide into the project, Captivate tries to determine the best Master Slide to apply to the new slide.
- The **Properties** panel makes it possible to change the Master Slide applied to a regular slide at any time

Creating a Theme

In this section, you will return to the `drivingInBe.cptx` file under `Chapter04` and create a new Theme. To do so, you will first apply one of the predefined Themes of Captivate to the project. You will then fine-tune the Master Slides and the Styles of this theme to create your own custom Theme.

1. Return to the `drivingInBe.cptx` file under `Chapter04`.
2. Navigate to **Themes** | **Show/Hide Themes panel** to turn the Themes panel on.

You will use the **Blank** Theme as a starting point to create your own custom Theme.

3. Apply the **Blank** Theme to the project.

By applying the **Blank** Theme to the project, you modify the overall look and feel as well as some of the styles of the project.

4. Navigate to **Themes** | **Save Theme As** to create a new Theme based on the **Blank** Theme.
5. Save the new Theme as `MFTC-Theme.cptm` under `Chapter04`.
6. Acknowledge the successful creation of the new Theme by clicking on the **OK** button.

Note that the file extension used for themes is `.cptm`.

With your new Theme saved, you can safely move on to the next step and customize the Master Slides of the Theme.

Customizing the Master Slides of the Theme

The idea behind the Master Slides is quite simple. The goal is to create a set of slides in which you place backgrounds and other objects that are common to many slides in the project (such as logos, headers, footers, and so on). Once the Master Slides are created, you can apply them to the standard slides of your project in order to share the elements defined on the Master Slide. If you are a PowerPoint or Keynote user, this process probably sounds very familiar.

1. If needed, open the **Master Slide** panel. By default, the **Master Slide** panel is situated at the bottom of the screen, next to the **Timeline** panel.

As shown in the following screenshot, the **Blank** Theme that you applied to the project already contains six Master Slides (shown as **(1)** in the following screenshot) in addition to the Main Master Slide (shown as **(2)** in the following screenshot).

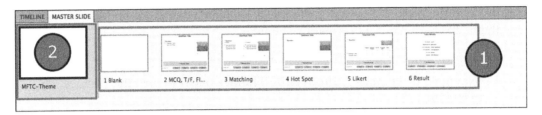

First, you will customize the Main Master Slide.

Customizing the Main Master Slide

The Main Master Slide is the first one in the **Master Slide** panel. The idea is to insert the main graphical elements shared by most (if not all) of the other Master Slides of the project on the Main Master Slides. Note that the name of the Theme (here, **MFTC-Theme**) appears below the Main Master Slide thumbnail.

1. In the **Master Slide** panel, click on the Main Master Slide to make it the active object.
2. If needed, open the **Properties** panel. Make sure it shows the properties of the Main Master Slide.
3. Navigate to **Insert** | **Image** to insert the mftcContentTemplate.jpg image under images on the Master Slide.
4. Right-click on the image you just imported. In the contextual menu that opens, click on the **Merge With the Background** menu item.
5. Take some time to read the information message that appears on the screen. Click on the **Yes** button to acknowledge the message and merge the image with the background.

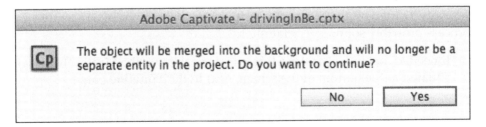

By merging a picture into the background, the picture becomes the slide itself. Consequently, it cannot be manipulated as an object anymore and it disappears from the **Timeline** panel.

Take a look at the **Master Slide** panel and note that all the Master Slides of the Theme are now using the background of the Main Master Slide.

Adding a Master Slide to the Theme

You will now add a new Master Slide to the project. You will name it the `Title` Master Slide and use another image as its background using the following steps:

1. With the Main Master slide selected in the **Master Slide** panel, navigate to **Insert | Content Master Slide** to insert a new Master Slide in the project.

The new Master Slide is inserted as Master Slide number 2. Note that, by default, it uses the background of the Main Master slide, which is not what you want in this case.

2. Select the newly inserted Master Slide in the **Master Slide** panel.
3. At the very top of the **Properties** panel, enter `Title` in the **Name** field and hit the *Enter* key to validate.

The new name appears below the Master Slide thumbnail in the **Master Slide** panel. The next step is to remove the default background image that is inherited from the Main Master Slide and to replace it with another background picture.

4. At the top of the **Properties** panel, deselect the **Use Master Slide Background** checkbox.
5. While still in the **Properties** panel, click on the folder icon situated below the **Background** field.
6. In the **Select Image from Library** dialog box, select the `MFTCTitleTemplate.jpg` image situated in the **Backgrounds** section of the **Library** panel.
7. Click on **OK** to apply the new background and to close the **Select Image from Library** window.

As depicted in the following screenshot, the new **Title** Master Slide now uses another background image than the one used by the other Master Slides of the project.

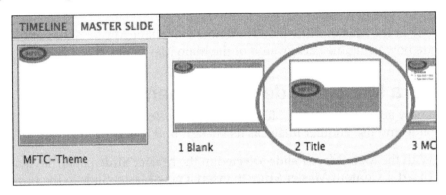

Adding Placeholders to the Master Slides

In addition to sharing the same background image, the title slides of your projects should contain a Text Animation with similar properties. To speed up the development of the future eLearning project that will use this Theme, you can add a Text Animation Placeholder on the **Title** Master Slide using the following steps:

1. In the **Master Slide** panel, select the new **Title** Master Slide.
2. Navigate to **Insert | Placeholder Object | Text Animation** to add a Text Animation Placeholder on the Master Slide.
3. Move the Placeholder object roughly to the center of the brownish area in the middle of the slide.

With the Text Animation Placeholder selected, note the **Effect** drop-down list of the **General** section of the **Properties** panel. It is identical to the one that is used when configuring an actual Text Animation.

4. In the **General** section, change the **Effect** option to **Waltz**.

The other options of the Text Animation (such as the text content) depend on the actual Text Animation object that will be placed in this Placeholder when developing the content.

Note that such a Placeholder object can only be inserted on Master Slides. In other words, it is not possible to insert a Placeholder object on a regular slide.

Applying the Master Slides to the slides of the project

In this section, you will use the Master Slides of your Theme to implement a consistent look and feel for all the slides of the project. You will start by applying the **Title** Master Slide to the first and last slides of the project.

1. Use the **Filmstrip** panel to go to slide 1 of the `drivingInBe.cptx` project.
2. Make sure that the **Properties** panel shows the properties of the slide and not the properties of one of the objects of the slide.
3. In the **General** section of the **Properties** panel, use the **Master Slide** drop-down list to apply the **Title** Master Slide to this particular slide.

Note how the name you added earlier to the Master Slide now helps you locate it in the drop-down list!

4. While still in the **General** section of the **Properties** panel, select the **Use Master Slide Background** and the **Master Slide Objects On Top** checkboxes.
5. Repeat the same sequence of actions on the last slide of the project.

On the first and last slides of the project, note that the Text Animation Placeholder from the **Title** Master Slide is displayed in addition to the existing Text Animation. This is not a problem because the Text Animation Placeholder will not be displayed to the learner. That being said, you probably want to keep your project nice and clean so that you can safely delete the Text Animation Placeholder on both the first and the last slides of the project.

You will now apply the **Blank** Master Slide to the other slides of the project.

1. Use the **Filmstrip** panel to return to slide 2.
2. In the **General** section of the **Properties** panel, confirm that the **Blank** Master Slide is in use.
3. Also make sure that the **Use Master Slide Background** and the **Master Slide Objects On Top** checkboxes are both selected.
4. Use the **Filmstrip** panel to go to slide 3 of the project.
5. Hold the *Shift* key while selecting slide 16 in the **Filmstrip** panel. This action selects from slide 3 to slide 16 (14 slides are selected).
6. In the **Properties** panel, choose the **Blank** Master Slide and select the **Use Master Slide Background** and the **Master Slide Objects On Top** checkboxes.

This single action applies the **Blank** Master Slide to all the selected slides at once! All the slides of the project should now share the same general look and feel with minimal effort on your side.

Modifying a Master Slide

The Master Slides already help you achieve a high level of consistency within your project. Now they will help you maintain this consistency over time.

A Master Slide can contain much more than just a simple background. It can contain many of the objects that are found on any regular slide (such as Text Captions, Highlight Boxes, and Images).

In the next exercise, you will add a Text Caption to the Main Master Slide and see how this change affects the Filmstrip slides of your project.

1. Return to the **Master** Slide panel situated at the bottom of the screen, next to the **Timeline** panel.
2. Select the Main Master Slide.
3. Navigate to **Insert** | **Standard Object** | **Text Caption** to insert a new Text Caption on the Master Slide.

While the **Standard Object** menu under **Insert** is open, note that some of the objects are grayed out and thus, unavailable for insertion on a Master Slide.

4. Replace the text in the Text Caption with Copyright MFTC - 2014.
5. Place your mouse cursor in the Text Caption, right before the **C** of **Copyright**.
6. In the **Format** section of the **Properties** panel, click on the **Insert Symbol** icon and insert the **Copyright** symbol followed by a space.

This process is illustrated in the following screenshot:

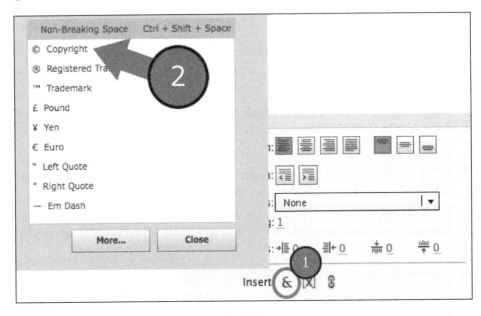

7. Hit the *Esc* key to leave the Text Editing mode and keep the copyright notice selected.
8. In the **Character** section of the **Properties** panel, change the font size of the entire Text Caption to `12` points and the font family to **Verdana**.
9. In the **Transform** section of the **Properties** panel, set the new Text Caption the following options.
    - Deselect the **Constrain proportions** checkbox
    - Change the size of the Text Caption to **W** = `150` and **H** = `30`
    - Change the position of the Text Caption to **X** = `10` and **Y** = `555`
10. In the **Transition** section, change the **Effect** option to **No Transition**, if needed.

By adding a copyright notice on the Main Master Slide, you have added a copyright notice on every single Master Slide and, consequently, on every standard Filmstrip slide in the project. Let's check it out!

11. Use the **Filmstrip** panel to return to the first slide of the project.

The copyright notice is visible at the bottom-left corner of slide 1.

12. Browse the remaining slides of the project one by one. Pay close attention to the copyright notice!

Not bad! The copyright notice is well-integrated with most of your slides. Only the first and last slides of the project, which use the **Title** Master Slide, must be adjusted. Also note that, thanks to the Master Slide system, the copyright notice has the very same appearance, size, and position on every single slide that displays it. Did you say consistency?

13. Return to the **Master Slide** panel and select the **Title** Master Slide.
14. In the **General** section of the **Properties** panel, deselect the **Show Main Master Slide Objects** checkbox.

This action removes the copyright notice from the **Title** Master Slide and, consequently, from all the slides of the project that are based on this Master Slide.

The Master Slide part of your customized Theme is complete for the moment. However, before moving on to the next section, don't forget to save the changes made to your custom Theme.

15. Navigate to **Themes | Save Theme** to save the new Master Slide configuration in your custom `MFTC-Theme.cptm` file.
16. Also save the `drivingInBe.cptx` file under `chapter04`.

Now that the Theme is saved, let's quickly summarize what you just learned:

- To create a new Theme, apply one of the predefined Themes to your project and navigate to **Themes** | **Save Theme As**
- A Theme is saved as a .cptm file
- The first element contained in a Theme is a set of Master Slides
- The Main Master slide is used to quickly define the general look and feel of the whole project
- By default, all the Master Slides of the project use the same background as the Main Master Slide
- Deselect the **Use Master Slide Background** checkbox of a specific Master Slide to customize that specific Master Slide, without using the elements of the Main Master Slide
- It is possible to prevent the objects of the Main Master Slide to appear on the individual Master Slides by deselecting the **Show Main Master Slide Objects** checkbox
- Navigate to **Insert** | **Content Master Slide** to insert a new Master Slide in the project
- The changes made on a Master Slide are reflected on the standard slides that are based on that Master Slide

In the next section, you will use Styles to fine-tune the look and feel of the objects of the project. You will also save these styles in the Theme so that they can be easily reused in subsequent projects.

Adding Styles to the Theme

To create new styles you will return to the topmost area of the **Properties** panel. You will save these new styles in the Theme at the end of the exercise.

Let's start by giving the proper look and feel to the standard objects of the project.

Styling the titles

In this section, you will repair the formatting of the Title Text Caption of slide 2. When done, you will create a new style and apply it to all the titles of your project.

1. Use the **Filmstrip** panel to return to slide 2 of the `drivingInBe.cptx` file under `chapter04`.

There should be two Text Captions on slide 2. The topmost Text Caption will be the title of the slide, but by applying the Blank Theme earlier in this chapter, the formatting of this Text Caption has been reset. You will now repair the formatting of this Text Caption so that it looks like a title again!

2. Select the Text Caption that reads **Drive in Belgium the safe way**. In the topmost area of the **Properties** panel, note that this Text Caption currently uses the **[Default Caption Style]** style.
3. In the **Character** section of the **Properties** panel, change the font family of the selected Text Caption to **Verdana** and the font size to `49` points.
4. Don't hesitate to slightly move the Text Caption if you feel it is needed.

Now that the Text Caption has recovered its proper look and feel, you will save its current formatting properties in a new style and apply that style to the other Text Caption of the same type throughout the entire project.

5. In the topmost area of the **Properties** panel, click on the **Create New Style** icon (icon 1).
6. Change the name of the new style to `MFTC-Title` and click on the **OK** button.
7. In the topmost area of the **Properties** panel, click on the **Apply this style to...** icon (icon 3).
8. In the drop-down list, choose **[Default Caption Style]**. This applies the new **MFTC-Title** style to all the Text Captions of the project that are currently using the **[Default Caption Style]** style.
9. Use the **Filmstrip** panel to browse through the slides of the project one by one.

Ensure that the remaining Title Text Captions of the project are formatted correctly.

Working with the Swatches panel

The **Swatches** panel is one of the newest additions to Captivate 7. It is part of the Captivate 7.0.1 update patch that was released in November 2013. The **Swatches** panel allows you to customize the set of colors available in your project.

> **Finding the exact version number of Captivate**
>
> To make it through this exercise, you need to have the latest Captivate update installed. To find out the exact version number of your Captivate installation, navigate to **Help | About Adobe Captivate** (Windows) or **Adobe Captivate | About Adobe Captivate** (Mac). At the time of this writing, the latest Captivate version is Captivate 7.0.1.237. If your version number is lower than that, the **Swatches** panel will not be available to you. See the official Adobe website for a detailed description of the Captivate 7.0.1 update patch and update instructions: http://www.adobe.com/support/captivate/downloads.html.

In the next exercise, you will take your first look at the **Swatches** panel using the following steps:

1. Open the **Swatches** panel. By default, the **Swatches** panel is situated on the right edge of the screen next to the **Properties** and **Library** panels.

The **Swatches** panel should look similar to what is shown in the following screenshot:

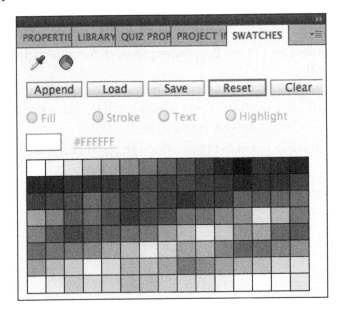

The main area of the **Swatches** panel is covered by lots of colored squares. Each of these squares is called a **Swatch** and can be used to apply a color to various elements of the selected Captivate object. In the upper portion of the **Swatches** panel are five buttons: **Append**, **Load**, **Save**, **Reset**, and **Clear**, which are used to append, load, save, reset, and clear the swatches. Also, note that the radio buttons for the **Fill**, **Stroke**, **Text**, and **Highlight** elements should all be disabled at this moment.

You will now select an object and change its colors using the **Swatches** panel.

2. Use the **Filmstrip** panel to go to slide 4 of the `drivingInBe.cptx` file under `Chapter04`.
3. Click on the rounded rectangle Smart Shape that you used as a picture frame.

Remember that in the previous chapter, you grouped this rounded rectangle with the image. By clicking once on the rounded rectangle, you actually select the entire group of objects, not the rounded rectangle alone!

4. Click on the rounded rectangle a second time to select this object within the group.

Note that white selection handles now surround the rounded rectangle and that green handles surround the entire group. The presence of these green handles is the visual clue telling you that the active selection is a single object within a group.

With the rounded rectangle selected, you should see that the **Fill** and the **Stroke** radio buttons of the **Swatches** panel are now enabled with the **Fill** option selected by default.

5. Click on any Swatch (in other words, any colored square) of the **Swatches** panel.

The color you clicked on should have been applied to the **Fill** property of the selected object.

6. In the **Swatches** panel, select the **Stroke** radio button.
7. Click on any other Swatch to apply the selected color to the **Stroke** property of the selected object.

This small experiment demonstrates how the **Swatches** panel works. You select an object on the stage and a property of this object using the radio buttons of the **Swatches** panel, and then click on a color Swatch to apply a color to the selected property of the selected object.

Importing custom Swatches to the Swatches panel

In my opinion, the ability to import and export Swatches to and from the **Swatches** panel is what makes it awesome! Thanks to this ability, you can export the Swatches created in other applications (such as Adobe Photoshop or Adobe Illustrator) and import them into Captivate.

In the next exercise, you will import the official brand colors of the MFTC Company into the project and use them to change the colors of the rounded rectangle Smart Shape.

1. While still in the **Swatches** panel, click on the **Load** button.
2. Navigate to the `MFTC-Colors.ase` file situated in the `Chapter04` folder and double-click on it.
3. A message informs you that this operation will remove the current colors from the **Swatches** panel. Click on **Yes** to discard the message and continue importing the custom swatches.

Five color Swatches are imported into the **Swatches** panel and replace the default set of colors. The imported colors are the official corporate colors of the MFTC Company that you must use in your projects to comply with the Company Policy.

Creating the .ase file

An **Adobe Swatch Exchange** (**ASE**) file is used to export Swatches from an Adobe Application and import them into other Adobe applications. Most Adobe applications can be used to create such a `.ase` file. In Captivate, use the **Save** button of the **Swatches** panel to save the current swatches to a `.ase` file. For this exercise, we have used an online service named **Adobe Kuler** to create the `.ase` file. You can find out more on Adobe Kuler and create your own `.ase` files at `http://kuler.adobe.com`.

Styling the Smart Shapes using the Swatches panel

Now that the official colors of the MFTC brand have been imported into the **Swatches** panel, you will use them to repair the formatting of the rounded rectangle Smart Shape of slide 4 using the following steps:

1. Make sure that the rounded rectangle of slide 4 is still selected.
2. Select the **Fill** radio button of the **Swatches** panel.
3. Click on the first Swatch (the light brown color) of the **Swatches** panel.

The light brown color is applied to the **Fill** property of the rounded rectangle. You will now apply another color imported from the .ase file to the **Stroke** property of the rounded rectangle.

4. With the rounded rectangle shape still selected on the stage, select the **Stroke** radio button of the **Swatches** panel.
5. Click on the second Swatch to apply the dark brown color to the **Stroke** property of the rounded rectangle.

Now that the colors are in place, you will return to the **Properties** panel to adjust the remaining properties of the rounded rectangle.

6. With the rounded rectangle still selected, return to the **Properties** panel.
7. In the **Fill & Stroke** section, make the object completely opaque by changing the Alpha value to 100 percent.
8. Finally, change the **Stroke Width** option to 3 pixels.

Make sure the rounded rectangle now looks similar to what is shown in the following screenshot:

Working with Styles, Master Slides, Themes, and Templates

In order to quickly apply this new formatting to the other Smart Shapes in the project, you will save the current formatting properties of the rounded rectangle in a style and apply this style to the other Smart Shapes of the project.

9. With the rounded rectangle still selected, click on the **Create New Style** icon (icon 1) of the **Properties** panel.
10. Name the new style `MFTC-SmartShape` and click on the **OK** button.
11. In the topmost area of the **Properties** panel, click on the **Apply this style to...** icon (icon 3).
12. In the drop-down list, choose the **[Default Smart Shape Style]** style.
13. Use the **Filmstrip** panel to go to slide 3.

Slide 3 contains the Curved Up Ribbon Smart Shape. It should have the same general look and feel as the rounded rectangle of slide 4. However, this Smart Shape contains some text that needs to be properly formatted.

14. Select the Curved Up Ribbon of slide 3.
15. In the **Character** section of the **Properties** panel, change the font family to **Verdana** and the font size to `28` points.
16. In the **Format** section, change the alignment to **Align Center** and **Align Top**.
17. In the topmost area of the **Properties** panel, click on the **Save changes to Existing Style** icon (icon 2) to update the style.

In this exercise, you have experimented with the all new **Swatches** panel of Captivate 7.0.1. Before moving on to the next section, let's quickly summarize the new material covered in this section:

- The **Swatches** panel is a new feature of Captivate 7.0.1. Therefore, it is necessary to install the latest Captivate update to enjoy the goodies of the **Swatches** panel.
- The **Swatches** panel lets you customize the set of colors available in Captivate.
- One of the most interesting aspects of the **Swatches** panel is the ability to import and export the color Swatches using the `.ase` files.
- The Adobe Swatch Exchange (`.ase`) files are used to export color Swatches from one Adobe Application and import them into another Adobe Application.
- Adobe Kuler (`http://kuler.adobe.com`) is an online service that allows you to create custom color Swatches and to export them as `.ase` files.

Saving the Styles in the Theme

In order to save the newly created Styles into the Theme, you simply need to save the Theme itself. By saving the Theme, you update the Master Slides, the Styles, and the Skin saved in the `MFTC-Theme.cptm` file.

1. Navigate to **Themes** | **Save Theme** to update the current Theme with the new styles.

From now on, each time you experiment with a new object in Captivate, you will create a style for this object and save the Theme to add the new style to the `.cptm` file. At the end of the book, your Theme will contain styles for almost every object within your project.

In the next section, you will discover the Captivate templates.

Working with Templates

The basic idea of a Template is to create a project that can be used as the starting point of another project. When creating a project from a Template, a stencil copy of the Template is created, which serves as the starting point of a new project. In the new project, the teacher can edit, remove, and add objects with no restrictions.

A Template can contain the same slides and objects as a regular project. The preferences applied to the Template become the default preferences of future projects that will be based on the Template. The Theme that is applied to a Template becomes the default Theme of future projects based on that Template.

In the next exercise, you will create a Template that will be used for all the demonstrations created by the developers at the MFTC Company. The instructional and visual designers at MFTC decided the following:

- All demonstrations should have a resolution of 800 x 600 pixels
- All demonstrations should use your custom MFTC Theme
- All demonstrations should begin with a **Title** Slide containing a Text Animation that uses the **Waltz** effect
- The second slide of each demonstration is a slide explaining the objectives of the demonstration
- The actual screenshot-based demonstration begins on the third slide
- When the demonstration is finished, a summary slide should emphasize the key points of what has been covered in the project
- After the summary, the last slide should contain a Text Animation similar to that of the first slide

Creating a Template

To help the company enforce these rules, you will create a Template that the eLearning developers will use to create future demonstrations. This Template will not only help in producing consistent content and design across projects, but also speed up the development process of the eLearning courses by reusing common designs, properties, and content.

1. Save and close every open project.
2. On the right column of the Welcome screen, click on the **Project Template** link under **Create New**. Alternatively, you can navigate to **File | New Project | Project Template**.
3. In the **New Project Template** box, select the **800 x 600** resolution and click on **OK**.

The first rule is already enforced! All the demonstrations that will be based on this Template will use the same **800 x 600** resolution.

4. Use the Themes panel to apply your custom MFTC-Theme to this Template. If the Themes panel is not open, navigate to **Themes | Show/Hide Themes Panel** to turn it on.

Second rule enforced! All future demonstrations based on this Template will use your custom `MFTC-Theme.cptm` file. Also, note that the new MFTC-Theme has been automatically added to the Themes panel.

5. Make sure that the **Properties** panel shows the properties of the first slide of the project.
6. In the **General** section of the **Properties** panel, use the **Master Slide** drop-down menu to apply the **Title** Master Slide of the Theme to the selected slide.
7. At the top of the **Properties** panel, change the slide name to `Intro Slide`.

Third rule enforced! The first slide of the Template contains a Text Animation Placeholder with the **Waltz** effect pre-selected!

8. Navigate to **Insert | New Slide From | Blank** to insert a new slide based on the **Blank** Master Slide of your Theme.
9. Use the **Properties** panel to change the name of this slide to `Objectives`.
10. Add two Text Captions to the new **Objectives** slide. Make sure these new Text Captions have the **MFTC-Title** style applied.
11. Position the first Text Caption in the upper area of the slide and change the Text to `Objectives of this demonstration`. Resize the Text Caption, if necessary.
12. Position the second Text Caption below the first one and apply the **transparentCaption** style to it.

The second slide of the Template should now look similar to what is shown in the following screenshot:

Fourth rule enforced! The second slide of the Template is ready to receive the objectives of the demonstration. The layout and styling of that content is already predefined in the Theme and in the Master Slides.

Adding Placeholder Slides

The third slide is where the actual screenshot-based demonstration should begin. When developing the Template, you do not know how long that demonstration will be and how many slides it will last. You only know that the demonstration begins on slide 3. To enforce this rule, add a Placeholder Slide to the Template.

In Captivate, there are two kinds of Placeholder Slides:

- A Recording Slide Placeholder is meant to be replaced by a screenshot-based recording using the techniques covered in *Chapter 2, Capturing the Slides*.
- A Question Slide Placeholder is meant to be replaced by a Question Slide. Quizzes and Question Slides will be covered in *Chapter 7, Working with Quizzes*.

In this case, a Recording Slide Placeholder is what you need. Use the following steps to insert a Recording Slide Placeholder to the Template:

1. If needed, use the **Filmstrip** panel to go to slide 2 in the Template.
2. Navigate to **Insert | Placeholder Slides | Recording Slide Placeholder** to add a Recording Slide Placeholder at the end of the Template.

Note that Placeholder slides can only be added to a Captivate template. If you try to insert a Placeholder Slide into a regular Captivate project, the elements of the **Placeholder Slides** menu item under **Insert** will be grayed out.

Fifth rule enforced! The Recording Slide Placeholder is added as slide 3 of the Template.

Note that the options of the **Properties** panel are all grayed out when the slide is selected. Also note that the icons of the vertical object toolbar, as well as most of the options of the **Insert** menu, are also grayed out. This is because this Placeholder is not an actual slide. Therefore, it has no properties to expose in the **Properties** panel and has no objects to align.

Adding the last slides

You will now create the last two slides of the Template. Because they will be very similar to the first two slides, you will copy, paste, and modify the first two slides of the project.

1. In the **Filmstrip** panel, select the first two slides of the project and use the *Ctrl + C* (Windows) or *Command + C* (Mac) shortcut to copy the slides.
2. Use the **Filmstrip** panel to go to the last slide of the Template (the Placeholder slide) and use the *Ctrl + V* (Windows) or *Command + V* (Mac) shortcut to paste the slides at the end of the Template.
3. Use the **Filmstrip** panel to reorder the slides you have just pasted. The copy of the **Intro Slide** should be the last one.
4. When you're done, go to slide 4 of the Template. In the **Properties** panel, change its name to Summary Slide.
5. Change the text of the Title Text Caption to Summary.
6. Move to the last slide of the Template and change its name to Ending Slide.

Sixth and seventh rules enforced! The last two slides of the Template are used to emphasize the key points learned during the demonstration and to add an Animation when the project is finished.

Saving the Template

For the sake of this example, you will consider this Template finished. Keep in mind though that you could go much further in the development of a Captivate Template. For example, you could use the **Preferences** dialog and define the project properties in the Template itself. These would become the default preference used by future projects based on that Template.

Chapter 4

1. Save the Template as `MFTC-Demo.cptl` under `Chapter08`.

Note that the file extension used for a Captivate Template is `.cptl` and not `.cptx` like for a regular project. Next, you'll create a new project from this Template.

Creating a new Captivate project from a Template

In this section, you will play the role of an eLearning developer who has to use the new Template to develop a new Captivate demonstration for the MFTC Company.

1. Close every open file so that you can see the Captivate Welcome screen.
2. In the right column of the Captivate Welcome screen, click on the **From Template** link under **Create New**.

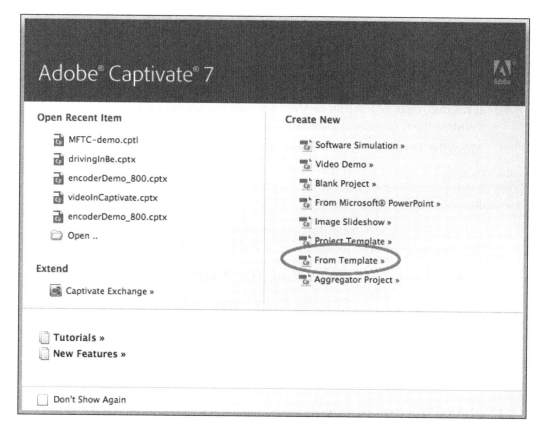

3. Navigate to the `MFTC-Demo.cptl` Template file under `Chapter04` situated in the exercises folder and choose it as the base of a new project.

Working with Styles, Master Slides, Themes, and Templates

The new project that opens in Captivate is a stencil copy of the Template you previously created. Note that the new project has the `.cptx` file extension.

Before moving on, you will quickly preview the project.

4. Use the Preview icon to preview the entire project.

When the project appears in the **Preview** pane, note that the Text Animation Placeholder object of slide 1 does not appear in the final output. Also, note that the recording slide Placeholder is not part of the final output as well. Actually, the slide count (shown at the top-left corner of the **Preview** pane) is 4 and not 5.

As long as the Placeholder objects and slides have not been replaced by actual objects and slides, they do not appear in the compiled version of the project.

5. Close the **Preview** pane to return to Captivate.
6. Use the **Filmstrip** panel to go to the first slide of the project.
7. Double-click on the Text Animation Placeholder to turn it into an actual Text Animation object.
8. Double-click on the Text Animation object to change its properties. Type `Welcome to the Demonstration` in the **Text Animation Properties** dialog. If needed, change the font to **Verdana** and the size to `52`. Click on **OK** to validate the change and generate the Text Animation object.
9. Move the Text Animation roughly to the center of the brown area of the slide.

Note how quick it was to insert this Text Animation object on the first slide. Rapid development is one of the advantages of using Themes, Templates, and Placeholder objects.

In the **Properties** panel, note that the default effect used by this object is the **Waltz** effect. This reflects what you decided on the **Title** Master Slide.

10. In the **Properties** panel, try to change the **Waltz** effect to any other effect of your choice.

No warning messages appear on the screen to tell you that this property is locked on the Template and cannot be changed. In other words, the teacher has the freedom to override the choices made on the Template. Remember that the Template set the default properties of slides and objects, but it does not force the teacher to use them in the final version of the project.

11. Use the **Filmstrip** panel to go to slide 3 of the project.

Slide 3 is the **Recording Slide Placeholder**. Remember that it does not show in the **Preview** pane while testing the project.

12. Double-click on the **Recording Slide Placeholder** slide.

Captivate switches to the recording mode and displays the red recording area. All the options discussed in *Chapter 2, Capturing the Slides,* are available in the Recording window, except for the size of the red recording area, which is blocked by the Template at **800 x 600** pixels.

13. Click on the **Cancel** button to return to the standard Captivate interface.
14. Close the project without saving it.

This exercise concludes your overview of the Templates. Before moving on to the next chapter, let's quickly summarize what has been covered in this section.

- A Captivate Template is a blueprint used as a starting point for standard Captivate projects.
- A Template can contain the very same objects and slides as a standard project.
- The Theme applied to a Template serves as the default Theme for all future projects based on that Template.
- Placeholder Slides are used to mark the location of a screen recording or the location of Question Slides in the Template.
- A Template sets the default properties and objects, but it does not strictly enforce them. In other words, the teacher can override the choices made on a Template when designing the project.
- A Template file has a `.cptl` file extension.

Summary

In this chapter, you concentrated on the cosmetic aspect of the project. You discovered that, when properly implemented, the look and feel of the project plays a critical role in providing a consistent learning environment for your students. Remember that, while taking your online courses, the students will most likely be alone in front of their computer. Therefore, it is important to create a consistent learning environment in which they feel comfortable enough to concentrate on learning the content and not on how the online course actually works.

In the first part of this chapter, you learned about the Styles and the Object Style Manager. You then used the predefined Themes of Captivate to better understand what Themes are and how they work. Next, you moved on to creating your own customized Theme and discovered the all new **Swatches** panel of Captivate 7.0.1. Finally, you have created a Template and used that Template to create a new project.

By using the Styles, the Master Slides, the Themes, the Swatches, and the Templates, you created professional-looking and consistent projects in a record time with minimal effort!

In the next chapter, you will concentrate on adding Animations and interactivity to your projects. To create this interactivity, you will learn about the interactive objects of Captivate. You will also learn about branching that allows you to define different actions based on the student's progression in the project. These interactive objects will allow you to convert your demonstration into a simulation.

Meet the community

In this section, I want to introduce you to Jim Leichliter. Jim is a Software Developer that specializes in the development of Captivate Widgets. He has always been very supportive and has agreed to feature my books on his home page. This collaboration of ours makes me better understand the amazing power of a community such as the one Jim and I are fortunate enough to be part of.

Jim Leichliter

Jim Leichliter of `CaptivateDev.com` is a Software Developer with 13 years of experience and has a love for eLearning. Not only does he build Captivate Widgets, but he also helps clients integrate Captivate with third-party systems to create mashups, interactive games, and reporting solutions.

Contact details

- Blog: `http://CaptivateDev.com`
- Twitter: `@CaptivatePro`
- E-mail: `Jim@CaptivateDev.com`

5
Adding Interactivity to the Project

In this chapter, you will continue the post-production phase of your project by adding interactivity to your Captivate files. This will make them even more interesting, sophisticated, engaging, and fun to use.

This interactivity is made possible by three interactive objects (Click Box, Text Entry Box, and Button) that have the ability to stop the playhead and wait for the learner to do or type something. This introduces a whole new level of complexity to the projects, as the student will receive feedback that depends on the action being performed. So, you will have to analyze the clicks and answers of the students, and act accordingly. This concept is known as **branching**.

Captivate also provides three types of Rollover objects. Even though Rollover objects don't stop the playhead, they do enable some kind of interactivity. These objects are hidden by default and are revealed when the student rolls the mouse on top of a sensitive area. Finally, Captivate includes an exciting new feature named the **Drag and Drop Interaction**. You will discover how you can use this feature to add some advanced and exciting interactivity to your eLearning content.

Thanks to these interactive objects and features, you will be able to convert your existing demonstration into a simulation. Other important tools, such as the **Find And Replace** feature, will be unveiled along the way.

At the end of this chapter, you will take a deeper look at your Video Demo project. You will discover the objects that can be inserted in a Video Demo and discuss some specific Video Demo features.

Adding Interactivity to the Project

In this chapter, you will:

- Insert Rollover Captions, Rollover Images, and Rollover Slidelet for enhanced interactivity
- Add text into a Smart Shape and convert it into a Rollover Smart Shape
- Insert buttons to give students more control over the timing of the project
- Convert your existing demonstration into a simulation by replacing the Mouse object with Click Boxes and Text Entry Boxes
- Use the Drag and Drop Interaction to add some sophisticated and exciting interactivity to your content
- Discuss the objects that can be added to a Video Demo project
- Use the Pan and Zoom feature of Video Demo

This will make for another chapter full of surprises and discoveries.

Preparing your work

For the exercises of this chapter, you will work with two different files. A third one will be created later on. Use the following steps to get Captivate ready:

1. Open Captivate and ensure that the **Classic** workspace is applied.
2. Navigate to **Window** | **Workspace** | **Reset 'Classic'** to return to the default **Classic** workspace.
3. Open the `encoderDemo_800.cptx` file under the `Chapter05` folder situated in your exercises folder.
4. Also, open the `drivingInBe.cptx` file under the `Chapter05` folder stored at the same location.
5. At the end of the chapter, you will use the `encoderVideo.cpvc` Video Demo project under the `Chapter05` folder.

All three files should be open in the Captivate interface. Make sure you use the right one when doing an exercise.

Working with Buttons

The **Button** object is the first interactive object of Captivate that you will focus on. Remember that an interactive object has the ability to stop the playhead and wait for the student to do something.

In the case of a Button object, a simple click triggers an action. Despite its apparent simplicity, the Button object is an essential part of every Captivate project as it lets the student control the timing of the online course.

In this exercise, you will add a Button below the video file you inserted in the previous chapter by performing the following steps:

1. Go to the `encoderDemo_800.cptx` file.
2. Use the **Filmstrip** panel to go to slide 2.
3. Navigate to **Insert | Standard Objects | Button** or the corresponding icon in the Objects toolbar to insert a new Button on the slide.
4. With the new Button selected, inspect the **Properties** panel.

When a Button is selected on the stage, the **Properties** panel shows the properties that are relevant to a Button. Take a look at the available sections; you'll notice three sections that were *not* present for the other objects you have used so far:

- **Action**: This section is used to determine what happens when the student clicks on the Button
- **Options**: This section gives you more choices to manage the interaction with the student
- **Reporting**: This section is used to report the interaction to an LMS server (this will be covered in depth in *Chapter 7, Working with Quizzes*)

These three sections of the **Properties** panel only appear when an interactive object is selected.

5. In the **General** section of the **Properties** panel, change the Button **Caption** to `Continue`.
6. In the **Action** section, open the **On Success** drop-down list.
7. Take some time to inspect the available options. When done, choose the **Go to the next slide** option.
8. Increase the width of the Button so the new text fits comfortably in the object.
9. Position the new Button in the bottom-right corner of the slide in the brownish area.

Now that the Button has the right look and performs the right action, your next task is to arrange it on the **Timeline** panel. With the Button being an interactive object that stops the playhead, there are a few more options than usual to take care of.

Adding Interactivity to the Project

On the **Timeline** panel, the Button object is separated into two areas. As shown in the following screenshot, the separator between the two areas is a *Pause* symbol. It represents the exact moment when the Button will stop the playhead and wait for the student to click:

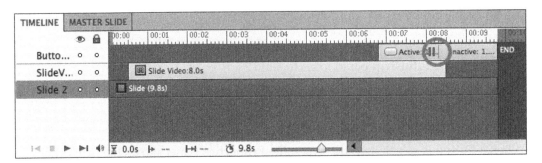

When the Button is clicked on, the action set in the **Action** section occurs. In this case, the action is **Go to Next Slide**. It means that when the student clicks on the Button, the playhead will jump from the Pause symbol directly to the first frame of the next slide. Consequently, the frames of slide 2 situated after the Pause symbol of the Button will not be played.

10. Use the **Timeline** panel or the **Timing** section:
    - Make the Button **Appear After 6.5 sec**
    - Have the Button **Pause After 1.9 sec**
    - Have the Button **Display For** the **Rest of Slide**
11. Make sure that the **Timeline** panel looks like the preceding screenshot.
12. Use the Preview icon's **Next 5 Slides** feature to test the new Button. When finished previewing, close the **Preview** pane.

Note that the Button pause can be removed by deselecting the **Pause After** checkbox situated in the **Timing** section of the **Properties** panel.

Formatting Buttons

In this section, you will use the various sections of the **Properties** panel to change the look of the Button using the following steps:

1. Still on slide 2 of the `encoderDemo_800.cptx` file under the `chapter05` folder, make sure the new Button is selected.
2. In the **General** section, open the **Button Type** drop-down menu.

The **Button Type** drop-down menu lists the three types of Buttons available in Captivate:

- **Text Button**: This Button is the default choice. It is a simple Button whose text can be customized in the **Properties** panel.
- **Transparent Button**: This Button is a transparent area that serves as a Button. Consider it as a sensitive area that can be added on top of a background picture.
- **Image Button**: This Button is an image (actually a set of three images) that is used as a Button. This gives you the ability to create Buttons of any size and any shape by simply drawing a Button in an image editing tool and import it in Captivate as an **Image Button**.

In this exercise, you will create a Button from an image that is on your hard disk using the **Image Button** option.

3. Choose the **Image Button** option in the **Button Type** drop-down menu.
4. Click on the folder icon situated next to the **Button Type** dropdown. Choose `images/buttons/mftcContinue_up.png` from the exercises files.

When browsing for the image file, notice that the `buttons` folder under the `images` folder contains *three versions* of each Button as shown in the following screenshot:

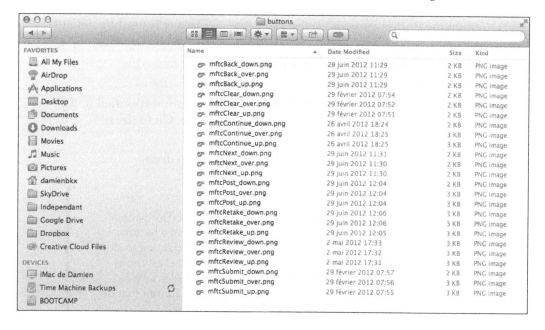

Adding Interactivity to the Project

- One version ends with _up. It is the normal state of the Button.
- Another version ends with _over. It is used to change the appearance of the Button when the student rolls the mouse over the Button.
- The third version ends with _down. It is used when the student has the mouse over the Button and the mouse Button down at the same time.

Captivate is able to recognize these three states provided all three images are stored in the same location and that they share the very same name with the exception of the _up, _over, and _down suffixes.

5. Use the **Properties** panel to create a new style after the current look and feel of the **Continue** button. Name this new style `MFTC-buttonContinue`.
6. Navigate to **Theme | Save Theme** to add the new style to the currently applied Theme.

> The Theme currently applied to the project is the `themes/mftc_800x600.cptm` Theme situated in your exercises folder.

7. Save the file and use the Preview icon to preview **Next 5 slides**. Alternatively, you can use the *F10* (Windows) shortcut or the *cmd + F10* (Mac) shortcut.
8. When the Button appears on the stage, the _up image is used by default.
9. Roll your mouse over the Button without clicking to see the _over state of the Button. Then, click and hold the mouse Button to see the _down state of the Button.
10. It is when you release the mouse Button that the action specified in the **Action** section of the **Properties** panel (in this case, **Go to the next slide**) is performed.
11. Close the **Preview** window, and save the file when done.

Finding the Images Buttons

When choosing **Image Button** in the **Properties** panel, Captivate proposes a list of predefined Image Buttons you can choose from. The image assets pertaining to these Buttons are located at `[Captivate install Path]/Gallery/buttons`. This folder also includes a more subfolder that contains a few extra **Image Button** that do not appear in the **Properties** panel by default.

Using Smart Shapes as Buttons

Still not convinced by the awesomeness of **Smart Shapes**? This section will give you yet another argument to convince you after all!

1. Return to the `drivingInBe.cptx` file under the `chapter05` folder.
2. Use the **Filmstrip** panel to go to slide 10 of the project.
3. Use the first icon of the Objects toolbar or the **Smart Shape** menu item under **Insert | Standard Object** to open the Smart Shape gallery.

In this section, you will use the Left Arrow Callout and the Right Arrow Callout Smart Shapes. These are identified in the following screenshot:

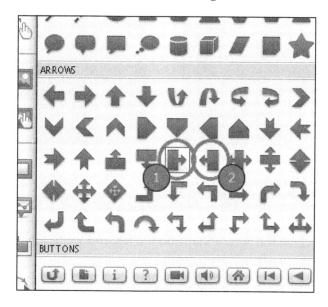

4. Click on the Right Arrow Callout icon (number **1** in the preceding screenshot), and draw it on the right-hand side of the slide.
5. Repeat this operation with the Left Arrow Callout shape (number **2** in the preceding screenshot), but draw it on the left-hand side of the slide.

Adding Interactivity to the Project

6. Use the tools of the Align toolbar and Smart Guides to give the same size to both Smart Shapes and to align them properly on the slide. When done, your slide should look like the following screenshot:

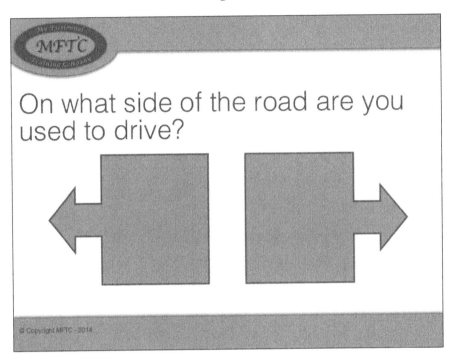

7. Double-click on the Smart Shape on the left and write `I'm used to driving on the left side of the road.`
8. Double-click on the Smart Shape on the right and write `I'm used to driving on the right side of the road.`
9. If needed, adjust the formatting of these Smart Shapes to your liking.

You now have two Smart Shapes in place on your slide. It's time to move on to the core of this section and turn these Smart Shapes into Buttons.

10. Take some time to inspect the **Properties** panel of these Smart Shapes.

Because you have written text into these objects, you should see eight sections in the **Properties** panel, including the **Character** and **Format** sections used to control the formatting of the text.

11. At the top of the **Properties** panel, select the **Use as Button** checkbox.

The **Action, Option,** and **Reporting** sections appear in the **Properties** panel to let you control the Button's behavior. You should now have 11 sections available in the **Properties** panel.

12. Repeat the preceding procedure for the second Smart Shape of the slide.

You will now arrange these two new Buttons on the **Timeline** panel.

13. Use the **Timeline** panel or the **Timing** section of the **Properties** panel to make the Button **Appear After 0 sec** and **Display For the Rest of Slide**.

14. Also select the **Pause After** checkbox to have both Smart Shape Buttons pause the playhead at **1.5 seconds** into the slide.

This is a particularity of the Smart Shapes used as Buttons. By default, they do not include the pause behavior. You must explicitly turn the pause behavior on in the **Timing** section of the **Properties** panel.

15. Finally, select the Text Caption present on this slide, and use the **Timing** section of the **Properties** panel to make it Appear After 0 sec and **Display For the Rest of Slide**.

Make sure the **Timeline** panel of slide 10 looks like the following screenshot before continuing with this exercise:

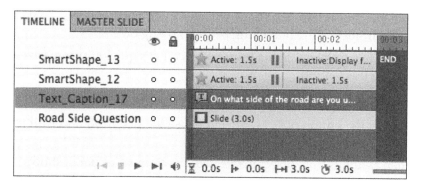

Branching with Buttons

Branching refers to providing a customized experience to the learners based on their actions in the project. In this exercise, you will create two different paths in the movie. If the learner clicks on the **I'm used to driving on the right side of the road** Smart Shape, he or she should be redirected to slide 11, where he or she has feedback specific to that answer. But if the learner clicks on the **I'm used to driving on the left side of the road** Smart Shape, he or she should be redirected to slide 12, where he or she will be shown a different feedback specific to the second answer. Use the following steps to set this branching up:

1. If needed, return to slide 10 of the `drivingInBe.cptx` file under the `chapter05` folder.
2. Select the **I'm used to driving on the right side of the road** Smart Shape.

Adding Interactivity to the Project

3. In the **Action** section of the **Properties** panel, change the **On Success** action to **Jump to slide**, and then select **slide 11** in the dropdown that appears below.
4. Select the **I'm used to driving on the left side of the road** Smart Shape.
5. In the **Action** section of the **Properties** panel, change the **On Success** action to **Jump to slide 12**.
6. Use the **Filmstrip** panel to go to slide 11 of the `drivingInBe.cptx` file under the `chapter05` folder.
7. Select the Button that is in the bottom-right corner of the slide, and apply the **MFTC-buttonContinue** style. Also, move the Button to the bottom-right corner of the slide on top of the brownish area.
8. In the **Action** section of the **Properties** panel, change the **On Success** action of the selected Button to **Jump to slide 13.**

The branching is now in place. You've effectively provided two different paths within your Captivate project. The chosen path depends on how the student answers the question on slide 10.

9. Save the file, and use the Preview icon to test your sequence. Make sure you test both sides of the branching before moving on.

This concludes the overview of the Button object. Let's quickly summarize what has been covered in this section:

- The Button object is one of the interactive objects of Captivate.
- As such, the Button object is able to pause the playhead and wait for the student to click on it.
- When an interactive object is selected, the **Properties** panel shows three additional sections in comparison to the sections available for non-interactive objects.
- One of these extra sections is the **Action** section used to define what happens when the Button is clicked.
- Captivate proposes three types of Buttons. These are **Text Button**, **Transparent Button**, and **Image Button**.
- Because the Button stops the playhead, it is separated into two areas on the **Timeline** panel. The separator represents the exact moment when the playhead is stopped.
- Image Buttons use three different images to create the _up, _over, and _down states of the Button.

- It is possible to convert a Smart Shape into a Button. In such a case, three sections are added in the **Properties** panel, including the **Action** section, to let you define the action to perform when the Smart Shape is clicked.
- Unlike a Button, a Smart Shape, used as a Button does not pause the playhead unless you explicitly select the **Pause After** checkbox in the **Timing** section of the **Properties** panel.

> **The Button object and the pedagogy**
>
> Two of the most important things to keep in mind while teaching are: to keep the students focused and to adapt your teaching to each student (the latter is known as **differentiated instruction**). Basically, it means that it is the course that has to adapt to the student and not the other way around (see `http://en.wikipedia.org/wiki/Differentiated_instruction` for more). The Button object helps you with both these concerns. While watching a long demonstration, your students' attention will inevitably drift away from the course. Each time you add a Button, you make the students active, which helps in refreshing their attention. Another benefit of the Button is that it lets each student manage the timing of the course. If you have a slide with a lot of text, it is a good idea to pause the playhead with a Button and let each student read the slide at his or her own pace.

Discovering Rollover objects

In this section, you will discover three more objects. These objects are known as the **Rollover objects**, because they are originally hidden and show up only when the user *rolls over* a specific area of the slide. This very behavior makes Rollover objects impossible to use on touch devices such as tablets and smartphones. This is the reason why Rollover objects are not supported in the HTML5 output of Captivate.

> **Making Rollover objects mobile friendly**
>
> On mobile devices, these Rollover objects can be replaced by other objects that mimic the rollover behavior. See Packt's *Adobe Captivate 7 for Mobile Learning* title at `http://www.packtpub.com/adobe-captivate-7-for-mobile-learning/book`.

Working with Rollover Captions

A **Rollover Caption** is a Text Caption that appears when the user places the mouse over a specific spot on the slide. Such a spot is known as the **Rollover Area**.

In the next exercise, you will add a Rollover Caption to the *Driving in Belgium* project by performing the following steps:

1. Return to the `drinvinInBe.cptx` file under the `chapter05` folder.
2. Use the **Filmstrip** panel to go to slide 15.

Slide 15 contains two Text Captions, four Images, and a Button that pauses the playhead at 2.5 seconds into the slide. The Text Caption in the top-right corner of the slide explains what you will achieve in this exercise.

3. Navigate to **Insert | Standard Objects | Rollover Caption** or the corresponding icon in the Objects toolbar to insert a new Rollover Caption.

A Rollover Caption inserts *two* objects on the slide. The first object is a basic Text Caption. The second object is the associated Rollover Area. The Text Caption will show only *if* and *when* the student rolls the mouse over the Rollover Area.

4. Change the text of the Rollover Caption to `No parking is allowed at any time!`.
5. Use the **Properties** panel to apply the **transparentCaption** style to the Rollover Caption.
6. Resize the Caption, and use the Smart Guides to position it to the right of the first road sign.
7. Select the Rollover Area, and position it, more or less, over the first road sign. Don't hesitate to resize the Rollover Area if necessary.
8. In the **Fill & Stroke** section, set the stroke **Width** to **0** to remove the stroke from the Rollover Area, and set the **Alpha** value to **0** percent. This makes the Rollover Area invisible.
9. Use the **Properties** panel to create a new style after the current formatting of the Rollover Area. Name the style `MFTC-RolloverArea`.
10. Use the **Timeline** panel or the **Timing** section to make the Rollover Area **Appear After 1 sec** and **Display For** the **Rest of Slide**.

When done, the slide should look like the following screenshot:

11. Use the Preview icon's **Next 5 Slides** feature to test the Rollover Caption.

The Text Caption is not displayed by default. It appears only *if* and *when* you roll your mouse over the Rollover Area.

12. Close the **Preview** pane, and save the file when done.

Working with Rollover Smart Shapes

In *Chapter 3, Working with Standard Objects*, you discovered the awesome Smart Shape object. You used it to draw a rounded rectangle around the AME logo. You also typed text into the *Curved Up Ribbon* Smart Shape. You will now discover yet more goodies of this type of object by performing the following steps:

1. Return to slide 15 of the `drivingInBe.cptx` file.
2. Select either the Rollover Area or the Rollover Caption that you added in the previous section.
3. Delete the selected object.

Note that both the Rollover Area and the Text Captions are deleted even though only one of these two objects was selected.

4. On the Object toolbar, click on the first icon to open the Smart Shape menu. Alternatively, you can navigate to **Insert | Standard Object | Smart Shape**.

Adding Interactivity to the Project

5. In the **Arrows** section, choose the Left Arrow Callout shape as shown in the following screenshot:

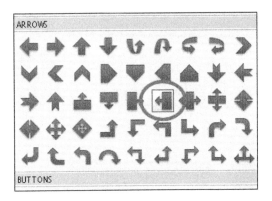

6. Draw a Left Arrow Callout shape to replace the Text Caption you deleted in step 3.

Note that there are three yellow squares around that particular Smart Shape. Each one of these yellow squares can be used to modify the Smart Shape in a specific way.

7. Use the yellow squares and the Smart Guides to make your Smart Shape look like the one in the following screenshot:

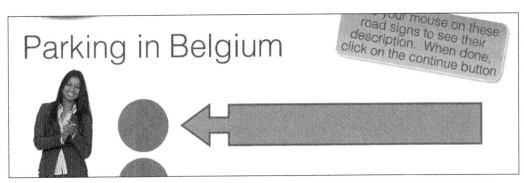

The **MFTC-SmartShape** style you created in the previous chapter should be applied by default to the Smart Shape. If it is not, use the **Properties** panel to manually apply the style to the Smart Shape.

8. Double-click on the Smart Shape.
9. In the Smart Shape, type `No parking is allowed at any time!`.
10. If necessary, fine-tune the size, position, and formatting of the Smart Shape to your liking.

11. With the Smart Shape selected, use the *Ctrl + D* (Windows) shortcut or the *cmd + D* (Mac) shortcut to duplicate the shape. Alternatively, you can also navigate to **Edit | Duplicate**.
12. Repeat the preceding operation to create a third copy of the Smart Shape.
13. Use the Smart Guides to position the Smart Shapes to the right of each road sign image and to align them together.
14. Change the text of the middle Smart Shape to `No parking allowed between the 1st and the 15th of the month`.
15. Change the text of the bottom Smart Shape to `No parking allowed between the 16th and the 31st of the month`.

So far, so good, there is nothing new in this exercise. Now that the stage is set, it is time to uncover another great feature of Smart Shapes: the **Rollover Smart Shape**.

You will associate a Rollover Area with each Smart Shape of slide 15. At runtime, the Smart Shapes will be hidden by default. They will become visible only *if* and *when* the student rolls the mouse over the corresponding rollover area.

16. Make sure you are still in slide 15 of the `drivingInBe.cptx` file.
17. Right-Click on the topmost Smart Shape.
18. Choose the **Convert to Rollover Smart Shape** item in the Contextual menu.

The Smart Shape is converted into a Rollover Smart Shape and a corresponding Rollover Area appears on the slide.

19. Move and resize the Rollover Area so it roughly covers the topmost road sign.
20. Apply the **MFTC-rolloverArea** style to make the Rollover Area completely transparent.
21. Repeat this sequence of actions with the remaining two Smart Shapes.
22. Use the **Timeline** panel or the **Timing** section to make all three Rollover Areas **Appear After 1 sec** and **Display For** the **Rest of Slide**.
23. Save the file when done.

The ability to convert a Smart Shape to a Rollover Smart Shape is yet another reason that makes the Smart Shape object awesome!

Adding Interactivity to the Project

This concludes the overview of the Rollover Caption and Rollover Smart Shape objects. The following is a quick review of the key points discussed in this section:

- Inserting a Rollover Caption adds 2 objects to the Slide.
- The first object is a regular Text Caption. The second object is a corresponding Rollover Area.
- At runtime, the Text Caption appears if and when the learner rolls the mouse over the Rollover Area.
- When a Smart Shape is converted to a Rollover Smart Shape, a corresponding Rollover Area appears on the stage.
- A Rollover Smart Shape is not displayed by default. At runtime, it shows only *if* and *when* the student rolls his or her mouse over the corresponding Rollover Area.

Now that you know how the Rollover Captions and Rollover Smart Shapes function, the next object may be easier to understand.

Working with Rollover Images

A **Rollover Image** is an image that shows only if and when the learner puts the mouse in the corresponding Rollover Area.

In the next exercise, you will add three Rollover Images to the `drivingInBe.cptx` file by performing the following steps:

1. If needed, return to the `drinvinInBe.cptx` file under the `chapter05` folder.
2. Use the **Filmstrip** panel to go to slide 16.

Slide 16 contains five Text Captions, one Image, and a Button that pauses the playhead at 7.5 seconds into the slide. The Text Caption in the top-right corner explains it all!

3. Navigate to **Insert** | **Standard Objects** | **Rollover Image** to insert a new Rollover Image.
4. Browse to the `priority.png` file under the `images` folder, and click on **open** to insert it onto the slide.

As with Rollover Captions and Rollover Smart Shapes, a Rollover Image inserts two objects on the slide: an Image and a corresponding Rollover Area. At runtime, the image will be displayed only *if* and *when* the learner rolls the mouse over the rollover area.

5. Use the Smart Guides to place the image to the right of the Text Caption that says **I have the right of the way**.

Chapter 5

6. Move and resize the Rollover Area so it covers more or less the entire **I have the right of the way** Text Caption.
7. With the Rollover Area selected, use the **Properties** panel to apply the **MFTC-rolloverArea** style.
8. Use the **Timeline** panel or the **Timing** section to make the Rollover Area **Appear After 6 sec** and **Display For** the **Rest of Slide**.
9. Add two more Rollover Images with the same formatting and timing properties:
    - Use the `noPriority.png` image under the `images` folder for the first one. Position it on the right of the **I do not have the right of the way** Text Caption. Use and resize the Rollover Area appropriately.
    - Use the `PriorityRight.png` image under the `images` folder for the second one. Position it on the right of the **Those coming from the right hand side have the right of the way** Text Caption.
10. Use the Smart Guides to properly position and align these objects on the slide.

When done, slide 16 should look like the following screenshot:

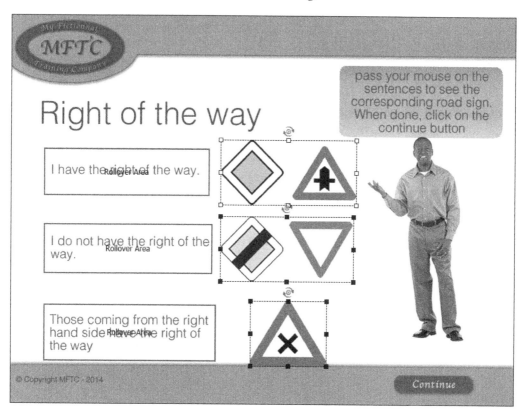

11. Save the file when done.
12. Use the **Filmstrip** panel to return to slide 15. Use the Preview icon's **Next 5 Sides** feature to test your Rollover Smart Shapes and your Rollover Images.

On these two slides (15 and 16), the role of the Button is critical in making the Rollover system work. It stops the playhead and lets the students go through the Rollover objects at their own pace and in the order they want. This is yet another example of the differentiated instruction concept.

Before moving on to the last Rollover object, this is a quick summary of what has been covered so far:

- The Rollover Image adds two objects to the slide: an image and a corresponding Rollover Area.
- When the project is played back, the image shows up only if and when the student rolls the mouse over the corresponding Rollover Area.

Working with Rollover Slidelets

The last Rollover object of Captivate is the **Rollover Slidelet**. As with every other Rollover object of Captivate, the Rollover Slidelet adds *two* objects to the slide: the Slidelet itself and a corresponding Rollover Area.

Inserting and formatting a Rollover Slidelet

In the next exercise, you will add a Rollover Slidelet to the *Driving in Belgium* project by performing the following steps:

1. If needed, return to the `drinvinInBe.cptx` file under the `chapter05` folder.
2. Use the **Filmstrip** panel to go to slide 14.
3. Navigate to **Insert | Standard Objects | Rollover Slidelet**. This adds the two objects that compose the Rollover Slidelet system to the slide.
4. Click on an empty area of the slide to deselect the Rollover Slidelet.
5. Click on the object with the thick blue border to select the Rollover Slidelet.

Make sure that **Rollover Slidelet Area** is written at the top of the **Properties** panel. If *Slidelet* is written instead, you did not select the right object.

The selected object is used as the Rollover Area of the Rollover Slidelet. You will position it on top of the **Convert Speeds to MPH** Text Caption and make it transparent.

6. Move and resize the selected object so it roughly covers the **Convert Speeds to MPH** Text Caption.
7. In the **Fill & Stroke** section of the **Properties** panel, deselect the **Show Border** and **Show Runtime Border** checkboxes.

By deselecting the **Show Border** checkbox, you make the **Rollover Slidelet Area** invisible. The **Show Runtime Border** checkbox adds a border that is visible at runtime when the student rolls over the **Rollover Slidelet Area**.

8. In the **Timeline** panel or in the **Timing** section, make the Rollover Slidelet **Appear After 15 sec** and **Display For** the **Rest of Slide**.

Note that, as expected, the **Timeline** panel shows a list of all the objects that are present on the slide. There should be 14 objects in addition to the slide itself.

9. Click on the other object of the Rollover Slidelet system to make it the active object. The word **Slidelet** should be written at the top of the **Properties** panel.

Take another look at the **Timeline** panel, and notice that the objects of the slide are not listed anymore. This is because the **Timeline** panel you are viewing at the moment is not the **Timeline** panel of the slide, but the **Timeline** panel of the Rollover Slidelet. This helps in understanding what a Rollover Slidelet really is.

A Rollover Slidelet is a slide within a slide. Consequently, objects (such as Text Captions, Images, and so on) can be inserted inside the Rollover Slidelet and arranged on its **Timeline**. At runtime, the Slidelet appears and plays its **Timeline** only if and when the student rolls the mouse over the corresponding Rollover Area (called **Rollover Slidelet Area** in this case).

You will now give the Slidelet the correct size, position, and format. Make sure the Slidelet is selected to perform the following actions:

10. In the **Transform** section, deselect the **Constrain proportions** box.
11. Give the Slidelet a **Width** value of **630** pixels and a **Height** value of **260** pixels.
12. Navigate to **Window | Align** to turn the Align toolbar on if necessary.

With the Slidelet selected, take a look at the Align toolbar. Only two icons should be available. These icons are named Center Horizontally on the Slide/Slidelet and Center Vertically on the Slide/Slidelet.

13. Click on both of these icons to position the Slidelet exactly at the center of the stage.
14. Return to the **Swatches** panel, and make sure that the `MFTC-colors.ase` swatch used in the previous chapter is still active (if not, click on the **Load** button of the **Swatches** panel to load the `MFTC-colors.ase` file under the `Chapter04` folder).

Adding Interactivity to the Project

15. Use the **Swatches** panel to apply the light brown color (swatch number 1) to the **Fill** property of the Slidelet, and the dark brown color (swatch number 2) to the **Stroke** property of the Slidelet.

16. In the **Fill & Stroke** section of the **Properties** panel:
    - Set the **Alpha** value to **90** percent
    - Set the **Width value** of the **Stroke** field to **3** pixels.

17. Make sure your Slidelet looks like the following screenshot:

Inserting objects in a Rollover Slidelet

Now that the Rollover Slidelet has the proper format, the proper position, and the proper size, you will insert three Text Captions in the Slidelet and organize them on its **Timeline** panel by performing the following steps:

1. To make sure the Slidelet is the active object, take a look at the **Timeline** panel, and confirm it shows the **Timeline** panel of the Slidelet, not the **Timeline** panel of the slide (no objects should appear on the **Timeline** panel).

2. Navigate to **Insert** | **Standard Objects** | **Text Caption** to insert a new Text Caption in the Slidelet.

While inserting the new Text Caption in the Slidelet, notice that some of the objects of the **Standard Objects** menu under the **Insert** menu are grayed out. It means that these objects cannot be inserted in a Slidelet. These objects are the interactive objects of Captivate, the Mouse and, of course, the Rollover Slidelet itself!

3. Type `Motorways - 120 km/H is approx. 80 MPH` in the new Text Caption.
4. Apply the **transparentCaption** style to the new Text Caption.
5. Resize the Text Caption, and position it in the upper area of the Slidelet.
6. Use the same procedure to add two more Text Captions in the Slidelet. Don't forget to apply the **transparentCaption** style to both Captions:
   - Type `National roads - 90 Km/h is approx and 60 MPH` in the second Text Caption
   - Type `Cities and towns - 50 Km/h is approx. 30 MPH` in the third Text Caption
7. Use the tools from the Align toolbar and the Smart Guides to position the three Text Captions properly in the Slidelet.
8. In the **Timeline** panel or in the **Timing** section, extend the duration of the Slidelet to **15 sec**.
9. Arrange the three Text Captions using the following properties:
   - The topmost Caption **Appears After 0 sec** and displays for **Rest of Slidelet**
   - The middle Caption **Appears After 2 sec** and displays for **Rest of Slidelet**
   - The bottom Caption **Appears After 4 sec** and displays for **Rest of Slidelet**
10. Select all three Text Captions, and use the **Properties** panel to apply a **Fade In Only** transition to all three Text Captions.

Adding Interactivity to the Project

The **Timeline** panel of your Rollover Slidelet should now look like the following screenshot:

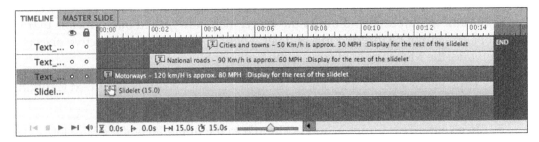

11. Save the file, and use the Preview icon's **Next 5 slides** feature to test the Rollover Slidelet.

When you've finished previewing your sequence, close the **Preview** pane.

This exercise concludes your exploration of the Rollover Slidelet. Before moving on to the next topic, let's summarize what you have learned in this section:

- Like every other Rollover object, the Rollover Slidelet adds two objects to the slide: the Slidelet and a corresponding Rollover Area.
- During the playback, the Slidelet shows up only if and when the student rolls the mouse over the associated rollover area.
- A Rollover Slidelet is a slide within a slide. As such, it has its own **Timeline** panel.
- Most of the objects that can be inserted on a regular slide can be inserted in a Rollover Slidelet.
- Some objects, however, cannot be inserted in a Slidelet. These are the interactive objects (the Click Box, Text Entry Box, and Button), the Mouse, and of course, the Rollover Slidelet itself.

This exercise only demonstrates part of what is possible with a Rollover Slidelet. Consult the Adobe Captivate help file at http://help.adobe.com/en_US/captivate/cp/using/WSEF20A87E-0F20-4fa6-A95E-B48C1EBCFCCC.html for more on Rollover Slidelet.

[210]

Creating a simulation

In this section, you will convert the `encoderDemo_800.cptx` demonstration into a simulation. Remember that when viewing a demonstration, the student is passive and only watches whatever happens on the screen. When viewing a simulation, however, the student is active and has to do things.

Technically, in Captivate, the difference between a demonstration and a simulation resides in the objects used. The object associated with a demonstration is the Mouse object. Remember that the Mouse object lets you show the mouse on the screen and control its movements. In order to convert the demonstration to a simulation, you'll have to remove the Mouse object from the project.

Hiding the mouse is one thing, but you'll have to replace it with something else. If you think about it, there are two kinds of actions that you need to be able to simulate: clicking and typing. That's why Captivate provides two interactive objects to let you replace the mouse in a simulation. The first object is the Click Box. It is used each time you need to make the student click somewhere. The second object is the Text Entry Box. You will use it when you need the student to type something. Those two interactive objects have the ability to stop the playhead and wait for the learner to interact.

The first step in converting your demonstration to a simulation is to create the simulation `.cptx` file using the following procedure:

1. Return to the `encoderDemo_800.cptx` file.
2. Navigate to **File** | **Save As** to create another version of this file.
3. Name the file `encoderSim_800.cptx`, and save it in the `Chapter05` subfolder of your exercises.

Hiding the Mouse object

Now that the simulation file exists, the next step is to remove the Mouse object.

Normally, there should be 19 slides in the project. In the **Filmstrip** panel, a Mouse icon at the bottom-right corner of the slides' thumbnails indicates that the Mouse object is used on slides 4 to 16.

For the following procedure, feel free to enlarge the **Filmstrip** panel as described in the *Working with panels* section of *Chapter 1, Getting Started with Captivate*.

Adding Interactivity to the Project

Use the following steps to hide the Mouse object throughout the entire project:

1. In the **Filmstrip** panel, select slide 4.
2. Hold down the *Shift* key, and select slide 16. This operation selects 13 slides from slide 4 to slide 16.
3. Hold down the *cmd* (Mac) or *Ctrl* (Windows) key, and click on slide 12 to remove it from the current selection.

Slide 12 is the Full Motion Recording slide that shows the scroll down action on the **Video** tab. The Mouse object does not show on this slide, so you can safely remove it from the selection.

4. To remove the Mouse object from the selected slides, navigate to **Modify | Mouse | Show Mouse** to deselect the **Show Mouse** option.
5. Go through the slides of the project to confirm that the Mouse object has been removed.

Your project is not yet a simulation, but with the removal of the Mouse object, it is not a demonstration anymore. The conversion is underway! Before moving on, there are a few more objects to remove/modify in the file.

One of the slides to modify is slide 2, where you will replace the video file with another one.

6. Go to slide 2, and remove the video file.
7. Navigate to **Video | Insert Slide Video** to insert a **Multi-Slide Synchronized Video**.
8. Use the `sim_en.flv` file under the `video` folder which is under the `flv` folder situated in the exercises folder.
9. At the bottom of the **Insert Video** dialog, make sure to select the **Modify slide duration to accommodate video** option and click on **OK** to validate.
10. In the **Transform** section of the **Properties** panel, position the video at **X** as `200` and **Y** as `196`.
11. Change the **Timeline** panel so that the video **Appear After 1 sec**. Make sure that the Button pauses the playhead just before the end of the video. The overall duration of the slide should be reduced to more or less five seconds.

Finally, you will update the Text Animations on the first and last slides of the project.

12. Use the **Filmstrip** panel to go to slide 01.
13. Select the Text Animation, and click on the **Properties** button situated in the **General** section of the **Properties** panel. The **Text Animation Properties** box opens.

14. In the box, change the word **demonstration** to `simulation` so that the sentence becomes **Adobe Media Encoder The Simulation**.
15. Use the same procedure to update the Text Animation on the last slide of the project.
16. Save the file when done.

With these updates done, you are now well on the way to convert this demonstration into a simulation. In the next section, you will change the necessary Text Captions to give the students precise instructions on what they have to do in the simulation.

Using Find and Replace

When developing a simulation, never forget that your students will be active and will have to do things on their own. As you do not want to mislead, and possibly lose, your students, it is critical to give them precise instructions on what they have to do at each step of the simulation. For the teacher, coming up with the proper instructions is not an easy task, but it is very important for the pedagogical approach to be successful, so don't hesitate to spend the necessary time to come up with the proper instructions. You will now use the **Find and Replace** feature to change the instructions given to the students throughout the entire project using the following steps:

1. Use the **Filmstrip** panel to go to slide 4 of the `encoderSim_800.cptx` file.

Note the message contained in the Text Caption of this slide. It says **The mouse will now click on the Add files icon**. This message was correct when in a demonstration, but in a simulation, you should change it in order to give the user a precise instruction to *click* on the item.

2. Browse the remaining slides of the project one by one.

Note that on most of the remaining slides, the message contained in the Text Caption follows the same pattern as the message of slide 4. In this exercise, you will use the **Find** and **Replace** feature to change the **The mouse will now click** part of the sentence into **Click**.

3. Navigate to **Edit | Find and Replace** to open the **Find And Replace** panel.

By default, the **Find And Replace** panel appears in the bottom-right corner of the screen, right below the **Properties** panel.

4. Type `The Mouse will now click` in the **Find** field.
5. Type `Click` (with a capital C) in the **Replace** field.

Before moving on, take some time to take a look at the other options provided by the **Find And Replace** panel.

Adding Interactivity to the Project

6. Leave all the other options at their default, and click on **Replace All**.
7. You should get a message saying that nine instances have been replaced. Click on **OK** to discard the confirmation box.
8. Use the **Filmstrip** panel to browse the slides of the project.

Confirm that the text displayed in the Text Captions has changed as expected. While browsing the slides, notice that the Text Caption of slide 5 uses a pattern that is slightly different from the Text Captions of the other slides.

9. Use the **Filmstrip** panel to go to slide 5, and select the Text Caption.
10. Manually modify the text contained in the caption so it reads **Double-click on the demo_en.mov video file**.

At each step of the simulation, the student now has a Text Caption explaining precisely what has to be done. This is a great thing, but it is not enough! To give the student complete information about the purpose of the simulation, you should provide some extra instructions at the beginning of the project.

11. In the **Filmstrip** panel, right-click on slide 3.
12. In the Contextual menu, click on the **Delete** command.
13. Read the message, and click on **OK** to confirm the deletion of the slide.

You will now replace the deleted slide with another one.

14. Open the `instructions.cptx` file under the `Chapter05` folder situated in your exercises folder.

This project contains a single slide that you will import into the `encoderSim_800.cptx` file using a simple copy and paste.

15. In the **Filmstrip** panel of the `instructions.cptx` file, right-click on the first (and only) slide.
16. In the Contextual menu, click on **Copy**.
17. Return to the `encoderSim_800.cptx` file.
18. In the **Filmstrip** panel, right-click on slide 2.
19. In the Contextual menu, click on **Paste**.
20. Apply the **MFTC-buttonContinue** style to the Button. Don't hesitate to resize and relocate the Button if necessary.

Remember that when inserting a new slide in a project, the new slide is inserted *after* the currently selected slide.

Take some time to examine the content of the new slide. It is a very important introduction slide. After reading this slide, the student will have all the required information to experience the simulation under the best possible conditions.

> **Let them be in charge!**
>
>
>
> The Button placed on the new slide 3 has *two* purposes. First, it pauses the playhead to let the learners read through the slide at their own pace. The second purpose of this button has to do with psychology. When doing a simulation, you confront the students with something they have to *do* for the first time. For some of them, this uncomfortable situation generates a lot of stress and anxiety. The button gives them time to put their thoughts together and take a deep breath before they give the go ahead to the simulation *themselves*. The button gives them the illusion that *they* are in charge. This helps them manage their anxiety. I have used this method successfully in many projects with great feedback from the students.

Working with Click Boxes

Your simulation is slowly taking shape but it still misses the object that will definitely make all the difference in making your project interactive. This object is what will replace the Mouse object you removed earlier. This object is the Click Box.

Just like the Button object, the Click Box is an interactive object. It is used to define a sensitive area on the screen. If the learner clicks inside the Click Box, the right action is performed and the simulation moves on to the next step. If the student clicks outside the box, the wrong action is performed, and the appropriate feedback should be displayed.

In the next exercise, you will add the required Click Boxes to the Encoder Simulation project by performing the following steps:

1. Use the **Filmstrip** panel to go to slide 4 of the encoderSim_800.cptx file.
2. Hide the Highlight Box by clicking on its eye icon in the **Timeline** panel.

You need to add the Click Box at the same spot where the Highlight Box is located. By hiding the Highlight Box, you clear the way for the Click Box to be added under the best possible conditions. Remember that when using the eye icon, as you just did, you hide the corresponding object in Captivate only, not in the resulting movie as seen by the students.

3. Navigate to **Insert | Standard Objects | Click Box** or the corresponding icon in the Objects toolbar to add the Click Box to the slide.

Adding Interactivity to the Project

Adding a Click Box adds up to four objects to the slide (it is ok if they don't all show on your screen). The first object is the Click Box itself. The three other objects are:

- **Success Caption:** This Caption will show only if the student performs the right action.
- **Failure Caption:** This Caption will show only if the student does not perform the right action.
- **Hint Caption**: This Caption will show when the student rolls the mouse over the Click Box. It behaves like a Rollover Caption using the Click Box as its Rollover Area.

You will now set up the Click Box so that it behaves the right way.

4. In the **Captions** section of the **Properties** panel, deselect the **Success** and **Hint** checkboxes if necessary. Leave only the **Failure** option selected.

By deselecting the **Success** and **Hint** options, the corresponding Captions disappear from the slide. There are two objects left: the Click Box itself and the associated Failure Caption.

5. Move and resize the Click Box so that it covers more or less the entire Add file icon of the background image.
6. Type `Sorry, you did not perform the right action` in the Failure Caption.
7. Select the Failure Caption object.
8. In the **Character** section of the **Properties** panel, change its font **Family** to **Verdana**.
9. At the top of the **Properties** panel, click on the Create new Style icon, and save the current formatting of the Failure Caption as `MFTC-Failure`.
10. If needed, resize the Failure Caption so the text fits comfortably in the Caption, and move it somewhere in the middle of the slide.

Sizing the Click Boxes

When sizing the Click Boxes, don't hesitate to make them a bit bigger than what is actually needed. The extra space will make it easier for your students to find the Click Box and perform the right action. Don't forget that you are teaching. You want your students to concentrate on the concepts to learn, so the exact location of a mouse click is a secondary concern. This extra space will also provide a big enough tap target for the students taking the course on a mobile device.

With the Click Box and the Failure Caption at the right location, it is time to focus on the actual actions that have to occur when the student interacts with the Click Box object.

11. Select the Click Box.
12. In the **Action** section of the **Properties** panel, confirm that the **On Success** action is set to **Go to the next slide**.
13. Deselect the **Infinite** option and set the number of **Attempts** to 2. This means that you let the student two chances to perform the right action.
14. Confirm the **Last Attempt** drop-down list is set to **Continue**.

The **Continue** action simply releases the playhead, while the **Go to the next slide** action directly moves the playhead to the next slide. This setup will help you do some branching without adding any extra slide to the project.

To finish with this slide, you will now organize the objects on the **Timeline** panel.

15. Use the Eye icon of the **Timeline** panel to reveal the hidden Highlight Box.
16. Make the Click Box **Appear After 3 sec** and pause the slide 1 second later.
17. Apply the same timing to the **Click on the Add files icon** Text Caption.
18. With the Text Caption selected, open the **Transition** section, and change the transition to **Fade In Only**.
19. Insert a new Text Caption on the slide. Type `The correct spot is currently highlighted. The simulation will now continue as if you performed the right action` in the new Text Caption.
20. Resize the new Text Caption, and move it somewhere in the middle of the slide.
21. In the **Timeline** panel or in the **Timing** section, make the new Text Caption **Appear After 4.5 sec** and **Display For** a **Specific Time** of `6.5` seconds.
22. Select the Highlight Box, and give it the same timing.
23. Reduce the length of the slide to **11** seconds.

Adding Interactivity to the Project

Make sure the **Timeline** panel of slide 4 looks like the following screenshot:

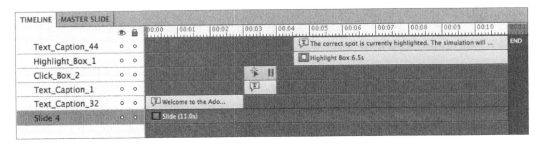

The Click Box will stop the playhead at 4 seconds into slide 4 and wait for the student to interact with the movie. If the student performs the right action, the playhead directly jumps to slide 5 without playing the second part of slide 4. If the student performs the wrong action, then the playhead is simply released and plays the Highlight Box and the Text Caption before moving on to slide 5. This is the first example of the branching concept without adding any extra slides to the project.

24. Save the file, and use the Preview icon's **Next 5 slides** feature to test your sequence.

It is necessary to test it twice. The first time, perform the right action and confirm that the playhead moves to the next slide. The second time, perform the wrong action twice, and confirm that the feedback messages and the Highlight Boxes are displayed before the simulation moves on to the next slide.

Extra Credit – adding the remaining Click Boxes

If everything works as expected, you can use the same procedure to add a Click Box and a failure message on slides 5, 6, 7, 8, 9, 10, 13, 15, and 16. Navigate to `chapter05/final/encoderSim_800.cptx` as reference. To help you out, the following are the general steps of the procedure to perform on each slide:

- Hide the Highlight Box using the Eye icon of the **Timeline** panel.
- Insert a Click Box, and make it cover the same spot as the Highlight Box.
- Set the Click Box so it accepts 2 attempts. It should *Jump to the next slide* on success and *Continue* after the last attempt.
- Make sure that the transition of the Text Caption is set to **Fade In Only**.
- Write a failure message in the Failure Caption.
- Apply the **MFTC-Failure** style to the Failure Caption.

- Create a Text Caption with extra feedback on the same model as the one you used on slide 4.
- Arrange the objects on the **Timeline** panel.
- Delete the objects that are not needed (extra Text Captions, Highlight Boxes, and so on).

When done, don't forget to save the file and preview your movie. In order to fully test the Click Boxes, it is necessary to preview the movie twice. The first time, perform the right actions and confirm that the simulation always jumps to the next slide. The second time, perform the wrong actions and confirm that the simulation displays the appropriate feedback messages.

Working with Text Entry Boxes

There is one last action to take care of on slide 14. That slide currently contains a Text Animation that automatically types the desired width of the video. In the simulation, you want the student to type this information. The interactive object that makes it possible is the **Text Entry Box**.

After the Button (including the Smart Shape used as a Button) and the Click Box, the Text Entry Box is the third and last interactive object that Captivate offers. Use the following steps to replace the Text Animation of slide 14 by a Text Entry Box:

1. Use the **Filmstrip** panel to go to slide 14 of the `encoderSim_800.cptx` file.
2. In the **Timeline** panel, use the Eye icon associated with the Text Animation that writes **400** in the **Width** field to hide it from the authoring environment.
3. Navigate to **Insert | Standard Objects | Text Entry Box** or the corresponding icon in the Objects toolbar to insert a new Text Entry Box.

The Text Entry Box system can add up to five objects to the slide (it is ok if they don't all show up on your slide):

- The Text Entry Box
- A Success Caption
- A Failure Caption
- A Hint Caption
- A **Submit** button (the **Submit** button is often hidden below the Success Caption)

You will now set up the Text Entry Box so it looks and behaves the way you want.

4. Move and resize the Text Entry Box object so it covers the **Width** field of the background image.

 Don't hesitate to use the *Zoom In* feature of Captivate to help you precisely size and position the Text Entry Box.

5. With the Text Entry Box selected, take a look at the **General** section of the **Properties** panel, and confirm that the **Validate User Input** checkbox is selected.

When the **Validate User Input** checkbox is selected, the **Correct Entries** box is displayed on the screen.

6. In the **Correct Entries** box, click on the + sign, and type 400. Do not tick the **Case Sensitive** option.

Thanks to this last action, the Text Entry Box is able to tell the right answer from the wrong answers. You can add as many correct entries as needed by clicking on the + sign (allowing alternate spelling of an answer to be accounted for). To remove an entry from the list, select it, and click on the – icon.

7. With the Text Entry Box selected, go to the **General** section of the **Properties** panel, and deselect the **Show Text Box Frame** option.
8. In the **Options** section, deselect the **Success** and **Hint** Captions if needed. Leave only the **Failure** Caption selected.
9. In the **Options** section of the **Properties** panel, also deselect the **Show Button** option to hide the **Submit** button.
10. In the **Transition** section, set the effect to **No transition** (if needed).
11. Type Sorry you did not perform the right action! in the Failure Caption. When done, resize the Failure Caption so the text fits comfortably in it, and move it somewhere in the middle of the slide.
12. Apply the **MFTC-Failure** style to the Failure Caption.
13. Select the Text Entry Box again.
14. In the **Action** section, open the **On Success** drop-down list, and choose **Go to the next slide**.
15. Deselect the **Infinite** option, and set the **Attempts** to 2.
16. Make sure the **Last Attempt** dropdown is set to **Continue**.
17. Confirm that the **Shortcut** option is set to **Enter**.

The **Shortcut** option lets you choose the keyboard key (or shortcut) the student will use to submit the content of the Text Entry Box. This **Shortcut** option can be used as an alternative to the **Submit** button or as a replacement to the **Submit** button when it is removed from the slide.

18. In the **Character** section, set the font **Family** to **Courier** and the text **Size** to **8**. This sets the formatting properties of the text that the student will type in the Text Entry Box.

Now that the Text Entry Box looks the right way and performs the right actions, you will move to the final step of this exercise: arranging the objects on the **Timeline** panel and providing the necessary feedback.

19. Select the Text Entry Box, and use the **Timeline** panel or the **Timing** section of the **Properties** panel to do the following:
    - Make the object **Appear After 0 sec**
    - Make it **Display For** a **Specific Time** of 1 second
    - Make it **Pause After 1 sec**

20. Select the Text Caption, and apply the same timing as for the Text Entry Box. In the **Transition** section, change the **Effect** field to **Fade In Only**.

The **Fade In Only** option is used to make sure that the Text Caption is still displayed at full opacity when the Text Entry Box pauses the playhead.

21. Insert a new Text Caption on the slide. Type The simulation will now perform the right action and continue. Resize the Text Caption so the text fits comfortably in the object, and place it somewhere in the middle of the slide.

22. In the **Timeline** panel or in the **Timing** section, make the new Text Caption **Appear After 1.5 sec** and **Display For** a **Specific Time** of 5.5 seconds.

23. Use the Eye icons of the **Timeline** panel to reveal the Text Animation again.

24. Make the Text Animation **Appear After 7.5 sec** and **Display For** a **Specific Time** of 1 second.

25. Adjust the duration of the slide accordingly.

Adding Interactivity to the Project

When done, make sure the **Timeline** panel looks like the following screenshot:

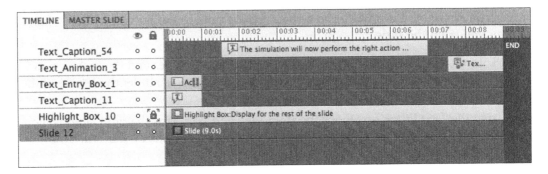

Don't forget to save the file and to test the new Text Entry Box in the **Preview** pane to make sure it works as expected.

Finishing touches

There are a few more things to do in order to completely finalize the simulation.

The first fine-tuning has to do with a limitation of Captivate. In a Captivate simulation, the Click Box object simulates a mouse click and the Text Entry Box object simulates a typing action, but there is no interactive object to simulate a drag-and-drop or a scrolling action.

Because of this limitation, you will now delete slides 11 and 12 of the simulation by performing the following steps:

1. In the **Filmstrip** panel, select both slide 11 and slide 12.
2. Right-click on any of the two selected slides, and choose **Delete** in the Contextual menu.
3. Click on the **OK** button to confirm the deletion of the slides.

The second thing to fine-tune is the double-click action on slide 5.

4. Use the **Filmstrip** panel to return to slide 5.
5. Use the **Timeline** panel to select the Click Box object.
6. In the **Options** section of the **Properties** panel, select the **Double-click** checkbox.

The last fine-tuning option takes place on slide 10. To better simulate the click over a link, you will turn the standard mouse pointer to a hand pointer over the Click Box.

7. Use the **Filmstrip** panel to return to slide 10.

8. Use the **Timeline** panel to select the Click Box object.
9. In the **Options** section of the **Properties** panel, select the **Hand Cursor** checkbox.

The conversion of the Encoder Demonstration into its simulation counterpart is now finished. To reach this milestone, you have used many objects and features of Captivate. Let's quickly summarize them as follows:

- The main object of a demonstration is the Mouse object. The main objects of a simulation are the Click Boxes and the Text Entry Boxes.
- To convert a demonstration to a simulation, you must first remove the Mouse object from the demonstration and then, replace it with Click Boxes and Text Entry Boxes.
- It is very important to provide specific and precise instructions to the learners at each and every step of the simulation.
- The **Find and Replace** feature is very useful to quickly modify the text contained in the Text Captions throughout the entire project.
- The three interactive objects of Captivate are the Button, the Click Box, and the Text Entry Box.
- When using Text Entry Boxes, you can decide if the text entered by the student must be validated or not.
- If the **Validate User Input** checkbox is on, you must provide the good answer(s) in the **Correct Entries** box.
- Each of these three objects implements the branching concept.
- Failure Captions, Hint Captions, and Success Captions can be added to these interactive objects.
- Captivate is not able to simulate drag-and-drop and scrolling actions in a simulation.

Working with the Drag and Drop Interaction

In this section, you will explore some of the amazing possibilities offered by the **Drag and Drop** Interaction. The Drag and Drop Interaction requires at least two objects. One serves as the **Drag Source** and the second one as the **Drop Target**:

- The Drag Source is the object that the user has to drag with his or her mouse
- The Drop Target is the object on which a Drag Source can be dropped

Adding Interactivity to the Project

It does not matter what those objects are. In this example, you will use images as both the Drag Source and the Drop Target, but you could as well use Text Captions, Highlight Boxes, Smart Shapes, and so on.

Of course, to make things more interesting, a single slide can contain multiple Drag Sources as well as multiple Drop Targets. Thanks to this new capability, you will be able to quickly and easily create complex and fun interactions.

Using the Drag and Drop Interaction wizard

For this first example, you will create a simple Drag and Drop Interaction. The goal is to ask your students how many **Miles per Hour** makes 120 **Kilometers per Hour**. They will have to drag the right answer and to drop it on top of the Drop Target. To create this first Drag and Drop Interaction, you will use the Drag and Drop Interaction wizard using the following steps:

1. Use the **Filmstrip** panel to go to slide 9 of the `drivingInBe.cptx` file under the `chapter05` folder.

As depicted in the following screenshot, this slide contains four images:

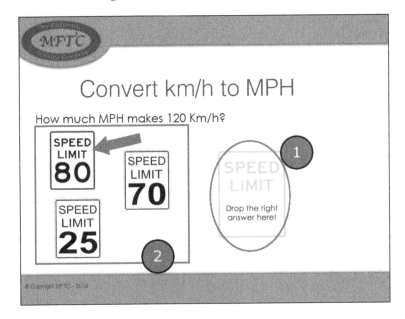

The image identified with the number **1** in the preceding screenshot is the Drop Target. The other three images, identified by the number **2**, are three Drag Sources. All three objects will be draggable, but only the image identified by the arrow (the 80 miles per hour image) is the right answer to the question.

2. Navigate to **Insert | Launch Drag and Drop Interaction Wizard** to start defining your first Drag and Drop interaction.

The Drag and Drop Interaction wizard is a three-step procedure that helps you quickly define a simple Drag and Drop Interaction. In the first step, you have to select the Drag Sources.

3. Click one by one on all three images identified as number **2** in the preceding screenshot.

As you click, the images are surrounded by a green outline indicating a Drag Source. If you made a mistake and select the wrong object, you can always use the little red minus sign to remove the object from the selection.

4. When all three Drag Sources are selected, click on the **Next** button at the top of the screen.

In the second step of the wizard, you have to choose the objects that serve as Drop Targets. In this example, you have a single Drop Target to select.

5. Select the image identified as **1** in the preceding screenshot to make it a Drop Target.
6. Note that a blue outline is used to identify the Drop Targets.
7. Click on the **Next** Button at the top of the screen.

The last step of the wizard is to tell Captivate the answer to the question by associating the Drag Sources with the proper Drop Target. In this example, you want to associate the 80 miles per hour image (identified by an arrow in the preceding screenshot) with the Drop Target.

8. Take the handle situated in the center of the 80 miles per hour image and move it on top of the Drop Target.

Adding Interactivity to the Project

9. Make sure your slide looks like the following screenshot before you click on the **Finish** button at the top of the screen:

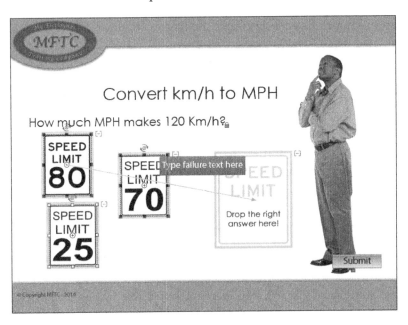

And now, the finishing touches.

10. Type a failure message in the Failure Caption.
11. Use the **Properties** panel to apply the **MFTC-failure** style to the Failure Caption.
12. Select the **Submit** button, and apply the **MFTC-buttonContinue** style. Move the button to the bottom-right corner of the slide in the brownish area.
13. Save the file, and use the Preview icon to test your first Drag and Drop Interaction.

Congratulations! You have created your first Drag and Drop Interaction in Captivate 7! It is not yet perfect, but your students will certainly enjoy it very much.

Using the Drag and Drop panel

The power of the Drag and Drop Interaction goes way beyond this first example. In the next exercise, you will explore the **Drag and Drop** panel and fine-tune the Drag and Drop Interaction you created in the previous section by performing the following steps:

1. Make sure you are still on slide 9 of the `drivingInBe.cptx` file under the `chapter05` folder.

2. Open the **Drag And Drop** panel situated on the right-hand edge of the screen next to the **Properties** and **Library** panels.

The **Drag and Drop** panel contains every single option pertaining to the Drag and Drop Interaction. The Drag and Drop Interaction wizard that you used in the previous section only gives you access to a very small subset of these options. The **Drag and Drop** panel is divided into five sections. At the very top of the **Drag and Drop** panel, notice the *trash can* icon that allows you to delete the Drag and Drop Interaction if needed.

3. In the **Action** section of the **Drag and Drop** panel, select the **Infinite** checkbox to give your students unlimited attempts to get the right answer.
4. Also select the **Reset All** radio button to have the Drag Sources moved back to their original location when a wrong answer is submitted.
5. Select the Drop Target image.

In the **General** section of the **Drag and Drop** panel, notice that the **Drop Target** options become available.

6. In the **Effects** drop-down menu, choose the **Zoom In** effect as shown in the following screenshot:

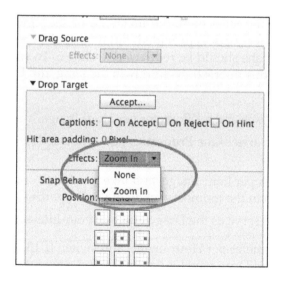

7. Select all three Drag Source images.

In the **General** section of the **Drag and Drop** panel, notice that the **Drag Source** options become available.

8. In the **Effect** drop-down menu of the **Drag Source** options, choose the **Glow** effect.

9. Save the file and use the Preview icon to test your updated Drag and Drop Interaction.

When testing your interaction, pay close attention to the effects you applied to the Drag Sources and to the Drop Target. You should see a yellow glow effect on the Drag Sources and a **Zoom In** effect on a Drop Target. Also notice that when you submit a wrong answer, the Drag Source automatically goes back to its original position.

Using the Drag and Drop Interaction for branching and navigation

In this section, you will use the Drag and Drop Interaction to enable navigation between the slides of your project using the following steps. This will give you yet another use case of the Drag and Drop Interaction as well as another example of the branching concept:

1. Still in the `drivingInBe.cptx` file, use the **Filmstrip** panel to go to slide 5.

Slide 5 contains three images along with a Text Caption. To answer the question in the Text Caption, the student will have to drag the image that represents the measurement unit he or she uses to measure speed on top of the Drop Target image. If the student chooses the Miles per Hour image, he or she should be redirected to slide 7, where specific feedback is provided. But if he or she chooses the Kilometer per Hour image, he or she should be redirected to slide 6. To spice it up a little bit more, you will create this interaction entirely in the **Drag and Drop** panel, without using the wizard!

2. Still on slide 5, select the Kilometer per Hour image.
3. In the topmost area of the **Properties** panel, notice that this image has a name (**KPH_image**).
4. Select the miles per hour image, and take good note of its name (**MPH_image**) in the topmost section of the **Properties** panel.

These two images will serve as the Drag Source of your interaction.

5. Select the Kilometer per Hour image, and switch to the **Drag and Drop** panel (if the **Drag and Drop** panel is not on display, navigate to **Window | Drag and Drop** to turn it on).

6. At the very top of the **Drag and Drop** panel, click on the Create New Interaction icon as shown in the following screenshot:

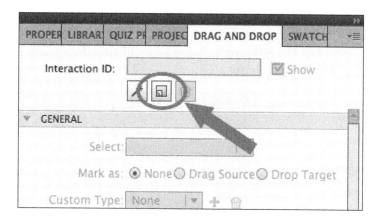

7. With the Kilometer per Hour image selected on the slide, use the **General** section of the **Drag and Drop** panel, to mark the selected image as a **Drag Source**.

8. Still in the **General** section of the **Properties** panel, open the **Select** drop-down menu, and choose the **MPH_image**. This selects the corresponding image on the stage.

9. Once selected, mark the **MPH_image** as another **Drag Source**.

Both the **MPH_image** and the **KMH_image** should be surrounded by a green outline identifying them as Drag Sources.

10. Select the Drop Target image, and use the same technique to mark it as a **Drop Target**.

When marked as a Drop Target, a blue outline appears around the image.

Now that the Drag Sources and the Drop Target of the interaction have been correctly identified, you will define what will happen when one or the other Drag Sources is dropped on the Drop Target.

11. With the Drop Target still selected, click on the **Accept** button situated in the **Drop Target** area of the **General** section of the **Drag and Drop** panel.

12. In the **Accepted Drag Sources** dialog, click on the **No Action** link associated with the **KMH_image** object.

Adding Interactivity to the Project

13. Open the **Action** drop-down menu, and choose the **Jump to slide** action. Then use the second drop-down menu to choose **Slide 6** as the destination.
14. Repeat the same sequence of action to associate the **MPH_image** object with the **Jump to slide 7** action.

Make sure the **Accepted Drag Sources** dialog looks like the following screenshot before continuing with this exercise:

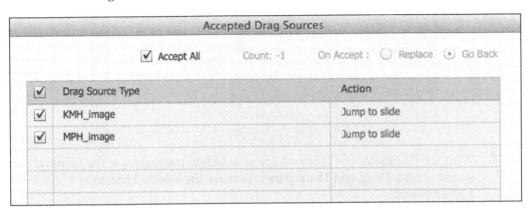

15. Click on the **OK** button to validate and to close the **Accepted Drag Sources** dialog.

The core parameters of your Drag and Drop Interaction are now in place. It is time for some fine-tuning.

16. Use the **Drag and Drop** panel to customize your interaction as you see fit. For example, you can add **Glow** effects on the Drag Sources and **Zoom In** effects on the Drop Targets.

When you are finished, there is one last thing to do to completely wrap up this exercise.

17. Use the **Filmstrip** panel to go to slide 6.
18. When slide 6 is selected, return to the **Properties** panel.
19. In the **Action** section of the **Properties** panel, change the **On Exit** action to **Jump to slide 10**.

With the completion of the preceding exercise, you have created another great branching experience that your student will certainly appreciate! If the student chooses the Kilometer per Hour image, he or she will be redirected to slide 6, where he or she will be provided with specific feedback before being sent to slide 10. If the student chooses the Miles per Hour image, he or she will be sent to slide 7, where a sequence of three slides will teach him or her how to convert Miles per Hour to Kilometers per Hour.

In *Chapter 7, Working with Quizzes*, you will create an even more sophisticated Drag and Drop interaction, but for now, let's quickly summarize what you already know about the Drag and Drop interaction:

- To create a Drag and Drop interaction, you need at least two objects on the slide. One of them is the Drag Source, and the other one is the Drop Target.
- A Drag Source is an object that the student can drag. A Drop Target is an object on top of which a Drag Source can be dropped.
- A single slide can contain many Drag Sources and many Drop Targets.
- The Drag and Drop interaction wizard is a three-step procedure that helps you create a basic Drag and Drop interaction.
- The **Drag and Drop** panel contains every option pertaining to the Drag and Drop interaction. It lets you fine-tune your interaction in many ways or even create an entire Drag and Drop interaction from scratch.

Drag and Drop extravaganza

Drag and Drop extravaganza is the title of an excellent webinar by Dr Allen Partridge, Adobe eLearning evangelist. This webinar will give you a much deeper look at the possibilities of the Drag and Drop interaction. You can access the Drag and Drop extravaganza webinar at http://www.adobe.com/cfusion/event/index.cfm?event=register_no_session&id=2252370&loc=en_us. Note that you need a free Adobe ID to access this content.

Objects and Animations in Video Demo projects

You now have a pretty good idea of all the objects available in Captivate 7. Before moving on to the next chapter, you will quickly return to the Video Demo project you created in *Chapter 2*, *Capturing the Slides*, and explore the objects that can be added in such a project.

Interactivity in Video Demo projects

Let's begin with the easiest and shortest topic.

Remember that a Video Demo project is a big Full Motion Recording and that it can only be published as a `.mp4` video file. To make it short, a Video Demo can only propose a linear video-like experience to the students. Consequently, there is no interactivity in a Video Demo project. In other words, the interactive objects (Buttons, Click Boxes, and Text Entry Boxes) as well as the Rollover objects of Captivate are *not* supported in Video Demo projects.

Standard objects in Video Demo projects

However, most of the standard objects of Captivate are supported in Video Demo projects. In this exercise, you will take a look at the objects that are supported in a Video Demo project using the following steps:

1. Open the `encoderVideo.cpvc` file under the `Chapter05` folder from your exercises folder.
2. Open the **Insert** menu to have a list of the objects that can be inserted in a Video Demo as shown in the following screenshot:

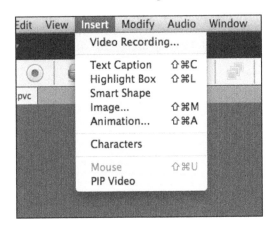

The **Insert** menu of a Video Demo project is much smaller than the **Insert** menu of a standard Captivate project. Take good note of the objects that are supported in a Video Demo. They all work the exact same way as the standard object you studied so far, so these objects have already been added to the project for you.

3. Browse the **Timeline** panel of the Video Demo to see how these objects have been inserted in this particular project. Don't hesitate to select them and inspect their properties in the **Properties** panel.

Animations in Video Demo projects

When it comes to Animations, there are two interesting features that are specific to Video Demo projects: **Pan & Zoom** and **Transitions**.

Using Pan and Zoom

The first one is the **Pan & Zoom** feature. It allows you to zoom to a specific area of the video and to move the camera during the movie. In the next exercise, you will add two **Pan & Zoom** Animations into this particular project by performing the following steps:

1. In the **Timeline** panel, move the playhead more or less to the **02:25** mark.
2. Navigate to **Window | Pan & Zoom** to turn the **Pan & Zoom** panel on.
3. In the **Pan & Zoom** panel, click on the **Add Pan & Zoom** button.

The **Pan & Zoom** panel updates and shows the available pan and zoom controls along with a thumbnail image of the current frame of the video in the topmost area of the panel. A blue bounding box with eight handles surrounds this thumbnail image.

4. Resize and move the blue bounding box so it covers only the **Video** tab part of the thumbnail (see **1** in the following screenshot).

Adding Interactivity to the Project

5. Decrease the **Speed** value of the **Pan & Zoom** Animation to 1.0 second (2) as shown in the following screenshot:

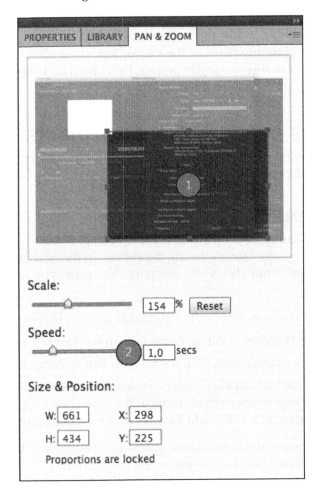

After this procedure, a Pan & Zoom icon appears in the **Timeline** panel. Click on this icon to load the properties of this **Pan & Zoom** Animation in the **Pan & Zoom** panel should you modify or delete this **Pan & Zoom** Animation later on.

You will now move the playhead ahead on the **Timeline** panel and add the corresponding *Zoom Out* Animation.

6. In the **Timeline** panel, move the playhead more or less to the **02:50** mark.
7. In the **Pan & Zoom** panel, click on the **Zoom Out** button to restore the view.

This last action adds a second **Pan & Zoom** Animation in the project as indicated by the second Pan & Zoom icon in the **Timeline** panel around the **02:50** mark shown in the following screenshot:

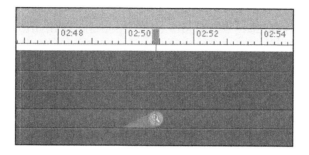

8. In the **Pan & Zoom** panel, decrease the **Speed** value of this Animation to `1.0` second.

Adding Transitions in Video Demos

Another way of adding some kind of Animations to a Video Demo project is by adding **Transitions**. A Transition defines how the Video moves from one video clip to the next.

In this case, you only have a single big video clip in your project, so the only places you can add Transitions to are the very beginning and the very end of the project. To add Transitions in the middle of a video clip, you first have to *split* the video into smaller sequences. You will then be able to add Transitions between these sequences. Let's check it out by performing the following steps:

1. In the **Timeline** panel, move the playhead to the **00:25** mark, where the front title of the video finishes (see **1** in the following screenshot).
2. At the bottom of the **Timeline** panel, click on the **Split** button (**2**) as shown in the following screenshot:

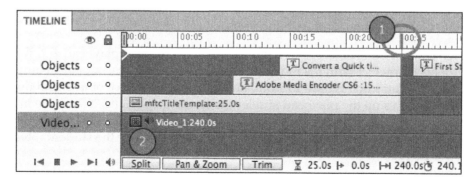

This effectively splits the video file into two separate sequences as indicated by the small diamond that appears in the **Timeline** panel at the exact location of the split. Because you now have two video clips in your project, it is possible to add a Transition between these two sequences.

3. Navigate to **Window | Transitions** to open the **Transitions** panel.
4. In the **Timeline** panel, click on the diamond situated between the two sequences that you have split.
5. In the **Transitions** panel, choose a Transition of your liking.
6. Repeat the same sequence of actions at the end of the project (more or less at the **03:52** mark of the **Timeline** panel).
7. When done, click on the Preview icon and choose to preview the video **Full Screen**.

During the preview, pay particular attention to the newly added **Pan & Zoom** Animations and **Transitions**.

8. When the preview is finished, click on the **Edit** button in the bottom-right corner of the screen to return in the edit mode.
9. Save and close the file when done.

This last exercise concludes your study of the objects of Captivate 7.

Summary

You are now deep into the post-production phase of your Captivate movie. Your projects are now very different from the original rushes. They have also become fully interactive and animated. To achieve these things, it has been necessary to add different kinds of objects to the slides and to use a lot of tools and features of Captivate.

In this particular chapter, you focused on the objects that allow you to add interactivity in your Captivate projects. First, you studied the Rollover objects. You used the Rollover Caption, Rollover Images, Rollover Slidelet, and Rollover Smart Shapes to add some interactivity to the project.

You then studied three objects that have the ability to stop the playhead and wait for the students to interact with the movie. The Click Box is used to simulate a mouse click; the Text Entry Box is used to simulate the typing of a piece of text; and the Button is used to stop the playhead and let the student experience the movie in a personalized fashion. These three objects also implement the branching concept by letting you choose two different actions depending on the way the student interacts with these objects.

You also discovered the Drag and Drop interaction that you used to add some very sophisticated interaction to the project.

In the final section of this chapter, you returned to the Video Demo project you created in *Chapter 2, Capturing the Slides*, in order to discover the objects that can be inserted in a Video Demo project. You also uncovered two features that are specific to Video Demo projects: **Pan & Zoom** and **Transitions**.

In the next chapter, you will focus on *sound and audio*. You will add sound effects to objects, background music to the project, and narration to the slides.

As you can see, there are still some very cool things to discover in Captivate!

Meet the community

In this section, I'll introduce you to two individuals from the same family. Together with two other members of the family, they own and manage Infosemantics, an Australian-based company specialized in eLearning development and Captivate widgets.

Rod Ward

Director of Infosemantics. Rod is a Technical Author, Information Designer, and eLearning Developer with over a decade of industry experience. Based in Perth since 1986, he has worked for companies large and small across Australia. Rod's specialties are the design and development of eLearning courses using sound instructional design principles and Adobe's suite of eLearning software tools. Rod is also the author of three e-books about Adobe Captivate, two about troubleshooting issues, and one about using Advanced Actions.

Tristan Ward

Tristan is a Flash, ActionScript and HTML5 expert. He builds many of the Flash Animations and interactivity add-ins included in Infosemantics' Captivate eLearning courses. Tristan is deservedly famous throughout the Adobe Captivate world for his *Widget King* blog, which contains many articles about creating AS3 Widgets using his WidgetFactory API, now the leading platform for creating AS3 Widgets for Captivate. He's also our go-to guy for video editing.

Contact details

- Website: http://www.infosemantics.com.au/
- Twitter: Rod @Infosemantics and Tristan @WidgetFactory
- Tristan's blog: http://www.infosemantics.com.au/widgetking

6
Working with Audio

In this chapter, the post-production phase of your projects will continue with the addition of audio files to your projects. In Captivate, you can add sound at three different levels:

- **Object level**: The sound associated with an object plays when the object appears on the screen. This is a great place to add small sound effects (whoosh, clings, bangs, tones, and so on) to the project.
- **Slide level**: The audio clip plays in sync with the slide. Most of the time, this option is used to add voice-over narration.
- **Project level**: The audio clip is used to add background music to the entire project.

This chapter will cover these three options in depth. The one where you will focus most of your attention is slide-level audio. Slide-level audio can either be recorded (with Captivate or with an external audio application) or generated by the **Text-to-Speech** engine of Captivate. Closed Captions can also be added to slide-level audio.

In this chapter, you will perform the following:

- Add sound effects to some objects
- Add background music to the project
- Record narration to the slides
- Import external sound files into Captivate
- Edit a sound clip in Captivate
- Generate narration with the Text-to-Speech engine
- Use the **Slide Notes** panel to convert Slide Notes to Closed Captions and Text-to-Speech
- Synchronize Closed Captions with the corresponding sound clip

Preparing your work

For the exercises of this chapter, you need to reset the Captivate interface and open two files.

1. Open Captivate. Make sure the **Classic** workspace is applied.
2. Navigate to **Window** | **Workspace** | **reset 'Classic'** to change the workspace back to default.
3. Open the `encoderDemo_800.cptx` file under `Chapter06` situated in your exercises folder.
4. Also, open the `drivingInBe.cptx` file under `Chapter06`.

In addition to these two files, one of the exercises requires a microphone — a simple microphone that can be found in any computer store is more than enough. If you have a built-in microphone in your computer, you're ready to go! If you do not have a microphone, don't worry, just read through that exercise; it has been designed to be optional so that the absence of a microphone will not compromise your progression.

Adding audio to objects

Sound can be added to each and every object in Captivate. The audio clip associated with an object plays when the object appears on the stage. Even though nothing prevents you from adding narration or music at the object level, most of the time, object-level audio is used to add sound effects to the movie.

In the next exercise, you will add a sound effect to the Adobe Media Encoder logo in the Encoder Demonstration project.

1. Go to slide 3 of the `encoderDemo_800.cptx` file under `Chapter06`.
2. Select the Adobe Media Encoder logo to make it the active object. The **Properties** panel gets updated.
3. Open the **Audio** section of the **Properties** panel and click on the **Add Audio** button. The **Object Audio** dialog opens.
4. At the bottom of the **Object Audio** dialog, click on the **Import (F6)...** button. The **Import Audio** box opens.

By default, the **Import Audio** dialog displays the contents of the `Sound` directory under `Gallery`. Remember that the `Gallery` folder is a collection of assets that ship with Captivate. In *Chapter 3, Working with Standard Objects*, you already used the `Gallery` folder to import the animated orange arrow.

> If the **Import Audio** dialog does not show the content of the Sound directory by default, remember that the Gallery folder is located at C:\Program Files\Adobe\Captivate 7\Gallery (Windows) or in Applications/Adobe Captivate 7/Gallery (Mac).

5. At the end of the list, choose the Whoosh 2.mp3 file and click on **Open**.

The sound clip is imported into the project, and the sound wave is loaded in the **Object Audio** dialog.

6. Click on the **Play** button situated in the top-left corner of the **Object Audio** dialog to control the imported sound.
7. Click on the **Save** button at the bottom-right corner of the box.
8. Click on the **Close** button to close the **Object Audio** box.

In the **Timeline** panel, a loudspeaker icon is added to the AME Logo layer indicating that an audio clip is associated with that particular object.

9. Use the Preview icon and click on **Next 5 Slides** to preview the next five slides and test the sound effect. Close the **Preview** pane when done.
10. In the top-right corner of the screen, click on the **Library** tab to open the **Library** panel.

Notice that the **Whoosh 2** sound clip has been added to the **Audio** section of the **Library** panel. This means that if you want to use the same sound effect elsewhere in the project, there is no need to import the file a second time.

> **Reusing an existing sound file**
>
> If the audio file you want to use is already present in the **Library** panel of the project, you can drag that audio file from the **Library** panel and drop it directly on top of the object you want to associate the sound effect with. This simple workflow also works with other types of assets present in the **Library** panel.

11. Don't forget to save the file when done.

>
> **Supported audio formats**
>
> Only `.wav` and `.mp3` sound clips can be imported in Captivate. When inserting a `.mp3` clip, Captivate automatically converts it to the `.wav` format. So, you end up with two versions of the same audio clip in the **Library** panel: a `.mp3` version and a `.wav` version. Internally, Captivate uses the `.wav` format because this uncompressed format maintains the highest possible sound quality while working with the file. You can therefore safely delete the `.mp3` version from the **Library** panel. When you publish the movie in Flash or HTML5, Captivate converts the `.wav` file back to `.mp3` and uses that `.mp3` file in the published movie.

Extra credit – adding sound effects to objects

In this section, you will add a sound effect to the Rollover Captions and Rollover Images of the *Driving In Belgium* project. These are the general steps to follow:

- Go to slide 15 of the `drivingInBe.cptx` file.
- Select the Rollover Caption that reads **No parking is allowed at any time!**. Make sure you select the Rollover Caption and not the corresponding Rollover Area.
- Open the **Audio** section of the **Properties** panel and click on the **Add Audio** button.
- Click on **Import** and select the `Electronic Beeping.mp3` sound file. Save and close the box.
- Open the **Library** tab. The `Electronic Beeping.mp3` sound clip should have been added to the **Audio** section of the **Library** panel.
- Drag-and-drop the Electronic Beeping sound clip from the **Library** panel to the remaining Rollover Captions of the slide (make sure you use the Captions and not their corresponding Rollover Areas).
- Go to slide 16 and associate the same sound clip with the three Rollover Images of the slide. Make sure you use Rollover Images and not the corresponding Rollover Areas.
- Save the file and use the preview feature to test the added sound clips.

[If you take a look at the **Timeline** panel while on slide 15 or 16 of the `drivingInBe.cptx` file, you'll notice that there are no objects showing the loudspeaker icon. This is because the objects listed in the **Timeline** panel are the Rollover Areas and not the corresponding Rollover Captions or Rollover Images you added the sound to.]

This concludes your overview of object-level audio. Let's have a quick summary of what you have learned so far:

- In Captivate, you can associate a sound clip with any object. The sound plays when the object appears on the screen.
- Usually, object-level audio is used to add sound effects to the movie.
- Only sound clips in `.wav` or `.mp3` format can be imported into Captivate.
- When an audio file is imported into the movie, it is automatically added to the audio section of the **Library** panel.
- When inserting a `.mp3` file, Captivate automatically converts it into a `.wav` file and uses that `.wav` file internally. The `.mp3` clip is used in the published movie. Both these audio files appear in the **Library** panel.
- It is possible to reuse a sound clip stored in the **Library** elsewhere in the project.
- When a sound clip is added to an object, a loudspeaker icon appears in the corresponding layer of the **Timeline** panel.

[**Is object-level audio always a sound effect?**

While object-level audio is the preferred place to add sound effects to project, it is not used just for sound effects. It may be used to read aloud descriptive text or pronounce a difficult word. This book only shows a typical use case, but don't hesitate to be creative in how you can actually use this feature!]

Adding background music to the entire project

In this section, you will associate an audio clip to the entire project. Usually, project-level audio is used to add background music. To make sure that music is being played during the entire project, you will use a 15 to 30 second sound clip (called a sample) and make it run in a loop for the duration of the movie.

Working with Audio

In the next exercise, you will add background music to the Encoder Demonstration.

1. Return to the `encoderDemo_800.cptx` file under `Chapter06`.
2. Navigate to **Audio** | **Import To** | **Background**.
3. Choose the `Loop Acoustic.mp3` file from the `/Sound` directory of the Captivate **Gallery** folder and click on **Open**.
4. The **Background Audio** dialog box opens.

The **Background Audio** dialog informs you that the duration of the loop of the `Acoustic.mp3` sound clip is 16 seconds (see the arrow in the following screenshot):

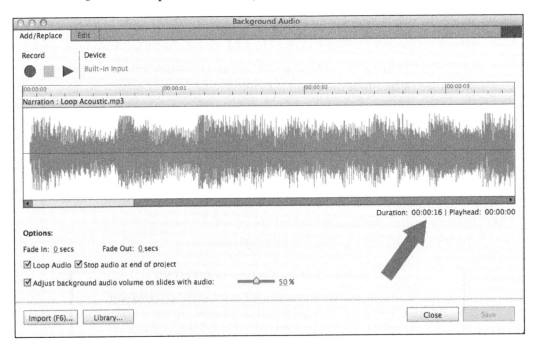

Some interesting options are situated in the lower part of the **Background Audio** dialog:

- When the audio clip has finished playing, the **Loop Audio** option makes it start over so the sound clip is played for the entire project.
- The **Stop audio at end of project** option should be selected at all times. If it is not ticked, the Background Audio will keep on playing even after the end of the project.

- The **Adjust background audio volume on slides with audio** option automatically lowers the volume of the background music on slides with associated audio. This option ensures that the slide audio is always louder than the Background Audio.

Most of the time, leaving these options to their default settings works just fine.

5. Accept the default settings and click on **Close** to close the **Background Audio** dialog.
6. Use the Preview icon and navigate to **Project** to preview the entire project.

During the preview, note that the Background Audio volume is not reduced when the video file plays on slide 2. The volume reduction of the Background Audio only works when an audio file is added at the slide level, which does not include the audio track of a video file.

7. When the preview is finished, close the **Preview** pane.
8. Use the **Filmstrip** panel to go to slide 2 of the project.
9. Make sure the slide is selected so that the **Properties** panel displays the properties of the slide.
10. In the **Audio** section of the **Properties** panel, select the **Stop Background Audio** checkbox as shown in the following screenshot:

11. Use the Preview icon again and navigate to **Project** to preview the entire project.

When the preview reaches the second slide of the project, the Background Audio should completely stop to let you see the video file. When you click on the **Continue** button to go to slide 3, the background music starts again and the project continues.

12. Close the **Preview** pane before continuing with this exercise.

If you need to modify the Background Audio or one of its associated options, navigate to **Audio | Edit | Background** to reopen the **Background Audio** dialog. Use the **Add/Replace** tab of the **Background Audio** dialog to use another sound clip and the **Edit** tab to modify the current sound clip.

When do you use Background Audio?

To be honest, I have never used Background Audio in a Captivate project. I find it annoying and distracting. It drives the students away from what I want them to focus on. That being said, there are probably some use cases for which Background Audio would be useful. If you run into one of these use cases, don't hesitate to use the feature. There is only one thing to keep in mind: you are teaching, so the background music you use, as well as any other features of your Captivate project, should serve the student's learning.

You will now remove the Background Audio that you have added to the project.

13. Navigate to **Audio | Remove | Background** to remove the Background Audio.
14. Confirm that you want to remove the audio clip.
15. Save the file when done.

Before moving on to the next section, here is a list of what you have learned about Background Audio:

- Audio can be added at the project level. Most of the time, this feature is used to add background music to the project.
- Use the **Audio** menu to add, edit, and delete the Background Audio.
- To make sure the background music plays for the entire duration of the movie, use a short sample of music and make it run in a loop.
- Captivate has an option to lower the volume of the Background Audio when a slide with an associated sound clip is played.
- Use Background Audio with care! It should not distract your students!

>
> **Using Background Audio the creative way**
>
> Background Audio does not need to be music. It can be, for instance, the sounds you may hear in a hospital setting when learning about hospital procedures. Again, this book only shows the most typical use case, and again, it is your imagination that will ultimately define how this feature is actually used.

Adding audio to slides

Adding audio to slides is by far the most interesting way to use audio in Captivate. Typically, slide-level audio is where you will add voice-over narration to the project.

Narration can be added directly during the filming; however, most of the time, it is recorded later in the process, imported into Captivate, and carefully synchronized with the rest of the slides' content. To get professional-sounding narration, it is best to use an external audio application; however, Captivate provides basic audio recording and editing tools.

>
> **Adobe Audition**
>
> Adobe Audition is an audio application from Adobe. Audition CC is available as part of a Creative Cloud subscription. Adobe Audition (formerly Cool Edit) is an awesome yet easy-to-use audio application. If Adobe Audition is available on your computer, use it to record and edit your audio clips instead of using Captivate.

Recording narration with Captivate

In this section, you will use Captivate to record an audio clip. To achieve this, your first concern is to carry the sound data from the microphone to Captivate by using your computer's audio interface.

>
> The following exercise requires a microphone. If you do not have a microphone available, just read through the steps. You'll have a chance to catch up on a subsequent exercise.

Working with Audio

Setting up the sound system

The exact setup procedure depends on your audio equipment and on your operating system, but basically, setting up the sound system can be divided into five phases:

- Plug the microphone into the audio input port of your computer (usually, it is the red plug of your sound card)
- Check out the audio options of your operating system (shown in the following screenshot)
- In the **System Preferences** window, use the **Input** tab of the **Sound** section (Mac OS)
- For Windows 7, use the **Manage Audio Devices** link in the **Hardware and Sound** section of the **Control Panel**
- Check out the audio options of Captivate

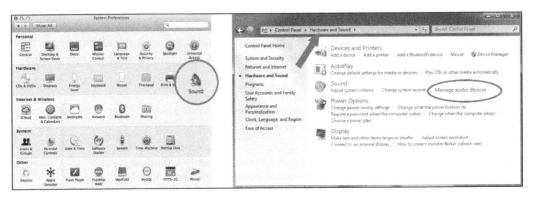

Once the audio options of the operating system are properly set up, you can safely move on to Captivate.

1. Return to the `encoderDemo_800.cptx` file.
2. Navigate to **Audio | Settings...** to open the **Audio Settings** dialog box.
3. Open the **Audio input Devices** drop-down list and select the audio device on which the microphone is attached.

If your computer has multiple audio input devices (such as a microphone and a line-in port), the **Audio Input Devices** drop-down list instructs Captivate about which device it has to listen to. This is the single most important part of the procedure. If a wrong device is selected, the audio data will never reach Captivate. In the following screenshot, we instruct Captivate to listen to the audio stream coming from the built-in microphone of the computer (the actual content of the drop-down menu depends on the audio drivers installed on your system):

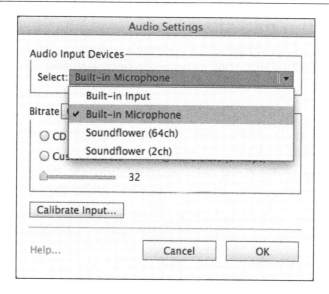

For the **Bitrate** options, the default should be fine. If you decide that the default audio quality is not good enough, you can test a new recording with a higher bitrate. Be aware that the higher the bitrate, the bigger the file. When choosing the bitrate, you have to find the most appropriate balance between the quality of the sound and the size of the resulting file.

4. Leave the **Bitrate** option at its default and click on the **Calibrate Input...** button.

Calibrating the input is finding the right sensitivity for the microphone. If it is set too high, you'll have a saturated sound with lots of clipping; however, if it is set too low, the recorded narration will be lost in the background noise. To help you out, Captivate provides an auto-calibrating feature. All you need to do is say a few words into the microphone in order to let Captivate evaluate the input sensitivity and find the right value. Let's give it a try!

5. In the **Calibrate audio input** dialog box, click on the **Auto Calibrate** button.
6. Speak normally into your microphone until you have a message saying that the microphone has been calibrated. (If you don't know what to say, just tell a joke! Don't worry, it is not recorded!)
7. Click on the **OK** button to validate the sensitivity value and to close the **Calibrate Audio Input** dialog.
8. Close the **Audio Settings** dialog box as well.

Recording the narration

Now that both the sound system and Captivate are properly set up, it is time to concentrate on the actual recording of the voice-over narration.

1. While still in the `encoderDemo_800.cptx` file, use the **Filmstrip** panel to go to slide 3.
2. Make sure the **Properties** panel displays the properties of the slide. In the **Audio** section, click on the **Add Audio...** button.
3. In the **Slide Audio** dialog, select the **SWF Preview** option. It will help you sync the narration with the rest of the slide during the recording.

The next step of the exercise is the actual recording of the sound clip! Before you press the **Record** button, it is necessary to take some time to rehearse the narration.

The following text is the script that you will record:

Want to insert a video in Captivate? Great! Video will make your eLearning content much more engaging and fun! But before you can import a video file in Captivate, you must first convert it into a video format that the Flash player can read. The Adobe Media Encoder is an application that has been designed to convert video and audio files to a proper format for your project. The good news is that the Adobe Media Encoder CS6 is part of your Captivate 7 bundle at no extra cost! Want to know how it works? Just click on the continue button.

Read these sentences out loud a few times. When you feel ready, move on to your first audio take!

4. Click on the red **Record Audio** button at the top-left area of the **Slide Audio** dialog. After a short countdown, read the preceding sentences out loud at a normal speed and with a normal voice.
5. When the recording is complete, click on the **Stop** button.
6. Control the quality of your take by clicking on the **Play** button. If you are not satisfied, start over with another take.
7. When you are satisfied with the result, click on the **Save** button and close the **Slide Audio** dialog.

If the recorded sound clip is longer than the slide, you will be prompted to extend the duration of the slide to the length of the sound clip. Click on **Yes** to finalize the integration of the new sound clip into the slide.

In the **Timeline** panel, the new sound clip is displayed as an additional layer situated below the slide layer. If needed, you can move the sound clip on the **Timeline** panel to better synchronize it with the rest of the slide, but you cannot use the **Timeline** panel to change the duration of the sound clip.

To quickly test the slide, use the **Play** button situated at the bottom-left corner of the **Timeline** panel. This button only plays the current slide without opening the **Preview** pane. This preview option does not let you test every single feature of the slide, but it is a quick and easy way to perform some basic testing and synchronization.

Recording narration is not an easy task, especially if you are not used to speaking into a microphone. Here are some basic tips and tricks to help you out:

- Write down the text that needs to be recorded and rehearse it a few times before the recording.
- Keep in mind that you don't have to make it right the first time. Try as many times as needed.
- Speak slowly, especially if you have an international audience where all the students do not speak the same language.
- Have a glass of water ready to avoid the dry-mouth effect. Remember that lots of students will hear the narration through a headset.
- Position the microphone within 4 to 6 inches of your mouth and slightly to the side to avoid pops and hisses on the letters S and P.
- If you have an external audio application available, use it to produce your sound clips and import them into Captivate.
- Standing up and gesturing while speaking can help you speak more clearly and confidently, and add more animation to your voice.

Working with Audio

With these simple tips and tricks, a basic computer microphone, and a bit of practice, you should be able to record some pretty good audio clips right away!

Whose voice should be recorded?

If you have the money, it is best to hire a narrator; however, most of the time, you will be recording your own voice or the voice of a colleague or friend. When choosing the person who will read the lines, always have your students in mind. For my very first big Captivate project, I had to develop a course in English, but most of the students were not native English speakers. We met with the customer and agreed to record the voice of a non-native English speaker. (It was an employee from the next-door office who was into theater.) The recorded English was not perfect, the accent was a bit strange, but it was not important because it was adapted to the audience.

Importing an external sound clip

When using an external audio application, the audio clips will be entirely produced in the external application and imported into Captivate when finished.

In the next exercise, you will import sound clips produced in Adobe Audition into the Captivate project.

1. Return to the `encoderDemo_800.cptx` file and use the **Filmstrip** panel to go to slide 3. Make sure the **Properties** panel displays the properties of the slide.
2. (This step is optional.) If you have completed the previous exercise, remove the recorded sound clip by clicking on the **Remove Audio** button situated in the **Audio** section of the **Properties** panel.
3. In the **Audio** section, click on the **Add Audio** button. The **Slide Audio** dialog box opens.
4. Click on the **Import Narration** button situated in the bottom-left corner of the dialog box.
5. Browse your computer to select the `slide03.mp3` file under `audio` situated in your exercises folder.
6. Click on **Open**. The selected file is imported into the project.
7. Click on the **Play** button to test the imported audio.

8. Save the changes by clicking on the **Save** button situated in the bottom-right corner of the **Slide Audio** dialog.
9. It is possible that the duration of the slide has to be increased to match the duration of the new audio file. Click on **Yes** if prompted to do so.
10. Close the **Slide Audio** dialog box.

After this procedure, the audio file appears in the **Timeline** panel as an extra layer situated below the slide layer. Remember that you can move this audio file to the **Timeline** panel so that the sound does not begin right away when the slide appears on the screen.

> **Sound synchronization**
>
> Sound can be very intrusive, so you must use it with care. One of the things that I always do on slides with voice-over narration (such as slide 3 of your project) is to move the sound clip on the **Timeline** panel half a second to the right, so the audio narration begins half a second into the slide. This simple trick dramatically diminishes the intrusive and aggressive feeling that poorly synchronized sound can induce.

Using the library to import the remaining audio files

In this section, you will import the remaining audio files and associate them with the slides of your project. To do so, you will use a slightly different workflow that involves the **Library** panel.

1. While still in the `encoderDemo_800.cptx` file under `chapter06`, open the **Library** panel situated at the right-hand side of the screen, next to the **Properties** panel.

Working with Audio

2. Click on the second icon of the Library toolbar. This icon is named Import and is shown in the following screenshot:

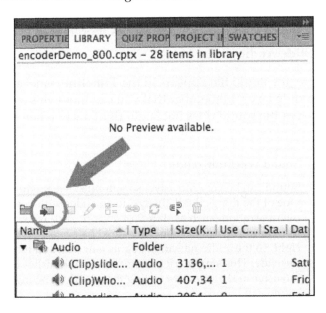

3. Browse to the `audio` folder of the downloaded exercises and select all the `.mp3` audio files it contains (except the `slide03.mp3` file that has already been imported).

4. Click on the **Open** button and let Captivate import the selected audio files one by one to the **Library** panel.

5. When the importation process is finished, you should have a message saying that **9 items have been successfully imported**. Click on **OK** to acknowledge the message.

All the required audio files have been imported into the project. Your next task is to associate each of the imported files with their corresponding slide.

6. Use the **Filmstrip** panel to go to slide 4 of the `encoderDemo_800.cptx` file under `chapter06`.

7. Drag the `slide04.mp3` file from the **Audio** section of the **Library** panel and drop it on top of slide 4. Make sure you drop it on the slide itself and not on one of the objects present on the slide. The **Slide Audio** dialog opens.

8. If needed, click on the **Play** button to control the imported audio file. When done, click on the **Close** button at the bottom-right corner of the **Slide Audio** dialog.

Yes, it is that easy to import external sound clips into Captivate! If you take a look at the **Filmstrip** panel, you'll notice a loudspeaker icon next to the slides you have added audio to.

Now, the rest of this exercise is easy! You will use the exact same drag-and-drop procedure to associate the remaining audio clips with their corresponding slides. The only potential problem you have to be mindful of is to drop the audio clip on top of the slide, and not on top of one of the objects included in the slide. Use the following table to make sure you associate each audio file with the right slide:

> To avoid any problems during the drag-and-drop of audio files to the slides, you can drag audio clips to the slide thumbnails in the **Filmstrip** panel as well. This makes the process go even faster and avoids the potential for associating the narration with an object rather than the slide.

Slide #	Audio clip	Slide #	Audio clip
5	slide05.mp3	10	slide10.mp3
6	slide06.mp3	11	slide11.mp3
7	slide07.mp3	16	slide16.mp3
8	slide08.mp3	18	slide18.mp3

Editing a sound clip in Captivate

Even though Captivate is not an audio-editing application, it does have some basic audio-editing capabilities.

In the next exercise, you will use the audio-editing capabilities of Captivate to finalize the chimes sound you recorded with the new System Audio feature of Captivate 7 back in *Chapter 2, Capturing the Slide*.

1. If needed, return to the `encoderDemo_800.cptx` file.
2. Use the **Filmstrip** panel to go to slide 17.
3. Make sure the **Properties** panel shows the properties of the slide.
4. Click on the **Edit Audio...** button situated in the **Audio** section of the **Properties** panel. Alternatively, you can also navigate to **Audio | Edit | Slide** to do the same thing.

Chapter 6

5. The **Slide Audio** dialog box opens on the **Edit** tab (shown as **(1)** in the following screenshot):

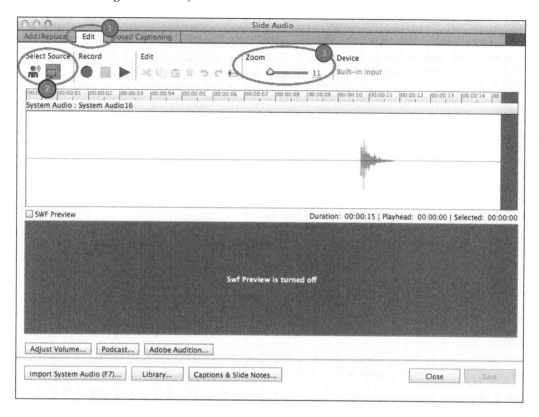

What's new in Captivate 7 is the ability to choose the audio source (shown as **(2)** in the preceding screenshot). This audio source can be Narration, System Audio, or both Narration and System Audio. The only sound clip associated with this slide is the chimes sound that is on the System Audio track as discussed in *Chapter 2, Capturing the Slide*.

6. Make sure the source selector (shown as **(2)** in the preceding screenshot) is set to **System Audio** only.
7. If needed, use the **Zoom** feature (shown as **(3)** in the preceding screenshot) to zoom out and have a look at the entire sound clip.
8. Click on the **Play** button to listen to the entire audio clip. Try to associate what you hear with the graphical representation of the sound as displayed in the **Slide Audio** dialog.

Working with Audio

In an audio clip, silence takes up as much space as the sound itself. Deleting the silence at the beginning and at the end of a sound clip is an operation that should be done systematically for every sound clip, as it helps in keeping the size of the resulting movie as low as possible.

9. Click-and-drag the clip from its beginning until the sound begins to select the silence located before the actual chimes sound and delete it.
10. Do the same with the period of silence located after the chimes sound.
11. Click on the **Play** button to test the new version of the clip.

Another thing that you can do is adjust the audio volume of the sound effect. You will now use the **Adjust Volume** feature of Captivate to finalize the System Audio chimes sound of slide 17.

12. Click on the **Adjust Volume...** icon situated in the bottom-left corner of the **Slide Audio** dialog.
13. Take some time to review the options of the **Adjust Volume** box, but do not change any of them at this time.
14. In the **Audio Processing** section of the **Adjust Volume** dialog box, select the **Normalize** option and click on the **OK** button.

Normalizing an audio clip is finding the best audio level for that particular sound clip.

> **Blog post**
>
> If you want to know more about the normalization process, I've written an entire blog post on this topic. It can be found at http://www.dbr-training.eu/index.cfm/blog/producing-high-quality-audio-content-for-captivate-part-1-normalization/.

The chimes sound effect you captured with the new System Audio feature of Captivate 7 is now final.

15. Click on the **Save** button situated at the bottom-right corner of the **Slide Audio** dialog.
16. Click on the **Close** button to close the **Slide Audio** dialog.

The last thing to do is to properly position the chimes sound on the **Timeline** panel.

17. Use the **Play** button in the bottom-left corner of the **Timeline** panel to spot the location where the yellowish progression bar reaches the end of its track, which marks the end of the encoding process.

18. Move the sound clip to the spotted location. Don't hesitate to click on the **Play** icon again to control the proper timing of the sound clip.

When done, the **Timeline** panel of slide 17 should look similar to what is shown in the following screenshot:

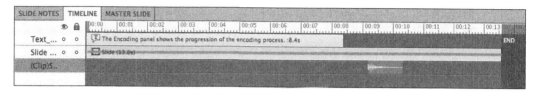

Extra credit – synchronizing the audio clips

Browse the remaining audio-enabled slides of the project and adjust the timing of the objects they contain so that they appear in sync with the narration.

Refer to the `encoderDemo_800.cptx` file under `Chapter06/final` for examples and inspiration, and don't forget to save the file when done.

This section concludes the first part of your exploration of audio added at the slide level. Before moving on, here is a quick summary of what has been covered:

- Most of the time, the audio added at slide level is used to add voice-over narration to the project.
- To insert a sound clip in your project, you can either record it entirely from within Captivate or import it from your hard disk.
- You must check the audio options of your operating system before recording the first sound clip with Captivate.
- Captivate has an auto-calibrating feature to help you find the right sensitivity for the microphone.
- When an audio clip is associated with a slide, the **Timeline** panel shows it as an extra layer situated below the slide.
- Captivate provides some basic sound-editing capabilities.
- In the **Slide Audio** dialog of Captivate 7, you can choose the audio source of the clip you are editing. This audio source can be Narration, System Audio, or both Narration and System Audio.
- The silence present at the beginning and at the end of an audio clip takes up as much disk space as the actual sound. It should be removed on every single sound clip used in Captivate.

- Normalizing an audio file is finding the right volume for that particular file. This operation should be done on every sound clip used in the project. (Note that it can be done in an external audio application before the clip is inserted in Captivate.)
- When inserting an audio clip onto a slide, the **Timeline** panel of that slide must be reorganized in order to make the audio and the objects of the slide play in sync.
- Use the **Play** button of the **Timeline** panel to quickly and easily test the synchronization between the audio and the objects of the slide.

Using Text-to-Speech to generate narration

The idea of the Text-to-Speech feature is to type the voice-over narration in the **Slide Notes** panel and have Captivate convert it to a sound clip. To convert typed text to sound clips, Captivate uses some pre-installed voice packages called **speech agents**.

Installing the Captivate speech agents

Due to their very large size, Adobe decided to make the installation of the Text-to-Speech agents optional. Captivate 7 ships with one voice-package that installs several speech agents for various languages.

The speech agents of Captivate can be downloaded from the following locations:

- `http://www.adobe.com/go/Cp7_win32_voices_installer`
  (for Windows 32 bit)
- `http://www.adobe.com/go/Cp7_win64_voices_installer`
  (for Windows 64 bit)
- `http://www.adobe.com/go/Cp7_mac_voices_installer` (for Mac)

 It is required to install the Text-to-Speech agents to do the exercise that follows.

Working with the Slide Notes panel

The basic idea of Text-to-Speech is to transform a piece of typed text into a sound clip. In Captivate, you use the **Slide Notes** panel to type the text you want to convert to speech.

By default, the **Slide Notes** panel is not part of the **Classic** workspace, so your first task is to turn it on.

1. Go to the `drivingInBe.cptx` file under `Chapter06`. Use the **Filmstrip** panel to go to slide 2.
2. Navigate to **Window | Slide Notes** to turn the **Slide Notes** panel on.

By default, the **Slide Notes** panel appears at the bottom of the screen next to the **Timeline** panel.

At the far right-hand side of the panel, the + icon is used to create a new slide note.

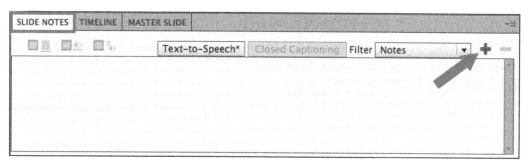

3. Click on the + icon to add a new slide note.
4. Type `So, you've decided to take a trip to Belgium!` in the new slide note.
5. Click on the + icon to add a second slide note after the first one.

This part is a bit tricky! Do not hit the *Enter* key when you have typed the first slide note. The *Enter* key does not validate the new slide note but creates a new paragraph in the slide note. Also, before adding a second slide note, make sure that your cursor is still within the first one; otherwise, the second slide note appears before the first one. If the second note appears before the first, you can use the - icon to delete the topmost note, or you can drag-and-drop the notes to reorder them.

6. Type `With the tips and tricks provided in this video, you'll soon be on your way to discover Belgium's treasures on a safely fashion.` in the second note.
7. Add a third note to the **Slide Notes** panel and type `Type your name in the box to get started!` in it.
8. If needed, drag and drop the notes within the **Slide Notes** panel to reorder them.

When typing the text in the **Slide Notes** panel, keep in mind that a machine will soon convert it into an audio clip. This machine will not work right if the spelling is not perfect, so double-check (and even triple-check) your spelling. If the spelling is wrong, you'll get unexpected (and sometimes hilarious!) results.

9. Use the **Filmstrip** panel to browse through the remaining slides of the project. Note that Slide Notes have already been added where needed.

Now that the Slide Notes have been correctly typed and carefully ordered, you can safely convert them to audio using the Text-to-Speech feature of Captivate.

Converting text to speech

Converting the text typed in the **Slide Notes** panel to speech is not difficult. All you need to do is to choose the note(s) to be converted, assign a speech agent to each note, and generate the audio file.

1. While still in the `drivingInBe.cptx` file under `Chapter06`, use the **Filmstrip** panel to return to slide 2.
2. At the top of the **Slide Notes** panel, click on the **TTS** checkbox to select all three notes as shown in the following screenshot:

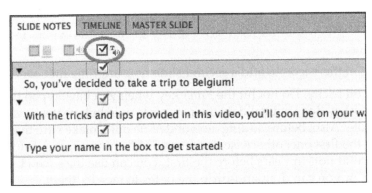

Most of the time, you'll want to convert every single slide note to speech. But, if needed, you can deselect the notes that do not need to be converted to speech.

3. Click on the **Text-to-Speech** button situated at the top of the **Slide Notes** panel. The **Speech Management** box opens.

The **Speech Management** box is where you assign a speech agent to the Slide Notes you selected for Text-to-Speech conversion. The number of available speech agents depends on the voice packs installed on the system. See the *Installing the Captivate speech agents* section for more details. Captivate also picks up third-party speech agents installed on the system.

For this exercise, you will use two speech agents: Kate and Paul. These speech agents are designed for US English text only and are included in the voices installer of Captivate.

4. In the **Speech Management** box, select all three Slide Notes (if needed). Open the **Speech Agent** dropdown and choose **Kate**.

For this first experience with Text-to-Speech, you will assign the same speech agent to every note.

5. Click on the **Generate Audio** button situated at the bottom-left corner of the box. A progress bar appears on the screen as the audio is generated.
6. When the progress bar disappears, click on the **Close** button to close the **Speech Management** dialog.
7. Return to the **Timeline** panel.

Surprise! The **Timeline** panel now shows a sound clip layer beneath the slide layer.

8. Move the sound clip half a second to the right.
9. Use the **Play** button of the **Timeline** panel to test the audio clip and the slide timing.

Normally, the timing of the slide should pretty much be fine, but if you want to adjust it, feel free to reorganize the objects on the **Timeline** panel.

10. Open the **Library** panel. In the **Audio** section, you should see an audio clip named **Text to Audio 1**. (It could be a different number if you did not get it right the first time when generating the audio clip.)
11. Right-click on the **Text to Audio 1** clip in the **Library** panel and choose the **Rename** command in the contextual menu.
12. Change the name of the audio clip to `TTS-Slide2` and hit the *ENTER* key to validate.

The ability to change the name of an item in the **Library** panel is yet another feature that helps you manage the assets of the project.

13. Use the **Filmstrip** panel to go to slide 4 and open the **Slide Notes** panel.
14. In the **Slide Notes** panel, mark all three Slide Notes for Text-to-Speech conversion and click on the **Text-to-Speech** button.
15. The **Speech Management** dialog opens.
16. Select all three notes. In the **Speech Agent** dropdown, choose **Paul** and click on the **Generate Audio** button.
17. When the audio generation is complete, close the **Speech Management** dialog and return to the **Timeline** panel.

Again, an audio layer containing the generated sound clip has been added to the slide. Adjust the timing of the objects and of the audio so that everything plays in sync.

> **Text-to-Speech versus manual voice-over recording**
>
>
> Is Text-to-Speech better than an actual recording? A real recording takes a lot of time and, consequently, costs a lot more money. But the result is perfect and can be tailored to fit the needs of a particular project. The Text-to-Speech feature is fast, easy, and cheap; however, the result may sound like an old Game Boy. Another thing to consider is how easy it is to update the project if needed. Updating a Text-to-Speech audio file is dead easy. Just change the text in the **Slide Notes** panel and regenerate the audio. Modifying a recorded sound clip is much more difficult and costly. You may have to rent a sound studio, hire the narrator a second time, and so on. No solution is perfect. The choice is yours…

Using the Speech Management window

To generate the remaining audio files of the project, you will use the **Speech Management** window. This feature will speed you up and make your job a little bit easier. The idea is to mark Slide Notes for Text-to-Speech conversion throughout the entire project and generate the audio clips all at once at the end.

1. Browse the slides of the project one by one. In the **Slide Notes** panel, confirm that every Slide Note is marked for Text-to-Speech conversion.
2. When the Slide Notes of the entire project are marked, navigate to **Audio | Speech Management** to open the **Speech Management** window.

The window that has just opened is very similar to the one you used to generate the audio files of slides 2 and 4, except that this window shows the Slide Notes of the entire project rather than those of the active slide only.

3. In the **Speech Management** window, select the Slide Notes of slides 2 and 4.
4. Click on the – icon to remove the selected notes.

This action does not delete the actual Slide Notes. It only clears the checkbox that marks the notes for Text-to-Speech conversion. You have to do this because the audio for slides 2 and 4 has already been successfully generated.

5. A speech agent has been assigned to each note. Note that it is possible to assign a different speech agent to different notes of the same slide. You can change the assigned agents if you want to, but make sure you use only **Kate** and **Paul**, as those two particular agents are designed to convert US English text.

If possible, try to match the Characters' images you inserted in *Chapter 3, Working with Standard Objects*. Use **Paul** for slides where the male Character is present and **Kate** on slides where the female Character is present.

6. When done, click on the **Generate Audio** button situated in the bottom-left corner of the **Speech Management** dialog.

Captivate generates all the needed audio files, assigns them to the correct slide, and adds them to the **Library** panel.

7. When done, close the **Speech Management** window.
8. Review every slide of the project and make the necessary adjustments in the **Timeline** panel.
9. When done, save the file and use the Preview icon to preview the entire project in the **Preview** pane.

This exercise concludes your overview of the Text-to-Speech feature of Captivate. Here follows a quick summary of the key points that have been covered:

- The basic idea of Text-to-Speech is to convert a piece of text into an audio clip
- To do it, Captivate uses speech agents
- Captivate ships with a bunch of speech agents that are packed into an extra installer available on the Adobe website
- Each speech agent is designed for a specific language
- The **Slide Notes** panel is used to type the text to be converted to speech
- You can choose to convert every slide note to speech or just some of them
- A different speech agent can be assigned to different notes of the same slide
- The generated sound clips appear in the **Audio** section of the **Library** panel where their properties can be modified
- The **Speech Management** window provides a quick and easy way to convert all the Slide Notes of the project to speech at once

Working with Audio

Using the Advanced Audio Management window

In the following exercise, you will open the **Advanced Audio Management** window and take a quick look at all of the audio present in your project. The steps are as follows:

1. Make sure you are still in the `drivingInBe.cptx` file under `Chapter06`.
2. Navigate to **Audio** | **Audio Management...** to open the **Advanced Audio Management** window.

The **Advanced Audio Management** window contains a list of all the slides of the project along with their associated audio file(s), if any.

3. In the bottom-left corner of the **Advanced Audio Management** window, select the **Show object level audio** checkbox (shown as **(1)** in the following screenshot):

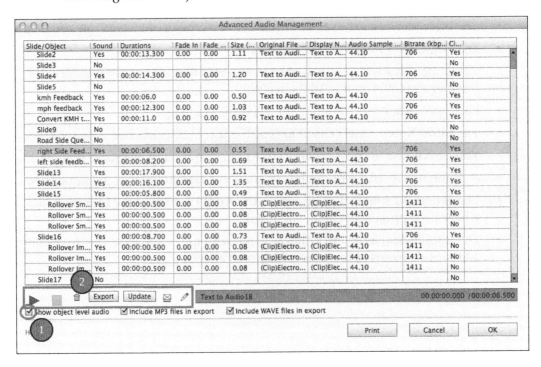

[266]

By selecting the **Show object level audio** checkbox, the list of audio files displayed in the **Advanced Audio Management** window includes all of the audio associated with the rollover objects of slides 15 and 16 of the project.

4. Select any of the audio files from the list.

When an audio file is selected in the **Advanced Audio Management** window, the buttons situated in the bottom part of the window are enabled (shown as **(2)** in the preceding screenshot). These buttons allow you to play the selected audio file, export it to a `.wav` and/or a `.mp3` file, edit the audio file, add Closed Captions, and more.

5. Take some time to inspect the controls of the **Advanced Audio Management** window. All the options should be self-explanatory.
6. Close the **Advanced Audio Management** window when done.
7. Save and close the `drivingInBe.cptx` file.

There really is nothing more to say about the **Advanced Audio Management** window. It is just a nice and easy way to have a general overview of all of the audio used in the project.

Adding Closed Captions to the slides

Closed Captions make your eLearning content more accessible and more interesting for the learners. There are many situations where Closed Captions are useful:

- They make your Captivate projects accessible for hearing-impaired students
- They make the project easier to understand for foreign students
- They are useful for learners who have to take the online course in an office and don't want to bother their colleagues with voice-over narrations

For these reasons (plus the ones not listed here), it is a good idea to use Closed Captions each time you add voice-over narration to a slide.

In Captivate, Closed Captions are always associated with a slide-level audio clip or with a Multi-Slide Synchronized Video inserted by navigating to **Video | Insert Video**.

As for Text-to-Speech narration, the text of the Closed Captions is found in the **Slide Notes** panel.

Working with Audio

In the next exercise, you will add Closed Captions to the Encoder Demonstration.

1. Return to the `encoderDemo_800.cptx` file under `Chapter06`. Use the **Filmstrip** panel to go to slide 3.

2. At the bottom of the screen, click on the **Slide Notes** tab to open the **Slide Notes** panel.

Slide 3 is the first slide of the movie you added narration to. There are six notes in the **Slide Notes** panel that exactly reflect what is said in the audio file associated with the slide.

3. At the top of the **Slide Notes** panel, click on the **Audio CC** checkbox situated right next to the **Text-to-Speech** checkbox. This operation is shown in the following screenshot:

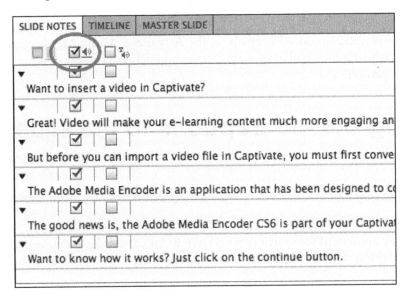

This action marks all the Slide Notes for Closed Captioning. Note that the **Audio CC** checkbox is available only if an audio file is associated with the slide. So, if you did not complete the previous exercises, you might not have the option to generate Closed Captions!

4. In the top-right corner of the **Slide Notes** panel, click on the **Closed Captioning** button.

[268]

Chapter 6

The **Slide Audio** box opens again, but this time, it shows the **Closed Captioning** tab (shown as **(1)** in the following screenshot):

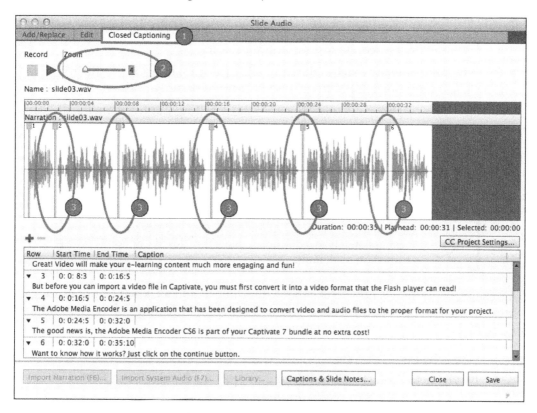

5. Use the zoom slider (shown as **(2)** in the preceding screenshot) to reduce the zoom level so you can see the entire sound clip.

Each of the vertical bars (shown as **(3)** in the preceding screenshot) represent one of the Slide Notes you marked for Closed Captioning.

6. Click on the **Play** button. While the audio is playing, note the current position of the yellow vertical bars as compared to the audio file.

7. If needed, adjust the position of the vertical bars and test again until all the Closed Captions are in sync with the audio.

8. When you are satisfied with the result, click on the **Save** button at the bottom-right corner of the **Slide Audio** dialog.

9. Close the **Slide Audio** dialog.

10. Repeat the procedure on each slide that has an associated audio file.

Don't forget to save the file when you are done!

[269]

Viewing Closed Captions

Now that Closed Captions have been added to every slide with associated audio, you will test the entire project in order to control the newly inserted Closed Captions.

1. Use the Preview icon to test the entire project.
2. When the preview reaches the third slide (the first one with audio and Closed Captions), notice that Closed Captions do not appear.

By default, Closed Captions do not appear in the resulting Captivate movie. It is up to the student to turn them on or leave them off while watching the movie.

To let the student turn them on and off, you need to add a Closed Captioning button on the Playback Controls bar that appears at the bottom of the movie in the **Preview** pane. To add this button, you need to use the **Skin Editor**.

[In *Chapter 11, Variables, Advanced Actions, and Widgets*, you will use an advanced action to have the Closed Captions turned on by default.]

This chapter only shows how to use the Skin Editor to add a Closed Captions toggle button to the Playback Controls bar. You will study other features of the Skin Editor in *Chapter 8, Finishing Touches and Publishing*.

3. Close the **Preview** pane.
4. Navigate to **Project | Skin Editor...** to open the floating **Skin Editor** panel.
5. On the left-hand side of the **Skin Editor** floating panel, select the **Closed Captioning** box to add a **CC** button on the Playback Controls bar.
6. Click on the **Settings...** button situated right below. The **CC Project Settings** dialog box pops up.

The **CC Project Settings** dialog box lets you fine-tune the formatting of the Closed Captions.

7. Choose a sans-serif font family (such as **Verdana** or **Arial**) and a font size of 12 points.
8. Click on the **OK** button to validate your choices and to close the **CC Projects Settings** dialog.
9. Click on the top-right corner of the floating **Skin Editor** panel to close it.

Everything is now ready to test the Closed Captions you have added to the project.

10. Use the Preview icon to test the entire project one more time.

11. When the project opens in the **Preview** pane, click on the **CC** button situated on the right-hand side of the Playback Controls bar to turn the Closed Captions on.
12. When the preview reaches slide 3, you should see the associated Closed Captions.

Make sure that Closed Captions play in sync with the audio. This contributes to making your projects accessible to students with disabilities.

Closed Captioning a video file

The last thing that you will do in this chapter is add Closed Captions to the video file you imported on slide 2 of the `encoderDemo_800.cptx` file. Note that you can add Closed Captions to a video file only if it has been imported as a Multi-Slide Synchronized Video.

1. Use the **Filmstrip** panel to return to slide 2. It is the slide where you imported the video file back in *Chapter 3, Working with Standard Objects*.
2. Click on the video to make it the active object. The **Properties** panel gets updated.
3. In the **Video** section of the **Properties** panel, click on the **Edit Video Timing** button. The **Edit Video Timing** dialog opens.

The **Edit Video Timing** dialog can be used to edit the imported video file. In this exercise, this is not exactly what you want to do. Actually, you only want to add Closed Captions to the video.

4. Click on the **Closed Captioning** tab situated at the top-left corner of the **Edit Video Timing** dialog.
5. Click on the + icon to add a new Closed Caption. Type `Hi, I'm Damien. I'll be your guide during this demonstration.`
6. Click on the + icon a second time to add a second Closed Caption. Type `To get started, click on the Continue button at the bottom of your slide.`

Note that two yellow vertical bars appear in the upper area of the **Edit Video Timing** dialog.

Watch out! It is possible that these two bars sit on top of each other at the same location, giving the false impression that there is only one vertical bar.

7. Move these vertical bars to synchronize Closed Captions with the video file. This is the exact same procedure as for Closed Captions associated with the slide audio.
8. Click on the play button in the top-left corner of the **Edit Video Timing** box to test the synchronization between the video and Closed Captions. It will probably be necessary to adjust the position of the vertical bars and to retest the video a few times before the yellow bars are properly positioned.

At the end of this procedure, the **Edit Video Timing** dialog should look similar to what is shown in the following screenshot:

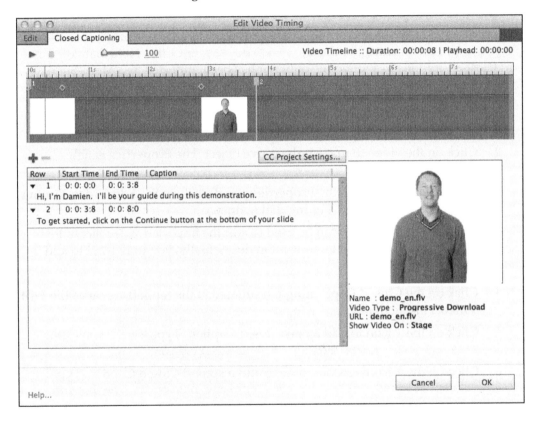

9. When done, click on **OK** to validate the changes and close the **Edit Video Timing** dialog.
10. Click on the Preview icon and choose to preview the entire project.
11. When the **Preview** pane appears, click on the **CC** icon of the Playback Controls bar to turn the Closed Captions on. Confirm that Closed Captions have been successfully added to the video file of slide 2.
12. Save the file when finished.

Extra credit – adding Closed Captions

Closed Captions can be added to every slide that has an associated audio file regardless of that audio file being imported from an external application or generated with the Text-to-Speech feature. In this section, you will add Closed Captions to the *Driving in Belgium* project. As a reminder, these are the basic steps to follow:

- Use the **Filmstrip** panel to go to a slide that has an associated audio clip. These slides can be easily identified thanks to the loudspeaker icon that appears next to the slide thumbnail.
- In the **Slide Notes** panel, convert every note to Closed Captions using the **Audio CC** checkbox.
- Click on the **Closed Captioning** button to open the **Slide Audio** dialog.
- Move the vertical yellow marks to synchronize Closed Captions with the audio clip.
- Use the **Play** button to test whether syncing between the audio and Closed Captions is good.
- Repeat the procedure on every slide with an associated audio.
- To test Closed Captions, don't forget to add the **CC** button to the Playback Controls bar by navigating to **Project | Skin Editor**.

This exercise concludes your overview of the Closed Captioning system of Captivate. Here is a quick summary of what has been covered:

- Closed Captions are associated either with a slide-level audio clip or with a Multi-Slide Synchronized Video.
- The text of Closed Captions associated with a slide-level audio clip is found in the **Slide Notes** panel.
- The **Slide Notes** panel is not displayed in the default **Classic** workspace. Navigate to **Window | Slide Notes** to turn it on.
- The text of the Closed Captions associated with a video file is found in the **Closed Captioning** tab of the **Edit Video Timing** dialog box.
- In the resulting movie, Closed Captions are turned off by default. It is the student who has to turn them on.
- Use the **Skin Editor** floating pane to add the **CC** button to the Playback Controls bar. The **CC** button is used by the student to turn Closed Captions on or off.

Summary

In this chapter, you have imported sound effects into objects, voice-over narration on slides, and background music on the entire project.

The first thing to keep in mind is that this chapter only introduces you to the most typical use cases. In practice, nothing prevents you from adding voice-over narration at object level, music at slide level, and sound effects at project level. There are certainly lots of creative ways to use sound in Captivate, with your creativity being the ultimate limit to what is possible to achieve.

To produce the needed audio files, Captivate offers the ability to record your own clips. But you can also import audio clips produced in an external application or convert text typed in the **Slide Notes** panel to speech using one of the speech agents provided by Captivate or already present on the system.

Wherever they are coming from, these audio files make your eLearning content much more interesting, interactive, accessible, and fun to use.

When adding voice-over narration, it is a good idea to add Closed Captions as well. Closed Captions greatly enhance the usability and accessibility of your Captivate movie. The same Slide Notes used for Text-to-Speech can also be used to generate Closed Captions.

With the addition of audio files to your projects, you have reached yet another milestone in the post-production phase. But before you can finally make your projects available to the outside world, there is one more feature to talk about.

In the next chapter, you will use one of the most powerful and widely used features of Captivate. By adding Quizzes and Question Slides into your projects, you will put yet another extraordinary tool in your teaching toolbox.

Meet the community

In this section, I want to introduce you to Allen Partridge. Allen is one of the Adobe eLearning evangelists. He is one of the main contributors to the official Captivate blog. He is also one of the favorite faces found in the countless Captivate videos that you can find on the official YouTube channel of Captivate. Allen is an awesome speaker and a wonderful teacher. His teaching background makes him an invaluable asset to the Captivate community. I had the chance to meet with Allen in the summer of 2013. It was one of the highlights of my trip to California and I keep a vivid memory of that moment.

Allen Partridge

Dr. Allen Partridge is an eLearning evangelist for Adobe. In addition to his work for Adobe Systems, he continues to serve on the doctoral faculty in the Communications Media and Instructional Technology program at Indiana University of Pennsylvania.

He has written several books and a host of articles on topics ranging from 3D game development to instructional design for new technologies. He is active in the explorations of immersive learning as well as traditional multimedia enhanced by eLearning and rapid eLearning. He works closely with the eLearning Suite and Captivate teams at Adobe, providing a channel to customer needs and concerns and helping facilitate communication among team members.

Contact details

- **Blog**: http://blogs.adobe.com/captivate/
- **Twitter**: @adobeElearning
- **Facebook**: http://www.facebook.com/adobecaptivate
- **LinkedIn**: http://www.linkedin.com/in/doctorpartridge
- **YouTube**: http://www.youtube.com/adobeelearning/

7
Working with Quizzes

Assessing students' knowledge has always been one of the primary concerns of anyone involved in some kind of teaching activity. When it comes to eLearning, addressing the assessment issue is both a pedagogical and a technical challenge.

On the pedagogical side, one of the factors that characterize the eLearning experience is the fact that the learners sit alone in front of their computer with no one around to assist them. As teachers, we have to leave lighthouses along the learner's path in order to make sure that the lonely learner does not get lost and confused. Constant assessment might help in keeping the students on track. By giving them many opportunities to test and validate their new knowledge, the students can immediately identify the areas of the course that deserve more attention and can build new knowledge on solid grounds.

On the technical side, Captivate contains a powerful quizzing engine that lets you insert different kinds of **Question Slides** in your projects. At the end of the quiz, Captivate is able to send a detailed report to a **Learning Management System (LMS)**. It is a server that is able to host eLearning content and track the learner's progression into the online courses it hosts.

In this chapter, you will perform the following:

- Insert various kinds of Question Slides in your Captivate projects using several different techniques
- Explore how some of the objects of Captivate can be added to the quiz
- Create a Question Pool and insert random Question Slides in the project
- Create a Pretest
- Explore and set Quiz Preferences
- Provide feedback to the students by using the branching capabilities of the Question Slides and the quiz

- Set up the reporting to an LMS server
- Discuss the SCORM and AICC standards used to communicate the quiz results to the LMS server
- Use the alternative quiz reporting features of Captivate in case no LMS is available

Preparing your work

For the exercises in this chapter, you will use both the Driving in Belgium and the Encoder Demonstration applications. Perform the following steps to prepare Captivate:

1. Open Captivate and ensure that the **Classic** workspace is currently applied.
2. Navigate to **Window** | **Workspace** | **Reset 'Classic'** to reapply the original default workspace.
3. Open the drivingInBe.cptx file under the Chapter07 folder.
4. Also open the encoderDemo_800.cptx file under the Chapter07 folder.

Introducing the quiz

During the first part of this chapter, you will insert a quiz at the end of the Driving in Belgium project. It is very important to introduce the quiz to the students and to explicitly explain what is going to happen. To help you do this, we have already prepared two slides for you, so all you have to do is copy and paste them into the Driving in Belgium project. These two slides are used to introduce the quiz to the students and give them precise instructions on how the quiz is supposed to be taken. So all you have to do is copy and paste them into the Driving in Belgium project using the following steps:

1. Make sure you are at Chapter07/drivingInBe.cptx.
2. Use the **Filmstrip** panel to go to slide 16.

Slide 16 is the last slide of the actual course. You want your quiz to be inserted in between slide 16 and the final slide of the project.

3. Open the dib_quizIntro.cptx file under the Chapter07 folder.
4. In the **Filmstrip** panel, select both slides of the dib_quizIntro.cptx file.
5. Press *Ctrl* + *C* (Windows) or *cmd* + *C* (Mac) to place both slides in the clipboard.
6. Return to slide 16 of the drivingInBe.cptx file.

7. Use the *Ctrl + V* (Windows) or the *cmd + V* (Mac) shortcut to paste the slides.

Remember that new slides are always inserted after the active slide. In this case, the two slides that you are pasting are included as slides 17 and 18 of the `drivingInBe.cptx` project. Also note how these two slides are picking up the Theme that is applied to the project.

8. Use the **Filmstrip** panel to return to slide 16.
9. Use the Preview icon to preview the **Next 5 slides**.

This gives you the chance to experience the new slides in a manner that is close to what your students will experience while taking the test.

10. When the preview is finished, close the **Preview** pane.
11. Close the `dib_quizIntro.cptx` project.

At the end of this procedure, there should be 19 slides in the project.

Creating Question Slides

In Captivate, a Question Slide is a very special kind of slide. When inserting the first Question Slide in a project, you automatically create a quiz. There are many options that you can set either for each specific Question Slide or for the entire quiz.

Captivate supports eight types of Question Slides. In this section, you will insert and explore each of these Question Types one by one.

A single quiz per project

Although very powerful, the quiz engine of Captivate has some limitations. While it is possible to insert regular slides in between the Question Slides, all the Question Slides of a project will always belong to the same quiz. In other words, there can only be a single quiz in each project. There are some workarounds to this limitation, some of which are described in this great blog post by Lieve Weymeis, available at `http://blog.lilybiri.com/creating-customized-question-slides-using-adv`.

Working with Quizzes

Inserting the first Question Slide

To get started, you will now insert the first Question Slide in your project using the following steps:

1. Return to the `drinvingInBe.cptx` file under the `Chapter07` folder.
2. Use the **Filmstrip** panel to go to slide 18.
3. Navigate to **Insert | Question Slide...**. The **Insert Questions** dialog box opens.

The **Insert Questions** dialog box provides a list of all the types of Question Slides available in Captivate. For this first example, you will add a single **Multiple Choice** question to the project.

4. In the **Insert Questions** dialog, select the **Multiple Choice** checkbox.
5. Open the **Graded** drop-down list associated with the **Multiple Choice** checkbox.

The drop-down list provides three options: **Graded**, **Survey**, and **Pretest**:

- **Graded**: This type of question has right and wrong answers. For example, *Is Belgium a multilingual country? (True/False)* is a question that has a right and a wrong answer, so it is a Graded question (by the way, the answer is *True*!).
- **Survey**: This type of question is used to gather the learner's opinion about something. As such, it has no right or wrong answer. For example, *Would you recommend this eLearning course to your friends? (Yes/No)* is a Survey question.
- **Pretest**: This type of question is not part of the quiz and its answer is not reported to the server. A Pretest is used to assess the student's knowledge before taking the course. It is possible to add branching based on the outcome of the Pretest. For example, the student that passes the Pretest can skip the course if he or she wants to, but the student that fails the Pretest has to take the course to gain the required knowledge.

In this case, you want to add a single Graded Multiple Choice question.

6. Select **Graded** in the drop-down list.

7. Make sure that the **Insert Questions** dialog looks like the following screenshot:

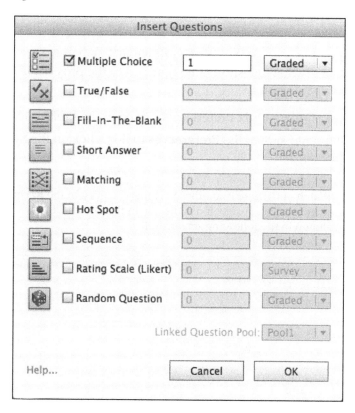

8. Click on the **OK** button to generate the Question Slide and to close the **Insert Questions** dialog.

Take a look at the **Filmstrip** panel. It now contains *21 slides*. This means that the operation you just completed has added *two* slides to the project.

As expected, the Multiple Choice question Slide has been inserted after the slide that was selected. In this case, the Multiple Choice question is slide 19. Because the new slide is the first Question Slide of the project, Captivate has also generated the **Quiz Results** slide as slide 20.

The **Quiz Results** slide contains a lot of automatically generated elements.

9. Use the **Filmstrip** panel to go to slide 20.
10. Inspect the various elements that have been automatically added to this slide.

Working with Quizzes

Most of these elements are self-explanatory. The only element that probably requires an explanation is the **Review Area**. This area is used to display feedback messages to the student at the end of the quiz. The content of that message depends on the outcome of the quiz.

The **Quiz Results** slide is generated by default when a new quiz is created (or in other words, when the first Question Slide is added to the project). It is possible to turn this slide off if you want to.

11. Navigate to **Quiz | Quiz Preferences...** to open the **Preferences** dialog.
12. On the left-hand side of the **Preferences** dialog, click on the **Settings** category of the **Quiz** section.

[Watch out! There is another **Settings** category in the **Recording** section. Make sure you use the one in the **Quiz** section, as shown in the following screenshot:]

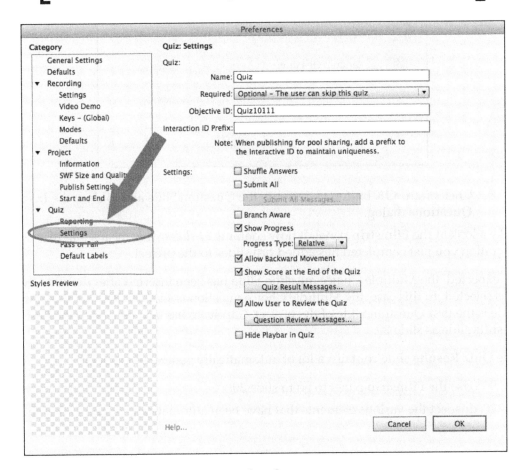

[282]

13. Deselect the **Show Score at the End of the Quiz** checkbox.
14. Click on the **OK** button to apply the changes and close the **Preferences** dialog.

When the operation is completed, take another look at the **Filmstrip** panel. Note that slide 20 is grayed out and that an eye icon appears under its thumbnail. This means that the slide is hidden. In other words, it is still in the project, but it won't be displayed to the student!

15. On the **Filmstrip** panel, click on the eye icon associated with slide 20.

This action turns the visibility of slide 20 back on. This action is equivalent to returning to the **Preferences** dialog to turn the **Show Score at the End of Quiz** checkbox back on.

Turning the visibility of slides on and off

Turning the visibility of slides on and off is not limited to the **Quiz Results** slide. You can actually use this handy feature on any slide of the project. Simply right-click on a slide in the **Filmstrip** panel and choose **Hide Slide** in the menu. This might be useful when a slide has been updated, but you want to retain a record of the original slide. It can also be used on multilingual projects to hide or show the slides pertaining to a particular language version.

Using the Multiple Choice question

The basic principle of a Multiple Choice question is to provide multiple possible answers to a given question. The student has to choose the correct answer from a predefined list.

In the following exercise, you will configure the Multiple Choice question you added in the previous section using the following steps:

1. Return to the `drivingInBe.cptx` file under the `Chapter07` folder.
2. Use the **Filmstrip** panel to go to slide 19.

Slide 19 is the first Question Slide of the project. As you can see, lots of objects have been automatically generated on this slide.

Watch out! It is possible that some objects sit on top of other objects. For example, move the orange *Incomplete Caption* to reveal the *Correct Caption*!

Working with Quizzes

The purpose of most of the generated objects should be obvious, but some of them require more explanation as follows:

- The **Review Area** is related to the **Review Quiz** button situated on the **Quiz Results** slide (currently slide 20). If the user clicks on that button at the end of the quiz, he or she will be allowed to review the quiz. In such a case, the **Review Area** is used to display an appropriate feedback message to the student.
- The student uses the four buttons at the bottom of the slide (**Clear**, **Back**, **Skip**, and **Submit**) to interact with the quiz. It is possible to control the visibility of each of those buttons either for the entire quiz or for each a specific Question Slide.
- The **Progress Indicator** in the lower-left corner of the slide can also be customized in the **Preferences** dialog.
- During the quiz, the feedback messages situated on the right-hand side of the slide are all hidden by default. They are automatically revealed depending on the student's answer to the question.

Every element of the Question Slide can be customized. If needed, you can even insert extra objects (such as Images, Animations, or additional Text Captions) using the same techniques as those for a standard slide.

Understanding the basic question properties

Text Captions are used to display the question and the list of possible answers. Your next task is to customize these answers using the following steps:

1. Double-click on the Text Caption that reads **Type the question here** to select it in the Edit mode. When done, triple-click on the same object to select its content.
2. Type `What are the three official languages of Belgium?`, and when you are done, hit the *Esc* key.
3. Resize the Text Caption so that the entire question sits on a single line of text.
4. If needed, move the Text Caption so that it does not overlap with any other slide element.
5. Double-click on the first possible answer to select it in the Edit mode, then triple-click on the same object to select its entire content. Type `French` as the first possible answer.
6. Use the same technique to write `English` as the second possible answer.

To make this question more interesting, you need to add some more possible answers to the list.

7. Open the **Quiz Properties** panel situated at the upper-right edge of the interface, next to the **Properties** and **Library** panels.
8. In the **General** section of the **Quiz Properties** panel, change the number of **Answers** to 5. Captivate generates three more answers on the Question Slide.
9. Type German, Dutch, and Spanish in the newly generated answers as shown in the following screenshot:

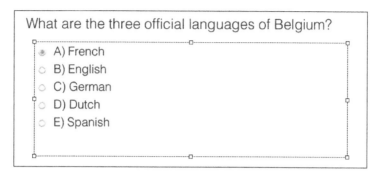

Currently, the Question Slide only accepts one of the answers from the list as the correct answer, but Belgium is a complicated country with three official languages! Fortunately, Captivate has an option that allows the Multiple Choice question to accept multiple correct answers.

10. In the **General** section of the **Quiz Properties** panel, select the **Multiple Answers** checkbox.

On the Question Slide, this action changes the radio buttons associated with each of the possible answers to checkboxes. You will now tell Captivate what the right answers are.

11. On the Question Slide, select all three correct answers (**French**, **German**, and **Dutch**).

Working with Partial Scoring

At this moment, the question is either entirely right (if the user selects all three correct answers) or entirely wrong (in every other case). **Partial Scoring** allows you to make this question partially correct if the student selects some of the right answers but not all. This advanced option is currently available on Multiple Choice questions only using the following steps:

1. In the **General** section of the **Quiz Properties** panel, select the **Partial Score** checkbox.

Note that by selecting the **Partial Score** checkbox, the **Points** and **Penalty** options of the **General** section are grayed out. When Partial Scoring is turned on, each possible answer of the Multiple Choice question is assigned a specific score.

2. Select the first possible answer of the Question Slide (**French**) and return to the **Properties** panel (don't confuse it with the **Quiz Properties** panel).
3. Open the **Advanced Answer Option** section of the **Properties** panel and change the **Points** of this answer to 5.
4. Select the second possible answer (**English**) and confirm it is worth **0 Points**.
5. Repeat the same procedure with the remaining possible answers. The **Dutch** and **German** answers should each grant **5 Points** to the student, while the **Spanish** answer is worth **0 Points**.

Now that Captivate is able to tell the right from the wrong answers, you can fine-tune some additional options of this Question Slide.

6. In the **General** section of the **Quiz Properties** panel, select the **Shuffle Answers** checkbox.

The **Shuffle Answers** checkbox asks Captivate to display the possible answers in a random order each time a student takes the quiz.

7. In the **Options** section of the **Quiz Properties** panel, deselect the **Incomplete** caption. This removes the yellow feedback message from the Question Slide.
8. Also deselect the **Next** checkbox to remove the **Skip** button from the slide.

Branching with Question Slides

The last thing to do with this Question Slide is implement branching based on how the student answers the question. Use the following steps to implement branching on this Question Slide:

1. In the **Action** section of the **Quiz Properties** panel, make sure the **On Success** action is set to **Continue.**
2. Also confirm that the **Attempts** option is set to **1**.
3. Open the **Last Attempt** drop-down list and inspect the available options.
4. Select the **Jump to slide** action and choose **4 Slide 4** in the **Slide** drop-down list that appears just below.

Slide 4 explains the multilingual status of Belgium. If the student does not answer this Multiple Choice question right, you want to redirect him or her to that slide in order to re-explain the particular topic.

5. Use the **Filmstrip** panel to return to slide 4 of the project.
6. In the **Properties** panel of the slide, take a look at the **Action** section.

The **Action** section of the **Properties** panel allows you to set special actions when the student enters or leaves the slide.

7. Open the **On Exit** drop-down menu and inspect the available options.
8. Choose the **Return to Quiz** action in the list.

If a Quiz is in progress, this action redirects the student to the current Question Slide. If no Quiz is in progress, this action has no special effect and the **Continue** action is assumed.

9. When done, use the **Filmstrip** panel to return to slide 19 of the project.

Finalizing the Question Slide

You're almost done! There are just some last things to do in order to completely finalize this first Question Slide.

1. Take some time to inspect the remaining options of the **Quiz Properties** panel, but do not change any of them at this time.

Pay particular attention to the following:

- You can still change the question **Type** (**Graded** or **Survey**) in the **General** section.
- You can set a **Time Limit** value to answer that particular question.

You will now take care of the two feedback messages.

2. Change the text of the green feedback message to `Great answer! Click anywhere to continue.`
3. Change the text of the red feedback message to `Sorry, your answer is not correct! The Official languages of Belgium are French, Dutch, and German. Belgian road signs might be in one or more of these languages. Click anywhere to continue.`
4. Move and resize these two feedback messages as you see fit. Remember that these messages will never be displayed at the same time, so it is not a problem if they overlap.

This concludes your exploration of the Multiple Choice question type. As you can see, there are a multitude of options available to help you fine-tune your assessments.

The Quizzing workspace

While setting up this first Question Slide, you had to switch between the **Properties** and **Quiz Properties** panels quite often. This can be cumbersome, but fortunately, Captivate has an easy solution. The **Quizzing** workspace rearranges the screen so that both the **Properties** and **Quiz Properties** panels are open at the same time. Feel free to switch to the **Quizzing** workspace for the other exercises of this section.

Importing Question Slides from a GIFT file

GIFT stands for **General Import Format Technology**. A GIFT file is a text file that allows you to use a simple text editor to write various types of questions. Such a text file can then be imported into various eLearning applications and systems, making it easy to share question banks across these systems.

New in Captivate 7 is the ability to import a GIFT file into your projects. Thanks to this new feature, you can import into Captivate questions that were originally created in another GIFT-compliant application. As of Version 7, Captivate can only import a GIFT file, but it cannot export the Question Slides of a Quiz into a GIFT file.

The GIFT format has been invented by Moodle, a popular open source LMS. To learn more about the GIFT format, see the following page on the official Moodle website: http://docs.moodle.org/26/en/GIFT.

In the following exercise, you will take a look at such a file and import it in the Driving In Belgium project using the following steps:

1. Open the `DIB-gift.txt` file under the `Chapter07` folder in a text editor such as Text Edit (Mac) or Notepad (Windows).

2. Take some time to read through this text file, making sure you don't change any of its content.

Even without knowing anything about the GIFT format, reading it is easy. This particular file contains three questions. The first one is a **Matching** question, the second a **Short Answer** question, and the last one is a **True/False** question.

3. Return to the `drivingInBe.cptx` file under the `Chapter07` folder and use the **Filmstrip** panel to return to slide 19.

4. Navigate to **Quiz | Import GIFT Format File** to import these three questions into Captivate.

5. Select the DIB-gift.txt file under the Chapter07 folder and click on **Open** to begin the importation process.

Captivate parses the GIFT file and creates three additional Question Slides in the project. These new slides are added after the selected one as slides 20, 21, and 22.

Creating a GIFT file

The GIFT file you just imported is a Moodle question bank that has been exported with the built-in export feature of Moodle. Some manual edits have been necessary to import it into Captivate with no errors. To learn more on creating question banks with Moodle, see http://docs.moodle.org/25/en/Question_bank. To learn more on exporting Moodle questions to a GIFT file, see http://docs.moodle.org/25/en/Export_questions.

Working with the Matching question

The first question that has been imported from the GIFT file is a Matching question. The basic idea is to provide two columns of elements. The student has to match an element of the first column with one or more element(s) of the second column. In the next exercise, you will take a look at the imported Matching question and modify some of its properties using the following steps:

1. Still at Chapter07/drivingInBe.cptx, use the **Filmstrip** panel to go to slide 20.
2. Take some time to inspect this slide and to compare it with the content of the GIFT file.

To make the question more interesting (and the answer more difficult to find), you will provide a different number of items in both columns.

3. In the **General** section of the **Quiz Properties** panel, increase the number of items of **Column 2** to 5.
4. Also select the **Shuffle Column 1** checkbox.

The **Shuffle Column 1** checkbox instructs Captivate to display the options of the first column in a random order each time a student takes the quiz.

You will now change the text of the two extra items of **Column 2**.

5. Type 30 km/h and Unlimited in the two extra items of **Column 2**.
6. Return to the **Quiz Properties** panel.
7. In the **General** section of the **Quiz Properties** panel, change the **Points** to 15.

Working with Quizzes

8. Select the **Motorway** item in the first column of the Matching question.
9. Open the drop-down list that appears in front of the **Motorway** item.

This drop-down list is used to tell Captivate the right answer. In this case, this operation is useless as the right answer is part of the information that has been imported from the GIFT file. Note that many items of the first column can match a single item of the second column. This ability can be used to create very interesting and complex Matching questions.

10. Click on an empty area of the slide to deselect the currently selected object and close the associated drop-down menu.
11. In the **Options** section of the **Quiz Properties** panel, deselect the **Incomplete** Caption to remove the yellow feedback message.
12. Also deselect the **Back** and **Next** options to remove the corresponding buttons from the slide.
13. Leave all the other options of the **Quiz Properties** panel at their current value.

Before moving on to the next question type, feel free to move and resize the objects of this slide per your taste. Remember that when it comes to aligning and resizing objects, some great tools are available on the Align toolbar. Make sure your slide looks like the following screenshot when done:

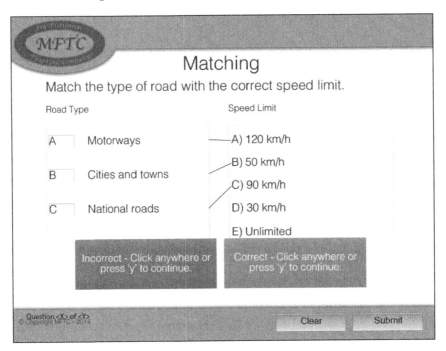

Working with the Short Answer question

The second question inserted from the GIFT file is a Short Answer question. In a Short Answer question, the student must supply a few words or a short sentence as the answer. Captivate then matches the supplied answer against a predefined list of correct answers. Let's take a look at the Short Answer question using the following steps:

1. Still at `Chapter07/drivingInBe.cptx`, use the **Filmstrip** panel to go to slide 21.
2. Take some time to inspect this slide and to compare it with the content of the GIFT file.
3. Select the big Answer Area situated in the middle of the slide. When selected, the **Correct Entries** box is displayed.
4. Compare the content of the **Correct Entries** box to the content of the GIFT file.

The **Correct Entries** box contains the list of entries that the answer provided by the student will be matched against. Note that you can add more correct answers by clicking on the + icon situated at the top-right corner of the **Correct Entries** box.

> **Coming up with the right question**
>
> As a teacher, coming up with the right question is always a challenge. This is especially true with the Short Answer question type. You need to find a question whose answer is obvious enough for a computer to correct, complicated enough to have some pedagogical value, and flexible enough to allow the students to type the same answer in different versions.

The main properties of this question are now in place. It's time for some fine-tuning.

5. In the **General** section of the **Quiz Properties** panel, change the **Points** value to 5 and the **Penalty** value to 1.

The **Penalty** value removes one point from the student's score if the wrong answer is given.

6. In the **Options** section of the **Quiz Properties** panel, deselect the **Incomplete** Caption. This removes the yellow feedback message and reveals the Success Caption that was underneath.

7. Also deselect the **Back** and **Next** options to remove the corresponding buttons from the slide.
8. Leave all the other options of the **Quiz Properties** panel at their current settings.
9. Don't hesitate to rearrange the elements of the slide as you see fit, keeping in mind that Success and Failure captions will never be displayed at the same time. Therefore, it is not a problem if they overlap.

That's it for the Short Answer question. Make sure your slide looks more or less like the following screenshot and save the file before moving on:

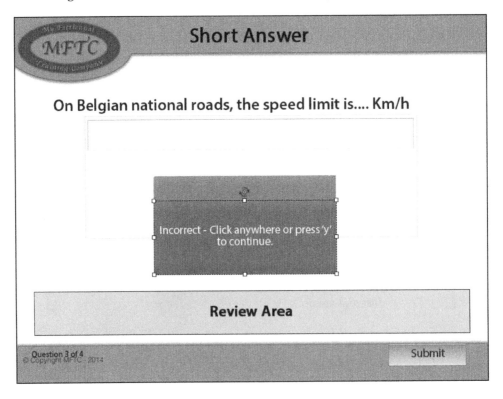

Working with the True/False question

The third question imported from the GIFT file is a True/False question. A True/False question actually is a Multiple Choice question with only two possible answers. By default, these two answers are *True* and *False*, but you can change these defaults to anything you like (such as Yes/No, Man/Woman, and so on) as long as there are no more than two different answers. Perform the following steps to explore and modify the imported True/False question type:

1. Still in the `drivingInBe.cptx` file, use the **Filmstrip** panel to go to Slide 22.

The GIFT file format does not allow you to change the default answers of a True/False question. In this case, these default values (**True** and **False**) do not integrate well with the question. Your first task is to adjust the possible answers so that the question actually makes sense.

2. Change the text of the **True** answer to `On the Left Side`. Resize the object accordingly.
3. Change the text of the **False** answer to `On the Right Side`. Resize the object accordingly.

This illustrates that the possible answers of a True/False question can actually be something else than *True* and *False*. The important point here is to ask a question that has no more than two possible answers, whatever these answers are.

4. Make sure that **On the Right Side** is selected as the correct answer.
5. In the **General** section of the **Quiz Properties** panel, change the **Points** to 5.

As usual, you will now fine-tune the other properties of this question slide.

6. In the **Options** section of the **Quiz Properties** panel, deselect the **Incomplete** Caption. This removes the yellow feedback message and reveals the Success Caption that was underneath.
7. Also deselect the **Back** and **Next** options to remove the corresponding buttons from the slide.
8. Leave all the other options of the **Quiz Properties** panel at their current settings.
9. Rearrange the elements of the slide as you see fit and customize the Success and Failure feedback messages at will.

Working with Quizzes

When done, your slide should look like the following screenshot:

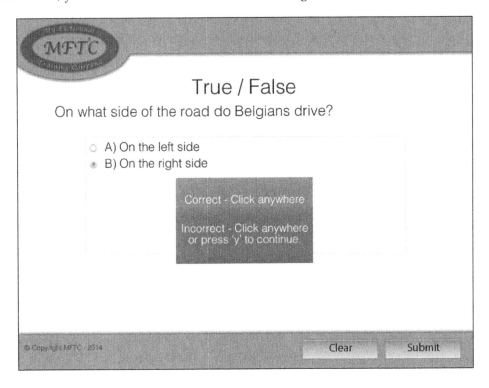

Adding the remaining Question Slides

To speed you up and let you focus on the Question Slide specifics, the remaining Question Slides of this project have already been created for you. They are stored at Chapter07/additionalQuestions.cptx. In this section, you will simply copy and paste the questions of the additionalQuestions.cptx file into the drivingInBe.cptx file:

1. Open the additionalQuestions.cptx file under the Chapter07 folder.
2. Use the **Filmstrip** panel of the additionalQuestions.cptx file to select the first slide of this project.
3. Press the *Shift* key and select slide 4 in the **Filmstrip** panel.

This action selects from slide 1 to slide 4. In other words, you have selected all but the last slide of the additionalQuestions.cptx file. The last slide of this project is the automatic **Quiz Result** slide of the quiz.

4. Use the *Ctrl + C* (Windows) or the *cmd + C* (Mac) shortcut to copy the selected slides to the clipboard.

5. Return to slide 22 of the `drivingInBe.cptx` file.
6. Use the *Ctrl* + *V* (Windows) or the *cmd* + *V* (Mac) shortcut to paste the slides.

Four Question Slides are added to the project after slide 22. At the end of this exercise, there should be 28 slides in the `drivingInBe.cptx` file.

7. Save the `drivingInBe.cptx` file.
8. Close the `additionalQuestions.cptx` file.

The stage is set for you to explore the remaining question types available in Captivate.

Working with the Fill-In-The-Blank question

The next question type is the **Fill-In-The-Blank** question. The idea is to take out one or more words from a given sentence. The student has to *fill in the blank(s)* either by typing the missing words or by choosing them from a drop-down list. Perform the following steps to use the Fill-in-The-Blank question type:

1. Use the **Filmstrip** panel to go to slide 23 of the `drivingInBe.cptx` file under the `Chapter07` folder.

Note the **On Belgian motorways, the speed limit is 120 km/h** sentence that has been typed for you. This sentence is the one from which some words will be taken out. In this case, you will delete the word **motorways** and replace it by a drop-down list of possible answers the students will have to choose from.

2. Select the word **motorways**.
3. In the **General** section of the **Quiz Properties** panel, click on the **Mark Blank** button.

Note that a dashed line now underlines the selected word. This is how Captivate marks the words that are taken out of the original sentence. You will now tell Captivate that you want to replace this word with a drop-down list.

4. Click on the underlined word until the **Correct Entries** box appears on the screen.
5. In the bottom-left corner of the box, change **User Input** to **Dropdown List** (see **1** in the following screenshot).
6. Click on the + icon (see **2** in the following screenshot) three times to add three additional entries in the list. There should now be four possible answers in the list.
7. Type `national roads`, `cities and towns`, and `railroad` as possible entries in the list.

Working with Quizzes

8. Show Captivate the right answer by selecting the **motorways** option (note that you can mark multiple entries as correct).
9. Select the **Shuffle Answers** checkbox.

The **Shuffle Answers** checkbox asks Captivate to display the options of the drop-down list in a random order each time a student takes the quiz.

Make sure your list looks like the following screenshot before moving on:

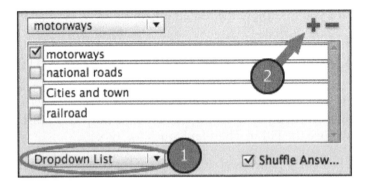

The other properties of this Question Slide have already been taken care of for you. Feel free to arrange the object contained on the slide as you see fit. You could, for example, apply the **[Default Failure Caption Style]** style to the Failure Caption and the **[Default Success Caption Style]** style to the Success Caption.

Spacing the answer

Captivate uses the width of the redacted words to generate the drop-down menu. If one of the items of the drop down is wider than the redacted word, it might not be completely visible in the drop-down menu. The workaround is to manually add some extra spaces in the Text Caption just after the redacted word.

That's it for the Fill-In-The-Blank question. Of course, it is possible to mark more than one blank in the same sentence. In such cases, Captivate awards points only if the whole sentence is correct. This question type does not support Partial Scoring and is therefore, completely right or completely wrong!

Working with the Hotspot question

The idea of the **Hotspot** question is to display an image on the slide and let the student choose the right spot(s) on this image. In this example, you will display road signs and ask the student to choose the sign that corresponds to a given situation using the following steps:

1. Return to the `drivingInBe.cptx` file under the `Chapter07` folder. Use the **Filmstrip** panel to go to slide 24.

Slide 24 has been imported from the `additionalQuestions.cptx` file. Note that an image containing various Belgian road signs has been added in the middle of the slide and that a single Hotspot is present. The student will be asked to click on the road sign(s) that gives the right of way.

In this example, two of the road signs present on the image are used to give the right of the way. Your next task is to add one more Hotspot to the slide and to position the Hotspots above the right answers.

2. In the **General** section of the **Quiz Properties** panel, change the number of **Answers** to 2.

This action generates a second Hotspot on the Question Slide.

3. Position the first Hotspot on top of the first road sign and the second hotspot on top of the last road sign. It may be necessary to resize the Hotspots.
4. Select one of the two Hotspots. In the **Fill & Stroke** section of the **Properties** panel, change the stroke **Width** to 0 to turn off the border of the selected Hotspot.
5. At the top of the **Properties** panel, click on the Create New Style icon.
6. Save the current formatting of the selected hotspot as `MFTC-transparentHotSpot`.
7. Apply the new **MFTC-transparentHotspot** style to the second hotspot.

The other options of this slide have already been taken care of for you. That being said, it is a good idea to take a closer look at the **Quiz Properties** panel to check out the available properties for a Hotspot question.

8. Arrange the elements of this slide as you see fit.

Working with Quizzes

At the end of this section, the Hotspot Question Slide should look similar to the following screenshot:

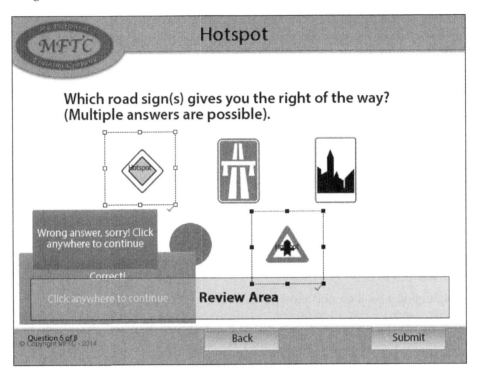

That's it for the Hotspot question! As you can see, there is nothing really difficult about this question type, just another great assessment tool in your teacher's toolset.

Working with the Sequence question

The idea of the **Sequence** question is to provide the student with a set of propositions that have to be arranged in the correct order. Perform the following steps to use the Sequence question:

1. Still at `Chapter07/drivingInBe.cptx`, use the **Filmstrip** panel to go to slide 25.
2. In the **General** section of the **Quiz Properties** panel, change the number of **Answers** to 5.

This action generates three additional steps. There should now be five steps in the sequence.

3. Change the text of the five steps to `Get a nice parking slot.`, `Turn off the engine.`, `Get out of the car.`, `Make sure the doors are locked.`, and `Visit Belgium!`.

Sizing the steps of the sequence

For some strange reason, it is not possible to change the height of an individual step after the text has been typed in. If needed, make sure to enlarge these Text Captions before typing the actual items of the sequence.

In this case, there is no need to show Captivate the right answer. Captivate will simply display these steps in a random order each time a student takes the quiz. The right answer is the order in which you typed the actions on the slide.

4. In the **General** section of the **Quiz Properties** panel, make sure the **Points** option is set to **10**. Also, add a **Penalty** value of **2** points.

These options instruct Captivate to add 10 points to the student's score in case the answer is right and to subtract 2 points from the score when the answer is wrong.

5. As usual, feel free to arrange the objects of this Question Slide as you see fit.

This concludes your overview of the Sequence question. There is one last question type to go through before you can give your quiz a first test run in the **Preview** pane.

Creating surveys with Likert questions

This one is a bit special. It is the only question type that *cannot be graded*. The **Rating Scale (Likert)** question is used to gather feedback and opinions, so there is no right or wrong answer for this type of question. The idea is to display statements on the screen and have the students specify their level of agreement to these statements using a rating scale.

Reporting Likert questions to an LMS

It is the LMS that determines what level of information may be extracted from the course. Some LMSs support a very detailed set of information, while other LMSs only support some basic information about the course and the quiz. Although Captivate sends a comprehensive report to the LMS, all the items of the Likert question might not be available for data analysis on the server. Check the documentation of your LMS to find out what exactly is supported. More on LMSs and reporting in the *Reporting scores to an LMS* section later in this chapter.

Working with Quizzes

In the following exercise, you will configure a Likert question using the following steps:

1. Go to slide 26 of the `drivingInBe.cptx` file under the `Chapter07` folder.
2. In the **General** section of the **Quiz Properties** panel, change the number of **Answers** to 3.
3. Open the **Rating Scale** drop-down list to reduce the scale to **3** items.

These actions create two extra statements and their corresponding objects on the slide. The **Rating Scale** option has left only three *levels of agreement* for each statement. This option is for the entire slide. It is not possible to set this option separately for each statement.

4. Change the text of the three statements to `I learned interesting things in this online course.`, `eLearning is a great learning solution`, and `I would recommend this course to a friend`.
5. Change the label of the three columns to `Disagree`, `Neutral`, and `Agree`.
6. Feel free to move and resize the objects of this slide as you see fit.

This question is a Survey question, so there is no right or wrong answer. Consequently, there are no green and red feedback messages available.

You will provide some feedback to the student by importing a regular slide in the middle of the quiz, right after the Survey question.

7. Open the `surveyFeedback.cptx` file under the `Chapter07` folder.

This file contains a single slide that will be used as the feedback message of the survey.

8. Copy and paste the single slide of the `surveyFeedback.cptx` file as slide 27 of the `drivingInBe.cptx` file.

This extra slide is situated after the Likert question, but before the **Quiz Results** slide. This illustrates the possibility to add a regular slide in the middle of the quiz.

 This extra slide also features another use of the **Characters** feature under the **Insert** menu. On this slide, transparent Text Captions have been carefully positioned right above the images of the actors. To give the illusion of text being written on the images, I have used two different **cursive fonts** and applied **Rotation** to both Text Captions.

9. Take some time to inspect the objects of this slide, their timing on the **Timeline**, and their properties in the **Properties** panel.

In this exercise, you have created a **Rating Scale (Likert)** Survey question and added an extra slide in the middle of the quiz to provide some feedback to the student.

Previewing the quiz

You now have one example of each possible question type in the project. Therefore, it is time to experience the Quiz hands-on! As you did not change any of the Quiz Preferences yet, you will live through the default Quiz experience. Perform the following steps to preview the Quiz:

1. Use the Preview icon to preview the entire project.
2. View the entire project as if it was the first time and take the Quiz as a regular student would.
3. When you reach the **Quiz Results** slide, click on the **Review Quiz** button.

The **Review Quiz** button takes you back to the first slide of the quiz. Use the Forward button of the Playback Controls to go through each Question Slide. Note how Captivate shows the right, wrong, incomplete, and expected answers.

When you get back to the **Quiz Results** slide, take some time to inspect the information it contains. Pay particular attention to the message in blue, written at the end of the slide (**Sorry you failed** or **Congratulations, you passed**). It is a general feedback message that depends on the outcome of the Quiz. Obviously, you have to set a *passing score* in order to let Captivate know when to display one or the other message.

4. Click on the **Continue** button to move on to the last slide of the movie.
5. When done, close the **Preview** pane to return to Captivate and save the file.

Remember that you did not change any of the Quiz Preferences yet. In the *The Quiz Preferences* section, you will review the options that allow you to customize the Quiz. But before that, you will take a deeper look at the Pretest feature.

Creating a Pretest

So far, you have created Graded and Survey questions. In this section, you will explore the Pretest questions. The Pretest questions are exactly the same as the Survey or Graded questions. What makes them special is the following:

- First, the Pretest questions are not part of the Quiz. Their result is not accounted for when generating the **Quiz Results** slide.

- Secondly, the Pretest questions are not part of the interaction report that is sent to an LMS (more on reporting to an LMS in the *Reporting scores to an LMS* section later in this chapter).

In the following exercise, you will insert a Pretest in the `encoderDemo_800.cptx` file using the following steps:

1. Open or switch to the `encoderDemo_800.cptx` file under the `Chapter07` folder.
2. Use the **Filmstrip** panel to go to slide 2.

Creating a Pretest question is a process that is very similar to creating a standard Graded or Survey question, so the Pretest has already been created for you in the `pretest.cptx` file under the `Chapter07` folder.

3. Open the `pretest.cptx` file under the `Chapter07` folder.
4. Use the **Filmstrip** panel to select slides 1, 2, 3, and 4 of the `pretest.cptx` file.
5. Copy the selected slides and return to the `encoderDemo_800.cptx` file.
6. In the **Filmstrip** panel of the `encoderDemo_800.cptx` file, right-click on slide 2 and paste the slides.

The four slides of the Pretest are inserted after slide 2. Slide 3 is a standard slide used to introduce the Pretest to the student. The actual Pretest is made of the next three slides. Slide 7 is automatically generated as the **Quiz Results** slide.

In order to better understand the Pretest feature, you will now test this project in the **Preview** pane to experience it hands-on.

7. Use the Preview icon to preview the entire project.

While in the **Preview** pane, there are some major changes to note. First, the Playback Controls Bar, at the bottom of the project, holds fewer controls than before! When a Pretest is inserted into a project, Captivate automatically disables most of the Playback Controls to prevent the student from skipping the Pretest.

After taking the entire quiz, the **Quiz Results** slide is displayed. Regardless of the answers you provided during the Pretest, your score will always be **0** and the **Total Questions** count will also always be **0**. Remember that the Pretest questions are *not* part of the actual Quiz!

8. Close the **Preview** pane when the preview is finished.
9. In the **Filmstrip** panel, right-click on the **Quiz Results** slide (slide 7) and click on **Hide Slide** in the Contextual menu.

Because the Pretest is not part of the Quiz, the **Quiz Results** slide of this project is useless and can be safely hidden.

In *Chapter 11, Variables, Advanced Actions, and Widgets*, you will use an Advanced Action to redirect the student to a different slide depending on the outcome of the Pretest.

At the end of this section, you have inserted one question of each type and explored the Pretest feature of Captivate. It is time to summarize what has been covered:

- There are eight types of Question Slides available in Captivate.
- Each question can either be a Graded, Survey, or Pretest question. The only exception to is the Rating Scale (Likert) question that can only be a Survey question.
- A Graded question has right and wrong answers. A Survey question is used to gather feedback and opinions from the students. As such, it does not have right or wrong answers. A Pretest question is not part of the quiz and is used to assess the student's knowledge before taking the online course.
- Navigate to **Insert** | **Question Slide** to insert Question Slides into the project.
- New to Captivate 7 is an option to insert questions from a GIFT file.
- When inserting the first Question Slide, Captivate automatically generates a **Quiz Results** slide. This slide can be hidden in the Quiz Preferences.
- The **Quiz Properties** panel is used to set up the options specific to each type of Question Slides.
- Each Graded question can be worth a different amount of **Points** when the student answers the question correctly. If the answer is not correct, it is possible to remove some points from the student's score by applying a **Penalty** value.
- Partial Scoring is available for Multiple Choice questions only.
- When a Pretest is inserted into a project, Captivate automatically turns off most of the Playback Controls to prevent the students from skipping the Pretest.

In the next section, you will concentrate on the Quiz Preferences.

Working with Quizzes

The Quiz Preferences

Now that you have a better idea of how a Quiz works by default, you will return to the **Preferences** dialog to take a deeper look at the available options using the following steps:

1. If needed, return to the `drivingInBe.cptx` file under the `Chapter07` folder.
2. Navigate to **Quiz** | **Quiz Preferences** to open the **Preferences** dialog.

By default, the **Preferences** dialog opens on the **Reporting** section. This section will be discussed later in this chapter.

3. On the left-hand side of the **Preferences** dialog, click on the **Settings** category of the **Quiz** section, as shown in the following screenshot:

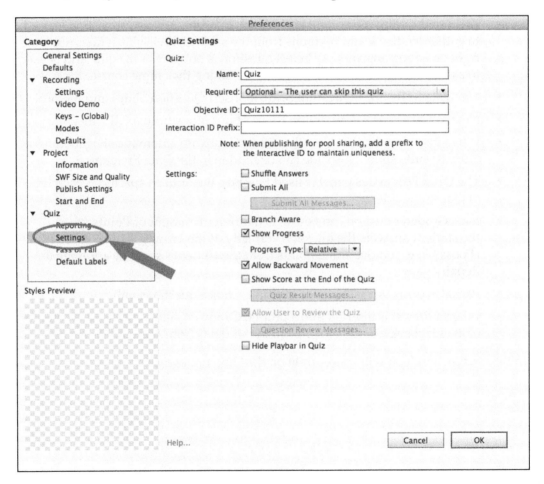

Take some time to review the options of this page.

[304]

4. Deselect the **Show Progress** checkbox. This removes the progress indicator situated in the bottom-left corner of the Question Slides.

The progress indicator is used to provide the students with an indication of their progress in the Quiz. The default progress indicator of Captivate can show the relative progress (**Question 1 of 3**) or the absolute progress (**Question 1**) to the student.

A customized progress indicator

Lieve Weymeis, also known as Lilybiri, is the queen of Advanced Actions. She has found a way to create a customized progress indicator using Advanced Actions and Variables. See her blog post at http://blog.lilybiri.com/customized-progress-indicator. Advanced Actions and Variables will be covered in Chapter 11, Variables, Advanced Actions, and Widgets.

5. Deselect the **Allow Backward Movement** checkbox.
6. Click on **Yes** to remove the (now not needed) **Back** buttons from the Question Slides.
7. Make sure the **Show Score at the End of Quiz** checkbox is selected.
8. Click on the **Quiz Results Messages...** button. The **Quiz Results Messages** dialog opens.

The **Quiz Results Messages** dialog is where you can customize the information that appears in the **Quiz Results** slide, at the very end of the Quiz.

9. Deselect the **Correct Questions** and **Total Questions** checkboxes.
10. Also, deselect the **Quiz Attempts** checkbox.

These actions remove the corresponding messages from the **Quiz Results** slide.

11. If needed, customize the **Pass Message** and **Fail Message**.

These are the messages that are displayed in **Review Area** of the **Quiz Results** slide at the end of the Quiz.

12. Click on the **OK** button to validate your changes and close the box.
13. Deselect the **Allow User to Review the Quiz** checkbox.

This action removes the **Review Quiz** button from the **Quiz Results** slide and **Review Area** from the Question Slides.

14. Select the **Hide Playbar in Quiz** checkbox.

Working with Quizzes

This option hides the Playback Controls during the Quiz. This is made to ensure students cannot use the Playback Controls to go back and forth in the Quiz or to skip the Quiz.

Also note the **Submit All** checkbox. When selected, the answers to the questions are all submitted together at the end of the Quiz. This allows the students to travel back and forth into the Quiz and change their answer to the questions.

15. Click on the **OK** button to validate the changes and close the **Preferences** dialog.
16. Use the **Filmstrip** panel to go to slide 28.

Slide 28 is the **Quiz Results** slide. Note that it contains less information than before and that the **Review Quiz** button has been removed. This matches the checkboxes configuration you created in the **Preferences** dialog.

Setting the passing score of a quiz

When the student reaches the **Quiz Results** slide, Captivate displays a message that depends on the outcome of the Quiz. To display this message, Captivate must be informed of what the passing score of the Quiz is. If the student reaches that passing score, Captivate displays the **Pass Message**; otherwise, the **Fail Message** is displayed.

In this section, you will set the passing score of the Quiz and add some branching.

First, you will import two more slides in the project and place them *after* the Quiz. One will congratulate the student who passes the Quiz, and the other one will ask the students who failed to take the test again later. Use the following steps to import these slides:

1. Open the `quizFeedback.cptx` file under the `Chapter07` folder.
2. Use the **Filmstrip** panel to select both the slides of this file and copy them.
3. Return to slide 28 of the `drivingInBe.cptx` file and paste the slides.

Chapter 7

After this procedure, the drivingInBe.cptx file should contain 31 slides, as shown in the following screenshot:

The stage is set! You will now return to the **Preferences** dialog to set the passing score of the Quiz and arrange branching.

4. Make sure you are *not* on slide 29 or 28 of the drivingInBe.cptx file.
5. Navigate to **Quiz | Quiz Preferences** to return to the **Preferences** dialog.
6. Click on the **Pass or Fail** category situated in the **Quiz** section of the **Preferences** dialog.

Working with Quizzes

The main **Pass or Fail** option is situated at the top of the dialog box. Note that there are two ways to set the passing score for a Quiz: as a *percentage* or as a certain amount of *points* to reach. Also, the total points are the sum of the points set for all the Question Slides of the Quiz (excluding the points of the Pretest slides, if any).

7. In the **Pass/Fail Options** section, set the passing score to 50 percent.

You will now configure the actions that have to take place when the student passes or fails the test.

8. In the **If Passing Grade** section, set the **Action** drop-down list to **Jump to slide**. Then, select **Quiz Passed Feedback** from the **Slide** drop-down list.

9. In the **If Failing Grade** section, allow the user one attempt and set the **Action** drop-down list to **Jump to slide**. Then, select **Quiz Failed Feedback** from the **Slide** drop-down list.

Setting the pass and fail options and adding some branching on the Quiz is that easy! Before moving on to the next step, take a quick look at the **Default Labels** preferences pane.

10. Click on the **Default Labels** category situated on the left-hand side of the **Preferences** dialog.

The **Default Labels** preferences are used to change the default text and the default formatting of the various elements of a Question Slide. It is best to change these options *before* the first Question Slide is added to the project. In this case, it is too late! But don't worry; you will take care of the formatting of the Quiz in an upcoming section.

11. Click on the **OK** button to validate the changes and close the **Preferences** dialog.

There is one more little thing to do in order to complete the branching system of the quiz.

12. Use the **Filmstrip** panel to go to slide 29.
13. Select the **Continue** button at the bottom-right corner of the slide.
14. In the **Action** section of the **Properties** panel, set the **on Success** action to **Jump to slide** and choose **slide 31** in the **Slide** drop-down list.
15. Use the Preview icon to test the entire project. When done, close the **Preview** pane and save the file.

Apart from the formatting, your Quiz is now up and running. In the next section, you will, however, add some spice to the mix by creating a Question Pool, but before that, let's make a quick summary of what you have just learned:

- By default, each Question Slide contains four buttons and a **Review Area**.
- By default, Captivate generates a **Quiz Results** slide and displays it at the end of the Quiz.
- By default, the **Quiz Results** slide contains the **Review Quiz** button that allows the student to return to each Question Slide and get feedback on the submitted answer.
- You can allow the students to go backward in the Quiz, but a submitted answer cannot be changed for another answer.
- The **Submit All** checkbox allows the students to change their answers until they submit all their answers together at the end of the Quiz.
- The **Preferences** dialog contains many options to let you fine-tune the student's experience. Some of these options are used to turn the objects of the Question Slides on or off.
- You can use the **Preferences** dialog to set the passing score of the quiz and to add branching that depends on the outcome of the Quiz.

Working with Question Pools

A **Question Pool** is a repository of Question Slides. The idea is to let Captivate randomly choose questions in the pool in order to create a unique Quiz for each student. You can have as many Question Pools as needed in a Captivate project, and each pool can contain an unlimited number of Question Slides.

Creating a Question Pool

In this example, you will create a single Question Pool, add six Question Slides to it, and ask Captivate to randomly choose one question from the pool and insert it into the Quiz.

Use the following steps to create a Question Pool:

1. Make sure you are still at `Chapter07/drivingInBe.cptx`.
2. Navigate to **Quiz | Question Pool Manager...** to open the **Question Pool Manager** dialog.

Working with Quizzes

The **Question Pool Manager** dialog is divided into two main areas:

- On the upper-left side of the box is a list of all the Question Pools of the project. Just above the list of pools, the **+** and **–** icons (see **1** in the following screenshot) are used to add or remove Question Pools.
- The right-hand side of the box shows the list of the Question Slides associated with the pool selected on the right-hand side. The **+** and **–** icons (see **2** in the following screenshot) are used to add new Question Slides into the selected pool or to remove existing Question Slides from the selected pool:

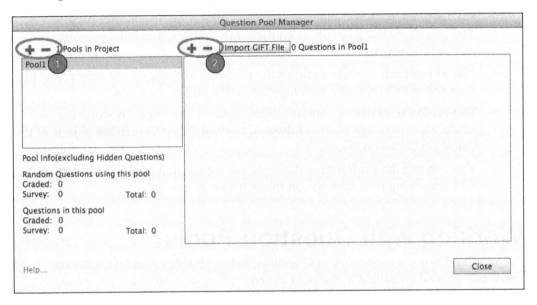

Notice that the first Question Pool named **Pool1** has been automatically created by Captivate when you opened the **Question Pool Manager** dialog. Notice also the **Import GIFT file** button that lets you import questions from a GIFT file directly into the selected Question Pool. You will now rename this Question Pool using the following steps:

3. On the left-hand side of the **Question Pool Manager** dialog, double-click on the **Pool1** entry of the list of pools.
4. Name the pool `DIB_pool1` and press the *Enter* key.
5. Click on the **Close** button to close the **Question Pool Manager** dialog.

Now that you have a Question Pool available, you will add questions to it.

Inserting questions in a Question Pool

You could have used the **Question Pool Manager** dialog to create new Question Slides directly into the pool, but you will use another technique. Instead of creating new Question Slides to fill the Question Pool, you will move some of the existing Question Slides of the Quiz into the new pool using the following steps:

1. Use the **Filmstrip** panel to go to slide 20. Hold the *Shift* key down and click on slide 25.

This operation selects six slides from slide 20 to slide 25.

2. In the **Filmstrip** panel, right-click on one of the selected slides.
3. In the Contextual menu, navigate to **Move Question to | DIB_Pool1**.

This operation removes the selected slides from the **Filmstrip** panel and moves them into the Question Pool.

4. Open the **Question Pool** panel that appears right next to the **Timeline** panel at the bottom of the screen. (If the **Question Pool** panel is not present on the screen, navigate to **Window | Question Pool** to turn it on.)

Six Question Slides should be displayed in the **Question Pool** panel indicating that they have been moved into the **DIB_pool1** correctly. Another way to access the same information is by using the **Question Pool Manager** dialog.

5. Navigate to **Quiz | Question Pool Manager** to open the **Question Pool Manager** dialog once again.
6. Make sure that the **DIB_pool1** Question Pool is selected on the left-hand side of the dialog and take a look at the right-hand side.

When the **DIB_pool1** is selected, the right-hand side of the **Question Pool Manager** dialog lists the six Question Slides included in the pool.

7. Click on the **Close** button to close the **Question Pool Manager** dialog.

The Question Pool is now ready for action! The next step is to randomly pick questions from the pool and add them to the main Quiz.

Share Question Pools with other projects

You may have noticed the **Import Question Pools** menu item under **Quiz**. Using this feature, you can easily import a Question Pool from another project into this project.

Working with Quizzes

Inserting random Question Slides into the main project

Remember that the idea of a Question Pool is to have a repository of questions available in order to generate random quizzes. In this section, you will randomly pick one question from the **DIB_pool1** Question Pool and insert it into the main Quiz using the following steps:

1. Use the **Filmstrip** panel to go to slide 19 of the `drivingInBe.cptx` file.

Slide 19 is the Multiple Choice question you created earlier in this chapter. It is the first question of the Quiz.

2. Navigate to **Quiz | Random Question Slide** to insert a random question into the main project.

Captivate inserts the random question *after* the selected slide.

Currently, the Quiz starts with the same Multiple Choice question of slide 19 for each student. The second question is randomly picked from the Question Pool at runtime. Finally, the Quiz ends the same way for every student with the survey on slide 21.

3. Use the **Filmstrip** panel to go to slide 20.
4. Take a look at the **Quiz Properties** panel.

The **Quiz Properties** panel of a **Random Question** slide holds only a fraction of the options in comparison to the **Quiz Properties** panel of a regular Question Slide. Two of the available options are the **Points** and **Penalty** properties.

5. If needed, open the **Question Pool** panel situated right next to the **Timeline** panel at the bottom of the screen.
6. Select any Question Slide in the **DIB_pool1** Question Pool.
7. When the selected question is loaded in the main area of the Captivate interface, take a look at the **Quiz Properties** panel.

Notice that, here again, the **Quiz Properties** panel holds fewer options than the **Quiz Properties** panel of a regular Question Slide. Two of the missing options are the **Points** and **Penalty** properties.

When combining the options of the **Quiz Properties** panel of the random Question Slide in the main project with the options of the **Quiz Properties** panel of a Question Slide within a Question Pool, you more or less obtain the **Quiz Properties** panel of a regular Question Slide.

8. Return to slide 20 of the main **Filmstrip** panel. In the **General** section of the **Quiz Properties** panel, make sure that the **Points** property is set to `10` and the **Penalty** property is set to `1`.

Now that you have a random question in the Quiz, you will give your random Quiz a try.

9. Use the Preview icon to test the entire project in the **Preview** pane.

When you reach the Quiz, pay close attention to the second question of the Quiz. Try to answer the questions correctly so that the **Quiz Passed Feedback** slide is displayed when the Quiz is over.

10. When you are done, close the **Preview** pane.
11. Use the Preview icon to test the entire project a second time.

When you reach the Quiz for the second time, notice that the second question is not the same as it was at the first attempt. Give wrong answers so that you fail the Quiz.

12. Make sure that the **Quiz Fail Feedback** slide is displayed at the end of the Quiz.

Your random Quiz is now up and running. It is time to make a quick summary of what you have just learned:

- A Question Pool is a repository of Question Slides from which Captivate randomly picks questions at runtime.
- A Captivate project can include as many Question Pools as needed. A Question Pool can contain as many Question Slides as needed.
- The **Import Question Pool** menu item under **Quiz** can be used to import a Question Pool of another project in the current project.
- Navigate to **Quiz | Question Pool Manager** to create new Question Pools and to add Question Slides in the available pools.
- GIFT files can be imported directly into a Question Pool.
- If the project already contains Question Slides, they can be moved to a Question Pool at any time. Questions in a Question Pool can also be moved to the main project using the same technique.
- A Quiz can be made up of a mix of regular Questions Slides and random questions from different Question Pools.
- The **Quiz Properties** panel of a **Random Question** slide contains only a fraction of the options available for a regular Question Slides. The remaining options are associated with each Question Slide in the **Question Pool** panel.

Working with Quizzes

Great! You now have a pretty good idea of what a Captivate Quiz is and of the myriad of options available. In the next section, you will quickly return to the Master Slide panel to finalize the look and feel of the Question Slides.

Styling the elements of the Question Slides

In this section, you will finalize the integration of the Quiz into the project by styling the elements that make up the Question Slides of the project. To do so, you will define formatting properties and apply Styles to Placeholder Objects of the Master Slides used by the Question Slides of the project. Perform the following steps to style the Question Slides:

1. Return to the **Master Slide** panel. If the panel is not open, navigate to **Window | Master Slide** to turn it on.

Note that the **Master Slide** panel contains five Master Slides that control the look and feel of the Question Slides and of the **Quiz Results** slide.

2. In the **Master Slide** panel, right-click on the **MCQ, T/F, FIB, Sequence** Master Slide and try to delete it.

Captivate informs you that at least one Quiz Master Slide of each type must be present in the project. The selected Master Slide therefore cannot be deleted. This particular Master Slide is used by the Multiple Choice, True/False, Fill-In-The-Blank, and Sequence Question Slides of the project.

3. Select the **MCQ, T/F, FIB, Sequence** Master Slide.
4. Select the **Question Title** placeholder.

In the topmost part of the **Properties** panel, notice that the style currently applied to the Question Title is **Default Question Title Style**.

5. In the **Character** section of the **Properties** panel, change the font **Family** to **Verdana**, change the font **Size** to **35**, and deselect the Bold icon.
6. In the topmost part of the **Properties** panel, click on the Create New Style icon.
7. Name the style `MFTC-questionTitle` and click on the **OK** button.
8. Click on the Apply this style to… icon situated right below the **Style** drop-down list.
9. In the box that opens, select the **[Default Question Title Style]** option and click on **OK**.

Chapter 7

This operation applies the new **MFTC-questionTitle** style to the other Question Title placeholders of the project. Don't hesitate to browse to the other Quiz Master Slides of the **Master Slide** panel to check it out. When done, make sure you return to the **MCQ, T/F, FIB, Sequence** Master Slide to continue with this exercise.

Thanks to the styles, it has been easy to apply the same formatting to all the Title Placeholders of the project. You will now give these objects the exact same size and position on each and every Quiz Master Slide.

10. Select the Title Placeholder of the **MCQ, T/F, FIB, Sequence** Master Slide.

11. Enter the following values in the **Transform** section of the **Properties** panel:
    - Deselect the **Constrain proportions** checkbox if needed
    - Position the Title Caption with **X** as 50 and **Y** as 100
    - Resize the Title Caption with **W** as 700 and **H** as 40

It is possible that the **Question Title** placeholder overlaps with other objects of the Master Slide.

12. In the top-right corner of the **Transform** section title bar, click on the small arrow icon. In the menu that opens, choose **Apply to all items of this type**, as shown in the following screenshot:

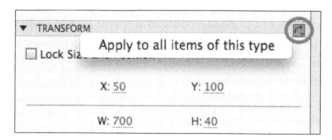

Thanks to this handy little feature, you can apply the current values of the **Transform** section to all other objects of the project that are of the same type. In this case, the Question Title of every Question Slide now has the same size and the same position.

You will now use the very same workflow for the **Question** Text Caption.

13. Still on the **MCQ, T/F, FIB, Sequence** Master Slide, select the **Question** placeholder. (**Question Placeholder** should be written at the top of the **Properties** panel.)

14. In the **Character** section, change the font **Family** to **Verdana** and the **Size** value to 25 points.
15. Save the new formatting as a new style named MFTC-question.
16. Apply the new style to every object that currently uses the **[Default Question Text Style]**.
17. In the **Transform** section of the **Properties** panel, enter the following values:
    - **X** as 50 and **Y** as 140
    - **W** as 700 and **H** as 70 (deselect the **Constraint Constrain Proportions** box if needed)
18. Use the small icon at the top-right corner of the **Transform** section to apply these values to other objects of the project that are of the same type.

Styling the quiz buttons

In this section, you will concentrate on the Question Slide buttons. Perform the following steps to style these buttons:

1. Return to the **MCQ, T/F, FIB, Sequence** Master Slide.
2. Select the **Submit** button of the Master Slide.
3. Make sure the **Properties** panel is displayed on the right-hand side of the screen.
4. In the **General** section, change **Button Type** to **Image Button**.
5. Click on the Folder icon situated right next to the **Button Type** dropdown. Choose the mftcSubmit_up.png image under images/buttons of the exercises files.

When browsing for the image file, notice that the buttons folder under images contains three versions of the **Submit** button representing each of the three possible states of the button.

6. Use the **Properties** panel to create a new style after the current look and feel of the **Submit** button. Name this new style MFTC-questionSubmit.
7. Use the very same procedure to change the look and feel of the **Clear**, **Next**, and **Back** buttons. Use the images stored in the images/buttons/ folder and create three new styles named MFTC-questionClear, MFTC-questionNext, and MFTC-questionBack.

Because all the buttons of the Question Slides share the same **[Default Quiz Button Style]** regardless of the action they perform (submit, clear, or else), you cannot use the Apply this style to… icon as you did for other elements of the Question Slide. Instead, you have to manually apply the new styles to the buttons of the remaining Master Slides.

8. Go to the **Matching**, **Hot Spot**, and **Likert** Master Slide and manually assign the four new styles to the corresponding buttons.

Now that all the buttons of your Master Slides have the right *look* you will use the **Transform** panel to assign these objects a precise *position*.

9. Return to the **MCQ, T/F, FIB, Sequence** Master Slide and select the **Submit** button.
10. Use the **Transform** section of the **Properties** panel to position the **Submit** button with **X** as 645 and **Y** as 550.
11. Select the **Clear** button and position it at **X** = 500 and **Y** = 550.

The **Clear** button currently overlaps with the **Next** button.

12. Use the same technique to move the **Next** button to **X** = 355 and **Y** = 550, and the **Back** button to **X** = 210 and **Y** = 550.

You will now use the **Apply to all items of this type** feature to apply these values to the buttons of other Quiz Master Slides as well.

13. Click on the **Submit** button to make it the active object.
14. Open the small icon at the top-right corner of the **Transform** section and click on the **Apply to all items of this type** icon.
15. Repeat the same operation with the **Clear**, **Next**, and **Back** buttons.
16. Save the file and use the Preview icon to test the entire project.

Cool! Thanks to the Master Slides, the Styles, and the Apply to All icon, you have been able to create an attractive look and feel for the Question Slides and to consistently use it throughout the Quiz.

The last thing to do is to save these new styles into the Theme so that you'll be able to reuse these Master Slides and Styles on your future projects.

17. Navigate to **Themes | Save Theme** to save these changes into our custom MFTC-Theme.cptm file.

Extra credit – styling the elements of the Question Slides

In this section, you will use the same tools to arrange the objects of the remaining quiz Master Slides. Feel free to lay them out as you see fit and to create new styles as needed. The following is a list of some tips and tricks to help you do the job:

- Stay in the **Master Slide** panel and apply your formatting and positioning to Placeholder Objects.
- Use the Styles whenever possible. They make it incredibly easy to apply the same formatting properties to lots of different objects.
- Use the small Apply to all icon at the top-right corner of the various sections of the **Properties** panel to quickly apply the same properties to many objects of the same type/style.
- Use the tools of the Align toolbar. Remember to navigate to **Window** | **Align** to turn the Align toolbar on. By default, it appears in the top-left area of the Workspace.
- Use the files of the `images/buttons` folder to define the look of the buttons of the **Result** Master Slide.

When you are done, don't hesitate to return to the main **Filmstrip** panel and to **Question Pool** to take a look at the slides and Question Slide of the project. You should see that they all share the same look and feel and that the objects present on these slides have consistent formatting. By modifying the look and feel of the Master Slides and by applying styles to the Placeholder Objects, you modified the actual objects on the actual slides as well.

> **Resetting the Master Slide**
>
> If a Master Slide is not properly applied to one of the standard Question Slides of the **Filmstrip** panel, use the **Reset Master Slide** button of the **Properties** panel to clear the overrides.

Now that your Quiz looks the way you want, you'll learn how to track the performances of the students taking the Quiz. This is where the LMS enters the stage.

Reporting scores to an LMS

LMS stands for **Learning Management System**. The help files of Captivate give the following definition for an LMS:

> *"You can use a learning management system (LMS) to distribute a computer-based tutorial created using Adobe Captivate over the Internet. A learning management system is used to provide, track, and manage web-based training."*

An LMS offers many services to both teachers and students involved in eLearning activities. Here follows a short list of the main services provided by an LMS:

- An LMS is a website that is able to host your eLearning courses.
- An LMS maintains a list of teachers and students. Thanks to this listing, an LMS can be used to enroll students in online courses and to define one or more teacher(s) for each course.
- An LMS is able to enforce the pedagogical decisions of the teacher. For example, the LMS can be programmed to give access to the next part of the course only if the current activity has been completed. Some LMSs can also enforce branching by automatically providing an additional activity for those students who have failed a Quiz and so on.
- An LMS is able to communicate with your Captivate-powered content. This gives you access to many pieces of information such as the number of students that have taken the course, the time it took to complete an activity, the results of the quizzes, and even a detailed report of every interaction performed by each student while taking the course.
- There are many other services that LMSs have to offer.

There are many LMSs available, and there are a myriad of companies, schools, and universities that have deployed an LMS to deliver, track, and manage their web-based trainings. Some LMSs are commercially licensed and can be quite expensive, but there are also several open source LMS platforms that are free and easily deployed on a web server.

Moodle

Moodle is the most popular and powerful open source LMS solution. Personally, I have used Moodle for many eLearning projects, and it has never let me down. However, Moodle has a fairly steep learning curve. Packt has published an impressive array of titles on Moodle, providing necessary documentation to get you started. More information on Moodle is available at `http://www.moodle.org`. More information about Packt books on Moodle is available at `http://www.packtpub.com/`.

For a list of the most popular LMSs, see the following web page on Wikipedia:

http://en.wikipedia.org/wiki/List_of_learning_management_systems.

Understanding SCORM, AICC, and Tin Can

Each LMS has its pros and cons and each contains a unique set of features. However, every LMS must be able to host eLearning content created by a myriad of different authoring tools (Adobe Captivate being the only one of the many eLearning authoring tools available).

It is important to keep in mind that you can create courses using a myriad of tools but at the same time, it is critical to ensure that theses courses can communicate with various LMSs. This is where SCORM, AICC and Tin Can come into play.

These are three internationally accepted standards used to make the communication between your eLearning content and your LMS possible. When choosing an LMS for your organization, make sure that the chosen solution is either SCORM, AICC, or Tin Can compliant. Captivate is SCORM, AICC, and Tin Can compliant, so Captivate courses can be integrated in virtually every LMS available in the market. Let's now discuss these three standards in more detail:

- **SCORM** stands for **Sharable Content Object Reference Model**. SCORM is maintained by the **Advanced Distributed Learning** (**ADL**) (http://www.adlnet.org/) project of the US Department of Defense. SCORM is a **reference model**. It means that it aggregates standards created by other organizations. The goal is to build a single standard based on the work done by other organizations that are active in the eLearning field. See the Wikipedia page on SCORM at http://en.wikipedia.org/wiki/SCORM.

- **AICC** stands for **Aviation Industry Computer-based Training Committee**. The idea was to provide a unique training and testing environment for the aviation industry in order to ensure the same training and testing standard for all the airline companies in the world. For more information, see the AICC page on Wikipedia at http://en.wikipedia.org/wiki/Aviation_Industry_Computer-Based_Training_Committee or the official AICC website at http://www.aicc.org/.

- **Tin Can** is the newest standard. The Tin Can API, now officially known as **Experience API** (**xAPI**), is an eLearning software specification that allows learning content and learning systems to speak to each other in a manner that records and tracks all types of learning experiences. Learning experiences are recorded in a **Learning Record Store** (**LRS**). LRSs can exist within traditional LMSs or on their own. You can find out more about the Tin Can API at http://tincanapi.com/.

Now that you have a better idea of what an LMS is and of its standards, you will enable reporting in your Captivate project.

Enabling reporting in Captivate

To have Captivate publish an LMS-ready package, you have to set options at different locations throughout the project.

In the next exercise, you will make your Quiz ready to be integrated in a SCORM-compliant LMS. You will first inspect the options available at the interaction level before moving on to project-level reporting options.

Reporting options at the interaction level

Each of the scorable objects of Captivate can be assigned with a unique **Interaction ID**. This Interaction ID is what makes data tracking by LMS possible. Perform the following steps to assign each interaction with a unique Interaction ID:

1. Use the **Filmstrip** panel to go to slide 19 of the drivingInBelgium.cptx file.
2. In the **Reporting** section of the **Quiz Properties** panel, make sure the **Report Answer** checkbox is selected.
3. Type MC_Languages in the **Interaction ID** field as shown in the following screenshot:

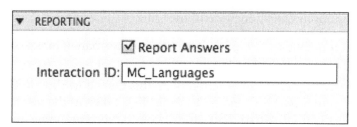

MC_languages is now the name under which this particular interaction will be reported to the LMS.

>
> **Coming up with unique Interaction IDs**
>
> In **MC_languages**, what is before the underscore is the type of interaction (**MC** stands for **Multiple Choice**, **TF** for **True/False**, and so on) and after the underscore is the topic of the question. This is how I come up with meaningful unique names for Interaction IDs. Feel free to use any other conventions in your projects as long as it ensures the uniqueness of the Interaction IDs.

Also notice that there is no space or special characters in the Interaction ID. Captivate enforces these restrictions by turning every space and every special character typed in the Interaction ID field into an underscore.

Extra credit – assigning Interaction IDs to quiz questions

Use the same technique to define an **Interaction ID** for each of the questions contained in this project. The following are the general steps to use:

- Select a Question Slide in the **Filmstrip** panel.
- Use the **Reporting** section of the **Quiz Properties** panel to assign a unique Interaction ID to each Question Slide. Use the convention explained previously to come up with meaningful, unique names.
- Don't forget the questions of **Question Pool**!
- Save the file when done.

Reporting the random Question Slides

In this section, you will take a closer look at the reporting options of a Random Question Slide using the following steps:

1. While in the `Chapter07/DrivingInBE.cptx` file, return to slide 20 of the **Filmstrip** panel.

Slide 20 is the Random Question Slide of the Quiz.

2. In the **Reporting** section of the **Quiz Properties** panel, make sure the **Report Answer** checkbox is selected.

Even though you assigned an Interaction ID to this Question Slide in the Question Pool, the decision to report the answer to the LMS is taken at the random Question Slide level in the main **Filmstrip**. This allows you to reuse the same question in different Captivate projects and decide, in each project, whether this particular question should be reported or not.

3. Save the file when done.

Using a Drag and Drop interaction as a Question Slide

The Question Slides that make up a Quiz are not the only interactions that can be reported to an LMS. There are a bunch of other objects that have this capability as well. One such feature is the brand new Drag and Drop interaction. This interaction has some built-in reporting capabilities that are very similar to those of a regular Question Slide.

In this section, you will import a new slide in the project, define a Drag and Drop interaction, and make this interaction part of the Quiz by configuring its reporting options:

1. Open the `Chapter07/dragAndDrop.cptx` file.
2. In the **Filmstrip** panel and select the first and only slide of this project.
3. Use the *cmd* + *C* (Mac) or *Ctrl* + *C* (Windows) shortcut to copy the selected slide.
4. Return to the `Chapter07/drivingInBe.cptx` file and use the **Filmstrip** panel to go to slide 20.
5. Use the *cmd* + *V* (Mac) or *Ctrl* + *V* (Windows) shortcut to paste the selected slide as slide 21 of the `drivingInBe.cptx` file.

The newly inserted slide contains a lot of objects. The Text Caption at the top of the slide explains what you will do. As far as Drag and Drop is concerned, each road sign image is a Drag Source, and the four black and white images at the bottom part of the slide are the Drop Targets.

6. Navigate to the **Insert | Launch Drag and Drop Interaction Wizard** menu item to start defining your Drag and Drop interaction.

The first step of the **Drag And Drop Interaction Wizard** consists of selecting the Drag Sources of the interaction. In this case, there are twelve Drag Sources to select.

7. Select all three prohibitory sign images (the red circles).
8. At the top of the screen, click on the **+** icon situated next to the **Add To Type** drop-down menu.
9. In the **Add new type** box, type `ProhibitorySgn` and click on **OK**.

Working with Quizzes

Grouping the Drag Sources into types will help you map these Drag Sources with their corresponding Drop Targets in the third and last step of the wizard. This process is depicted in the following screenshot:

10. Repeat this process with other types of road signs. Refer to the following table for precise instructions:

What to select	Tip	Name of type
Mandatory signs	The blue circles	`mandatorySgn`
Warning signs	The red triangles	`warningSgn`
Information signs	The blue rectangle	`informationSgn`

After this part of the process, you should have defined the twelve Drag Sources of your slide.

11. Click on the **Next** button situated in the top-right part of the screen to go to the second step of the wizard.

The second step of the wizard is where you define the Drop Targets of the interaction.

12. Select all four black and white images in the lower part of the slide.
13. These images are surrounded with a blue outline indicating the Drop Targets of the interaction.
14. Click on the **Next** button situated in the top-right part of the screen to go to the third step of the wizard.

The third step of the wizard is where you map the Drag Sources with their corresponding Drop Targets.

15. Select the little circle situated in the middle of any one of the warning signs (any red triangle). Drop that little icon on the warning sign to Drop Target.
16. Thanks to the Drag Source types you created in the first step of the wizard, all three warning signs are automatically mapped to that Drop Target.
17. Repeat the same operation with the remaining three types of road signs.

At the end of this process, your slide should look like the following screenshot:

18. Click on **Finish** to close the **Drag and Drop interaction Wizard**.

Apart from the larger number of objects involved, the process of creating this Drag and Drop interaction is very similar to the process you used to define the other Drag and Drop interaction, earlier in this book. But the wizard can only take you that far, and, in this case, you need to go a bit further.

In the next part of this exercise, you will use the **Drag and Drop** panel to further refine the settings of this Drag and Drop interaction.

19. Open the **Drag and Drop** panel situated on the right edge of the interface, next to the **Properties** and **Library** panels. (If the **Drag and Drop** panel is not present, navigate to **Window | Drag and Drop** to turn it on.)
20. In the **Interaction Properties** section of the **Drag and Drop** panel, click on the **Correct Answers** button.

The **Correct Answers** dialog contains many options to let you decide what the correct answer of the Drag And Drop interaction is. It currently shows you the four Drop Targets and their associated Drag Sources in a list. In this case, you want the student to drag two road signs of each type in the corresponding Drop Target.

21. In the **Count** column of the list, double click on **3** to change the number to 2.

This is how you tell Captivate that dropping two road signs of each type on the corresponding Drop Target is enough for the answer to be correct.

22. Leave the other options of the **Correct Answers** dialog at their current values.
23. Make sure the **Correct Answers** dialog looks like the following screenshot and click on **OK** to validate:

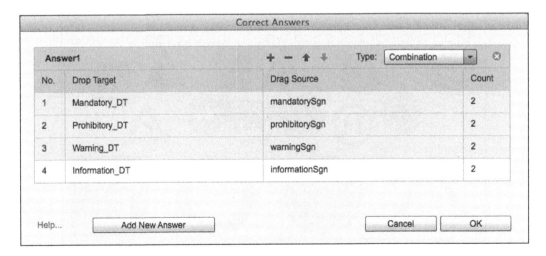

After all these steps, the main options of your Drag and Drop interaction are now in place. The next step is to make it part of the Quiz.

24. Open the **Reporting** section of the **Drag and Drop** panel.

The options of the **Reporting** section of the **Drag and Drop** panel are similar to the **Reporting** options of a regular Question Slide. It is therefore very easy to include the Drag and Drop interaction into the Quiz and to report the results to the LMS.

25. Select the **Include in Quiz** checkbox situated in the **Reporting** section of the **Drag and Drop** panel.
26. Also select the **Report Answer** checkbox to have this interaction reported to the LMS.

Your Quiz now contains three Graded questions and one Survey question.

Feel free to further customize this Drag and Drop interaction with the techniques you learned in *Chapter 5, Adding Interactivity to the Project*. For example, you could use the **Drag and Drop** panel to add either a Glow or Zoom In effect on the Drag Sources and Drop Targets. You can also apply the **MFTC-questionSubmit** style to the **Submit** button of the interaction, reposition this button in the lower-right corner of the slide, turn the **Reset** button on and apply the **MFTC-questionclear** style, and so on. There are a bunch of actions you can perform to finalize this Drag and Drop interaction. Don't forget to save the file before moving on to the next section.

Using the other scorable object

In addition to regular Question Slides and Drag and Drop interaction, some other objects in Captivate can also be part of the Quiz. In this section, you will return to the Encoder Simulation you created in *Chapter 5, Adding Interactivity to the Project*, and explore how Click Boxes, Buttons, and Text Entry Boxes can be added to the Quiz.

1. Open the `Chapter07/encoderSim_800.cptx` file. Use the **Filmstrip** panel to go to slide 2.
2. Select the **Continue** button in the lower-right corner of the slide.

With the button selected, take a look at the **Properties** panel and note that it contains a **Reporting** section.

3. Open the **Reporting** section and take a look at the available options.
4. Use the **Filmstrip** panel to go to slide 4. Select the Click Box and take a look at the **Reporting** section of the **Properties** panel.
5. Use the **Filmstrip** panel to go to slide 12. Select the Text Entry Box and take a look at the **Reporting** section of the **Properties** panel.

Each of these three interactive objects can be added to the Quiz by selecting the **Include in Quiz** checkbox. Once included in the Quiz, these objects have the very same reporting capabilities as a regular Question Slide and their points value is added to the points value of the entire Quiz.

When selecting the **Include In Quiz** checkbox, and not the **Report Answer** checkbox, you include an interactive object in the Quiz without reporting the interaction to the LMS. Captivate then uses these objects to generate the **Quiz Results** slide but does not report these interactions to the LMS.

6. Close the `encoderSim_800.cptx` file without saving the eventual changes.

In this section, you have assigned a unique Interaction ID to the interactions that you want to report to the LMS. You have also explored the scorable objects of Captivate and learned that the reporting capabilities are not limited to Question Slides only.

The Advanced Interaction dialog

Navigate to **Project** | **Advanced Interaction** to open the **Advanced Interaction** dialog. This floating panel provides a list of all the scorable objects of the project in addition to a great summary view on their current settings.

In the next section, you will explore project-level reporting options.

Setting up project-level reporting options

When every interaction that you want to report has a unique Interaction ID, it is time to focus on project-level reporting options. This is where you will configure the settings that will report the data to the LMS.

Before putting in all this effort, it is important to check what level of information your LMS can receive and what is the standard (SCORM, AICC, or Tin Can) that your LMS uses. In this exercise, you will report the data to Moodle. A quick look in the Moodle documentation (`http://docs.moodle.org/26/en/SCORM_FAQ`) tells you that Moodle is SCORM 1.2 compliant.

Perform the following steps to create a SCORM 1.2 package that can be integrated into Moodle:

1. If needed, return to the `Chapter07/DrivingInBe.cptx` file.
2. Navigate to **Quiz** | **Quiz Preferences** to open the **Preferences** dialog. In the left-hand side of the **Preferences** dialog, make sure that you are on the **Reporting** category.

3. At the top of the page, select the **Enable reporting for this project** checkbox.

When I conduct a Captivate class, I often refer to this checkbox as being the *main circuit breaker* of the reporting system.

4. Open the **LMS** drop-down menu.

The LMS drop-down lists some of the most popular LMSs and lets you quickly apply specific settings that are optimized for each LMS.

5. Choose **Moodle** as the LMS.

This action automatically adjusts most of the options of **Reporting Preferences** to values that a Moodle LMS expects.

6. Open the **Standard** drop-down list.

The **Standard** drop-down menu probably is the single most important option of this **Preferences** page. It allows you to choose the reporting standard used to report the scoring and tracking of data to the LMS. By choosing **Moodle** as the LMS in the previous step, this option has been automatically set to **SCORM 1.2**.

7. Make sure you choose the **SCORM 1.2** option in the drop-down list.

You will now decide how Captivate will report the status of the course. If there is a Quiz in the project, you probably want the status to be either *Pass* or *Fail*. If the project does not contain a Quiz and you just want to track the completion status of the project, choose *Complete/Incomplete*. Knowing your LMS and how it receives and deals with the information is important for making these decisions. In this case, Moodle can accept both representations of the status, but it might not be true for every LMS.

8. In the **Status Representation** section, choose the **Incomplete -> Passed/Failed** option.

You will now instruct Captivate that you want to consider this piece of eLearning content as complete when the student has passed the Quiz.

9. In the **Success/Completion Criteria** section, choose the **Slide views and/or quiz** option.

10. Deselect the **Slide Views** checkbox, but leave the **Quiz is Passed** checkbox selected.

Finally, you need to decide what data you want to see reported to the LMS. Basically, you can choose to report only the final score of the student or to report the final score plus some details about each interaction. In this case, you want to report the score of the student in percent as well as the interaction data.

11. In the **Data To Report** section, choose to report **Quiz Score** as **Percentage**.

12. Make sure the **Interaction Data** checkbox is selected.

Working with Quizzes

At the end of this procedure, make sure your **Preferences** dialog looks like the following screenshot:

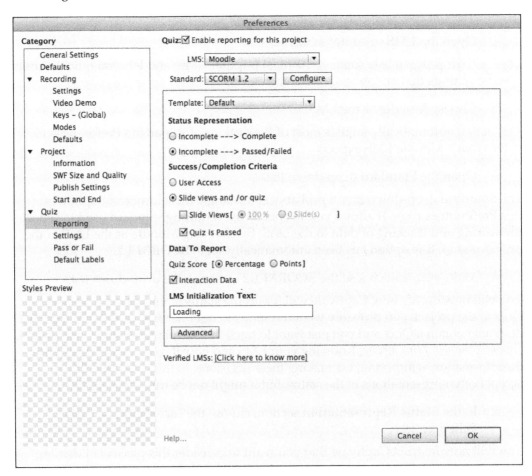

Because you are using the SCORM standard, there is one extra step to go through. This extra step is the creation of the SCORM manifest file.

> **Enabling reporting in a quizless project**
>
> These reporting options are not limited to projects containing a Quiz. Reporting can be used to track only the completion status of a project. Some LMSs are able to reveal the next activity of a course when, and only when, they receive the complete status report from the current activity.

Creating a SCORM manifest file

A SCORM manifest is a `.xml` file named `imsmanifest.xml`. This manifest file is an essential component of any SCORM package. It is used to describe the course to the SCORM-compliant LMS. Without this file, the LMS is unable to integrate Captivate projects in a course or gather the tracking data sent by the project.

If this sounds too technical for you, don't worry! Captivate can generate that manifest file for you by using the following procedure:

1. While in the **Reporting** category of the **Preferences** dialog, click on the **Configure** button situated next to the **SCORM 1.2** standard at the top of the box.

The first section of the **Manifest** dialog is the **Course** section. The **Course** section is used to enter the metadata of the project. This metadata is used by the LMS to display the course information to the student and to enhance the integration of the project into the LMS.

2. In the **Course** section of the **Manifest** dialog, enter the following information:
    - **Identifier**: `DrivingInBe101`
    - **Title**: `Driving in Belgium`
    - **Description**: Enter any meaningful description here

The second part of the **Manifest** dialog is named **SCO**.

SCO stands for **Shareable Content Object**. This concept is at the heart of the SCORM standard. In the SCORM specification, a course can be composed of many activities. Each of these activities must have a unique SCO identifier. Using a SCORM Packager application (such as the *Multi SCO Packager* or *Reload*), it is possible to integrate a Captivate project in a larger SCORM-compliant course containing lots of other content made by lots of other applications. This is why it is important to specify the SCO identity of your Captivate project. By default, Captivate generates a random SCO that is based on the name of the project.

3. Enter `DrivingInBe101` in the SCO **Identifier** field.
4. Enter `Driving in Belgium` in the SCO **Title** field.

The **Manifest** dialog should now look like the following screenshot:

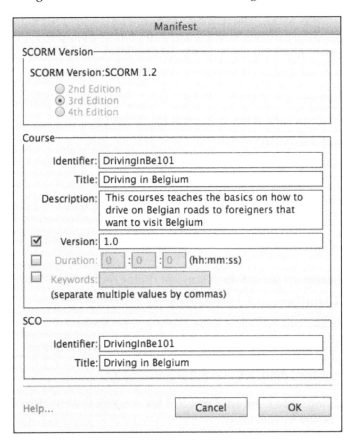

5. Click on **OK** to validate the changes and close the dialog box.
6. Also click on the **OK** button of the **Preferences** dialog.
7. Make sure you save the file when done.

The project is now ready to be published as an SCORM package. This step will be covered in *Chapter 8, Finishing Touches and Publishing*.

Using Acrobat.com as an alternate reporting method

If you do not have access to an LMS, Captivate provides an alternate reporting method. This alternate method uses the Acrobat.com cloud service to replace the LMS used in the traditional reporting workflow.

Acrobat.com is a set of cloud-based services from Adobe. One of the greatest things about Acrobat.com is the free 5 GB storage space that can be used to share large files with other people (and more specifically with your students). But Acrobat.com is not only about file storage and sharing. It is a whole array of free and pay-for cloud-based services, including the ability to convert files to PDF online, form design, and much more.

> The exercises in this section require that you, as well as each of your students, have an Acrobat.com account. A free Acrobat.com account is one of the goodies brought to you by your Adobe ID, so if you already have an Adobe ID, you're all set for this section. If you do not have an Adobe ID, it is easy to create one for free on the www.adobe.com website or on the www.acrobat.com website. If you do not want to sign up for a free Acrobat.com account, you will not be able to perform the exercises of this section. Just read through the steps to have an idea of the workflow.

In the next exercises, you will use Acrobat.com as an alternate reporting method. Make sure you have an Adobe ID before starting this procedure.

Configuring the Captivate project for Acrobat.com reporting

First of all, you will create a copy of the current project and configure Captivate for Acrobat.com reporting using the following steps:

1. Navigate to **File | Save As** to create a copy of the current file. Save it in the Chapter07 folder under drivingInBe_acrobat.cptx.
2. Use the **Filmstrip** panel to go to slide 24 of the Chapter07/drivingInBe_acrobat.cptx file.

Slide 24 should be the automatically generated **Quiz Results** slide. Note that this slide contains a single button labeled **Continue**.

3. Navigate to **Quiz | Quiz Preferences** to open the **Reporting** category of the **Preferences** dialog.
4. Open the **LMS** drop-down list and choose **Acrobat.com** as the LMS.
5. Click on the **Configure** button situated right below.
6. In the topmost area of the **Configure Acrobat.com Settings** dialog, enter your Adobe ID credentials.

Working with Quizzes

7. In the lower area of the **Configure Acrobat.com Settings** dialog, enter the following information:
   - **Company/Institute**: MFTC
   - **Department**: Training
   - **Course**: Driving In Belgium

Note that all these fields are mandatory, as shown in the following screenshot:

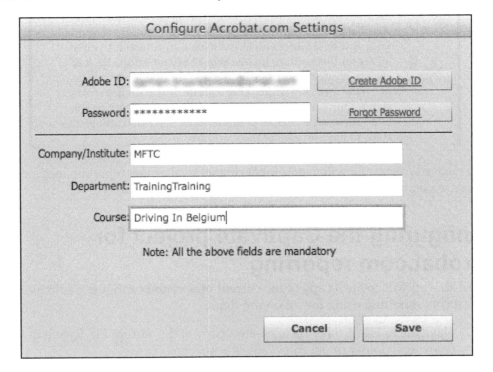

8. Click on the **Save** button. Captivate logs in to the Acrobat.com service and retrieves the necessary information.
9. Click on **OK** to close the **Preferences** dialog.

Notice that the **Quiz Results** slide (slide 24) now contains a second button labeled **Post Results**. When the student clicks on this button, the Quiz results are uploaded to the Acrobat.com service.

Uploading files to Acrobat.com

Now that the project is properly configured, you will take advantage of the File Sharing service provided by Acrobat.com to upload your project and share it with your students using the following steps:

1. Navigate to **File | Collaborate | Share files on Acrobat.com** to open the corresponding dialog box.
2. Enter your Adobe ID credentials in the box and click on the **Sign In** button. Captivate connects to the Acrobat.com service and moves on to the second step of the wizard.
3. Select the **PDF** checkbox to have Captivate convert the project into a PDF file and send it to Acrobat.com.
4. Click on the **Next** button to go to the next step of the wizard.
5. In the **To** field, enter the e-mail addresses of the students you want to share your project with.

Optionally, you can type a nice introduction message for your students. Also note that your own e-mail address is automatically added to the **CC** field.

6. Click on the **Send** button to convert the project to PDF, upload the PDF file to Acrobat.com, and send the e-mail messages to the selected students.

This operation can be quite lengthy depending on the size of the project and the speed of your Internet connection.

Add students to the course

Thanks to your e-mail address being added automatically in the **CC** field, a copy of the project is sent to yourself. You can then allow students to access the course by sending them the link to the file. Note that each student needs an Adobe ID to download the course from Acrobat.com and to report the results of the Quiz.

Taking the Quiz

Once the students have access to the download link, they can log in to Acrobat.com using their own Adobe ID and download the PDF File. In the following exercise, you will pretend to be a student in order to download the project and experience the online course as a student would, using the following steps:

1. By now, you should have received an e-mail from Acrobat.com with a link to the shared PDF file. Click on the link to open the Acrobat.com website.

2. Once on the Acrobat.com website, sign in with your Adobe ID credentials and click on the **Sign in** button. You will be automatically redirected to the shared file.
3. Click on the **Download** button situated at the top-left corner of the Acrobat.com screen to download the file to your computer.
4. Open the downloaded file with Adobe Acrobat or Adobe Reader and take the course as if you were a student.
5. Once you reach the **Quiz Results** page, click on the **Post Results** button.
6. Follow the onscreen instructions to sign in to Acrobat.com and upload your Quiz result to the cloud.
7. When the movie is finished, close the Adobe Acrobat or Adobe Reader application.

When viewing such a PDF file, it is important to use the official Adobe Acrobat or Adobe Reader application. Third-party PDF readers (such as Foxit Reader) might not implement all the required features that make the Acrobat.com integration work as advertised.

Using the Adobe Captivate Quiz Results Analyzer

For the last step of the process, you will examine how the Quiz results from the Acrobat.com server can be retrieved and analyzed.

To achieve these goals, you will use another application that is part of the Captivate bundle. This application is named **Adobe Captivate Quiz Results Analyzer**.

Adobe Captivate Quiz Results Analyzer is an Adobe AIR application, which means that it works in the exact same way on every platform, but it also means that the AIR runtime must be installed on your computer to run **Adobe Captivate Quiz Results Analyzer**.

 More information on Adobe AIR can be found at the following URL: `http://www.adobe.com/products/air.edu.html`

You will now open the **Adobe Captivate Quiz Results Analyzer** application and use it to retrieve the scoring data of your Quiz. The procedure is described in the following screenshot and steps:

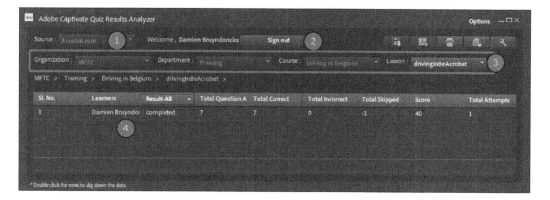

1. Open the Adobe Captivate Quiz Result Analyzer 7 application.
2. At the top of the screen, select **Acrobat.com** in the **Source** drop-down list (**1**) and click on the **Sign in** button.
3. Enter your Adobe ID credentials and sign in to Acrobat.com. Once you have signed in, your name and a **Sign out** button (**2**) appear in the top-left corner of the interface.
4. Choose **MFTC** in the **Organization** drop-down list, **Training** in the **Department** drop-down list, and **Driving In Belgium** in the **Course** drop-down list (**3**).
5. When done, click on the **Generate Report** button.
6. Double-click on the **drivingInBeAcrobat** lesson to drill down through the data and have a list of all the students who have taken the Quiz.

As shown in the preceding screenshot, only one student (yourself) has taken the Quiz (**4**).

It is possible to go even deeper into the data and see the details of each interaction within the Captivate project.

7. Double-click on your name to have a detailed report on your performances in the Quiz.

Take some time to browse through the available data. Notice how the Interaction IDs you typed earlier in Captivate are used to generate this report. Right above the report, use the breadcrumb to go back up the data tree and display the report of another user, of another lesson, or of another course.

Working with Quizzes

8. In the top-left corner of the application, click on the Export to CSV icon to export the current report to CSV, as shown in the following screenshot:

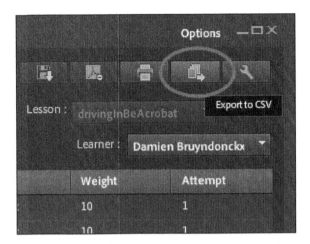

The exported CSV file can be opened with any spreadsheet application (such as Microsoft Excel or Apple Numbers) in order to be further analyzed.

This exercise concludes your exploration of the alternate reporting method using Acrobat.com as the LMS. Before moving on to the next chapter, let's make a quick summary of what you have learned in this section:

- If no LMS is available, you can use Acrobat.com as an alternative reporting method.
- This solution requires the teacher (you) and every student to have a valid Adobe ID.
- Acrobat.com is a set of online services provided by Adobe. These services include a free 5 GB storage space to share large files with colleagues, customers, or students.
- To use Acrobat.com as the LMS, follow this basic four-step workflow:
    ○ Configure the Acrobat.com reporting in the Quiz Preferences
    ○ Upload your file to Acrobat.com
    ○ Let the students take the Quiz
    ○ Use the **Adobe Captivate Quiz Results Analyzer** application to visualize, analyze, and export the Quiz results
- **Adobe Captivate Quiz Results Analyzer** is an AIR application that is part of the Captivate installation. It is used to retrieve and analyze the data stored on the Acrobat.com LMS.

To finish off with this topic, I've included a link to a nice video from the Adobe TV website. This video explains how to use Acrobat.com as an alternate reporting method and has been created using Adobe Captivate. It is available at `http://tv.adobe.com/watch/publish-and-track-results/reporting-without-having-to-use-lms/`.

Summary

With the addition of Question Slides and Quizzes your project is not a simple demonstration or simulation anymore. It is a highly interactive eLearning package that is able to integrate nicely in virtually every LMS in the market. On the pedagogical side, you have discovered the eLearning answer to the assessment challenge, which is one of the primary concerns of any teacher. On the technical side, you have discovered the SCORM, AICC, and Tin Can standards that make communication between the eLearning content and the LMS possible.

In this chapter, you learned about each of the eight question types of Captivate. You created a Question Pool before exploring the **Quiz Preferences** settings and the myriad of options available. In the second part of this chapter, you learned how the Quiz results and other interactions can be reported to an LMS. Finally, you discovered how Acrobat.com can be used as an alternative reporting method if you don't have access to an LMS.

In the next chapter, you will move on to the third and last step of the Captivate production workflow: the Publishing step.

Meet the community

In this section, I want to introduce you to Kevin Siegel. He is an awesome technical writer and has written several Adobe Captivate courses. As an Adobe Captivate Certified Instructor, I teach a lot of Captivate classes for various customers using Kevin's courseware. Besides his great courseware, he maintains a great blog on Captivate and eLearning that you definitely want to bookmark.

Kevin Siegel

Kevin Siegel is the Founder and President of IconLogic, Inc. He has written more than 100 step-by-step computer training books on Adobe Captivate, Adobe RoboDemo, Adobe DreamWeaver, QuarkXPress, Adobe InDesign, Camtasia Studio, and more.

He spent five years in The United States Coast Guard as an award-winning photojournalist and has more than two decades of experience as a print publisher, technical writer, instructional designer, and eLearning developer. He is a certified technical trainer, has been a classroom instructor for more than 20 years, and is a frequent speaker at trade shows and conventions. He holds multiple certifications from companies such as Adobe and the CompTIA.

His company, IconLogic, offers online trainings on Captivate that are attended by students worldwide. The company also offers full development and one-on-one mentoring on Captivate and other eLearning development tools.

Contact details

- **Kevin's e-mail**: ksiegel@iconlogic.com
- **IconLogic's website**: www.iconlogic.com
- **IconLogic's blog**: www.iconlogic.blogs.com

8
Finishing Touches and Publishing

With the work done in the previous chapters, your time in the post-production studio is almost over. There are just a couple of things left to be done before the project can finally be published.

Most of these final changes are options and features that you will set for the entire project. It includes checking the spelling, entering the project metadata, choosing how the project starts and ends, and so on. The most important of these final changes is probably the creation of a Skin in the Skin Editor. It allows you to customize the Playback Controls bar and create a Table of Contents of the project among other things.

In the second part of this chapter, you will focus on the third and last step of the Captivate production process: publishing the movie. Publishing the movie is the process by which you make your Captivate projects available to the outside world. Most of the time, you'll publish your movies in the Adobe Flash format or the HTML5 format so that any student can enjoy the content of your online course across devices. However, Captivate can also publish the movie in many other formats, which you will also learn about.

In this chapter, you will perform the following actions:

- Check the spelling of the entire project
- Set the Start and End preferences of the movie
- Enter the project metadata to enhance the accessibility of the project
- Export the properties of a project and import them back in another project
- Customize the project Skin
- Add a Table of Contents
- Publish the project in various formats

- Publish a SCORM package
- Use the Multi-SCORM Packager

At the end of this chapter, you will be ready to leave the post-production studio and publish your eLearning content online.

Preparing your work

First, you will make Captivate ready for this chapter by performing the following steps:

1. Open Captivate.
2. Make sure that the **Classic** workspace is applied.
3. Navigate to **Window | Workspace | Reset 'Classic'** to reset the workspace to its default look.

This little procedure ensures that the way Captivate appears on your computer and in the screenshots of this chapter is consistent.

Finishing touches

With the completion of *Chapter 7, Working with Quizzes*, you can consider that the slides of the Encoder Demonstration project are all final. There are, however, a few more things to do before the movie can be published. In this section, you will focus on these small finishing touches.

Checking spelling

Checking the spelling is probably one of the most fundamental finishing touches. After all, you are a teacher, and teachers know how to write with no mistakes. The Spell Checker of Captivate works like any other Spell Checker found in any other text-authoring applications.

In Captivate 7, the Spell Checker has the ability to check the text typed in various locations throughout the project. This includes the text typed in Text Captions, Smart Shapes, Slide Notes, Text Animations, Buttons, and in the Table of Contents.

Before using the Spell Checker, you will take a quick look at its options using the following steps:

1. Open the `encoderDemo_800.cptx` file under `Chapter08`.
2. Open the **Preferences** dialog of Captivate by navigating to **Edit | Preferences** (Windows) or **Adobe Captivate | Preferences** (Mac).
3. On the left-hand side of the **Preferences** dialog, click on the **General Settings** category.
4. Click on the **Spelling Preferences...** button to open the **Spelling Options** dialog, as shown in the following screenshot:

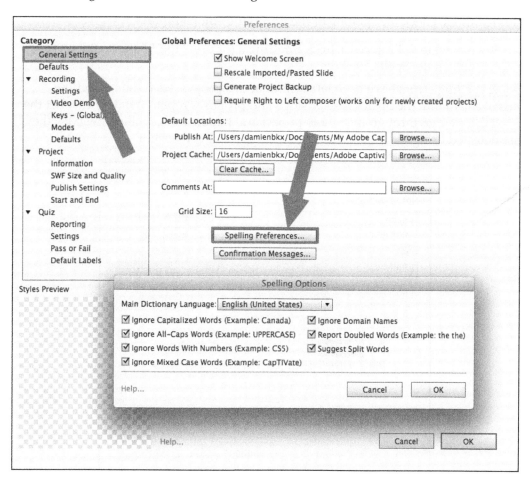

The main option of this box is **Main Dictionary Language**. Notice that, by default, the checkboxes of the **Spelling Options** dialog box are all selected.

Finishing Touches and Publishing

5. Open the **Main Dictionary Language** drop-down list and take some time to inspect the available languages. Is yours in the list?

6. For this exercise, make sure you choose **English (United States)** as **Main Dictionary Language**.

7. Take some time to inspect the other options of the dialog box. They should be pretty much self-explanatory. Make sure they are all selected before moving on.

8. Click on the **OK** button to close the **Spelling Options** dialog, then on **OK** again to validate the changes and close the **Preferences** dialog.

Now that you have a better idea of the available Spell Checker options, you will use this feature to check the spelling of the Encoder Demonstration.

9. Navigate to **Project | Check Spelling...** (or press the *F7* shortcut key) to launch the Spell Checker.

Some spelling errors have been left behind in this project. Each time a spelling mistake is found, the Spell Checker stops and proposes replacement words. Let the Spell Checker go through the whole project and handle each spelling mistake; they are detected using the dialog shown in the following screenshot.

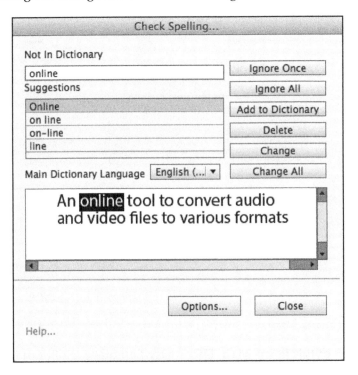

At the end of the **Check Spelling** window are two important buttons.

10. Click on the **Options...** button at the end of the **Check Spelling...** dialog.

The same **Spelling Options** dialog you accessed through the **Preferences** dialog opens.

11. Leave all the **Spelling Options** at their current settings and click on **OK** to close the **Spelling Options** dialog.
12. At the bottom-left corner of the **Check Spelling...** dialog, click on the **Help...** link.

Such a **Help...** link can be found at the bottom-left corner of many dialog boxes throughout Captivate. It opens the default browser and displays the **Adobe Captivate Help** page that specifically explains the options of the current dialog box. The **Help...** link is an easy and fast way to access specific help content.

13. Take some time to review the currently opened help page. When done, close your browser and return to Captivate.

When the spell check is over, a box informs you that the check is complete and that a certain number of corrections have been made (in my case, four errors were corrected).

14. Click on the **OK** button to discard the information box.
15. Make sure you save the file before moving on.

With the spell check complete, the final phase of the post-production process is now underway. Checking the spelling in Captivate is as easy as checking the spelling in any other text-authoring application. Just remember that it is an essential part of any professional eLearning project.

The following is a quick summary of what has been covered in this section:

- Captivate contains a Spell Checker that works in the same way as any other Spell Checker found in virtually every text-authoring application.
- The Spell Checker of Captivate has the ability to check the spelling of all the text typed throughout the application. This includes the text typed in Text Captions, Slide Notes, Text Animations, Buttons, and in the Table of Contents.
- The **Spelling Options** can be accessed through the **Preferences** dialog or directly from the **Check Spelling** dialog.
- The **Help...** link found at the bottom-left corner of many dialog boxes opens the default browser and displays the help page specifically dedicated to that dialog box. It is a quick and easy way to access specific help content.
- Checking the spelling is an essential part of any professional eLearning project.

Finishing Touches and Publishing

Exploring the Start and End preferences

The second final touch you will focus on will let you decide how the movie should start and how it should end. This is very important to fine-tune the student's experience and to optimize the performance of the project when viewed over the Internet.

In the following exercise, you will explore the available Start and End preferences using the following steps:

1. If needed, return to the `encoderDemo_800.cptx` file under `Chapter08`.
2. Navigate to **Edit** | **Preferences** (Windows) or **Adobe Captivate** | **Preferences** (Mac) to open the **Preferences** dialog.
3. On the left-hand side of the **Preferences** dialog, select the **Start and End** category situated in the **Project** section.

Remember that the categories pertaining to the **Project** section of the **Preferences** dialog are specific to the current project only. Your screen should now display the dialog shown in the following screenshot:

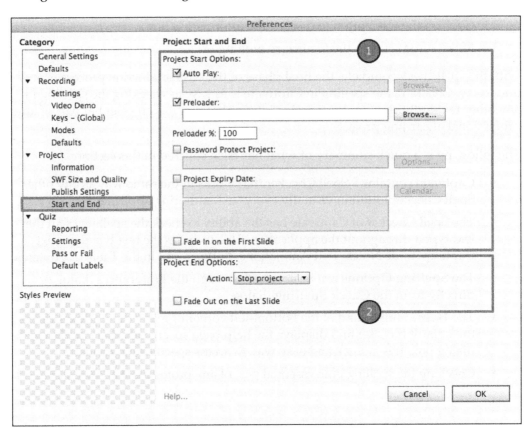

[346]

The **Start and End** preference page is divided into two sections. At the top of the page is **Project Start Options**, shown as **(1)** in the previous screenshot. At the end of the page is **Project End Options**, shown as **(2)** in the previous screenshot.

The following options are available under the **Project Start** section:

- **Auto Play**: If this option is selected, the project will start playing as soon as it finishes loading. If it is not selected, the student will have to click on the **Play** button to view the movie. In such a situation, you can use the **Browse** button to choose an image that will be displayed until the student clicks on the **Play** button (such an image is often called a poster image).

- **Preloader**: The **Preloader** checkbox is an image or a Flash animation (.swf) that is displayed while the movie is loading. If **Preloader** is selected and no preloader file is supplied, Captivate uses its default preloader, but you can also create your own custom preloader or choose one from the **Gallery**.

- **Preloader %**: This is, to me, the most important option of this **Preferences** pane. It represents the percentage of the file that has to be downloaded before the movie starts to play. If set to 50 percent, it means that the movie will start playing when 50 percent of the entire file is downloaded. The remaining 50 percent will be loaded while the beginning of the movie is being played. Use this option when the project is large and contains lots of audio or video. It reduces the waiting time of the student, which provides a much smoother learning experience.

> Here is an interesting blog post from the Iconlogic blog. Kevin Siegel details how to use the **Preloader** and **Preloader** % options to broadcast your corporate brand. It is available at http://iconlogic.blogs.com/weblog/2010/10/adobe-captivate-5-preloadyour-corporate-brand.html.

- **Password Protect Project**: This option is self-explanatory. Share the password only with those individuals who should be granted access to the project. Use this option if the project contains confidential information or if you want to share a beta release of the project with a limited team of reviewers.

- **Project Expiry Date**: Use this option to set an expiration date for the project. The project will not be accessible if a student wants to access it after the expiration date.

- **Fade In on First Slide**: This option is turned on by default and provides a smoother transition when the student enters the course.

The following options are available under the **Project End Options** section:

- **Action**: The **Action** drop-down list is used to select an action that will be fired when the project is complete. By default, the **Stop project** action is selected.
- **Fade Out on Last Slide**: This option is turned on by default.

Now that you have had an in-depth overview of the available options, you can set the **Start and End** preferences of this particular project.

4. Set the **Preloader** % option to 50.

This particular movie contains a lot of sound, and sound takes a lot of time to download. With the **Preloader** % option set to 50, the time spent by a student waiting for the movie to download is divided by two.

5. Leave the remaining options at their default settings and click on **OK**.
6. Don't forget to save the file when done.

This concludes your overview of the **Start and End** preferences. Let's make a quick list of what you have learned so far:

- In the **Preferences** dialog, the pages pertaining to the **Project** section are specific to the current project only.
- In the **Start and End** category, Captivate exposes lots of options and features to let you decide how the project should start and what happens when it has finished playing.
- Use these options to enhance the user experience, enforce some basic security, and optimize the loading time of the movie.

Discussing the project metadata and accessibility

Metadata is data about data. In the Captivate files you are creating, the main data consists of the slides and all the objects and features that make up the project. Metadata is information such as the slide count, the author of the project, the description of the project, the resolution, and so on. All this information is data about data, or, to use a proper word, metadata.

Some of this metadata (such as the slide count, the resolution, the length, and so on) are automatically generated by Captivate, while other metadata has to be manually entered.

Metadata is essential if you want to create accessible projects. An accessible project is a project that can be accessed by people with disabilities. There are many things that you can do in a Captivate project to make it accessible. One of those things is to take the time to enter the metadata. This metadata is used by assistive devices of those with disabilities (devices such as Braille readers, screen readers, text-to-speech utilities, and so on) to provide the best possible learning experience to these students.

Section 508

Many countries around the world have adopted some kind of accessibility standards, rules, and even laws. Most of the time, these standards are based on the **Web Accessibility Initiative** (**WAI**, see www.w3.org/WAI), a document developed by the **World Wide Web Consortium (W3C)**. In U.S. legislation, these standards are implemented as an amendment of the U.S. Rehabilitation Act of 1973. This amendment is commonly known as Section 508. When a project is 508 compliant, it simply means that it complies with the accessibility requirements of this legal document.

In the following exercise, you will take the first step toward making this project accessible by using the **Project Info** dialog to enter the metadata of the project using the following steps:

1. If needed, return to the `encoderDemo_800.cptx` file under `Chapter08`.
2. Navigate to **Edit** | **Preferences** (Windows) or **Adobe Captivate** | **Preferences** (Mac) to open the **Preferences** dialog.
3. On the left-hand side of the **Preferences** dialog, click on the **Information** category situated in the **Project** section.

The upper section of the **Project Information** preferences is used to manually enter the missing metadata, while the bottom section displays the automatically generated metadata. The bottom section displays the estimated **Time**, **Resolution**, the number of **Slides**, and the number of **Hidden Slides**.

4. Type `My Fictional Training Company-MFTC` in the **Company** field.
5. Type `2014-MFTC` in the **Copyright** field.
6. Enter `Adobe Media Encoder - Demonstration` in the **Project Name** field.
7. Type `This project shows the students how to use the Adobe Media Encoder to convert a Quick Time movie into Flash Video` in the **Description** field.
8. Fill the remaining fields (**Author**, **Email**, and **Website**) with your own name, e-mail address, and website URL. Note that none of these fields are mandatory. If you do not have a website, just leave the field blank.

Finishing Touches and Publishing

The **Preferences** dialog should now look similar to what is shown in the following screenshot:

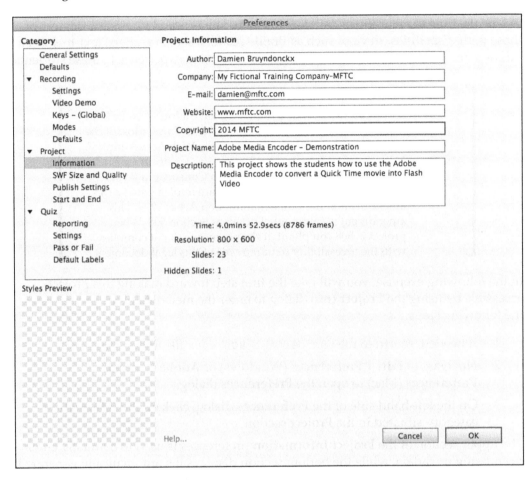

9. Click on the **OK** button when done to close the **Preferences** dialog.

Back in the main Captivate interface, the **Project Info** panel gives you easy access to some of the metadata.

10. Click on the **Project Info** tab situated next to the **Properties** and the **Library** tabs in the upper-right edge of the workspace.

11. The **Project Info** panel opens and displays the automatically generated metadata.

The **Project Info** panel only displays some of the metadata. It cannot be used to create new metadata or modify the existing metadata.

By entering the project metadata, you have taken the first important step toward making your project 508 compliant. This is a very good point, but there is a lot more that can be done throughout Captivate to further enhance the accessibility of the project. For example, you can add accessibility text to each individual slide using the **Properties** panel. There are some great blog posts on this subject as well as some very interesting pages in the official Captivate documentation:

- The accessibility page from the official Captivate documentation is available at `http://help.adobe.com/en_US/captivate/cp/using/WSc1b83f70210cd1011d7107e311c7efcf707-8000.html`
- The Captivate Accessibility overview page on the Adobe website is available at `http://www.adobe.com/accessibility/products/captivate/overview.html`
- Some useful tips and tricks regarding Project Info in Captivate 5 on the IconLogic blog by Kevin Siegel is available at `http://iconlogic.blogs.com/weblog/2011/01/adobe-captivate-5-dont-quote-me.html`

This concludes our little discussion on project accessibility and metadata. Here is a quick summary of what has been covered:

- Metadata is data about data.
- Metadata is essential to make projects accessible.
- Captivate automatically generates some of the metadata, while other metadata has to be entered manually.
- An accessible project is a project that can be accessed in good conditions by people with disabilities. These particular students use some specific input and output devices (such as Braille readers, text-to-speech utilities, and so on). These devices work better if you take the time to enter some extra metadata in your projects.
- The accessibility guidelines and standards are commonly known as Section 508 in reference to an amendment of the U.S. Rehabilitation Act of 1973.
- For some institutions, creating projects that comply with Section 508 is required by law. Check with your legal department.
- Use the **Project Information** preferences to manually enter the project metadata.

Exploring other project preferences

There are some more project preferences available in Captivate that are good to explore before publishing. Most of the time, the default settings for these particular options work just fine, so you won't modify any of these options in the Encoder Demonstration Project.

In the following exercises, you will simply take a look at these preferences and briefly discuss some of them:

1. If needed, return to the `encoderDemo_800.cptx` file under `Chapter08`.
2. Navigate to **Edit** | **Preferences** (Windows) or **Adobe Captivate** | **Preferences** (Mac) to open the **Preferences** dialog.
3. Open the **SWF Size and Quality** category situated in the **Project** section.

This particular **Preferences** page provides some options to control how the Captivate project is converted into Flash upon publication. If you want more information about any one of these options, don't hesitate to click on the **Help...** link at the bottom-left corner of the **Preferences** dialog.

4. Click on the **Publish Settings** category situated in the **Project** section in the left column of the **Preferences** dialog.

This **Preferences** page displays some additional options about how the project will be converted to Flash or HTML5. Once again, the default options work just fine for the vast majority of the project. We will briefly discuss some of these options:

- **Frames Per Second**: Use this option if you want to embed your Captivate project in another Flash project that has a frame rate which is different than 30 frames per second, or if you want to insert a video in your project that was created with a different FPS value. Otherwise, leave this option at its default value of 30 fps.
- **Publish Adobe Connect metadata**: This option adds some metadata to the project, thus producing a slightly larger SWF file. This metadata is designed to facilitate the integration of the Captivate project in the Adobe Connect LMS from Adobe. If you do not have access to an Adobe Connect server, there is no point in clicking on this option.

> See this great blog post by Michael Lund (also known as the Captivate Guru) about how the Adobe Connect metadata affects the size of the resulting file. It is available at http://www.cpguru.com/2008/12/30/reducing-the-file-size-of-your-captivate-projects/.

- **Enable Accessibility**: This option also adds extra information to the Captivate project, but it makes the project 508 compliant. If this option is not selected, the accessibility options set throughout the project are useless.
- **Externalize Resources**: When publishing to Flash, Captivate produces a single SWF file containing the whole project. Consequently, this file can be very large and hard to download for the students. Externalizing resources tells Captivate to generate many smaller SWF files that reference each other. This option may help in optimizing the download time of a large project, but it makes it more difficult to push the Captivate project online once published. Note that some assets (such as inserted video files) are always externalized. Also note that when publishing to HTML5, all the resources are always externalized.

Other options of the **Preferences** page should be self-explanatory. Don't hesitate to click on the **Help...** link if you need more information.

5. Click on the **Cancel** button to close the **Preferences** dialog and discard the eventual changes you've made along the way.

This concludes the tour of project preferences. You will now export the preferences of this project and import them into another project.

Exporting project preferences

Remember that the options pertaining to the **Project** section of the **Preferences** dialog are specific to the current project only.

If you want to apply the very same set of preferences to another project, Captivate lets you export the preferences of the current project and reimport them in another project. In the following exercise, you will export the preferences of the Encoder Demonstration and apply them to the Encoder Simulation:

1. If needed, return to the `encoderDemo_800.cptx` file under `Chapter08`.
2. Navigate to **File | Export | Preferences...** to export the preferences of the demonstration.
3. Save the preferences file as `encoderDemo_800_Preferences.cpr` under `Chapter08`. It should be the default name proposed by Captivate.
4. Click on **OK** to discard the information box telling you that the export is successful.

Note that the file extension of such a preference file is `.cpr`.

You will now open the simulation and import the preferences of the demonstration. At the end of this process, both files will share the exact same project preferences.

5. Open the `encoderSim_800.cptx` file under `Chapter08`.
6. Navigate to **File | Import | Preferences** to import a preference file in the project.
7. Browse to the `encoderDemo_800_Preferences.cpr` file under `Chapter08` and click on **Open**.

After a short while, an information box should appear on the screen telling you that the preferences were successfully imported.

8. Click on **OK** to discard the information box.
9. Navigate to **Edit | Preferences** (Windows) or **Adobe Captivate | Preferences** (Mac) to open the **Preferences** dialog of the `encoderSim_800.cptx` file.
10. Open the **Information** category situated in the **Project** section of the **Preferences** dialog.

The same metadata you entered in the Encoder Demonstration should have been applied to the simulation.

11. Change the **Project Name** field to `Adobe Media Encoder - Simulation`.
12. Change the project's **Description** field to `This project guides the student in using the Adobe Media Encoder to convert a QuickTime movie into Flash Video.`
13. Leave the other metadata at their current value, click on **OK** to validate the changes, and close the **Preferences** dialog.
14. Navigate to **File | Save All** to save both the Encoder Demonstration and the Encoder Simulation in one action.

The following list is a quick summary of what you have learned about the remaining project preferences:

- Most of the time, the default settings of the **SWF Size and Quality** and **Publish Settings** pages of the **Preferences** dialog work just fine.
- These settings help you control the size of the resulting Flash file and optimize the download time of the project. On the other hand, they can be quite technical and require some knowledge about Flash to be used with full efficiency.
- It is possible to export the preferences of one project and import them back into another project.

Working with the Skin Editor panel

The Skin of a project is a collection of elements that are, for the most part, displayed around the slides. It means that the elements of the Skin are not part of the actual eLearning content. They are used to interact with the Captivate movie and to enhance the overall user experience. A Skin is made of the following three elements:

- **The Playback Controls bar**: This is the most visible element of the Skin. It contains the necessary buttons and switches used by the student to control the movie during playback. It also contains a progress bar that tracks the student's progression in the Captivate movie.
- **The Borders**: The Skin Editor lets you create Borders around your movies. You can turn each of the four Borders on or off and choose their width, color, and texture.
- **The Table of Contents**: The last element of a Skin is the Table of Contents. By default, it is turned off, but it is very easy to turn it on and generate a Table of Contents for the project.

Captivate is shipped with a handful of predefined Skins that you can apply as is to your projects for rapid development. However, you also have the option of customizing any of the existing Skins and saving it with your own unique Skin name.

Also remember that the Skin is the third element of a Theme. The other two elements are the Styles and the Master Slides. This has already been covered in *Chapter 4, Working with Styles, Master Slides, Themes, and Templates*.

In this section, each of the three elements of the Skin will be discussed one by one. While doing so, you will slowly create a unique Skin that you will save and apply to other projects. Some more features of Captivate 7 will be uncovered along the way.

Customizing the Playback Controls bar

The first and most visible element of the Skin is the Playback Controls bar. By default, it appears below the project and contains the necessary buttons and switches to let the student control the playback of the project.

In the following exercise, you will explore the available options and create a customized Playback Controls bar for your projects:

1. Return to the `encoderSim_800.cptx` file under `Chapter08`.
2. Navigate to **Project** | **Skin Editor** to open the **Skin Editor** floating pane.

The **Skin Editor** floating pane should look similar to what is shown in the following screenshot:

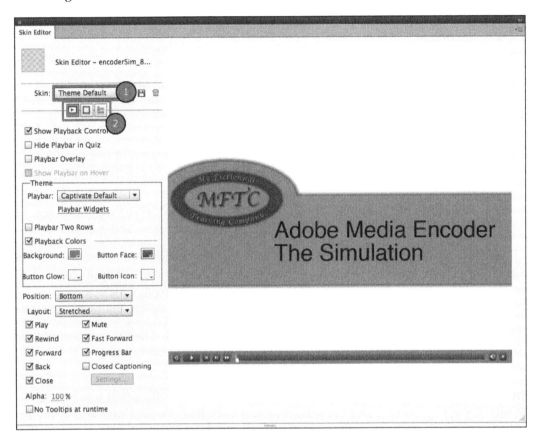

The **Skin Editor** floating pane is divided into two main areas. On the left-hand side are the Switches, Boxes, and Buttons you will use to customize the various elements of the Skin. On the right-hand side is a live preview of the first slide of the project. This area of the **Skin Editor** floating pane is automatically updated as you turn the options of the left area on and off.

Notice that the colors used by the playback controls match the colors of the other elements of the slide. This is the Skin stored in the applied Theme that is already in action!

In the upper-left area of the **Skin Editor** floating pane, notice two important controls. The **Skin** drop-down list (marked as **(1)** on the previous screenshot) is used to choose and apply one of the predefined Skins of Captivate to the project. Right below, there are three icons (marked as **(2)** in the preceding screenshot). Each of them represents one of the elements of the Skin: the Playback Control, the Borders, and the Table of Contents.

3. Open the **Skin** drop-down list and choose any Skin you want.
4. The chosen Skin is applied to the movie and the preview area of the **Skin Editor** floating pane is updated.
5. Open the **Skin** drop-down list again and apply the **Theme Default** Skin to the project.

The **Theme Default** Skin is the one that is stored in the Theme applied to the project. You will use that Skin as the starting point to create your own customized Skin.

6. Deselect the **Show Playback Control** checkbox.

When the preview updates, notice that the playback controls are not displayed anymore and that a grey bottom border appears where the Playback Controls used to be. This is shown in the following screenshot:

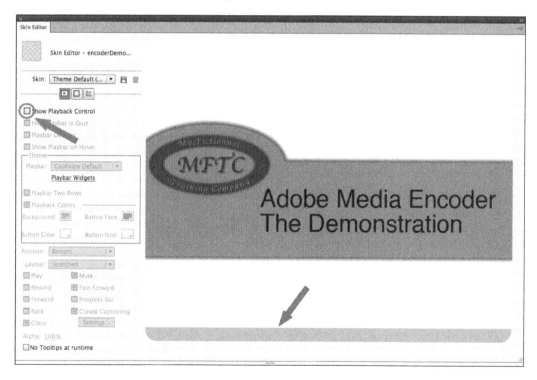

This is very interesting and deserves further investigation.

Finishing Touches and Publishing

By default, when a Playback Controls bar is applied, a bottom border that has the same width as the Playback Controls bar is also automatically applied to the movie. The idea is to put the Playback Controls on top of that bottom border so that they do not overlap with the movie. This is a very good thing and, most of the time, it works just fine. That being said, this system increases the overall height of the project. If you remember the discussion we had in *Chapter 2, Capturing the Slides* about the resolution of the movie, this can be quite a problem in some situations.

You will now set the Skin so that the Playback Controls are displayed without adding a single pixel to the height of the movie.

7. Click on the **Borders** icon. It is the second of the three icons situated just below the **Skin** drop-down list.
8. Deselect the **Show Border** checkbox.
9. Return to the previous screen by clicking on the **Playback Control** icon situated right below the **Skin** drop-down list.
10. Select the **Show Playback Control** checkbox to turn the Playback Controls back on.
11. Right below **Show Playback Control**, select the **Playbar Overlay** checkbox. This is the option that actually allows the Playback Controls bar to overlap with the slide.

This is how you can accommodate Playback Controls without adding a single pixel to the height of the movie.

12. Close the **Skin Editor** floating pane.
13. Use the Preview icon and click on **Next 5 Slides** to test the new Playback Controls configuration.
14. When the preview is over, close the **Preview** pane.

In this example, you want the Playback Controls to be situated outside of the actual movie and on top of the bottom border. You will now return to the **Skin Editor** floating pane to revert your latest changes before further exploring the other available options.

15. Navigate to **Project | Skin Editor** to reopen the floating **Skin Editor** pane.
16. Open the **Skin** drop-down list. Notice that the Skin currently in use is the **Theme Default (Modified)** Skin.
17. Apply any Skin of the list to the project.
18. Once the chosen Skin is applied, open the **Skin** drop-down list again.
19. Choose the **Theme Default** Skin.

The original **Theme Default** Skin is reapplied to the project. Basically, what you just did is reset the **Theme Default** Skin.

20. Deselect the **Rewind, Forward, Back, Close,** and **Fast Forward** checkboxes.
21. Make sure the **Play, Mute, Progress Bar,** and **Closed Captioning** checkboxes are selected.

After this operation, the Playback Controls bar should now contain only three buttons along with the Progress bar. You will now change the settings for the Closed Caption.

22. Click on the **Settings** button situated right below the **Closed Captioning** checkbox.
23. In the **CC Project Settings** dialog, choose the **Verdana** font family, change the font **Size** to 14 and the number of **Lines** to 2.
24. Click on the **OK** button to close the **CC Project Settings** dialog.
25. Take some time to inspect the remaining options of the Playback Controls bar. Make sure you do not change any of them before moving on to the next step.

With the completion of this exercise, you can consider the Playback Controls bar as final. Let's give it a try by using the **Preview** pane.

26. Close the floating **Skin Editor** pane.
27. Click on the Preview icon and then on **Project** to preview the entire project.

When the movie starts to play, take a look at the Playback Controls bar situated below the project. It contains three buttons and the Progress bar as specified in the **Skin Editor** floating pane during the preceding exercise. Don't hesitate to click on the CC button to have a look at the changes you made in the **CC Project Settings** dialog.

28. Close the **Preview** pane.

In the next section, you will discover the second element of a Captivate Skin: the Borders.

Working with Borders

Borders are the second main element of a Captivate Skin. As discussed in the previous section, *Customizing the Playback Contol*, adding a Playback Controls bar automatically adds a corresponding bottom border so that the Playback Controls do not overlap with the slide elements.

Finishing Touches and Publishing

In the following exercise, you will further experiment with Borders' properties:

1. While still in the `encoderSim_800.cptx` file, navigate to **Project | Skin Editor** to return to the **Skin Editor** floating pane.
2. Click on the **Borders** icon situated right below the **Skin** drop-down list.

In the Borders page of the **Skin Editor** floating pane, notice that the Borders are currently enabled and that the bottom border is turned on, as shown in the following screenshot:

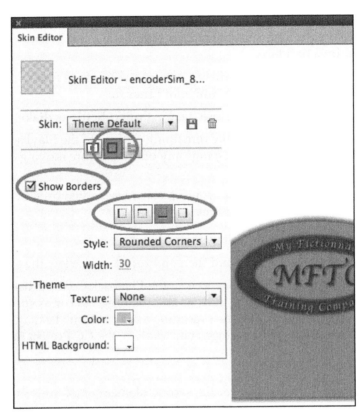

You will now turn all four borders on and explore the available formatting options.

3. Click on the left border, right border, and top border icons to turn the corresponding borders on.
4. In the **Style** drop-down list, choose the **Square Edge** style.
5. Click on the **Color** chooser. When the color palette opens, click on the Color Picker. It is the eyedropper icon situated in the top-right corner of the **Color** chooser.

6. Take a close look at your mouse pointer. It should look like an eyedropper. With this pointer active, click anywhere on the brown background where the **Adobe Media Encoder – The Demonstration** text animation is located

The Color Picker tool takes the color of the pixel you click on and applies it to the border. This tool is an incredibly fast and easy way to make two different elements share the very same color.

7. Open the **Texture** drop-down list and choose any texture you want.
8. Change the **Width** option of the borders to `80`.

The previous steps illustrate the available options of the Borders. You will now arrange these options to fit the particular needs of the Encoder Simulation.

Let's start with the most obvious change to be made: turning off this awful texture! (I do not like textures. They make the project look like my grandmother's kitchen!)

9. Open the **Texture** drop-down list again and choose **None** at the very top of the list.

This action turns the **Texture** option off. With the **Texture** option turned off, the brownish border reappears.

10. Turn the top, left, and right borders off. Leave only the bottom border on.
11. Reduce the **Width** option of the border to `30` pixels.
12. Close the floating **Skin Editor** pane and save the file.

With the completion of the preceding exercises, the first two elements of the Skin (Playback Controls and Borders) are now in place. In the next section, you will focus on the third and last element of the Skin: the Table of Contents.

Adding a Table of Contents

The Table of Contents is the third and last element of the Skin. By default, the Table of Contents is turned off.

In the following exercise, you will turn the Table of Contents on and explore the available options:

1. While still in the `encoderSim_800.cptx` file under `Chapter08`, navigate to **Project | Table of Contents...** to open the floating **Skin Editor** pane on the **Table of Contents** page.
2. Click on the **Show TOC** checkbox to turn the Table of Contents on.

By default, the Table of Contents appears on the left-hand side of the project and lists every single slide. At this moment, the slides are named **Slide 1**, **Slide 2**, and so on.

In the next section of this exercise, you will experiment with two ways of changing the name of the slides in the Table of Contents.

The first way is to change the name of the slide directly in the **Skin Editor** floating pane using the following steps:

3. Right below the **Show TOC** checkbox, double-click on the **Slide 1** title.
4. Change the name of the slide to Introduction and press the *Enter* key.

After a short while, the Preview area displays the updated Table of Contents.

The second way of changing the slide name involves closing the **Skin Editor** floating pane and using the **Properties** panel of each slide to specify a slide label.

5. Close the floating **Skin Editor** panel.
6. Use the **Filmstrip** panel to select slide 2. Make sure the **Properties** panel shows the properties of the slide and not the properties of any of the slide element.
7. At the top of the **Properties** panel, type Video Slide in the **Label** field.
8. Press *Enter* to validate the change.

When it is done, take another look at the **Filmstrip** panel. The slide label should be displayed below the corresponding thumbnail.

9. Use the same technique to enter a label for other slides of the project:
    - **Slide 3**: Change the label to Simulation Instructions
    - **Slide 4**: Change the label to Beginning of the Simulation
    - **Slide 17**: Change the label to Ending slide
    - Leave the **Label** field of the other slides empty
10. Navigate to **Project | Table of Content** to reopen the floating **Skin Editor** pane on the **Table of Contents** page.

11. Click on the Reset TOC icon situated below the list of TOC entries, as shown in the following screenshot:

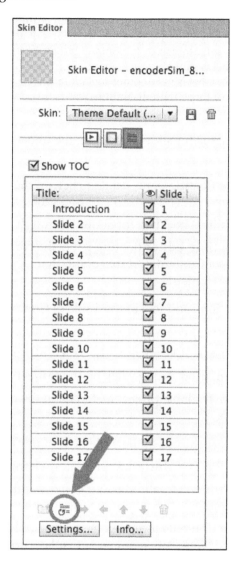

When clicking on this icon, Captivate inspects the slides of the project and regenerates the entries of the Table of Contents. Notice that the slide label, if any, is used as the title of the corresponding TOC entry.

Also, notice that there is no label for slide 1. This tells you that manually changing the name of the slide in the TOC editor does *NOT* add a corresponding label to the slide.

> **About slide labels**
>
> In the current exercise, you are using slide labels to generate the entries of the Table of Contents, but adding labels to slides serves many other purposes as well. First of all, it makes the project easier to use and maintain, but the main benefit of the slide label is probably the enhanced accessibility it provides. The slide label is yet another metadata used by the assistive devices of those with disabilities and is mandatory to make the eLearning project 508 compliant.

You will now re-enter a name for slide 1 and hide the unnecessary slides from the Table of Contents.

12. In the **Skin Editor** floating pane, double-click on the **Slide 1** title in the list of TOC entries. Retype `Introduction` and press the *Enter* key.
13. Uncheck the visibility checkbox for slides 5 through 16.

In the preview area of the **Skin Editor** floating pane, the corresponding slides disappear from the Table of Contents. At this point, there should be only 5 slides mentioned in the Table of Contents.

You will now finalize the look and feel of the Table of Contents.

14. Click on the **Info...** button situated at the bottom of the **Skin Editor** floating pane, below the list of TOC entries. The **TOC Information** dialog opens.
15. In the **TOC Information** dialog, click on the **Project Information** button.

This last action copies the available project metadata to the corresponding fields of the **TOC Information** box.

16. Type `Encoder Simulation` in the **Title** field of the **TOC Information** dialog.
17. At the bottom of the **TOC Information** dialog, change the font to **Verdana**.
18. Click on the **OK** button to validate your choices and close the **TOC Information** dialog.

At this point, the Table of Contents is almost ready. The only remaining problem is the extra space the Table of Contents requires to display properly. To address this problem, you will ask Captivate to position the Table of Contents on top of the slide and to provide a way to toggle its visibility on and off.

19. Click on the **Settings...** button situated at the bottom of the **Skin Editor** floating pane, below the list of TOC entries.
20. At the top of the **TOC Settings** dialog, change the **Style** option to **Overlay**.
21. In the **Color** section, click on the **Background** color and use the eyedropper tool to apply the same brownish color as the one used on the slide itself.

22. Change the **Alpha** value to 65 percent to create a semitransparent Table of Contents.
23. Take some time to explore the other available options and feel free to modify them at will. When done, your screen should look similar to what is shown in the following screenshot:

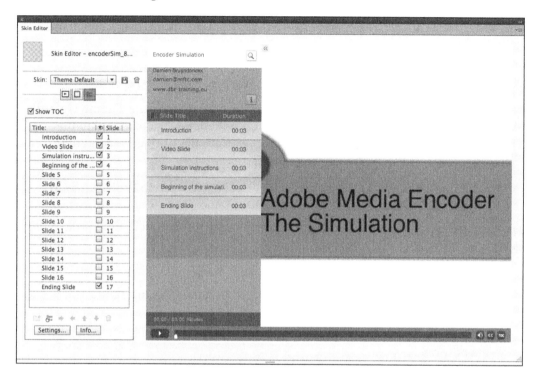

24. When you are happy with your Table of Contents, click on **OK** to validate your choices and close the **TOC Settings** dialog.
25. Close the floating **Skin Editor** pane and save the file.

Your Table of Contents is now ready. It is time to give it a try in the **Preview** pane.

26. Click on the Preview icon to preview the entire project.

When the **Preview** pane opens, notice the small double-arrow in the top-left corner of the slide.

27. Click on that small double-arrow to reveal the Table of Contents.
28. Click on the same icon to turn off the Table of Contents again.

Notice the new **TOC** button at the right edge of the Playback Controls bar.

Finishing Touches and Publishing

29. Click on the **TOC** icon situated at the right edge of the Playback Controls bar to reveal the Table of Contents.
30. Click on the **TOC** icon again to turn off the visibility of the Table of Contents.
31. Close the **Preview** pane and save the file.

With the addition of the Table of Contents, the Skin of your project is now final. It looks so great (no kidding!) that you want to apply it to other projects you are working on.

Applying the same Skin to other projects

To create the Skin of the Encoder Simulation, you started from the **Theme Default** Skin and you customized it. In this section, you will make the current Skin the **Theme Default** Skin, save the Theme, and apply it to other projects using the following steps:

1. While still in the `encoderSim_800.cptx` file, navigate to **Project | Skin Editor** to reopen the floating **Skin Editor** pane.

The **Skin** drop down indicates that the **Theme Default (Modified)** Skin is currently in use.

2. Click on the **Save As** icon situated next to the **Skin** drop-down list.
3. In the **Save As** box that pops up, leave the **Theme Default** name as it is and click on **OK**.
4. Confirm that you want to replace the existing **Theme Default** Skin with a new one.
5. Close the floating **Skin Editor** pane.

The new Skin is now saved as the Default Skin of the applied Theme. You will now save the Theme in a new file and apply that theme to the Encoder Demonstration.

6. Navigate to **Theme | Save Theme As** to save the current theme as a new file.
7. Save the Theme in your exercise folder as `mftc_theme_final_800.cptm` under `themes`.
8. Switch to (or open) the `encoderDemo_800.cptx` file under `Chapter08`.
9. When in the Demonstration project, navigate to **Theme | Apply a New Theme**. Browse to the `mftc_theme_final_800.cptm` file under `themes` and click on **Open**.
10. Click on **Yes** to confirm that you want to apply the new Theme to the Demonstration project.

11. Take some time to go through the slides of your project as some styles must be reapplied after applying the Theme to the project.

Both your demonstration and your simulation now share the very same theme. It means that they share the same set of Styles, the same Master Slides, and the very same Skin.

12. Navigate to **Project | Skin** to open the **Skin Editor** floating pane of the `encoderDemo_800.cptx` file under `Chapter08`.

On the **Playback Controls** page of the **Skin Editor** floating pane, note that some of the checkboxes are not available. This is due to the presence of a Pretest in this project. When a Pretest is present in the project, most of the controls of the Playback Controls bar cannot be turned on. That being said, all the other properties of the Playback Controls bar (such as colors) are derived from the Theme and are the same as in the simulation file.

13. Click on the **TOC** icon situated below the **Skin** drop-down menu to jump to the **TOC** page of the Skin.
14. Click on the **Show TOC** checkbox to turn the TOC on.

By default, the Table of Contents is not activated. When turned on, note that the TOC has the exact same look and feel as in the Simulation project.

15. Deselect the **Show TOC** checkbox to turn the TOC off.
16. Close the floating **Skin Editor** panel.
17. Save the file when done.

Apply this Skin to future projects

If you want to apply this Skin by default to future projects, one of the possible approaches is to apply the Theme that contains the Skin to a Captivate Template (a `.cptl` file). All Captivate Projects made from that template would therefore inherit the Skin applied to that template.

Here is a quick summary of what has been covered in the Skin Editor section of this chapter:

- A Skin is a collection of three elements: Playback Controls, Borders, and the Table of Contents.
- By default, adding a Playback Controls bar to the project automatically adds a corresponding border. The idea is to place the Playback Controls on top of the border to avoid overlapping between the Playback Controls and the project.

Finishing Touches and Publishing

- You can customize the Playback Controls bar in many ways using the Skin Editor.
- You can also turn the Borders on and off, and change their width, their color, or their texture.
- By default, the Table of Contents is turned off.
- It is possible to add labels to the slides. Slide labels serve three purposes: they make it easier for the developer to work with the project, they provide enhanced accessibility, they and are used to automatically generate the TOC.
- The **Skin Editor** floating pane provides many options to fine-tune the Table of Contents.
- Captivate ships with predefined Skins for rapid development.
- When you modify one of the predefined Skins, you actually create a new Skin that can be saved and reapplied to another project.
- The Skin of a project is one of the elements of the applied Theme. All the projects that have the same Theme inherit the same Skin.

Now that all the *finishing touches* have been taken care of, you will move on to the final phase of the general Captivate production workflow and make your eLearning content available to the outside world.

Publishing a Captivate project

So far, you have been working on .cptx files, which is the default native file type of Captivate. The .cptx file format is great when creating and designing projects, but it has two major disadvantages:

- It can become very large. Consequently, it is difficult for you to upload the file on a website and for the student to download and view it.
- Opening a .cptx file requires Captivate to be installed on the computer system.

Publishing a Captivate movie is converting (the proper word is *compiling*) the .cptx file into a format that can be easily downloaded and viewed by the students.

The primary format to publish your projects is the .swf format. SWF (pronounced swif) stands for ShockWave Flash. It is the file format used by the free Adobe Flash player plugin installed in more than 98 percent of the computers connected to the Internet. It has two advantages as compared to the .cptx file:

- A .swf file is usually much lighter than its .cptx counterpart, making it much easier to upload and download across the Internet.

- Any browser equipped with the free Adobe Flash plugin is able to open and play the .swf file. This makes it incredibly easy to deploy the courses made by Captivate.

That being said, the .swf format has some major disadvantages of its own:

- It requires the Adobe Flash Player plugin to be installed. If, for whatever reason, the plugin is not available, the .swf file cannot be played back.
- It cannot be modified. To modify a .swf file, you need to reopen the corresponding .cptx file, modify it in Captivate, and publish another version of the .swf file.
- The Flash Player plugin is no longer available for mobile devices. Consequently, a .swf file cannot be played back on a smartphone or on a tablet device.

That's why other publishing formats are available in Captivate. The most popular alternative to the .swf format is the HTML5 format. When published in HTML5, the project can be played back in any modern browser without the need for an extra plugin. An HTML5-enabled project can also be played back on mobile devices such as iOS and Android devices.

HTML5 also has its caveats. At the time of writing (January 2014), HTML5 is still a very new technology. Consequently, some features of Captivate are not yet supported in HTML5, and HTML5 support is not entirely consistent across browsers.

In this section, you will explore the various publishing options available in Captivate.

Publishing a Video Demo project

Due to its very nature, a Video Demo project can only be published as a .mp4 video file. In the following exercise, you will return to the encoderVideo.cpvc project and explore the available publishing options:

1. Open the encoderVideo.cpvc file under Chapter08.
2. Make sure the file opens in Edit mode.
3. If you are not in Edit mode, click on the **Edit** button at the lower-right corner of the screen. (If the **Edit** button is not displayed on the screen, it simply means that you already are in Edit mode.)

Finishing Touches and Publishing

When the file is open in Edit mode, take a look at the main toolbar at the top of the interface.

4. Click on the **Publish** icon or navigate to **File | Publish**.

The **Publish Video Demo** dialog opens.

5. In the **Publish Video Demo** dialog, make sure the **Name** of the project is encoderVideo.
6. Click on the ... button and choose the publish folder of your exercises as the destination of the published video file.
7. Open the **Preset** dropdown. Take some time to inspect the available presets. When done, choose the **Video - Apple iPad** preset.
8. Make sure the **Publish Video Demo** dialog looks similar to what is shown in the following screenshot and click on the **Publish** button:

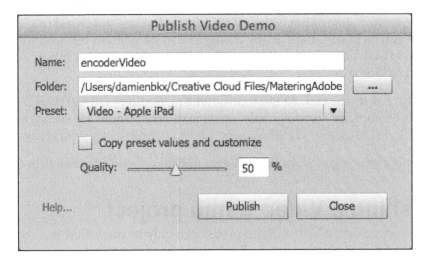

Publishing a Video Demo project can be quite a lengthy process, so be patient. When the process is complete, a message asks you what to do next. Notice that one of the options enables you to upload your newly created video to YouTube directly.

9. Click on the **Close** button to discard the message.
10. Use Windows Explorer (Windows) or the Finder (Mac) to go to the publish folder of your exercises.
11. Double-click on the encoderDemo.mp4 file to open the video in the default video player of your system.

Remember that a Video Demo project can only be published as a video file. Also remember that the published `.mp4` video file can only be experienced in a linear fashion and does not support any kind of interactivity.

Publishing to Flash

In the history of Captivate, publishing to Flash has always been the primary publishing option. Even though HTML5 publishing is a game changer, publishing to Flash is still an important capability of Captivate. Remember that this publishing format is currently the only one that supports every single feature, animation, and object of Captivate.

In the following exercise, you will publish the Encoder Demonstration project in Flash using the default options:

1. Return to the `encoderDemo_800.cptx` file under `Chapter08`.
2. Click on the **Publish** icon situated right next to the Preview icon. Alternatively, you can also navigate to **File | Publish**.

The **Publish** dialog box opens as shown in the following screenshot:

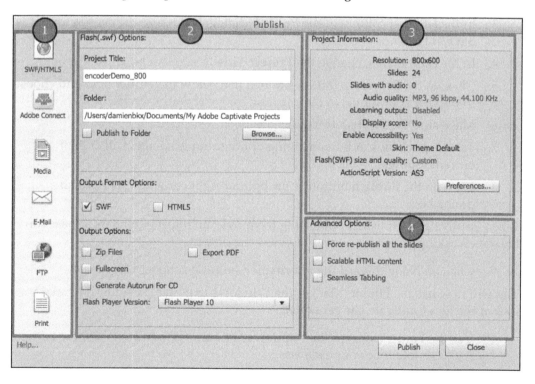

Notice that the **Publish** dialog of a regular Captivate project contains far more options than its Publish Video Demo counterpart in `.cpvc` files. The **Publish** dialog box is divided into four main areas:

- **The Publish Format area (1)**: This is where you choose the format in which you want to publish your projects. Basically, there are three options to choose from: **SWF/HTML5**, **Media**, and **Print**. The other options (**E-Mail**, **FTP**, and **Adobe Connect**) are actually suboptions of the **SWF/HTML5**, **Media**, and **Print** formats.
- **The Output Format Options area (2)**: The content of this area depends on the format chosen in the Publish Format **(1)** area.
- **The Project Information area (3)**: This area is a summary of the main project preferences and metadata. Clicking on the links of this area will bring you back to the corresponding preferences dialog boxes. Most of these boxes have been discussed earlier in this chapter.
- **The Advanced Options area (4)**: This area provides some additional advanced publishing options.

You will now move on to the actual publication of the project in the Flash format.

3. In the leftmost column of the **Publish** dialog, make sure the chosen format is **SWF/HTML5**.
4. In the central area, change the **Project Title** to `encoderDemo_800_flash`.
5. Click on the **Browse…** button situated just below the **Folder** field and choose to publish your movie in the `publish` folder of your exercises folder.
6. Make sure the **Publish to Folder** checkbox is selected.
7. Take a quick look at the remaining options, but leave them all at their current settings.
8. Click on the **Publish** button at the bottom-right corner of the **Publish** dialog box.

When Captivate has finished publishing the movie, an information box appears on the screen asking whether you want to view the output.

9. Click on **No** to discard the information box and return to Captivate.

You will now use the Finder (Mac) or the Windows Explorer (Windows) to take a look at the files Captivate has generated.

10. Use the Finder (Mac) or the Windows Explorer (Windows) to browse to the `publish` folder of your exercises.

Chapter 8

Because you selected the **Publish to Folder** checkbox in the **Publish** dialog, Captivate has automatically created the encoderDemo_800_flash subfolder in the publish folder.

11. Open the encoderDemo_800_flash subfolder to inspect its content.

There should be five files stored in this location:

- encoderDemo_800_flash.swf: This is the main Flash file containing the compiled version of the .cptx project
- encoderDemo_800_flash.html: This file is an HTML page used to wrap the Flash file
- standard.js: This is a JavaScript file used to make the Flash player work well within the HTML page
- demo_en.flv: This is the video file used on slide 2 of the movie
- captivate.css: This file provides the necessary style rules to ensure there is proper formatting of the HTML page

If you want to embed the compiled Captivate movie in an existing HTML page, only the .swf file (plus, in this case, the .flv video) is needed. The HTML editor (such as Adobe Dreamweaver) will recreate the necessary HTML, JavaScript, and CSS files.

Captivate and Dreamweaver

Adobe Dreamweaver CC is the HTML editor of the Creative Cloud and the industry-leading solution for authoring professional web pages. Inserting a Captivate file in a Dreamweaver page is dead easy! First, move or copy the main Flash file (.swf) as well as the needed support files (in this case, the .flv video file), if any, somewhere in the root folder of the Dreamweaver site. When done, use the Files panel of Dreamweaver to drag and drop the main .swf file onto the HTML page. That's it! More information on Dreamweaver can be found at http://www.adobe.com/products/dreamweaver.html.

You will now test the compiled project in a web browser. This is an important test as it closely recreates the conditions in which the students will experience the movie once uploaded on a web server.

12. Double-click on the encoderDemo_800_flash.html file to open it in a web browser.
13. Enjoy the final version of the demonstration you have created!

Now that you have experienced the workflow of publishing the project to Flash with the default options, you will explore some additional publishing options.

Using the Scalable HTML content option

Back in *Chapter 2, Capturing the Slides*, there was a discussion about choosing the right size for the project. One of the solutions was to use the **Scalable HTML content** option of Captivate. Thanks to this option, the eLearning content is automatically resized to fit the screen on which it is viewed. Let's experiment with this option hands on using the following steps:

1. If needed, return to the `encoderDemo_800.cptx` file under `Chapter08`.
2. Click on the **Publish** icon situated right next to the Preview icon. Alternatively, you can also navigate to **File** | **Publish**.
3. In the leftmost column, make sure the chosen format is **SWF/HTML5**.
4. In the central column, change the **Project Title** to `encoderDemo_800_flashScalable`.
5. Click on the **Browse...** button situated just below the **Folder** field and ensure that the publish folder is still the `publish` folder of your exercises.
6. Make sure the **Publish to Folder** checkbox is selected.
7. In the **Advanced Options** section (lower-right corner of the **Publish** dialog), select the **Scalable HTML content** checkbox.
8. Leave the remaining options at their current value and click on the **Publish** button at the bottom-right corner of the **Publish** dialog box.

When Captivate has finished publishing the movie, an information box appears on the screen asking whether you want to view the output.

9. Click on **Yes** to discard the information box and open the published movie in the default web browser.

During the playback, use your mouse to resize your browser window and notice how the movie is resized and always fits the available space without being distorted.

> The Scalable HTML content option also works when the project is published in HTML5.

Publishing to HTML5

Publishing to HTML5 was the killer new feature of Captivate 6 when it was released in June 2012. One of the main goals of HTML5 is to provide a plugin-free paradigm. This means that the interactivity and strong visual experience brought to the Internet by plugins should be supported natively by browsers and their underlying technologies (mainly HTML, CSS, and JavaScript) without the need for an extra third-party plugin.

Because no more plugins are necessary to deliver rich interactive content, any modern browser should be capable of rendering the interactive eLearning courses created by Captivate. This includes the browsers installed on mobile devices such as tablets and smartphones.

This is an enormous change not only for the industry, but also for Captivate users and eLearning developers. Thanks to HTML5, your students will be able to enjoy your eLearning content across all their devices. The door is open for the next revolution of our industry: the mLearning (for Mobile Learning) revolution.

Blog posts

To get a better idea of what's at stake with HTML5 in eLearning and mLearning, I recommend these two blog posts available at http://blogs.adobe.com/captivate/2011/11/the-how-why-of-ipads-html5-mobile-devices-in-elearning-training-education.html by Allen Partridge on the official Adobe Captivate blog and http://rjacquez.com/the-m-in-mlearning-means-more/ by RJ Jacquez.

Using the HTML5 Tracker panel

At the time of writing (January 2014), HTML5 is still under development. Some parts of the HTML5 specification are already final and well implemented in most browsers, while other parts of the specification are still under discussion. Consequently, some features of Captivate that are supported in Flash are not yet supported in HTML5.

In the following exercise, you will use the HTML5 Tracker to better understand what features of the Encoder Demonstration are (un)supported in HTML5:

1. If needed, return to the `encoderDemo_800.cptx` file.
2. Navigate to **Window** | **HTML5 Tracker** to open the **HTML5 Tracker** floating panel.

The **HTML5 Tracker** floating panel informs you that some of the features used in this project are not supported in HTML5, as shown in the following screenshot:

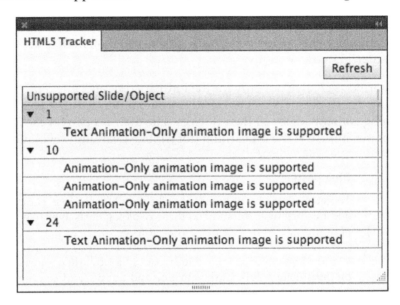

On slide 1 and slide 24, Text Animations are not supported in HTML5. It is the same for the orange-arrow Animations you inserted on slide 10 back in *Chapter 3, Working with Standard Objects*. This does not prevent the project from being published in HTML5; just be aware that the objects listed in the **HTML5 Tracker** floating panel will not function as expected.

3. Close the **HTML5 Tracker** panel.

[A comprehensive list of all the objects and features that are not supported in the HTML5 output is available in the official Captivate Help pages at http://help.adobe.com/. Make sure you read that page before publishing your projects in HTML5.]

In the next exercise, you will publish a version of the Encoder Demonstration in the HTML5 publishing format.

Publishing the project in HTML5

The process of publishing the project in HTML5 is very similar to the process of publishing the project to Flash. Perform the following steps to publish the project in HTML5:

1. If needed, return to the encoderDemo_800.cptx file.
2. Click on the **Publish** icon or navigate to **File | Publish** to open the **Publish** dialog box.
3. In the leftmost column of the **Publish** dialog, make sure you are using the **SWF/HTML5** option.
4. Change the **Project Title** to encoderDemo_800_HTML5.
5. Click on the **Browse...** button and choose the publish folder of the exercises as the location where the file will be published.
6. Make sure the **Publish to Folder** checkbox is selected.
7. In the **Output Format Option** section, select the **HTML5** checkbox. Once done, deselect the **SWF** checkbox.

This is the single most important setting of the entire procedure. Note that you can select both the SWF and HTML5 options.

8. In the **Advanced Options** area of the **Publish** dialog, deselect the **Scalable HTML content** checkbox.
9. Leave the other options at their current value and click on the **Publish** button.

Captivate informs you that some features used in this project are not supported in HTML5. This is something you already anticipated while looking at the **HTML5 Tracker** panel.

10. Click on **Yes** to discard the message and start the publication to HTML5.

Finishing Touches and Publishing

The process of publishing to HTML5 is much longer than the publication to Flash. One of the reasons is that Captivate needs to open the Adobe Media Encoder to convert the .flv video used on slide 2 and the Full Motion Recordings of slide 17 and 22 to the .mp4 format.

When the publish process is complete, a second message appears asking whether you want to view the output.

11. Click on **No** to discard the message and return to the standard Captivate interface.

You will now use the Windows Explorer (Windows) or the Finder (Mac) to take a closer look at the generated files.

12. Use the Windows Explorer (Windows) or the Finder (Mac) to go to the encoderDemo_800_HTML5 folder under the publish folder of the exercises.

You should find a bunch of files and folders in the encoderDemo_800_HTML5 folder, under publish, as follows:

- index.html: This file is the main HTML file. This is the file to load in the web browser to play the course.
- /ar: This folder contains the needed audio assets in .mp3 format.
- /dr: This folder contains the needed images. Notice that the mouse pointers, the slide backgrounds, as well as all the Text Captions are exported as .png images.
- /vr: This folder contains the needed video files in .mp4 format.
- /assets: This folder contains the needed CSS and JavaScript files.

You will now test this version of the project in a web browser.

13. Double-click on the index.html file to open it in the default web browser.

When testing the HTML5 version of the project in a web browser, notice that standard Text Captions have been used to replace the unsupported Text Animations of slide 1 and 24. On slide 10, the Animations have been replaced by static images.

Apart from the few problems mentioned in the HTML5 Tracker, Captivate does a pretty good job of converting the demonstration to HTML5.

That being said, HTML5 publishing is still an emerging technology. The room for improvement is enormous. In the coming years, more parts of the HTML5 specification will be finalized and new techniques, tools, and frameworks will emerge. You will then be able to better implement HTML5 across devices, both in Captivate and throughout the Internet.

Adobe Captivate 7 for Mobile Learning

Adobe Captivate 7 for Mobile Learning is a Packt Publishing title that covers the HTML5 publishing process of Captivate 7 in great detail. To get more information about this title, just visit the Packt Publishing website at http://www.packtpub.com/adobe-captivate-7-for-mobile-learning/book.

Publishing an eLearning-enabled project

As a Captivate user, publishing an eLearning-enabled project is not very different from publishing a normal project in Flash or HTML5. Behind the scenes, however, Captivate generates a whole bunch of files to enable SCORM or AICC reporting. In the next exercise, you will publish the SCORM-enabled *Driving in Belgium* project using the following steps:

1. Open or switch to the drivingInBe.cptx file under Chapter08.
2. Use the Publish icon or navigate to **File | Publish** to open the **Publish** dialog.
3. In the leftmost column of the **Publish** dialog, choose to publish the movie in the **SWF/HTML5** format.
4. Use the **Browse...** button next to the **Folder** field to choose the publish folder of your exercise as the publishing destination.
5. In the **Output Format Options** section, make sure the **SWF** option is the only one selected.

Finishing Touches and Publishing

At the bottom of the middle column of the **Publish** dialog, note that the **Zip Files** option has been automatically selected by Captivate. This is because this particular project has been configured to enable reporting to a SCORM-compliant LMS as indicated in the **Project Information** section of the **Publish** dialog.

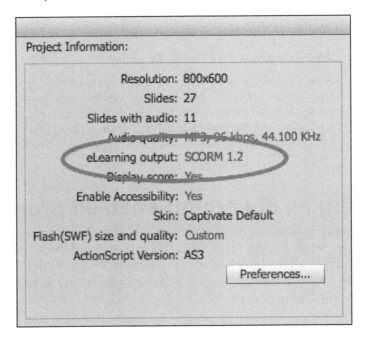

When the **Zip Files** checkbox is selected, Captivate publishes the movie and creates a `.zip` archive containing all the generated files. This is the reason why the **Publish to Folder** checkbox is disabled. Using this technique, you simply have to upload that single `.zip` file to the LMS. A SCORM-compliant LMS is able to unzip the package and properly deploy the files it contains.

6. Take some time to inspect the remaining options of the **Publish** dialog, but leave them all at their current value.
7. Click on the **Publish** button.
8. Acknowledge the **Publish Complete** message by clicking on the **OK** button.

You will now take a look at the generated `.zip` file.

9. Use the Finder (Mac) or Windows Explorer (Windows) to navigate to the `publish` folder of the exercises files.

You should find the `drivinInBe.zip` file in this folder.

10. Unzip the file to take a closer look at its content.

This is where the magic takes place! In the unzipped version of the file, you should find the same files as when you published a regular non-SCORM project (that is, the `.swf` file, a corresponding `.html` file, the `standard.js` JavaScript file, and the `captivate.css` file). However, because you decided to produce a SCORM-compliant package, Captivate has generated lots of extra files. These extra files are used to enable communication between the LMS and the Captivate project.

The most important of these extra files is `imsmanifest.xml`. This file is the SCORM Manifest. It must be stored at the root of the SCORM package. Feel free to open this file in your favorite text editor to take a look at its content (but make sure you do not modify it). The manifest file describes the course structure to the LMS using a SCORM-compliant XML format. These files are shown in the following screenshot:

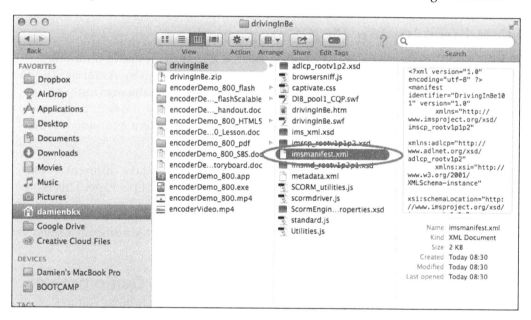

The actual extra files that Captivate generates depend on the standard being used (SCORM, AICC, or Tin Can) and the chosen version of SCORM.

Test your SCORM packages for free

If you do not have a SCORM- or Tin-Can-compliant LMS available, you can still test the SCORM and Tin Can features of your Captivate project by setting up a free account with SCORM Cloud at `https://cloud.scorm.com/sc/guest/SignInForm`. SCORM Cloud is a web-based LMS. Their free service can be used as a great testing platform, but if you want to use SCORM Cloud to host your real online courses, you'll have to upgrade to a paid subscription plan. There is a great blog post about creating an LMS-ready file in Captivate and uploading it to SCORM Cloud available at `http://blogs.adobe.com/captivate/2011/11/demystifying-captivate%E2%80%93lms-integration.html`.

Working with the MultiSco packager

In *Chapter 7, Working with Quizzes*, you discovered that the concept of **Sharable Content Objects (SCO)** is at the heart of the SCORM specification. As far as SCORM is concerned, the eLearning-enabled content you published in the previous section is a SCO. One of the key pieces of information contained in the `imsmanifest.xml` file is the unique SCO identifier of this particular piece of content as entered in the **Manifest** dialog box of Captivate.

One of the most interesting aspects of SCORM is the ability to take different SCOs, arrange them in a course, and publish them as a single SCORM package. This is precisely what the MultiSco packager enables you to do.

In the next exercise, you will create one more SCO and use the MultiSco packager to package multiple SCOs into a single package.

Creating a SCORM package from the Video Demo project

As discussed earlier in this chapter, a Video Demo project can only be published as a `.mp4` video file. The publishing options available for a Video Demo project do not allow for the creation of a SCORM package. But, there is a trick! In the next exercise, you will import a `.cpvc` Video Demo project inside a standard Captivate project and publish it as a SCORM package using the following steps:

1. Return to Captivate and close every open file.
2. On the Welcome screen, click on the **Create New Blank Project** item. Alternatively, you can navigate to **File | New Project | Blank Project**.

3. In the **New Blank Project** dialog, select the predefined size of **800 x 600** and click on **OK**.

Captivate creates a new project that is 800 pixels in width and 600 pixels in height. The next step is to insert the Video Demo CPVC project inside this new project.

4. Navigate to **Insert | CPVC Slide** to insert the Video Demo project into the current project.
5. Browse to the `encoderVideo.cpvc` file under `Chapter08` and click on **Open**.
6. In the **Filmstrip** panel, right-click on slide 1 and delete it.
7. Save the file as `EncoderVideo.cptx` under `Chapter08`.

The **CPCV Slide** menu item under **Insert** is a brand new feature of Captivate 7. It allows you to insert the Video Demo project inside a regular project. As far as Captivate is concerned, this project is a standard project that uses the `.cptx` file extension. The Video Demo project can therefore be published as a SCORM package.

8. Navigate to **Quiz | Quiz Preferences...** to open the **Preferences** dialog on the **Quiz Reporting** page.
9. At the top of the page, select the **Enable reporting for this project** checkbox.
10. Open the **LMS** drop-down menu and choose **Moodle** as the LMS.
11. Click on the **Configure** button to create a SCORM Manifest.
12. Enter the following values in the **Manifest** dialog:

Course Identifier	`encoderVideo`
Course Title	`The Adobe Media Encoder Video Demo`
Course Description	`This video shows the student how to convert a Quick Time movie into Flash Video`
SCO Identifier	`encoderVideo`
SCO Title	`The Adobe Media Encoder Video Demo`

13. Click on **OK** to validate and close the **Manifest** dialog.

There is no Quiz in this particular file, but it does not mean that you have nothing to track! In a Quiz-less project, SCORM can be used to track the completion status of the project by the students.

14. In the **Status Representation** section, make sure that the **Incomplete ---> Complete** option is selected.

Finishing Touches and Publishing

15. In the **Success/Completion Criteria** section, select the **Slide Views** checkbox and deselect the **Quiz** checkbox.
16. Since there is no Quiz in this project, deselect the **Interaction Data** checkbox situated in the **Data To Report** section.
17. Make sure your reporting **Preferences** look similar to what is shown in the following screenshot and click on **OK** to validate and close the dialog:

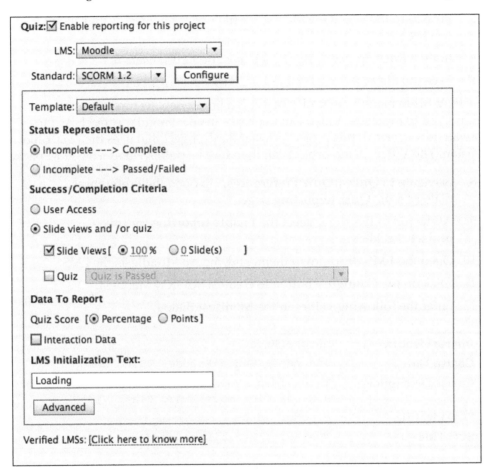

Now that the Quiz Reporting Preferences have been correctly entered, the last step is to publish this project as a SCORM package.

18. Use the **Publish** icon or navigate to **File | Publish** to open the **Publish** dialog.
19. In the leftmost column of the **Publish** dialog, choose to publish the movie in the **SWF/HTML5** format.
20. Use the **Browse...** button next to the **Folder** field to choose the publish folder of your exercise as the publishing destination.
21. In the **Output Format Options** section, make sure the **SWF** option is the only one selected.
22. In the **Output Options** section, make sure that the **Zip Files** option is selected.
23. Leave all the other options at their default value and click on **Publish**.
24. When the publication process is finished, use the Finder (Mac) or the Windows Explorer (Windows) to browse to the publish folder of your exercises.

You should see a second SCORM package named encoderVideo.zip. This ZIP file contains all the assets that are necessary to integrate the Video Demo project into a SCORM-1.2-compliant LMS such as Moodle.

Creating a single course package from multiple SCOs

The publish folder of your exercises should now contain two separate SCORM packages: drivingInBe.zip and encoderVideo.zip. Each of these two packages have a unique SCO identifier defined in the imsManifest.xml file situated inside the package.

Using the MultiSco packager, you will now combine these two SCOs into a single SCORM course. At the end of this procedure, you will have a single .zip file containing both modules. This single .zip file can be uploaded as is into a SCORM-compliant LMS such as Moodle.

Perform the following steps to create the SCORM package:

1. Return to Captivate and navigate to **File | New Project | Multi-SCORM Packager...** to open the **multiscoPackager** AIR application.

Finishing Touches and Publishing

The **multiscoPackager** application is an external AIR application that is part of your Captivate installation. As shown in the following screenshot, **multiscoPackager** proposes three course templates, the leftmost template being the simplest one:

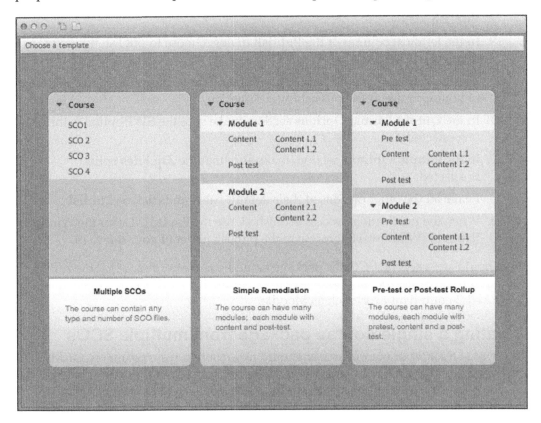

In *Chapter 7, Working with Quizzes*, you learned that Moodle is SCORM-1.2-compliant. This means that you need to generate a SCORM-1.2-compliant package if you want to upload your course to Moodle. In the **multiscoPackager** application, only the simplest template is SCORM-1.2-compliant.

2. Click on the first (leftmost) template named **Multiple SCOs**.
3. In the **Course Manifest Details** dialog, perform the following steps:
    - Select **1.2** in the **Version** drop-down menu under **SCORM Version**.
    - Type `mftc_bestOfSeries` in the **Identifier** field.
    - Type `The best of MFTC` in the **Title** field.

- Type `Experience the best courses of the MFTC company in this sample Course package` in the **Description** field.
- Type `1` in the **Version** field

4. Click on **OK** to validate the changes and close the **Course Manifest Details** dialog.

The information you just typed in the **Course Manifest Details** dialog box will be merged with the Manifest files of each individual SCO contained in this course in order to create a single SCORM manifest for the entire course. The next step is to add multiple SCOs into the course.

5. Click on the **+** icon situated in the top-right corner of the **multiscoPackager** application.
6. Browse to the `publish` folder of your exercise and select the `drivingInBe.zip` package. Click on **Open** to add the package to the course.
7. Repeat the same operation to add the `encoderVideo.zip` package of your `publish` folder to the course.

You can add as many SCORM packages as needed into the course. Notice the icons at the bottom-right corner of the **multiscoPackager** application. They allow you to reorder or delete the SCOs inside the course.

Now that every SCO has been added to the course, the last step is to publish the course as a single SCORM package.

8. Click on the **Publish Course** icon situated at the top-left corner of the **multiscoPackager** application.
9. In the **Publish SCO package** dialog, change the **Publish Folder** field to choose the `publish` folder as the output folder of the package.
10. Click on the **Publish** button. When the process is complete, click on **OK** to acknowledge the successful creation of the SCORM package.
11. Close the **multiscoPackager** application.
12. Use the Finder (Mac) or the Windows Explorer (Windows) to browse to the `publish` folder of your exercises.

You should see the new `mfct_bestOfSeries.zip` package that has been created by the **multiscoPackager** application. This package contains both the `drivingInBe` and `encoderVideo` modules. Feel free to unzip the package to check its content out. You should be able to locate a single `imsManifest.xml` file as well as the assets pertaining to each of the two modules you added to the course.

When using the Multi-SCORM Packager, remember the following points:

- Each individual component needs to be published as a SCORM package that contains an `imsManifest.xml` file. Such a package is called a **Sharable Content Object (SCO)**.
- A single SCO can be used in many different course packages.
- A single course can contain an unlimited number of SCOs.
- The generated course package can be uploaded as a single unit to a SCORM-compliant LMS.
- There are different versions of SCORM. Make sure you create course packages that are compliant with whatever SCORM version your LMS supports.
- The Multi-SCORM Packager of Captivate proposes three course templates to choose from. Make sure the chosen Template can be used with the version of SCORM that you are targeting.

This concludes your exploration of the Multi-SCORM Packager of Captivate 7.

For more information on the Multi-SCORM Packager, refer to this help article on the Adobe website at `http://helpx.adobe.com/captivate/using/multi-scorm-packager.html`.

Publishing to PDF

Another publishing option available in Captivate is to publish the project as an Adobe PDF document. This process is very close to the Flash publishing process covered previously. When converting to PDF, Captivate first converts the project to Flash and then embeds the resulting `.swf` file inside a PDF document. To read the Flash file embedded in the PDF document, the free Adobe Acrobat Reader simply contains a copy of the Flash player plugin.

Publishing the Captivate project to PDF is a great way to make the eLearning course available offline. The students can, for example, download the PDF file from a website and take the course on a train or on an airplane where no Internet connection is available. However, be aware that if the course is viewed offline or outside an LMS, Quiz scores and the course completion status are not tracked.

In the following exercise, you will publish the Encoder Demonstration to PDF:

1. Return to the `encoderDemo_800.cptx` file under `Chapter08`.
2. Click on the **Publish** icon situated right next to the Preview icon. Alternatively, you can navigate to **File** | **Publish**.
3. In the leftmost column of the **Publish** dialog, make sure the chosen format is **SWF/HTML5**.
4. In the central area, change the **Project Title** to `encoderDemo_800_pdf`.
5. Make sure the publish **Folder** field still points to the `publish` folder of the exercises.
6. Make sure the **Publish to Folder** checkbox is still selected.
7. At the end of the Format Options area, select the **Export PDF** checkbox.
8. Click on the **Publish** button situated at the lower-right corner of the **Publish** dialog.

When the publishing process is complete, a message tells you that Acrobat 9 or higher is required to read the generated PDF file.

9. Click on **OK** to acknowledge the message. A second information box opens.
10. Click on **No** to discard the second message and close the **Publish** dialog.
11. Use the Finder (Mac) or the Windows Explorer (Windows) to browse to the `encoderDemo_800_pdf` folder under your `publish` folder.

There should be six files in the `encoderDemo_800_pdf` folder under your `publish` folder. Actually, publishing to PDF is an extra option of the standard publishing to Flash feature.

12. Delete all but the PDF file from the `encoderDemo_800_pdf` folder under your `publish` folder.
13. Double-click on the `encoderDemo_800_pdf.pdf` file to open it in Adobe Acrobat.
14. Notice that the file plays normally in Adobe Acrobat. This proves that all the necessary files and assets have been correctly embedded into the PDF file.

In the next section, you will explore another option of Captivate: publishing the project as a standalone application.

Finishing Touches and Publishing

Publishing as a standalone application

When publishing as a standalone application, Captivate generates a .exe file for playback on Windows or a .app file for playback on Macintosh. The .exe (Windows) or .app (Mac) file contains the compiled .swf file plus the Flash player.

The advantages and disadvantages of a standalone application are similar to those of a PDF file. That is, the file can be viewed offline on a train, on an airplane, or elsewhere, but the features requiring an Internet connection will not work.

In the following exercise, you will publish the Captivate file as a standalone application for Mac or Windows using the following steps:

1. If needed, return to the encoderDemo_800.cptx file under Chapter08.
2. Click on the **Publish** icon situated right next to the Preview icon. Alternatively, you can navigate to **File** | **Publish**.
3. Click on the **Media** icon situated at the leftmost column of the **Publish** dialog box. The middle area is updated.
4. Open the **Select Type** drop-down list. If you are on a Windows PC, choose **Windows Executable (*.exe)**. If you are using a Mac, choose **MAC Executable (*.app)**.
5. If needed, change the **Project Title** to encoderDemo_800.
6. In the **Folder** field, make sure that the publish folder is still the current value.

Take some time to inspect the other options of the **Publish** dialog. One of them allows you to choose a custom icon for the generated .exe (Windows) or .app (Mac) file.

7. Leave the other options at their current value and click on the **Publish** button.

When the publish process is complete, an information box asks whether you want to see the generated output.

8. Click on **No** to clear the information message and to close the **Publish** dialog.

Now that the standalone application has been generated, you will use the Finder (Mac) or the Windows Explorer (Windows) to take a look at the publish folder and test the newly created applications.

9. Use the Finder (Mac) or the Windows Explorer (Windows) to browse to the publish folder of the exercises.
10. Double-click on the encoderDemo_800.exe (Windows) file or the encoderDemo_800.app (Mac) file to open the generated application.

The Captivate movie opens as a standalone application in its own window. Notice that no browser is necessary to play the movie.

This publish format is particularly useful when we want to burn the movie on a CD-ROM. When generating a Windows executable (`.exe`), Captivate can even generate an `autorun.ini` file so that the movie automatically plays when the CD-ROM is inserted in the computer.

Publishing as a .mp4 video file

When publishing a project as a video, Captivate generates a `.mp4` file and proposes various video presets for the conversion. Actually, Captivate first generates a `.swf` file and then converts it into a video file.

After the video conversion, the video file will play on any media player that is capable of reading the `.mp4` format. It is an ideal solution if you want to upload the resulting movie to YouTube or if you want to make it available to non-Flash devices. However, the generated `.mp4` video file permits only a linear experience, that is, no more interaction and no more branching are possible. The student experiences the video from the beginning to the end in a linear fashion, as is the case while watching a motion picture in a movie theatre or on TV. Consequently, converting a Captivate project to a video file is well suited for a demonstration, but does not work well with simulations.

In the following exercise, you will convert the Encoder Demonstration into a `.mp4` video using the following steps:

1. If needed, return to the `encoderDemo_800.cptx` file under `Chapter08`.
2. Click on the **Publish** icon situated right next to the Preview icon. Alternatively, you can also navigate to **File** | **Publish**.
3. If needed, click on the **Media** icon situated on the leftmost column of the **Publish** dialog box.
4. Open the **Select Type** drop-down list and choose **MP4 video (*.mp4)**.
5. If needed, change the **Project Title** to `encoderDemo_800`.
6. Open the **Select Preset** drop-down list. Take some time to inspect the available options and choose **YouTube Widescreen HD**.
7. Make sure the **Folder** field still points to the `publish` folder of the exercises.
8. Click on the **Publish** button at the bottom-right corner of the **Publish** dialog.

Publishing to a video file can be quite a lengthy process, so be patient. First, you will see that Captivate converts the project into a .swf file. When that first conversion is over, Captivate opens a second window named **Adobe Captivate Video Publisher** and converts the .swf file to a .mp4 video. At the end of the whole process, the **Adobe Captivate Video Publisher** dialog proposes to publish the generated video to YouTube or to open it.

9. Close the **Adobe Captivate Video Publisher** window.
10. As usual, use the Finder (Mac) or the Windows Explorer (Windows) to take a look at the publish folder of your exercises.
11. Double-click on the encoderDemo_800.mp4 file. The video opens in the appropriate media player.

The generated video file can be uploaded to YouTube, DailyMotion, or any other video-hosting service. You can also host the video on your own internal video-streaming server (such as a Flash Media server) if you have one available.

Publishing to YouTube

Captivate includes a workflow that allows you to publish your Captivate movie to a video file and upload it to your YouTube account even without leaving Captivate.

In the following exercise, you will convert your Captivate file to a video and upload it to YouTube.

This exercise requires a YouTube account and the creation of a new channel on your account. If you do not have a YouTube account, you can create one for free on the YouTube website or read through the steps of the exercise.

Perform the following steps to upload the video to YouTube:

1. Return to the encoderDemo_800.cptx file under Chapter08.
2. Click on the **YouTube** icon situated in the main toolbar.

When clicking on the **YouTube** icon, Captivate generates the slides as if you were publishing the movie in the Flash format. When that first conversion is complete, Captivate opens the **Adobe Captivate Video Publisher** window and converts the .swf file to .mp4. So far, the process is exactly the same as the one used in the previous section. At the end of the process, however, Captivate opens another window.

3. Enter your username and password to log in to your YouTube account.

4. Once logged in, enter the relevant project information:
   - Enter the title of the movie in the **Title** field. This is the only required field.
   - Enter a description in the **Description** field. By default, the description entered in the **Project Info** preferences pane (if any) is used.
   - Enter a list of comma-separated tags. These tags will help YouTube reference your video so that other YouTube users can find it easily.
   - Choose the best **Category** for your video.
   - Choose the level of **Privacy** (private or public).
5. Select the **I have read the terms & conditions** checkbox and click on the **Upload** button.

Captivate uploads the video to YouTube. When the process is complete, the **Adobe Captivate Video Publisher** window shows the direct link of our video on YouTube.

6. Click on the **Close** button to close the **Adobe Captivate Video Publisher** window.

As you can see, Captivate makes it incredibly easy to publish a project to YouTube!

> For more information on YouTube's privacy settings and the difference between a public and private video, visit `https://support.google.com/youtube/answer/157177?hl=en`.

Publishing to Microsoft Word

The last important publishing option to cover is the publication of the Captivate movie as a Microsoft Word document. There are four formats available: Handout, Lesson, Step-by-Step guide, and Storyboard.

> This publication option requires that both Adobe Captivate and Microsoft Word be installed on the same system. If you do not have Microsoft Word installed on your computer, just read through the steps of this exercise to have an idea of the workflow.

In the next exercise, you will publish your Captivate movie as a Microsoft Word file using the Handout template:

1. Return to the `encoderDemo_800.cptx` file under `Chapter08`.
2. Click on the `Publish` icon situated right next to the Preview icon. Alternatively, you can navigate to **File | Publish**.
3. Click on the **Print** icon situated at the end of the leftmost column of the **Publish** dialog box.
4. In the middle column, change the **Project Title** to `encoderDemo_800_handout`.
5. Make sure the **Folder** field still points to the `publish` folder of the exercises.
6. In the **Export Range** section, make sure that **All** is selected. You could publish a smaller selection of slides if needed.

That's it for the usual options. Before clicking on the **Publish** button, you have a few more options available in the rightmost column of the **Publish** dialog.

7. In the rightmost area of the **Publish** dialog, open the **Type** drop-down list. Inspect the available options and choose the **Handouts** type.
8. In the **Handout Layout Options** section, leave the **Use table in the output** option selected.
9. Open the **Slides Per Page** dropdown and choose to have two slides on each page of the Word document.
10. Select the **Caption Text**, **Slide Notes**, and **Include mouse Path** checkboxes.
11. Take some time to inspect the remaining options, but leave them all at their current value.
12. When ready, click on the **Publish** button.

Captivate generates the Word document according to the options set in the **Publish** dialog. When done, an information box appears asking whether you want to view the generated file.

13. Click on **No** to discard the information box and close the **Publish** dialog.
14. Use the Finder (Mac) or the Windows Explorer (Windows) to browse to the `publish` folder of your exercises.
15. Double-click on the newly created `encoderDemo_800_handout.doc` file.

The file opens in Microsoft Word. Take some time to inspect the generated Word document. Can you find the effect of each of the boxes you selected in the **Publish** dialog?

Extra credit – publishing to Word

In this section, you will test the remaining Microsoft Word publishing options by generating a Lesson, a Step-by-Step guide, and a Storyboard. These are the general steps to follow:

- Open the **Publish** dialog box.
- In the leftmost column, ensure that the **Print** option is selected.
- Give the project a meaningful Project Title.
- In the rightmost area of the **Publish** dialog, change the **Type** to **Lesson**, **Step by Step**, or **Storyboard**.
- Experiment with other options as well. Each Type has a specific set of options available, which are, for the most part, self-explanatory.
- When ready, click on the **Publish** button.
- Use the Finder (Mac) or the Windows Explorer (Windows) to browse to the publish folder and test your files in Microsoft Word.

Other publishing options

When you open the **Publish** dialog box, there are three options in the leftmost column that were not covered in previous sections:

- **Adobe Connect**: This is a server product from Adobe. One of the services offered by this enterprise solution is an LMS that integrates nicely with Captivate. If an Acrobat Connect server is available in your network, you can use this publishing option to convert the Captivate project to Flash or HTML5 and upload the resulting file to the Adobe Connect server. For more information, see this video on the official Captivate YouTube channel at http://www.youtube.com/watch?v=L1JtdeysJaU.
- **E-mail**: This option converts the Captivate project to Flash or a standalone application and attaches the resulting file in an e-mail message. The message can be further customized in your e-mail client software.
- **FTP**: This option converts the Captivate file to Flash or a standalone application and uploads the resulting file(s) to a **File Transfer Protocol (FTP)** server.

These three options are not special. They just combine one of the main publishing options covered earlier with some kind of extra file transport action in order to facilitate a workflow.

This last exercise concludes your overview of the publishing options of Captivate. So, let's have a quick summary of what has been covered:

- Publishing is the third and last step of the Captivate workflow.
- Captivate provides four main publishing formats: publishing to Flash or HTML5, publishing as a standalone application, publishing as a video file, and publishing as a Microsoft Word document.
- When publishing in a Flash format, Captivate generates a .swf file that can be played back by the free Adobe Flash Player plugin.
- The generated .swf file can be embedded in a PDF document for offline viewing. This option requires Adobe Acrobat or Adobe Reader 9, or later versions.
- Publishing in HTML5 was a new capability of Captivate 6 when it was released in June 2012. A project published in HTML5 can be played back on virtually any mobile device, including iOS and Android devices.
- Not every feature of Captivate is supported in HTML5. Use the HTML5 Tracker to find out which slides/objects of your project are not supported.
- When publishing as a standalone application, Captivate produces either a .exe file for playback on Windows or a .app file for playback on a Mac.
- Captivate can produce a .mp4 video that can be optimized for YouTube and for playback on a mobile device.
- When publishing as a .mp4 video, PDF file, or standalone application, the published project can no longer connect to the Internet. Consequently, some features that require an Internet connection (such as communicating with an LMS) do not work.
- When the project is published as a video file, it can only be experienced as a linear video that plays from the beginning to the end. Consequently, interactivity and branching are not supported.
- A Video Demo project can only be published as a .mp4 video file.

Summary

At the end of this chapter, you can proudly turn off the lights and leave the post-production studio. You have gone through the three major steps of the production process, uncovering lots of Captivate features, tools, and objects along the way!

In this particular chapter, you first focused on some final changes you can apply to the project before the actual publishing phase. You have checked the spelling, decided how the movie should start and end, added metadata to the project, and created a unique Skin, among other things. When all these final changes had been taken care of, the movie was finally ready for publication.

In the second part of this chapter, you concentrated on the **Publish** dialog box where you gained experience of the main publishing features of Captivate. Publishing is the process by which the movie is made available to the outside world.

Publishing to Flash is the main publishing option of Captivate. The Flash format supports every single feature of Captivate. When published in HTML5, the project can be played back on any device equipped with a modern web browser. This includes a vast majority of mobile devices such as iOS and Android smartphones and tablets. HTML5 publishing opens the doors for mLearning, which is the next revolution of our industry.

Other publishing formats of Captivate include publishing as a standalone application, publishing as a `.mp4` video file, and publishing as a Microsoft Word document. The `.mp4` video files produced by Captivate can easily be uploaded to YouTube without even leaving the application.

Congratulations on achieving this important milestone! In the remaining chapters of the book, you will focus on some of the most advanced features of Captivate. In the next chapter, you will learn about how Captivate can be used with other applications such as Microsoft PowerPoint or Adobe Photoshop.

You still have lots of interesting features to discover, so stay tuned and let's meet in *Chapter 9, Using Captivate 7 with Other Applications*!

Meet the community

In this section, I want to introduce you to Joe Ganci. He is a veteran eLearning developer and instructional designer. He has reviewed two of my Captivate books (including this one). I feel very fortunate to have people such as Joe participating in the review process of this book. The first time I contacted him via e-mail, he was kind enough to include a small quote in French (my native language) in his reply. This is incredible attention to detail that I will never forget…Thank you Joe.

Joe Ganci

Joe Ganci is an eLearning consultant with a long track record. His design approaches and his innovative use of tools, such as Adobe Captivate, Articulate Storyline, Adobe Presenter, Articulate Studio, ZebraZapps, Interact, and others, has caused many to improve how they design and develop their eLearning and to implement new and better methods. His personal and hands-on style of consulting keeps his services constantly in demand, and he is privileged to have visited with many clients from all over the world.

He has been involved in every aspect of learning development since 1983. He holds a degree in Computer Science and is a published author, having written several books, research papers, and articles about eLearning. He is widely considered a guru for his expertise in eLearning development and conducts classes and seminars at commercial companies, government facilities, leading universities, and at many industry conferences, where he often serves as the keynote speaker. He is on a mission to improve the quality of eLearning with practical approaches that work.

Contact details

- **Web**: http://elearningjoe.com/
- **Twitter**: @elearningjoe
- **E-mail**: joe@elearningjoe.com

Using Captivate 7 with Other Applications

In this chapter, you will explore how Captivate can be used with other applications. These external applications include Adobe products, such as Adobe Flash Professional and Adobe Photoshop, but Captivate can also integrate with third-party applications, such as Microsoft Word and Microsoft PowerPoint.

There are many benefits to using Captivate with these external applications. If your company already has a significant amount of training material made using PowerPoint, you'll be able to recycle this existing material and build on what already exists, rather than starting everything from the ground up again. By integrating Microsoft Word in the workflow, you can export Text Captions and Slide Notes to a Microsoft Word document and send it out to a translation service where the translators won't need any knowledge of Captivate to help you localize your eLearning content. By exporting the Captivate project to Flash Professional, you will be able to leverage the full power of the Flash Platform in your Captivate project.

In this chapter, you will:

- Create a new Captivate project from a PowerPoint presentation
- Add a PowerPoint slide in the middle of an existing Captivate project
- Explore the round-trip editing workflow between Captivate and PowerPoint
- Localize a Captivate project by exporting Text Captions and Slide Notes to Microsoft Word and reimport them into Captivate once translated
- Export the project to an XML file
- Import a Photoshop document into Captivate
- Export the Captivate project to Flash Professional

Preparing your work

To begin with this chapter, you won't need any of the files you worked with earlier, so the only thing to do is to reset the workspace of Captivate using the following steps:

1. Open Captivate.
2. Ensure that the **Classic** workspace is applied.
3. Navigate to **Window** | **Workspace** | **Reset 'Classic'**. This will reapply the default **Classic** workspace to the Captivate interface.

Most of the exercises of this chapter require external applications to be installed on your system along with Captivate. If you do not have access to these applications, just read through the steps of the exercises to have a basic idea of the workflows.

Integrating Captivate with PowerPoint

In this section, you will discover the tight integration that unites Microsoft PowerPoint and Adobe Captivate. This integration includes many features, such as creating a new Captivate project from a Microsoft PowerPoint presentation and including some slides of a presentation in an existing Captivate project.

> Captivate shares these features with another software product from Adobe named **Adobe Presenter**. Adobe Presenter is a Microsoft PowerPoint plugin. In PowerPoint 2007 and later versions, Presenter installs an extra ribbon at the top of the PowerPoint interface. Presenter can be used to publish a PowerPoint presentation to Flash using a technique that is similar to what is used in Captivate. Presenter also includes the ability to add narration and subtitles to a PowerPoint presentation and features the same quiz engine as the one used in Captivate. One of the best features of Presenter is the Adobe Presenter Video Creator, which allows you to create stunning professional screencasts. Adobe Presenter is only available on Windows. The Video Creator feature is the only part of Presenter that has been ported to Mac. Mac users, look for the free **Adobe Presenter Video Express** in the Mac App Store. More info can be found at http://www.adobe.com/products/presenter.html.

Converting an existing presentation to Captivate

In this first exercise, you will convert an existing PowerPoint presentation into a new Captivate project. To do so, you will use a simple workflow that allows you to open a PowerPoint file from the Welcome screen of Captivate. But first, let's have a look at the original PowerPoint presentation.

Viewing the presentation in PowerPoint

If PowerPoint is available on your system, take a look at the presentation before converting it into a Captivate project. Perform the following steps to view the presentation in PowerPoint:

1. Open Microsoft PowerPoint.
2. When in PowerPoint, open the `Chapter09/presentations/AdobeCaptivate.ppt` presentation situated in the exercise files.
3. Navigate to **Slide Show** | **View Slide Show** or hit the *F5* shortcut key to start the slideshow.

While viewing the presentation, focus your attention on the following:

- The presentation is made of 11 slides
- There is a transition between all the slides of the presentation
- On the first and last slide, the text is animated using an effect that has no equivalent in the **Effects** panel of Captivate
- The presentation is mainly composed of text and images, and most of it is animated
- Some of the effects used to animate the objects of PowerPoint have an equivalent in Captivate, but some others do not
- Sometimes, a mouse click is needed to go to the next step of the presentation, but sometimes not
- Some slides of the presentation include Slide Notes
- Slide 10 includes two links to the Adobe website

Spelling errors and typos have been intentionally left over in the presentation. Please, refrain from correcting them. They will be used to demonstrate the round-tripping workflow between Captivate and PowerPoint in a short while.

4. Close PowerPoint without saving the changes made to the presentation.

You will now convert this presentation into a Captivate project and see how the PowerPoint features previously listed are carried over (or not) into Captivate.

Creating a Captivate project from a PowerPoint presentation

In this section, you will convert the file you have viewed in PowerPoint into a Captivate project.

> **.ppt or .pptx?**
>
> Captivate imports .ppt files only. When importing a .pptx file, it must be converted to .ppt before being imported into Captivate. The conversion from .pptx to .ppt requires that PowerPoint be installed on the computer. When importing a .ppt file, that conversion is not needed, and PowerPoint is therefore not mandatory. That's the reason why we chose to use .ppt files in this book instead of the newer .pptx file format. We do also provide the .pptx files in the exercise folder for you to experiment with them if desired.

Before starting this exercise, make sure the PowerPoint presentation is closed. Perform the following steps to convert the PowerPoint presentation into a Captivate project:

1. Return to Captivate. The exercise begins on the Welcome screen of Captivate.
2. On the right-hand side column of the Captivate Welcome screen, click on the **Microsoft PowerPoint** link under **Create New** (or if the Welcome screen has been turned off, navigate to **File | New Project | Project From MS PowerPoint**) as shown in the following screenshot:

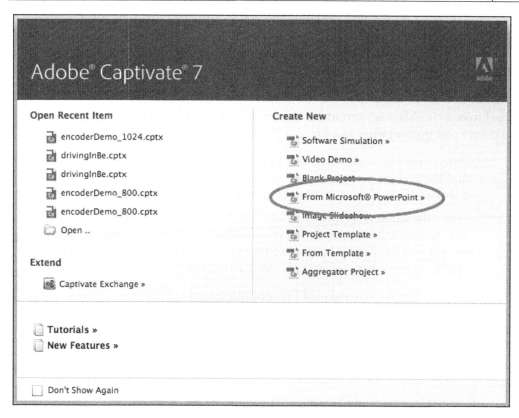

3. Browse to the Chapter09/presentations/AdobeCaptivate.ppt file situated in the exercises folder, and click on **Open**.

Captivate converts the PowerPoint slides into Captivate slides one by one. This operation can be quite lengthy, so be patient. When the conversion is finished, Captivate opens the **Convert PowerPoint Presentations** dialog box.

4. At the top of the dialog box, change the **Name** of the project to AdobeCaptivateIntro.

5. Open the **Preset Sizes** drop-down list and change the size of the project to **800 x 600**.

Captivate lets you choose which PowerPoint slides to import in the project. Use the **Clear All** and **Select All** buttons to quickly select or deselect the entire set of slides. In this case, you want to import the entire PowerPoint presentation into Captivate, so make sure all the PowerPoint slides are selected before moving on.

6. At the end of the dialog box, set the **Advance Slide** option to **On mouse click**.
7. Make sure the **Linked** checkbox is selected.

It is very important to get these last two options right! The **Advance Slide** option lets you decide how Captivate advances from one slide to the next. By choosing **On mouse click**, you ask Captivate to generate a Click Box on top of every imported slide. This Click Box stops the playhead and waits for the student to click anywhere on the slide to continue to the next step of the project.

The **Linked** checkbox is even more important. Captivate proposes two ways to insert a PowerPoint presentation in a project. They are as follows:

- When **Linked** is not selected, you create an **Embedded** presentation. It means that the PowerPoint presentation is entirely integrated into Captivate and does not maintain any kind of link with the original PowerPoint file.
- When the **Linked** checkbox is selected, the PowerPoint presentation is also embedded into Captivate, but Captivate maintains a link between the project and the original PowerPoint file. This link can be used to update the Captivate file when a change is made to the PowerPoint presentation.

Make sure the **Convert PowerPoint Presentations** dialog looks like the following screenshot before moving on:

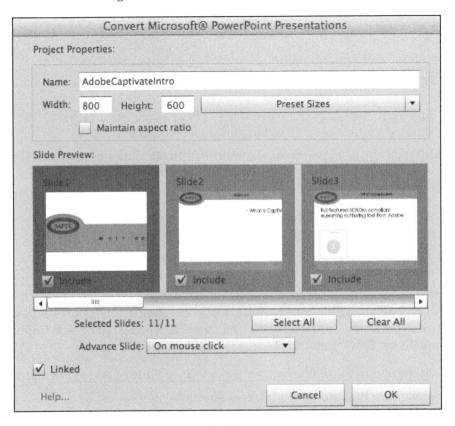

8. Click on the **OK** button.
9. Take some time to read the message that appears on the screen. Click on **Yes** to acknowledge the message and clear the message box.

This message tells you that the size of the imported presentation is not the same as the size of the Captivate file it is imported in. However, Captivate does a good job of converting the size while maintaining good quality of the project, so you can safely acknowledge the message and move on with the exercise.

Captivate creates a new project from the original PowerPoint presentation. This process can take some time, so be patient. When the importation is finished, an eleven-slide project is loaded into the Captivate application. In the **Filmstrip** panel, notice that each slide has a **Name** field that is derived from the slide title as entered in PowerPoint.

You will now test the movie to see how well (or how badly) Captivate handles the PowerPoint conversion process.

10. Save the file as `Chapter09/AdobeCaptivateIntro.cptx`.
11. Use the Preview icon or *F4* on the keyboard to preview the entire project.

Take the time to test the entire project noticing that:

- Captivate does a pretty good job of converting a PowerPoint presentation into a Captivate movie
- Most animations are carried over from PowerPoint even if a corresponding effect does not exist in Captivate
- The transitions are correctly imported and played back
- On slide 9, the links are functional

The conversion of the PowerPoint presentation to a Captivate project is now complete. Note that all the objects of Captivate can be inserted on these slides using the same techniques as those used for the regular slides of Captivate. Also, regular Captivate slides can be added anywhere in the project.

12. Close the **Preview** pane when done.

What you just experienced in the **Preview** pane is how the students will experience the project. You will now take a closer look at the Captivate editing environment to discover other properties from the original presentation that are carried over in Captivate.

13. If needed, use the **Filmstrip** panel to return to the first slide of the project.
14. Use the **Window | Slide Notes** menu item to open the **Slide Notes** panel. Remember that, by default, this panel appears at the bottom of the screen, next to the **Timeline**.

Slide Notes typed in Microsoft PowerPoint have been imported in the **Slide Notes** panel of Captivate. Remember that these **Slide Notes** can be converted to Text-to-Speech and to Closed Captions. The fact that Captivate imports this data from PowerPoint is a great productivity feature and a huge timesaver.

> Warning: If Slides Notes are added to the original PowerPoint file after it has been converted into Captivate, Slide Notes will not be synced!

15. Use the **Filmstrip** panel to go to slide 2.
16. At the bottom of the screen, open the **Timeline** panel.

In PowerPoint, this slide holds quite a few pieces of text arranged in a bulleted list. You would expect the same slide in Captivate to contain a lot of Text Captions. Unfortunately, the PowerPoint to Captivate conversion process does not go that far. In Captivate, each PowerPoint slide is considered as a single animated object. The individual components of this animation are not shown in the **Timeline** panel.

This can be a big problem if you want to modify a PowerPoint slide that was imported to Captivate. However, you selected the **Linked** checkbox when importing the slides, so Captivate knows where the original PowerPoint file is located. This enables you to easily update the slides if needed.

Round Tripping between Captivate and PowerPoint

Round Tripping is the process by which you can invoke PowerPoint from within Captivate, edit the presentation in PowerPoint, and return to the updated Captivate project. If you are working on Windows, PowerPoint can even be displayed right within the Captivate interface, so you won't even have to leave the Captivate environment. If you are working on a Mac, you'll be redirected to the actual PowerPoint application.

> The following exercise requires both PowerPoint and Captivate to be installed on your computer. On Windows, Office 2003 (SP3) or higher is required. On Mac, Office 2004 and up will do.

In the next exercise, you will modify a slide in PowerPoint and return to Captivate using the following steps:

1. Still in the `Chapter09/AdobeCaptivateIntro.cptx` file, use the **Filmstrip** panel to go to slide 4.
2. Right-click anywhere on the slide, and navigate to **Edit With Microsoft PowerPoint | Edit Presentation** as shown in the following screenshot:

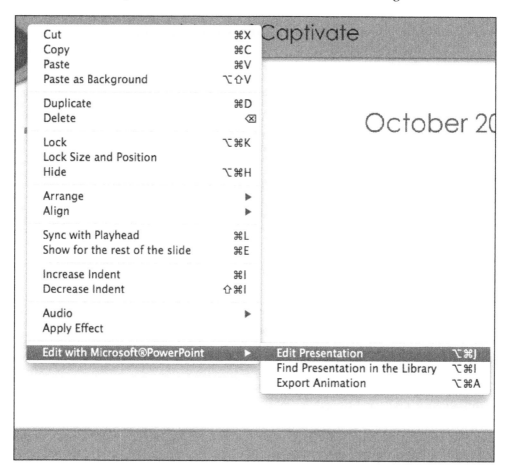

 If you get a message saying that Captivate is unable to open the PowerPoint presentation because of a permission problem, return to PowerPoint to make sure the presentation is closed before starting this procedure in Captivate.

Using Captivate 7 with Other Applications

What follows depends on the operating system you are working on. On Windows, PowerPoint opens within the Captivate interface, allowing you to edit the presentation using all the tools and features of PowerPoint without even leaving Captivate. On Mac, PowerPoint automatically opens in its own separate window and loads the presentation you want to edit.

Pay close attention to the remaining steps of this exercise. The Round Tripping experience on Windows is very different to the one on Mac.

3. (Mac only) When PowerPoint is open, go to slide 4 of the PowerPoint presentation.
4. (Mac and Windows) On slide 4, change **October 204** to October 2004.
5. (Mac only) Navigate to **File** | **Save** of PowerPoint to save the presentation.
6. (Mac only) Return to Captivate. A message asks if you want to import the updated presentation. Click on **Yes**, and let Captivate make the necessary changes in the project. This is shown in the following screenshot:

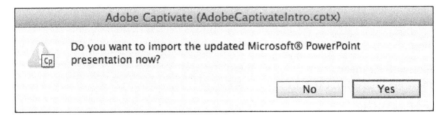

7. (Mac only) Close the PowerPoint application manually.
8. (Windows only) Click on the **Save** button situated in the upper-left corner of the interface. PowerPoint closes and the Captivate project is automatically updated.
9. (Mac and Windows) Save the Captivate file when done.
10. (Mac and Windows) Use the Preview icon to preview the entire project.

When the preview reaches slide 4, pay close attention to the text in the main textbox. The modification done in PowerPoint should be reflected in the Captivate project.

Updating a linked PowerPoint presentation

In the next exercise, you will open PowerPoint and modify the presentation in the PowerPoint application. This is very different from what you did in the previous exercise, where the workflow was triggered from within Captivate. You will then return to Captivate and update the project accordingly. The steps are as follows:

1. Return to PowerPoint and open `Chapter09/presentations/AdobeCaptivate.ppt`.
2. Go to slide 3 of the presentation, and change **SCROM** to `SCORM` in the main textbox.
3. Save the presentation and close PowerPoint.
4. Return to Captivate.

Because you selected the **Linked** checkbox when converting the PowerPoint presentation, Captivate is able to pick up the change made in the PowerPoint file and should display the same message as in the previous screenshot. If the message is not displayed automatically, the **Library** panel offers a way to manually update the Captivate project.

5. If the message shown in the previous screenshot is displayed on your screen, click on **No** to close the message without updating the Captivate project.
6. Open the **Library** panel situated next to the **Properties** panel on the right-hand side of the screen.
7. In the **Presentations** section of the **Library** panel, locate the **AdobeCaptivate** presentation.

Notice the red dot in the **Status** column as shown in the following screenshot. It indicates that the linked PowerPoint presentation and the Captivate project are out of sync:

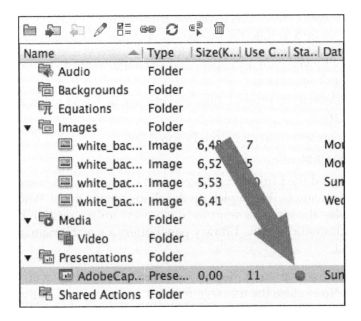

8. In the **Library** panel, click on the red dot associated with the **AdobeCaptivate** presentation.

This refreshes the linked presentation and puts the Captivate project and the PowerPoint presentation back in sync. At the end of the process, the **Status** color should turn back to green.

Using the **Library** panel, there are a few more operations that can be done on a PowerPoint presentation.

9. Still in the **Library** panel of Captivate, right-click on the **AdobeCaptivate** presentation.

10. In the Contextual menu, click on the **Change To "Embedded"** menu item as shown in the following screenshot:

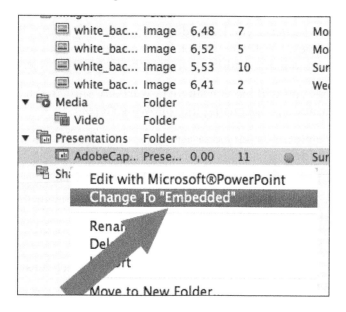

11. Click on **OK** to clear the acknowledgement message.

After this operation, the link between the Captivate project and the PowerPoint presentation is broken. The changes made to the external PowerPoint file will no longer be picked up by Captivate.

12. In the `Presentations` folder of the **Library** panel, right-click on the **AdobeCaptivate** presentation again.
13. In the Contextual menu, click on the **Change To "Linked"** menu item.
14. Browse to the `/Chapter09` folder of the exercises files, and save the file as `Chapter09/presentations/AdobeCaptivate_linked.ppt`.
15. Again, click on the **OK** button to clear the message.
16. Save the Captivate project when done.

This operation saves the embedded PowerPoint presentation as a new PowerPoint file and creates a link between this new file and the Captivate project. It is not possible to actually recreate the link to the original PowerPoint file. Instead, you create a new PowerPoint file and link that new file to the Captivate project.

Inserting a PowerPoint slide in a Captivate project

In the previous two sections, you learned how to convert an entire PowerPoint presentation into a new Captivate project. But sometimes, only a few PowerPoint slides must be inserted in the middle of an existing Captivate project.

In the next exercise, you will insert a single PowerPoint slide in the middle of the Encoder Demonstration project using the following steps:

1. Open the `chapter09/endoderDemo_800.cptx` file situated in the exercises folder.
2. Use the **Filmstrip** panel to go to slide 23 of the project.

Slide 23 should be the last slide of the screenshot-based demonstration and the second to last in the project.

3. Navigate to **Insert | PowerPoint Slide...**.
4. In the box that opens, make sure that **Slide 23** is selected as shown in the following screenshot:

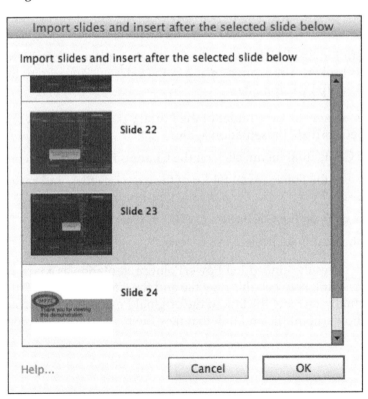

The imported PowerPoint slide(s) will be inserted after the slide selected in this dialog box.

5. Click on the **OK** button and navigate to the `Chapter09/presentations/mediaEncoder.ppt` presentation situated in the exercises folder. Click on the **Open** button.
6. In the **Convert PowerPoint Presentations** dialog, open the **Advance Slide** drop-down list, and select the **Automatically** option.

This time, you do not want Captivate to generate an extra Click Box on top of the slide as you did when converting a PowerPoint file earlier in this chapter.

7. Leave the other options at their current value, and click on the **OK** button.
8. Take some time to read the message, and click on **Yes** to acknowledge and clear it.

The PowerPoint slide is inserted as slide 24 of the Encoder Demonstration project. You will now add a Captivate object on top of the imported PowerPoint slide.

9. Open the **Timeline** panel, and extend the duration of the slide to **13** seconds.
10. Navigate to **Insert | Standard Objects | Button** or the corresponding icon in the vertical Object toolbar to insert a new button on the slide.
11. At the top of the **Properties** panel, use the **Style** drop-down menu to apply the **MFTC-ButtonContinue** style to the new button.

The **MFTC-ButtonContinue** style is defined in the **MFTC_theme_final_800** Theme that is applied to the project.

12. In the **Action** section of the **Properties** panel, make sure that the **On Success** action of the new button is set to **Go to the next slide**.
13. Move the button so that it sits in the brownish area in the lower-right corner of the slide.
14. In the **Timeline** panel, move the button to the very end of the slide **Timeline**.
15. Use the Preview icon to test the entire project.
16. Save the file when done.

In this exercise, you have inserted a PowerPoint slide in the middle of an existing Captivate project. This presentation is available in the **Library** panel of the project and can be edited using the same Round Tripping capabilities as discussed earlier in this chapter.

This exercise also demonstrates the ability to add standard Captivate objects on top of the imported PowerPoint slides.

> **Controlling the user experience**
>
> Importing the PowerPoint slides with the **Advance Automatically** feature and adding your own buttons on top of the imported slides allow you to better control the user experience of the imported projects. Lots of Captivate developers adopt the workflow described in this exercise rather than let Captivate create a Click Box on top of every single PowerPoint slide as you did in the first exercise of this chapter when choosing **Advance On a Mouse Click**.

This concludes your overview of the integration between Microsoft PowerPoint and Adobe Captivate. Before moving on, it is time to emphasize the key points of what has been covered. They are as follows:

- It is possible to convert an entire PowerPoint presentation into a Captivate project.
- Captivate can import both a .ppt file and a .pptx file. A .ppt file can be imported in Captivate even if PowerPoint is not installed on the computer. When importing a .pptx file, however, PowerPoint must be installed on the system along with Captivate.
- When converting PowerPoint to Captivate, most animation, effects, and transitions are carried over even if they are not natively supported by Captivate.
- Each PowerPoint slide is imported as a single animation. In the **Timeline** panel, it is not possible to access each individual object of the original PowerPoint slide.
- An imported presentation cannot be updated in Captivate. To update a presentation, it is necessary to use PowerPoint.
- An imported PowerPoint presentation is either an Embedded presentation or a Linked presentation. An Embedded presentation is entirely integrated into the Captivate project. A Linked presentation is also integrated in the Captivate project, but it maintains a link with the original PowerPoint presentation. This link can be used to keep the PowerPoint presentation and the Captivate project in sync.
- Round Tripping is a concept that enables you to invoke PowerPoint from within Captivate, update the presentation in PowerPoint, and import the changes back into Captivate.

- The actual Round Tripping experience depends on the operating system in use (Mac or Windows).
- It is possible to insert only a few PowerPoint slides in the middle of an existing Captivate project.
- All the objects of Captivate can be inserted on top of the imported PowerPoint slide(s).

In the next section, you will use a workflow that involves Captivate and Microsoft Word to localize a Captivate project.

Importing PowerPoint versus animating native Captivate objects

In the early versions of Captivate, the **Effects** panel did not exist, and so it was very common to create slides in PowerPoint and insert them into Captivate. Ever since the **Effects** panel was introduced in Captivate 5, any native object of Captivate can be animated in ways that are very similar to what is found in PowerPoint. I think that the PowerPoint integration is a great tool to recycle existing content made in PowerPoint or to involve non-Captivate developers in the production process, but new content should be developed entirely in Captivate whenever possible.

Localizing a Captivate project using Microsoft Word

In this section, you will create the French version of the Encoder Demonstration. To produce the French version of the project, there are three basic things to do. They are as follows:

- Recapture the screenshots of the demonstration using the French version of the Adobe Media Encoder application
- Translate Text Captions and Slide Notes
- Translate the other assets (such as a video file or additional imported images)

In the following exercise, you will concentrate on the second step of this process, which is translating Text Captions and Slide Notes:

1. Open the `Chapter09/encoderDemo_800_fr.cptx` file.
2. Use the **Filmstrip** panel to go to slide 4 of the project.

Notice that the background of slide 4 is a screenshot of the French version of Adobe Media Encoder. The same is true for the other screenshot-based slides of the project. Notice also that, for the purpose of this exercise, the Pretest has been removed from the French project. Apart from these (not so) small details, this project is the very same project as the English one you created during the previous chapters.

To get the French screenshots in the English project, we followed these simple steps:

- We installed a French version of Adobe Media Encoder on our computer (actually in a virtual machine), and we used it to re-record the same screenshots as the ones you recorded in *Chapter 2, Capturing the Slides*.
- We opened the English version of the project and used the **Save As** menu item to save it as `encoderDemo_800_fr.cptx`.
- We navigated to **File | Import | External Library...** to open the **Library** panel of the French project into the English project.
- We inserted **Backgrounds** of the external **Library** to the corresponding English slides and used the **Merge With Background** feature to override the old English background with the new French background.

After this simple procedure, the file you just opened was ready for the second step of the process, that is, the translation of Text Captions and Slide Notes in Microsoft Word using the following steps:

 The following exercise requires Microsoft Word to be installed on the computer along with Captivate.

3. Make sure you are still in the `Chapter09/encoderDemo_800_fr.cptx` file.
4. Navigate to **File | Export | Project Captions and Closed Captions...** to export Text Captions and Slide Notes to a Word document.
5. Save the file as `Chapter09/encoderDemo_800_frCaptions.doc`.

When the export is complete, Captivate displays a message asking if you want to see the generated Word document.

6. Click on **Yes** to open Microsoft Word and view the generated document.

The Word document generated should look like the following screenshot:

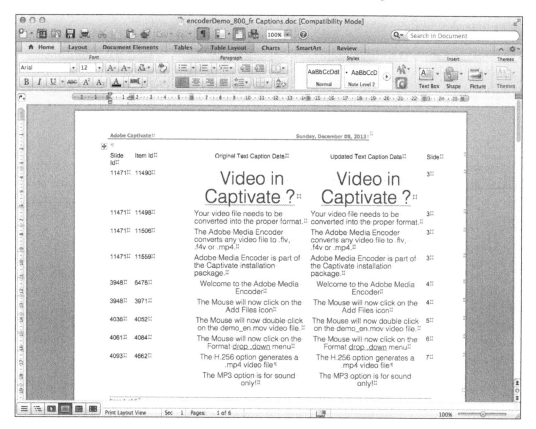

The generated Word document is a five-column table. The first two columns hold the **Slide ID** and **Item ID**. *Those two columns should not be tampered with.* When the translated text is imported back into the project, these two pieces of information will be used by Captivate to uniquely identify the object into which the text needs to be imported.

The third column is the original text as written in the source language. The fourth column is where the translator will do their job. The translated text should be entered in the fourth column of the table.

Finally, the last column is the slide number on which the object is found.

7. Change the text in the fourth column of the Word document.

If you don't know French, don't worry. For the sake of this exercise, you can translate the first few captions in any language you want (or just update the text in any way!). After completing this task, save and close the Word document.

You will now import the updated Text Captions and Slide Notes back into the Captivate project.

8. Return to Captivate in the `encoderDemo_800_fr.cptx` file.
9. Navigate to **File | Import | Project Captions and Closed Captions...**.
10. Import the `Chapter09/encoderDemo_800_frCaptions.doc` file.

Captivate imports the Word document, reads the data it contains, and updates the Text Captions and Slide Notes of the project. This process can be quite lengthy, so be patient. When the import process is complete, use the **Filmstrip** panel to browse through the slides of the project, and see the updated Text Captions and Slide Notes.

11. Don't forget to save the `encoderDemo_800_fr.cptx` file when done.

This simple workflow is only one step in the translation of an eLearning project into a foreign language. At this point of the exercise, the screenshots, Text Captions, Smart Shapes with text, and Slide Notes have been updated. However, the localization work is not over. Text Animation (on slide 1 and slide 22) is not yet translated; the video file on slide 2 needs to be updated; and all the narration must be re-recorded in French and imported in the project.

These remaining actions are beyond the scope of this book, but all the techniques needed to complete them have been discussed in the previous chapters.

Exporting the project to XML

In this section, you will export the project as an XML file. Exporting the Captivate project to `.xml` gives you access to a much wider range of properties and content than the Export to Microsoft Word feature you used in the previous section. According to the official Adobe Captivate blog, the exported XML file contains the following:

Text Captions, Text Animation, Rollover Captions, Default text, and correct entries in Text Entry Box, Success/Failure/Hint Captions and button text for all interactive objects, Text Buttons, Slide Notes, Text and Rollover Captions in Rollover Slidelets, Quiz Buttons and Feedback captions, Project Info, Project Start and End options, text messages for password, and Expiry Messages

[See the original post at http://blogs.adobe.com/captivate/2009/05/quick_editing_of_text_using_xm_1.html.]

Here are the steps to export our project to an XML file:

1. If needed, return to the chapter09/encoderDemo_800.cptx file.
2. Navigate to **File** | **Export** | **To XML**.
3. Export the project as chapter09/encoderDemo_800.xml in the exercises folder.

When the export is finished, Captivate asks if you want to open the resulting XML file.

4. Click on **No** to close the message box and return to Captivate.

The resulting XML can be opened and updated with any XML editor. When the editing is done, the **From XML...** menu item under **File** | **Import** can be used to import the updated data back into Captivate.

Importing a Photoshop file into Captivate

Photoshop is one of the most famous applications from Adobe. It is an amazing image-editing tool aimed at the professional designer. Many design companies around the world use Photoshop as one of their primary tools to develop the look and feel of the projects they work on.

It is therefore very common to have a designer make use of Photoshop to create the look and feel of a Captivate project. This is why the Captivate engineering team came up with a specific feature to import a Photoshop file into Captivate.

In Photoshop, each piece of the image is stored on a separate **layer**. At the bottom of the layer stack is the background layer. The other layers are arranged on top of the background in a way that is similar to what is found in the **Timeline** panel of Captivate.

Thanks to the **Import from Photoshop** feature the layers created in Photoshop can be imported into Captivate. Each layer will become a separate image in the Captivate file. You will see the benefit of this approach during the next exercise.

The following screenshot is the Photoshop file, as seen in Photoshop CC. The **Layers** panel of Photoshop has been enhanced for better viewing:

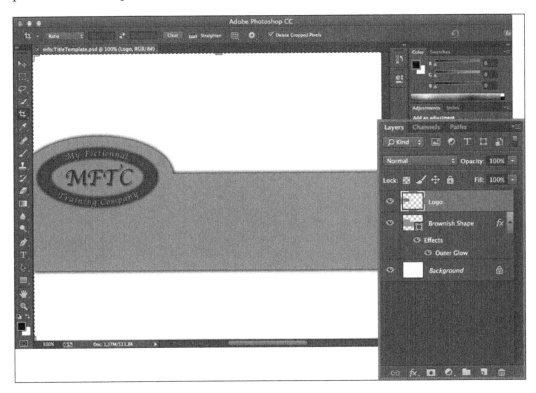

Notice that the preceding screenshot has three layers. They are as follows:

- At the bottom of the stack, the **Background** layer is a white rectangle that covers the whole image.
- Right above it is the **Brownish Shape** layer. It is the brownish area at the center of the slide. Notice that an **Outer Glow** effect is applied to this layer.
- At the top of the stack, the **Logo** layer holds the **MFTC** logo.

You will now import this Photoshop document in the Driving in Belgium project in order to create a new version of the introduction slide.

For the sake of clarity, close every open project before starting the following exercise:

1. Open the `Chapter09/drivingInBe.cptx` file.
2. When the project is open, make sure you are on slide 1.
3. Navigate to **Insert | Blank Slide** to insert a new slide in the project. This new slide is inserted as slide 2.

Notice that Captivate automatically applies the **Blank** Master Slide to the new slide. That's why the copyright notice is displayed in the bottom-left corner of the slide. In the **Properties** panel, note that the **Use Master Slide Background** checkbox is deselected, which explains why the new slide is blank and does not display the default project background.

4. In the **Properties** panel, open the **Master Slide** drop-down list and apply the **Title** Master Slide on slide 2.
5. Select and delete the Text Animation placeholder.

Slide 2 should now be completely blank! Now, let's start the actual Photoshop importation.

6. Still on slide 2, navigate to **File | Import | Photoshop File** to start the procedure.
7. Import the `Images/mftcTitleTemplate.psd` Photoshop file situated in the exercises folder. (Notice that the file extension of a Photoshop file is `.psd`, which stands for Photoshop document.)

Captivate opens the **Import "mftcTitleTemplate.psd"** dialog box. This is shown in the following screenshot:

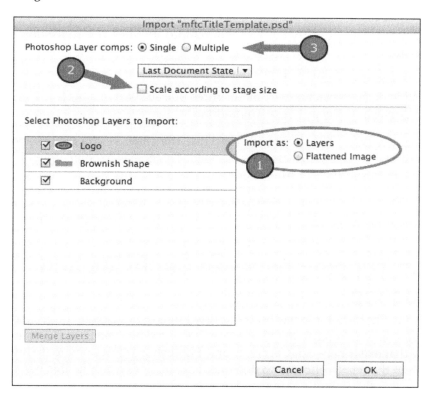

First of all, notice that you can import all **Layers** of the original Photoshop file or import a **Flattened Image** (**1**). A **flattened image** is an image where all the layers have been combined into one single image.

Notice also the **Scale according to stage size** checkbox (**2**). If selected, the Photoshop image will be automatically enlarged or reduced to fit the size of the Captivate project.

Photoshop users should notice the **Photoshop Layer comps** option at the top of the dialog (**3**).

8. Make sure that **Import as Layers** (**1**) is selected.
9. In the main area of the dialog, deselect the **Background** layer. (You do not want to import that blank rectangle.)
10. Click on the **OK** button to import the remaining two Photoshop layers in Captivate.
11. When the importation is complete, switch to the **Timeline** panel of slide 2.

This is where the Import from Photoshop feature shows its awesomeness. Two images have been imported on slide 2. This means that a separate image has been created for each of the imported layers. These two images can each be arranged on the **Timeline** panel and animated using the **Effects** panel of Captivate.

12. Return to slide 1, copy the Text Animation, and then return to slide 2 and paste it.
13. When done, delete the first slide of the project.

The first slide of the project now contains three objects: two images from the imported Photoshop file and Text Animation.

14. Arrange these three objects on the **Timeline** panel as you see fit. Don't hesitate to use the **Effects** panel as well. The goal is to come up with the greatest introduction slide ever!

Inserting a Photoshop file in Captivate is that easy. In the next section, you will examine the Round Tripping workflow between Captivate and Photoshop.

Round Tripping between Captivate and Photoshop

Now that the Photoshop file has been imported into the Captivate project, let's pretend you want to modify the Photoshop file a little bit. The Round Trip editing workflow that exists between Captivate and Photoshop allows you to do it without re-importing the whole Photoshop document again. Let's examine this workflow hands-on using the following steps:

> The following exercise requires Photoshop to be installed on your system along with Captivate. If Photoshop is not available on your computer, just read through the steps to have an idea of the workflow.

1. Make sure you are still on slide 1 of the `Chapter09/drivingInBe.cptx` file.
2. Select either one of the two images that you imported as part of the Photoshop document in the previous section (the **MFTC** logo or the brownish area).
3. Right-click on the selected image, and choose **Edit PSD Source File**.

This action opens the `.psd` file in Photoshop. Note that all the layers of the `.psd` document are available in Photoshop, not only the one you right-clicked on in Captivate. From here, you can use all the tools of Photoshop to modify your image.

4. Feel free to modify the image using the tools of Photoshop.
5. When done, save and close the Photoshop file.
6. Captivate automatically updates the components of the `.psd` document.

This simple procedure illustrates the tight integration that exists between Captivate and Photoshop. If you have Photoshop available on your system, this Round Trip editing workflow will greatly facilitate your authoring experience.

To wrap up this section, you will now take a quick look at the **Library** panel of Captivate to see how the Photoshop files appear in it.

7. Still on slide 1 of the `Chapter09/drivingInBe.cptx` file, right-click on the **MFTC** logo.
8. Choose **Find in the Library** in the Contextual menu.

This action opens the **Library** panel and selects the **MFTC** logo. Note that the logo is part of a folder that has the same name as the Photoshop file. This folder is used to bind all the images (in other words, all the layers) of the original Photoshop document as shown in the following screenshot:

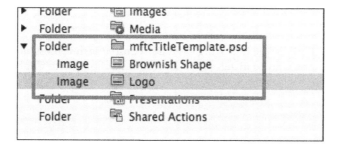

9. When done, save and close every open file.

In the next section, you will export the Captivate project to Flash Professional, but before that, let's quickly summarize what has been covered in this section:

- Photoshop is a professional image-editing application developed by Adobe.
- Photoshop uses a layer-based system to create complex compositions.
- Captivate contains a specific tool to import a Photoshop file into the project.
- You can import a flattened image into Captivate or maintain the layers found in the Photoshop file during the importation.
- If the Photoshop layers are maintained, each layer is imported as a separate image in Captivate. This allows you to arrange these images on the **Timeline** panel and apply different effects to the different parts of the imported image.
- You can edit the original .psd file using the Round Trip editing workflow between Captivate and Photoshop.
- In the **Library** panel, the Photoshop document is a folder.

Exporting to Flash Professional

Adobe Flash Professional and Captivate have a lot in common. Both applications are used primarily to generate .swf files that can be played back by the free Flash Player plugin.

That being said, the Flash technology has a lot more to offer than what is actually used by Captivate. Adobe Flash Professional is the ultimate Flash authoring tool. By using Adobe Flash Professional, a Flash developer is able to leverage the full power of the Flash technology.

It is possible to export a Captivate project to Flash Professional where a Flash developer is able to tweak the Captivate projects in many ways that are not possible in Captivate.

In the next exercise, you will export the Captivate project to Flash Professional CS6 or CC.

 Parts of the following exercise require Flash Professional CS6 or CC to be installed on the computer along with Captivate.

Chapter 9

The steps to export the Captivate project to Flash Professional CS6 or CC are as follows:

1. Open the `Chapter09/encoderDemo_800.cptx` Captivate file.
2. Depending on the version of Flash available on your system, navigate to **File** | **Export** | **To Flash CS6** or **File** | **Export** | **To Flash CC**.
3. In the **Export To Flash Options** dialog box, change **Location** to the `Chapter09` folder of the exercise files.
4. Make sure the **Publish to Folder** checkbox is selected.
5. Take some time to explore the remaining options of the dialog, but leave them all at their current setting.
6. Click on the **Export** button as shown in the following screenshot:

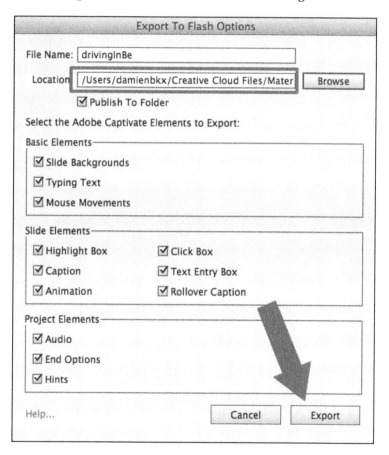

Captivate generates the slides and exports the project as a Flash file, with a `.fla` extension.

7. Use Finder (Mac) or Windows Explorer (Windows) to navigate to the `Chapter09/drivingInBe` folder of the exercises.
8. If Flash Professional CC or CS6 is available on your system, double-click on the `drivingInBe.fla` file to open it in Flash Professional.

When in Flash Professional, the Flash developer has access to the underlying code of your Captivate project as shown in the following screenshot:

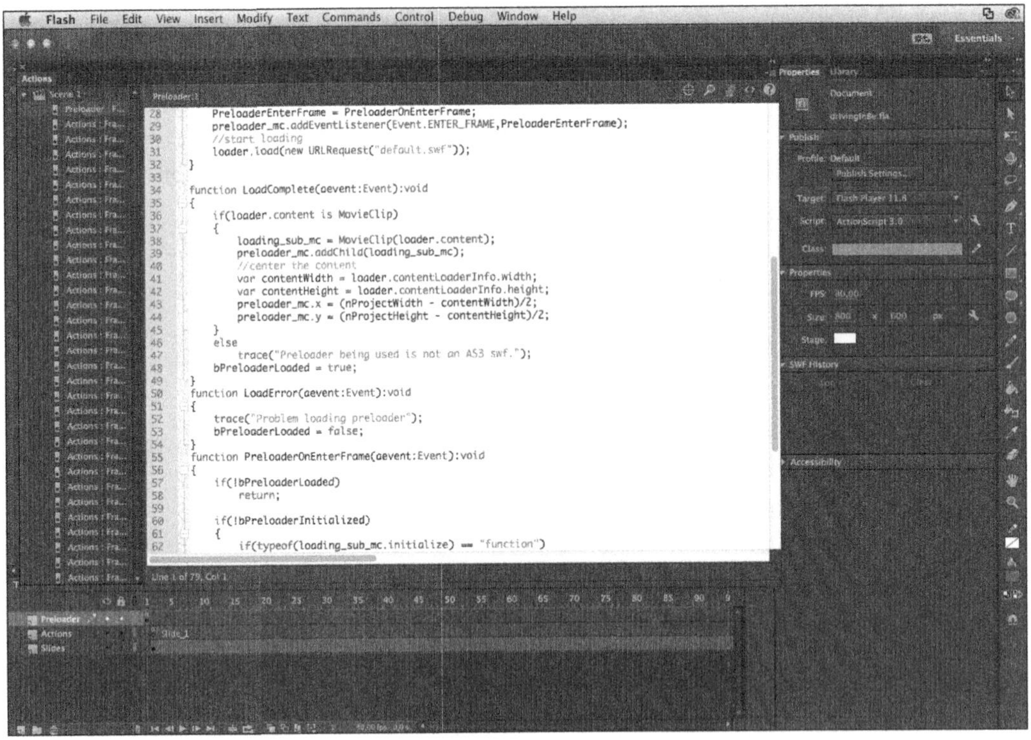

Learning how to leverage all that power in Flash Professional is beyond the scope of this book, but give the generated `.fla` file to a trained Flash developer, and they will know what to do with it!

This discussion concludes the overview of the export to the Flash feature. Let's quickly summarize what has been covered in this section:

- Both Adobe Flash Professional and Adobe Captivate are used to generate Flash content.
- Captivate only uses a small portion of the power of Flash.
- It is possible to export the Captivate project to Flash to leverage the full power of the Flash technology.

- Exporting the Captivate project to Flash generates a `.fla` file that can be opened by the Adobe Flash Professional application. When the project is finished, it is necessary to use Flash Professional to compile it into a `.swf` file. The `.swf` file type is the one that the Flash player is able to read.

Summary

In this chapter, you have learned some of the workflows that integrate Captivate with other applications. Some of these applications, such as Photoshop and Flash, are part of the Adobe product line, and others, such as Microsoft Word and Microsoft PowerPoint, are third-party applications.

By using the PowerPoint workflows, you are able to recycle existing content made in PowerPoint. When it comes to localization, you can export Text Captions and Slide Notes as Microsoft Word documents, send them to a translation service and import them back into Captivate. There is no need for the translators to know anything about Captivate to make this workflow work. When importing a Photoshop file into Captivate, you can decide to maintain the layers of the original Photoshop file, which gives you a great deal of flexibility to further customize the imported images using the tools and effects of Captivate. Exporting the project to Flash gives you access to the full power of the Flash technology.

When used correctly, these workflows are huge time-savers that help you to streamline the production process of your eLearning content.

Your projects are almost finished now. In the next chapter, you will learn how to set up a review process and make your project available to a team of reviewers. Each of these reviewers will add their comments to the project and send them back to you using various techniques, including e-mail and Acrobat.com. You will then import these comments into the Captivate project and address the reviewer's feedback.

Meet the community

In this section, I want to introduce you to Richard Jenkins. He works for Adobe as an eLearning Solutions consultant. He has also authored the *Foreword* section of this book. When I first contacted him about the *Foreword* section, he was very surprised, as he had never written a foreword before. So, congratulations and thank you Richard on your very first foreword.

Richard Jenkins

Richard John Jenkins' background lies in photojournalism, film, screenwriting, neon art and design, multimedia, web publishing tools, technology training, and search engine marketing industries. During his varied career, he aligned himself with Macromedia Inc. (acquired by Adobe Systems). He was invited to join Macromedia's Systems Engineer (SE) team in 1998, focusing on the Hi-ED and K12 markets. As part of the Macromedia Education SE team, he evangelized Macromedia's products to tens of thousands of people at over 250 schools, 25 user groups, 137 companies, plus presented at dozens of public seminars, workshops, webinars, and webcast all over the U.S. and Canada. Currently, he is Adobe's eLearning Solutions consultant who supports Adobe's North American eLearning team, from where he evangelizes the eLearning solutions and technologies far and wide. In his so-called spare time, he is a fine artist who creates stylized hanging art mobiles along with abstract pastels and paintings in the Russian and German Expressionist style. When he is not creating art or working, he spends his time with his three little kids who are obsessed with computer games, endlessly walking the family dog, and stealing away a little quality time holding hands with his Starbucks-addicted wife.

Contact details

- **Blog**: http://blogs.adobe.com/captivate
- **E-mail**: Jenkins@Adobe.com

10
Reviewing a Captivate Project

Despite your great level of professionalism and frequent testing throughout the development phase of the project, you have, more than likely, made grammatical, design, and functional errors. These mistakes should be corrected before final publishing. All authors must have their projects rigorously reviewed before publication; it is no different with eLearning authors. The problem is that you have been working so hard and so long on these projects that you are just not able to see those little details anymore.

By letting reviewers in on the project, you bring in fresh eyes, open minds, and different perspectives. Most of the time, their feedback is an invaluable asset that helps you take a step back and see what your projects are really capable of in the real world, outside the eLearning studio.

This is not only about going the extra mile. Such a review process is an essential part of any professional project.

In this chapter, you will:

- Discover more about the review process in general
- Initiate a review process using your own internal server or Acrobat.com
- Install and use the Captivate Reviewer to generate comments
- Import the comments from various reviewers into Captivate
- Use the Captivate commenting tools to approve, reject, and respond to comments

Preparing your work

In this chapter, you will work with the Encoder Demonstration project. Perform these basic steps to get Captivate ready:

1. Open Captivate.
2. Ensure that the **Classic** workspace is the one being used.
3. Navigate to **Window** | **Workspace** | **Reset 'Classic'** to reapply the default interface.
4. Open the `encoderDemo_800.cptx` file under `Chapter10`.

Captivate is now ready for the exercises of this chapter.

The review process at a glance

There are two kinds of individuals and three important steps that make up a standard review process.

Obviously, the two kinds of individuals are as follows:

- **Author(s) of the project**: That's you! You have created the project, and you are the one who initiates and manages the reviewing workflow. You know the project by heart, and you have Captivate installed on your computer.
- **Reviewer(s)**: These are the people who will view and comment on your work. Some of them might know about Captivate, but some don't know anything about the technical part of your work (which is exactly what you need to have fresh and open-minded feedback). Typically, reviewers do not have Captivate available on their systems.

Now, let's take a look at the reviewing workflow. What are the steps of this process and what are the tools and strategies available in Captivate to facilitate each of these steps?

In Captivate, the reviewing process can be summarized in the following three steps:

- **The Distribution Step**: In the Distribution Step, you make the project available to the reviewers. Basically, you have two options to do this: your own internal server (in other words, a location that can be accessed by every reviewer; it can be a shared network drive on your company's network or a folder shared on a third-party cloud-based service such as Dropbox) or Acrobat.com. In both cases, an e-mail can be sent to the reviewers to invite them to the review. Note that a single review can include reviewers from Acrobat.com mixed with reviewers using an internal server.

- **The Commenting Step**: In this step, each reviewer watches the course and inserts comments in the project. As most of the reviewers do not have Captivate installed on their system, Adobe has created the **Adobe Captivate Reviewer** AIR application. The reviewers can use this special commenting application to create their comments. Note that it is not possible to create new comments from within Captivate, so the reviewers that have Captivate available still have to use the Adobe Captivate Reviewer application to create their comments.

- **The Collection Step**: The Collection Step takes place in Captivate. In this step, you import the comments sent by the reviewers into the project. The comments can be downloaded automatically from Acrobat.com or your own internal server (or cloud-based service), or they can be inserted manually in the project from an XML file sent by a reviewer as an e-mail attachment. Once all the comments are inserted in Captivate, you can review and address them by approving, rejecting, and commenting on your reviewer's comments.

Thanks to this workflow, you will be able to engage with your reviewers in real interactive conversations about your content. In some situations, the reviewers can even see each others' comments almost in real time and converse about the course. This is much more fun and efficient than asking your reviewers to send their comments by e-mail or in a Microsoft Word document. In the next few pages, you will learn about each of these three steps, starting with the Distribution Step.

Distributing the project

In this step, you make the project available to the reviewers. To allow the reviewers to view and comment on the project without using Captivate, you actually have to publish the project. To do so, you will use yet another publication format than the ones you have already used in *Chapter 8, Finishing Touches and Publishing*. Perform the following steps to distribute the project:

1. Use Windows Explorer (Windows) or the Finder (Mac) to browse to the `encoderDemo_review` folder under `Chapter10`.

2. Note that this folder contains a subfolder named `comments`. The comments made by the reviewers will be stored at that location.

3. Return to Captivate. If needed, open the `encoderDemo_800.cptx` file under `Chapter10`.

4. When the file is open, navigate to **File | Collaborate | Send for Shared Review** to open the **Send for Shared Review** dialog. Alternatively, you can also use the **Collaborate** icon of the main toolbar.

5. At the top of the dialog, make sure that the name of the project is **encoderDemo_800**. Make the necessary adjustments if needed.
6. Open the **How do you want to collect comments from your reviewers?** drop-down list and choose the **Automatically collect comments on my own internal server** option.

This option is also the one to choose if you decide to use a third-party cloud-based service such as Dropbox to make the project available to your reviewers.

Make sure that the **Send for Shared Review** dialog looks similar to what is shown in the following screenshot before continuing:

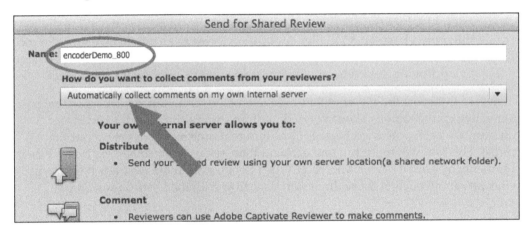

7. Click on the **Next** button to move on to the second step of the wizard.

The second step of the wizard is where you choose the location you want to publish your Captivate Review file and the associated comments. If possible, you want to use a folder that can be accessed by all reviewers (a shared folder on a network drive or a folder in the cloud). In this case, you will use the `helpViewer_review` folder under `Chapter10` and pretend it is a shared location.

8. Click on the **Browse** button.
9. Choose the `encoderDemo_review` folder under `Chapter10` as the `Publish` folder.
10. Choose the `comments` folder under `Chapter10/encoderDemo_review` as the `comments` folder.

If you need to send an invitation e-mail to the reviewers, you can select the **SendMail** checkbox; however, for this exercise, you will not (the two suboptions of the **SendMail** checkbox will be discussed in the next section).

11. Make sure the **SendMail** checkbox is not selected and click on **Publish**.

12. When the process is complete, save and close the `.cptx` file.

Captivate generates the slides using a process similar to the one you used in the *Publishing a Captivate project* section of *Chapter 8, Finishing Touches and Publishing*. When this process is finished, you can take a look at what really happened by using Windows Explorer (Windows) or the Finder (Mac) to explore the generated file.

13. Use Windows Explorer (Windows) or the Finder (Mac) to navigate to the `encoderDemo_review` folder under `Chapter10`.

This folder contains the `encoderDemo_800.crev` file. A `.crev` file is a special kind of `.swf` file used for commenting within a Captivate project. The `.crev` file can only be opened by the Adobe Captivate Reviewer application.

In the **Send for Shared Review** dialog, the two suboptions of the **SendMail** checkbox are used to attach the `.crev` file as well as the Adobe Captivate Reviewer AIR application to the generated e-mail.

Exploring the .crev file

The `.crev` file is actually a `.zip` package. If you want to explore the contents of the `.crev` package, change the `.crev` extension to `.zip` and use any archive utility to unzip the file. In the archive, you should find the usual `.swf` file plus an extra `.properties` file that can be opened with Text Edit (Mac) or Notepad (Windows). Make sure you rename the `.zip` file with the original `.crev` extension before continuing with the exercises of this chapter.

Your Captivate project is now published as a `.crev` file in a location where it can be accessed by the team of reviewers. You are now ready for the second step of the reviewing workflow.

Commenting a Captivate project

To demonstrate the second step of this workflow, you will pretend to be one of the reviewers. You will use the Adobe Captivate Reviewer application to add your comments to the project.

Installing the Adobe Captivate Reviewer application

The Adobe Captivate Reviewer is a free AIR application. Normally, it should have been installed with the rest of the Captivate 7 package. On Mac, the Adobe Captivate Reviewer 7.app file can be found in /Applications/Adobe. On Windows, it is situated in the Adobe folder under C:\program files\. For reviewers who do not have Captivate, see the following page on the official Captivate blog for downloads and installation instructions: http://blogs.adobe.com/captivate/captivate-6-review-app. Also, remember that the AIR runtime must be installed on the system in order to install and run an AIR application.

[To install the AIR runtime, use the following URL: http://get.adobe.com/air/.]

The next exercise begins when the Adobe Captivate Reviewer application is up and running on your system.

Using the Captivate Reviewer to create new comments

With the Captivate Reviewer application installed and the .crev file available to the reviewers, all the required conditions are met to start adding comments to the Captivate project. Perform the following steps to create new comments:

1. Open the Adobe Captivate Reviewer AIR application. (On Windows, run it as an administrator.)
2. If it is the first time you run the application, enter your name and your e-mail address and then click on the **Login** button.

Even though the button says **Login**, the information you typed is not validated in any way, so you can enter any name/e-mail you please.

3. When the application is ready, click on the **Load Adobe Captivate Movie** button situated in the middle of the screen.
4. Browse to the encoderDemo_800.crev file under Chapter10/encoderDemo_review that you published in the *Distributing the project* section earlier in this chapter.

The movie loads in the Adobe Captivate Reviewer application.

Chapter 10

> If you are not using a shared drive to store your comments, Adobe Captivate Reviewer will display a message asking you to export the comments and send them back to the author when finished. Just discard this message. It does not interfere with the correct completion of this exercise.

Note the icons situated at the lower-left and lower-right corners of the application, as shown in the following screenshot:

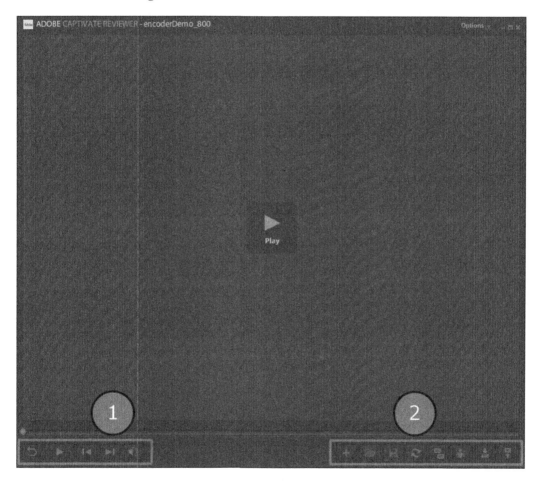

- In the lower-left corner of the application are the Playback Controls (marked as **(1)** in the preceding screenshot). These icons are used to control the movie as it plays in the Adobe Captivate Reviewer application. The usual Play/Pause, Forward/Rewind, and Mute buttons (plus a few others) can be found in this area.

[435]

- In the lower-right corner of the application are the icons used to manage the comments (marked as **(2)** in the preceding screenshot). The first icon for instance is used to create a new comment. Roll your mouse over the icons situated in that area to get a brief description of each available tool. Most of the time, the purpose of these icons is self-explanatory.

Now that you have a better idea of how the Adobe Captivate Reviewer works, it is time to play the lesson and add some comments.

5. Click on the **Play** button to start playing the course in the Captivate Reviewer.

> If the playback of the project freezes in the Adobe Captivate Reviewer, use the Next and Previous icons in the lower-left corner of the application (and leave a comment to signal the bug to the author!).

6. When you feel that a comment is needed, click on the **Add Comment** icon.

A comment is added at the current location of the playhead and the movie is paused.

7. Type your comment in the box and click on the **Add** button.
8. The comment is added and the movie continues playing.

Note the small dot that stays on the progress bar. It marks the exact location of the comments you just added in the movie. This process is shown in the following screenshot:

9. Use the same procedure to add more comments to the file.

Add as many comments as needed to the movie, just like a real reviewer would do.

10. When done, click on the **Save Comments** icon situated in the lower-right corner of the application.

When you click on the **Save Comments** icon, an XML file with your comments is saved in the `comments` folder under `Chapter09/encoderDemo_Review` as specified in Captivate when you initiated the shared review. Remember that this folder is supposed to be in a location that can be easily accessed by every reviewer.

Exporting comments

The reviewers that do not have access to the shared location shall receive the `.crev` file as an e-mail attachment. These reviewers must open the `.crev` file with the Captivate Reviewer Application installed on their system and add comments to the project as described in the *Using the Captivate Reviewer to create new comments* section.

Because they do not have access to the shared folder where the comments are saved, they must export their comments rather than save them.

To export the comments, use the Export Comments icon of the Captivate Reviewer application. The Export Comments icon is highlighted in the following screenshot:

This procedure generates an XML file that needs to be sent back to the author of the project. In the next section, you will return to Captivate and import those XML files in the project.

Collecting and addressing comments

When the reviewers have sent their comments back (on a shared drive, using a cloud-based service, by e-mail, or using Acrobat.com), you can move on to the third and last step of the reviewing workflow. In this step, you will import the comments into the main Captivate project and address the reviewers' feedback:

1. Return to Captivate and open the `encoderDemo_800.cptx` file under `Chapter10/commentFiles`.
2. Navigate to **Window** | **Comments** to open the **Comments** panel.

By default, the **Comments** panel appears at the bottom-right corner of the interface. At the very bottom of the **Comments** panel is a set of eight icons used to manage the comments. Two of these icons can be used to import comments into the project. They are as follows:

- The Import Comments icon (marked as **(1)** in the following screenshot) is used to manually import the comments into Captivate. These comments are stored in the XML files sent as e-mail attachments by the reviewers with no access to the comments' storage location.
- The Refresh icon (marked as **(2)** in the following screenshot) is used to import the comments of the reviewers that have access to the shared folder where the comments are stored.

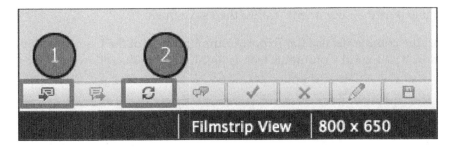

You will now import the three XML files situated in the commentFiles folder under Chapter10. For the sake of this example, you will pretend that three different reviewers with no access to the comments' storage location sent these three XML files as e-mail attachments.

3. Click on the Import Comments icon **(1)** situated at the bottom of the **Comments** panel.
4. Import the bill@mftc.com.xml file under Chapter10/commentFiles.
5. Repeat this operation with the other two XML files of the commentFiles folder under Chapter10.

After importing those three files, there should be 10 comments from three different reviewers in the project.

Addressing comments in Captivate

Take a look at the **Filmstrip** panel and note that there is an additional icon next to some of the slides. This icon is used to mark the slides with one or more associated comment(s). In the case of this project, slide 2 is the first slide that has one (or more) comment(s) associated. Perform the following steps to address these comment(s):

1. Use the **Filmstrip** panel to go to slide 2.
2. Take a look at the **Timeline** panel of slide 2.

There should be two gray dots somewhere on the **Timeline** panel. They mark the exact position of the comments associated with this slide.

3. Roll your mouse over the first gray dot. A yellow message displays the comment.
4. When you click on the gray dot, the corresponding comment is selected in the **Comments** panel.
5. Click on the **Accept** button situated at the bottom of the **Comments** panel.
6. If needed, add a message in the message box. When done, click on the **OK** button to validate your reply.
7. In the **Timeline** panel of slide 2, click on the second gray dot. This action selects the corresponding comment in the **Comments** panel.

This particular comment asks you to modify the look and feel of the **Continue** button.

8. Apply the **MFTC-ButtonContinue** style to the button and use the icons at the bottom of the **Comments** panel to accept the comment.
9. In the **Comments** panel, click on the second comment to select it.

When clicking on the second comment of the **Comments** panel, Captivate automatically takes you to the fifth slide of the project where that comment is located. In the **Timeline** panel of slide 5, note that there are three comments associated with that particular slide as indicated by the three dots present in the Timeline panel.

10. Move your mouse over each of the three dots of the **Timeline** panel to read the comments.

According to these comments, all three reviewers have a hard time reading the question!

11. Open the **Properties** panel and make sure it shows the properties of the slide.
12. At the top of the **Properties** panel, click on the **Reset Master Slide** button.

This action reapplies the associated Master Slide to this particular slide. After this operation, the question and the answers do not overlap anymore, but some extra buttons are displayed at the bottom of the slide.

13. In the **Options** section of the **Quiz Properties** panel, deselect the **Back** and the **Next** checkboxes to remove the corresponding buttons from the slide (it might be necessary to select then deselect the checkboxes for the buttons to be effectively removed).
14. Return to the **Comments** panel and accept all three comments of slide 5.

Address the remaining comments of the project. You can either **Accept**, **Reject**, or **Reply** to a comment.

The ability to reply to the comments makes it possible to start real conversations with the reviewers around various aspects of the project being reviewed. This capability is one of the main benefits of such a review process.

15. When done, click on the **Save Comments** icon to save your new comments and replies.

Earlier in this section, you discovered two ways of importing comments into the Captivate project. The method to use depends on whether the reviewers have access to the shared location where the comments are stored. The very same discussion is valid the other way around now that you have to make your new comments and replies available to the reviewers:

- The reviewers who have access to the comments on a shared drive will use the **Refresh** button of their Adobe Captivate Reviewer application to import the new comments and participate in the discussion.
- For the other reviewers, you have to use the **Export Comments** icon to create a new .xml file that has to be sent by e-mail. Those reviewers will have to manually import this updated XML file into their Adobe Captivate Reviewer application to see the comments and participate in the discussion.

Using Acrobat.com in the review process

Alternatively, Acrobat.com can be used as the storage location for the comments. This makes it much easier to distribute and refresh everyone's comments, but it requires that every individual involved in the review process has a free Acrobat.com account.

 For more information on using Acrobat.com in a review process, see the blog post from the official Adobe Captivate blog at http://blogs.adobe.com/captivate/2010/08/using-acrobat-com-for-adobe-captivate-project-reviews.html.

Ending a review

When the eLearning developer decides that the review has come to an end, there is one last operation to do in Captivate using the following steps:

1. At the top of the **Comments** panel, click on the **End Review** icon.
2. Confirm that you want to end the review and delete all the comments.

This short exercise concludes your overview of the commenting workflow in Captivate. Before moving on to the last chapter, let's make a quick listing of what has been covered in this chapter:

- Captivate offers a reviewing workflow that allows you to gather the feedback of individuals not involved in the development of the project.
- Such feedback is of vital importance in order to come up with truly professional and efficient eLearning content.
- Basically, Captivate offers two options to manage the workflow: Acrobat.com or your own internal server. When choosing Acrobat.com, it is required that each reviewer has a free Acrobat.com account.
- The reviewing workflow of Captivate is composed of three main steps. In the Distribute Step, you initiate the workflow and make the project available to the reviewers. The Comment Step is where the reviewers add their comments to the project, and the Collect Step is where you gather everyone's comments and address them in Captivate.
- Third-party cloud-based services (such as Dropbox or Microsoft SkyDrive) can be used to make the project available to the reviewers and to store their comments.

- To add their comments to the project, the reviewers use the free Adobe Captivate Reviewer AIR application. Thanks to this application, it is not necessary to own Captivate in order to participate in a Captivate Review.
- The `.crev` file is a special kind of `.swf` file used for commenting. It is the preferred file type of the Captivate Reviewer AIR application.
- In Captivate, it is possible to **Approve**, **Reject**, and **Reply** to comments.

Summary

Having several revision cycles with different reviewers will make your projects more professional and consistent. When reviewing an eLearning project, reviewers not only analyze the content and the grammar, but also test all interactive objects and features of the course.

For the success of such a review process, it is important to choose the reviewers wisely. Try to have a wide variety of reviewers, some of who are very specific about grammar, others who know the content, and some others who will test the functionalities. It's also a good idea to have someone who is from the target audience.

In this chapter, you have explored the three basic steps of the review workflow (Distribute, Comment, and Collect).

In the next chapter, you will discover some of the most powerful and advanced features of Captivate. Thanks to the **Variables** and the **Advanced Actions**, you will be able to add an even higher degree of interactivity and customization to your projects. You will also learn about the **Widgets** and the **Smart Learning Interactions** used to extend the capabilities of Captivate.

Captivate still has a few gems waiting to be uncovered in the next and final chapter of this book. See you in *Chapter 11, Variables, Advanced Actions, and Widgets*.

Meet the community

In this section, I want to introduce you to Michael Lund, also known as CpGuru. He is an eLearning designer and a Captivate expert located in Denmark. He is one of the key members of the worldwide Captivate community and specializes in the development of Captivate Widgets. Make sure you take a look at his blog and at his awesome collection of Widgets.

Michael Lund

Michael, also known as CpGuru, has been a part of the Adobe Captivate community since Version 2 and started experimenting early on with pushing Captivate to the limit and expanding its functionality with custom Flash components. He is an active participant on the Adobe Captivate forums and a community champion on http://captivate.adobe.com/.

He runs the website www.cpguru.com where he provides tips and tricks on common issues and problems with Adobe Captivate and tutorials on how to achieve more advanced things with Adobe Captivate.

The site also has a number of free and commercial Widgets for Adobe Captivate that can help you achieve more with your Adobe Captivate projects. Michael also provides freelance support and troubleshooting and develops custom Adobe Captivate Widgets if you need to achieve something special in your projects.

Contact details

- **Twitter**: @cpguru_com
- **E-mail**: support@cpguru.com
- **Website**: www.cpguru.com

11
Variables, Advanced Actions, and Widgets

In this chapter, you will take advantage of the Flash foundations of Captivate. The Flash technology includes a programming language named **ActionScript**. This language is one of the most powerful tools included in the Flash platform. It can be used to implement virtually anything Flash is capable of (and that means a lot of things indeed!). When publishing a Captivate project to Flash, a lot of ActionScript code is generated behind the scenes. It is the Flash Player that executes this ActionScript at runtime. If you decide to publish your projects to HTML5, Captivate generates a lot of JavaScript code instead. It is the browser that executes this JavaScript code at runtime.

Captivate exposes part of this technology to the eLearning developer. Now let's be honest, you won't actually be writing real ActionScript or JavaScript in Captivate (being an ActionScript or JavaScript developer is a full-time job that requires proper training and real programming skills), but you will be able to create some small scripts anyway, using buttons, drop-down lists, and dialog boxes. In Captivate, these small scripts are named **Advanced Actions**.

Thanks to Advanced Actions, you will be able to dramatically enhance the eLearning experience of the students. For example, you can:

- Dynamically generate text in Text Captions based on student input
- Show and hide objects in response to system or user events
- Trigger a sequence of actions instead of a single action when a Click Box or a Button is clicked, and so on

Most of the time, Advanced Actions need to store and read data in the memory of the computer, so you need a robust system to manage these pieces of data. This task is handled by **Variables**. Basically, a variable is a named space in the memory of the computer in which you can store pieces of data. When referencing the name of a variable, you can access the data it holds and use this data in Advanced Actions.

Individuals with advanced programming skills can also create **Widgets**. Widgets are used to extend the original toolset of Captivate. They are written in ActionScript and/or JavaScript. The tools used to develop Widgets include Adobe Flash Professional and Flash Builder. Smart Learning interactions are a special kind of Widget compatible with both the Flash and the HTML 5 output. They are used to add sophisticated interactions into your Captivate projects. Many premade Widgets and Smart Learning interactions are included in Captivate by default. You can also find more Widgets and Interactions on the web.

In this chapter, you will:

- Learn about and use System Variables
- Store student input in a User Variable
- Use variables to generate text dynamically
- Create Standard and Conditional Advanced Actions
- Insert and customize Widgets
- Insert and customize a Smart Learning interaction

Preparing your work

In this chapter, you will return to the Driving In Belgium project, but first, you will get Captivate ready by performing the following steps:

1. Open Captivate.
2. Make sure that the **Classic** workspace is applied and navigate to **Windows** | **Workspace** | **Reset 'Classic'** to reapply the default interface.
3. Open the `drivingInBe.cptx` file under the `Chapter11` folder situated in the exercises folder.

Great! Captivate is now ready to take you into the Variables adventure.

Working with Variables

Every single programming language in the world makes use of **Variables** to store and retrieve data to and from the memory of the computer. ActionScript and JavaScript are no exception! In Captivate, it is enough to know that a variable is a named space in the memory of the computer in which data can be read or written.

To make it short, a variable is made of two things:

- **A name**: This name must comply with strict naming rules and conventions. In ActionScript for instance, the name of a variable cannot contain any spaces or special characters (for example, @, é, è, ç, à, #, ?, /, and so on). When writing a script, the programmer uses the name of the variable to access the data it holds.
- **A value**: The value is the piece of data that the variable contains. This value can change (vary) during the execution of the script or each time the script is executed, hence the name *variable*.

For example, `v_firstName = "Damien"` defines a variable:

- `v_firstName`: This is the name of the variable
- `Damien`: This is the value of the variable

Next time the script is executed, you might have `v_firstName = "Bill"` or `v_firstName = "Linda"`, depending on the first name of the student who is taking the course.

In most programming languages, when a variable is created (the proper word is *Declared*), the programmer must specify the type of data that the variable will hold (data types include Text String, Integer, Date, Boolean, and so on), but Captivate has decided to keep things simple, so you won't have to worry about data types in your Captivate scripts.

System and user-defined Variables

In Captivate, there are two kinds of Variables available:

- **System Variables**: These Variables are automatically created by Captivate. You can use them in your scripts to retrieve information about the movie, or the system, or even to control various aspects of the movie.
- **User Variables**: These Variables are your own custom Variables that you create for your own specific use.

Exploring System Variables

Enough talking for now! Let's go back to Captivate to start your hands-on exploration of Variables by performing the following steps:

1. Return to the `drivingInBelgium.cptx` file under the `Chapter11` folder in Captivate.
2. Navigate to **Project** | **Variables** to open the **Variables** dialog box.
3. Open the **Type** drop-down list, and choose **System** (see **1** in the following screenshot):

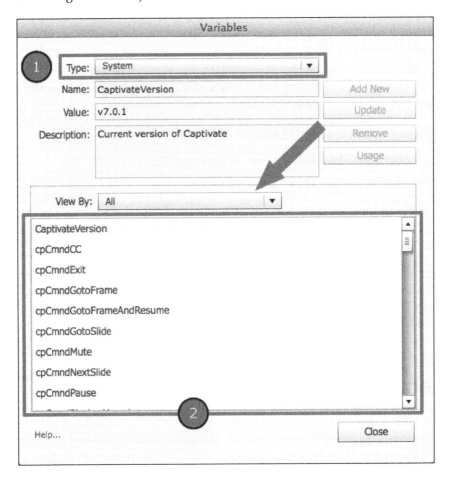

When selecting **System** in the **Type** dropdown, the list of the available System Variables appears in the main area (marked as **2** in the preceding screenshot) of the **Variables** dialog. Notice the **View By** dropdown (see the arrow in the preceding screenshot) that lets you filter the Variables by their category.

4. Open the **View By** dropdown, and take some time to examine the available options. When done, select the **Movie Information** category.

The Variables not pertaining to the **Movie Information** category are filtered out of the **Variables** dialog.

5. Select the **CaptivateVersion** variable.

The upper area of the **Variables** dialog now displays the information of the **CaptivateVersion** variable. The **CaptivateVersion** variable gives you access to the current version number of Captivate.

6. Take some time to review the other **System** Variables available.
7. When done, click on **Close** to close the **Variables** dialog.

Now that you have a better idea of the available System Variables, you will use some of them to dynamically generate the content of some Text Captions.

Generating text dynamically

You can include Variables in your Text Captions and in various other places where text is supported. To be more exact, you will use the names of the Variables to specify the piece of data you want to print on the screen. At runtime, the Flash Player (if the project is published in Flash) or the web browser (if the project is published in HTML5) will replace the name of the Variable with the current value of the variable.

In the next exercise, you will create a small note on the last slide of the project containing the version of Captivate used to create the movie using the following steps:

1. Return to the `drivinginBe.cptx` file under the `Chapter11` folder and use the **Filmstrip** panel to go to the last slide of the project (slide 27).
2. Insert a new Text Caption on the last slide. Type `This project is powered by Captivate` in the Text Caption.
3. Apply the **Transparent Caption** style to the Text Caption, and move it to the bottom-left corner of the slide.
4. In the **Timeline** panel, make the caption **Appear After 0 sec** and **Display for** the **Rest of Slide**.

So far, so good! This is just about inserting and formatting a new Text Caption. Now, what you want is to automatically insert the version number of Captivate at the end of the Text Caption.

5. Double-click on the new Text Caption, and place your cursor at the end of the text, after the word **Captivate**.
6. Add a space in the Text Caption after the word **Captivate**.

Variables, Advanced Actions, and Widgets

7. In the **Format** section of the **Properties** panel, click on the Insert Variable icon as shown in the following screenshot:

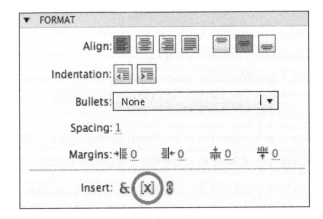

This action opens the **Insert Variable** dialog. You will use this dialog box to choose the variable, the value of which is to be appended to the Text Caption.

8. In the **Insert Variable** dialog, change **Variable Type** from **User** to **System** if necessary.
9. In the **View By** drop-down list, choose the **Movie Information** category.
10. Open the **Variables** dropdown, and choose the **CaptivateVersion** variable from the list.
11. Click on **OK** to add the variable to the end of the Text Caption.

Thanks to this sequence of actions, you have added the **CaptivateVersion** system variable to the end of the new Text Caption. Actually, it is the name of the variable that has been added to the Text Caption. The Text Caption now reads **This project is powered by Captivate $$CaptivateVersion$$**. At runtime, the $$CaptivateVersion$$ part of the sentence will be automatically replaced by the value of the CaptivateVersion variable.

You will now test the new Text Caption in the **Preview** pane.

12. Use the **Filmstrip** panel to return to slide 26.
13. Use the Preview icon to preview the movie **From This Slide**.
14. When the last slide appears in the **Preview** pane, pay close attention to the newly added Text Caption.
15. Close the **Preview** pane when done, and save the file.

Normally, the Text Caption should read something like **This project is powered by Captivate 7.0.0**!

This first experience with Variables teaches you what **Dynamic Text** is. It is a piece of text that is generated on the fly at runtime.

Extra credit – generating a Quiz Results slide for the Pretest

In this section, you will create a **Quiz Results** slide for the Pretest you added to the Encoder Demonstration project. To do it, you will use the `cpQuizInfoPretestScorePercentage` system variable. This system variable gives you access to the result of the Pretest expressed as a percentage.

The general steps of this exercise are the following:

- Open both the `encoderDemo_800.cptx` and `pretestFeedback.cptx` files under the `Chapter11` folder
- Copy the two slides of the `pretestFeedback.cptx` file, and paste them as slides 8 and 9 of the `encoderDemo_800.cptx` project
- On slides 8 and 9, replace the **XXX** part of the Text Captions with the **cpQuizInfoPretestScorePercentage** system variable
- Set the actions of the buttons of the two new slides to implement proper branching:
    - On slide 8, the *Skip* button jumps to the last slide of the project
    - On slide 8, the *Take it anyway* button jumps to slide 10
    - On slide 9, the *Let's go* button jumps to slide 10
- Preview the project several times to ensure that every Text Caption shows the right information and that every button takes the student to the right slide

At the end of this section, the branching associated with the Pretest is not completely finished just yet. You will address this issue using a Conditional Advanced Action in the *Using a Conditional Action to implement branching with the Pretest* section later in this chapter. Don't forget to save and close the files when done!

Using user-defined Variables

What is true with System Variables is also true with User Variables. In the next exercise, you will create a User Variable to store the first name of the student taking the course. To capture the value of that variable, you will ask the student to type his or her first name in a Text Entry Box that you will associate with the User Variable.

Creating a User Variable

First of all, you will create your own User Variable using the following steps:

1. Return to the `drivingInBe.cptx` file under the `Chapter11` folder.
2. Navigate to **Project** | **Variables** to open the **Variables** dialog box.
3. Make sure that **User** is selected in the **Type** dropdown.

Note that Captivate 7 has already generated two User Variables. These variables expose the name and the ID of the student when the course is hosted on an LMS.

4. Click on the **Add New** button to create a new variable.
5. Type `v_name` in the **Name** field.

This will be the name of your new variable. Remember that the name of a variable must comply with a strict set of rules and conventions, which is as follows:

- A variable name cannot contain any space
- A variable name cannot contain any special characters

In addition to these rules, some names are reserved by ActionScript and JavaScript and cannot be used as the names of our user-defined variables.

> See the Captivate Help page at `http://help.adobe.com/en_US/captivate/cp/using/WSDF6E7000-1121-4808-B61B-CCAB6A554AD3.html` for a complete list of ActionScript-reserved names.

6. Leave the **Value** field empty.
7. Optionally, add a meaningful **Description** to the new variable.
8. Click on **Save** to create the variable, and **Close** the **Variables** dialog.

Now that the variable exists, you will add a Text Entry Box on the second slide of the project to capture the value to be stored in it.

Capturing values with Text Entry Boxes

First of all, you must insert the new Text Entry Box on slide 2 of the *Driving In Belgium* project using the following steps:

1. Use the **Filmstrip** panel to go to slide 2 of the `drivingInBe.cptx` file under the `Chapter11` folder.
2. Navigate to **Insert** | **Standard Objects** | **Text Entry Box** or the corresponding icon in the vertical Objects toolbar to create a new Text Entry Box.

As covered in *Chapter 5, Adding Interactivity to the Project*, Captivate inserts up to five objects that make up the Text Entry Box system (three feedback Captions, one **Submit** button, and the Text Entry Box itself). In the case of this particular Text Entry Box, you do not need all these objects, so your first task is to disable the objects you do not need.

3. Make sure the Text Entry Box is the selected object (the **Text Entry Box** mention appears at the top of the **Properties** panel).
4. In the **Options** section of the **Properties** panel, deselect the **Success**, **Failure**, and **Hint** checkboxes if needed. The corresponding captions disappear from the slide.

Now comes the option that will mark the change between a regular Text Entry Box and a Text Entry Box used to capture data.

5. In the **General** section of the **Properties** panel, make sure the **Validate User Input** checkbox is *not* selected.

There are no right or wrong answers for this particular Text Entry Box, so you do not need to validate what the user types in the object against a list of correct entries. Consequently, the Correct Entries Box associated with the object is not displayed. Instead, you will associate this Text Entry Box with the custom v_name variable you created in the previous section.

6. In the **General** section of the **Properties** panel, open the **Variable** drop-down list.
7. Select the v_name variable from the list of available variables.

Your Text Entry Box is now associated with the v_name variable. It means that whatever the student types in the Text Entry Box at runtime will become the value of the v_name variable.

8. In the **Action** section of the **Properties** panel, change the **On Success** action to **Go to the next slide**.
9. Move and resize the **Text Entry Box** and the associated **Submit** button so it fits nicely on the stage.
10. Use the **Properties** panel to apply the **MFTC-buttonSubmit** style to the **Submit** button.
11. In the **Character** section of the **Properties** panel, adjust the formatting to your taste. The choices you make here apply to the text that the student will type in the box.
12. Move the Text Entry Box to the end of the **Timeline** panel.

The Text Entry Box is now ready to capture the first name of the student and to store that particular value in the v_name variable.

Using user-defined variables to dynamically generate text

The last step of this exercise is to use the v_name variable and its associated value to dynamically generate the content of a Text Caption using the following steps:

1. Use the **Filmstrip** panel to go to slide 3 of the drivingInBelgium.cptx file under the Chapter11 folder.
2. Double-click in the **Welcome** Text Caption, and place your cursor at the end of the word.
3. Use the Space bar to add a space after the word **Welcome**.
4. In the **Format** section of the **Properties** panel, click on the Insert Variable icon.
5. In the **Insert Variable** dialog, choose to insert v_name as the **User** variable.
6. Change the **Maximum length** value to 30 characters to accommodate longer first names.
7. When the **Insert Variable** dialog looks similar to the following screenshot, click on the **OK** button:

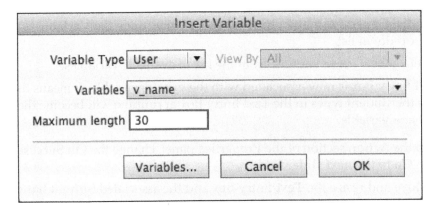

This action inserts the v_name variable in the new Text Caption and encloses it in double $ signs. The full text of the Caption now is **Welcome $$ v_name$$**. Remember that at runtime, the **$$v_name$$** part of the sentence will be automatically replaced by the first name of the student as typed in the Text Entry Box of the previous slide.

8. When done, save the file and use the Preview icon to preview the whole **Project**. On the second slide, type your first name in the Text Entry Box, and click on the **Submit** button. On slide 3, your name should be displayed in the Text Caption.

9. Close the **Preview** pane, and save the file when done.

This exercise concludes your first exploration of System and User Variables. Before moving on to creating more variables and using them in Advanced Actions, let's quickly summarize what you have learned so far:

- A variable is a named space in the memory of the computer. When referencing the *name* of a variable, you can access the *data* that the variable holds.
- There are two types of variables in Captivate. The System Variables are automatically created by Captivate. The User Variables are yours to create.
- It is possible to add Variables in Text Captions. This creates dynamic texts in the project.
- A dynamic text is a text that is generated on the fly at runtime. The Flash Player or the JavaScript engine of the browser simply retrieves the current value of a given variable to generate the content of a Text Caption.
- A Text Entry box can be associated to a User Variable. Whatever value typed by the student in the Text Entry Box at runtime becomes the value of the variable. Once captured and stored in a variable, that piece of data can be used in any script or in any Text Caption.

Working with Advanced Actions

An Advanced Action is a small script that is executed at runtime by the Flash Player or by the JavaScript engine of the web browser. These Advanced Actions can be used to manipulate the data contained in Variables or to manipulate the objects of Captivate.

In Captivate, there are three families of Advanced Actions:

- **Standard Actions**: These actions are simple procedures that are always executed the same way.
- **Conditional Actions**: These actions are a bit more complex. They can evaluate if a given condition is true or false and act accordingly. Consequently, they do not always perform the same set of actions each time they are executed.
- **Shared Actions**: These actions are new to Captivate 7. These actions can be reused throughout a given project or even shared across projects.

In the next exercise, you will create a couple of Standard Actions to get a sense of what they can achieve.

Using Standard Action

The Standard Action is the simplest form of Advanced Actions that can be created in Captivate. A Standard Action is simply a list of instructions that the Flash Player or the JavaScript engine of the browser executes one by one and in order at runtime.

Automatically turning on Closed Captions with Advanced Actions

Your first Advanced Action will manipulate one of the many System Variables of Captivate to automatically turn the Closed Captions on when the movie starts.

First, you will use the following steps to find out the name of the variable to manipulate:

1. Still in the `drivingInBe.cptx` file, navigate to **Projects | Variables** to open the **Variables** dialog.
2. Make sure the **Type** drop-down list is set to display the **System** Variables.
3. In the **View By** dropdown, choose the **Movie Control** category.
4. Select the first variable of the list named `cpCmndCC`.

The description says it all! This variable is a *Boolean* variable. It means that it can only have two values: 1 or 0. When the value of the variable is set to 1, the Closed Captions are turned on, but if it is set to 0, the Closed Captions do not appear. So basically, what you have to write is an Advanced Action that assigns the value 1 to the `cpCmndCC` System Variable.

5. Close the **Variables** dialog.
6. Navigate to **Project | Advanced Actions** to open the **Advanced Actions** dialog.
7. In the top-left corner of the dialog, type `displayCC` in the **Action Name** field.

Note that the name of the action must comply with the same strict rules as those complied by the name of the variables (no spaces and no special characters).

8. In the **Actions** area of the dialog, double-click on the first line of the table.

This adds a first step to the Advanced Action. In the first column, a yellow warning sign indicates that the action is invalid in its current state. In the second column is a drop-down menu containing a list of possible actions.

9. Open the **Select Action...** dropdown, and take some time to inspect the list of possible actions.
10. When done, choose the **Assign** action in the list.

11. Open the **Select Variable** dropdown, and take some time to inspect the available Variables.

The **Select Variable** drop-down list opens and proposes a list of Variables whose value can be changed. (For instance, the `CaptivateVersion` variable you used earlier is not listed, because you cannot change the value of this variable. It is a read-only variable).

12. At the very top of the list, select the `cpCmndCC` variable.
13. Open the second **Variable** drop-down list, and choose **Literal**.
14. Type 1 in the field that appears, and press *Enter*.

The whole sentence becomes `Assign cpCmndCC with 1`. In plain English, it translates to *Turn the Closed Captions on*. Notice that the yellow warning sign in front of the action changed into a green checkmark. This is an indication that Captivate understands the first instruction of your Advanced Action, which is very good news!

15. Double-click on the second line of the table to add a second step into the action.
16. In the **Select Action...** dropdown, choose the **Continue** action. This ensures that the project will continue playing normally after the Closed Captions have been turned on.

The warning sign at the beginning of the second line of the table immediately turns to a green checkmark, because the `Continue` action does not require any kind of extra parameter to work.

Make sure the **Advanced Actions** dialog looks like the following screenshot before continuing with this exercise:

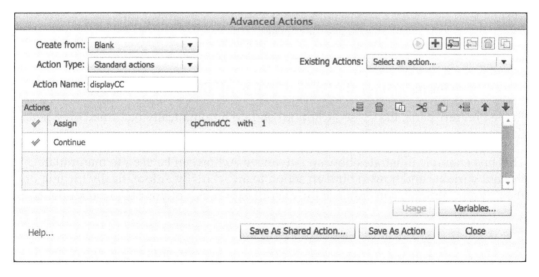

17. Click on the **Save As Action** button at the bottom of the dialog to save the Advanced Action.
18. Acknowledge the successful saving of the Advanced Action, and **Close** the **Advanced Action** dialog.

Your Advanced Action is now ready, but one last piece of the puzzle is still missing. You need to tell Captivate *when* you want your action to be executed. In other words, you need to bind the action to the **event** that will trigger the action.

In Captivate, there are lots of events you can bind actions to. Some of them are **system events** (for example, the start of a movie, the beginning of a slide, and so on), and some of them are **student-driven events** (typically, a click on a button). In this case, you will ask Captivate to execute the action when the playhead enters the second slide of the movie. This is an example of a system event.

19. Use the **Filmstrip** panel to go to slide number 2. Make sure that the **Properties** panel shows the properties of the slide.
20. In the **Action** section of the **Properties** panel, open the **On Enter** drop-down list.
21. Take some time to inspect the possible actions. When done, choose the **Execute Advanced Action** item.
22. Make sure that the **displayCC** action appears in the **Script** dropdown as shown in the following screenshot:

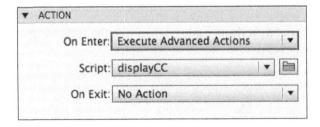

23. Save the file and use the Preview icon to preview the entire **Project**.

In the **Preview** pane, the Closed Captions should automatically be turned on when the preview reaches slide 2.

This first example illustrates how an Advanced Action can be used to manipulate a System Variable and how to bind an action to an event. By automatically turning on the Closed Captions, you enhance the overall experience of your beloved students.

Don't forget that other System Variables can be manipulated in the very same way, allowing you to do things such as muting or unmuting the sound, setting the audio volume, jumping to a slide, hiding or showing the Playback Controls, and more.

Extra credit – turning Closed Captions off

The last slide of the project with associated audio (and consequently with associated Closed Captions) is slide number 16, so it is safe to turn the Closed Captions off at the end of slide 16. In this section, you will build a second Advanced Action that turns the Closed Captions off by assigning the value 0 to the `cpCmndCC` System Variable. Captivate should execute this second Advanced Action when the student clicks on the **Continue** button of slide 16.

The main steps are as follows:

- Navigate to **Project | Advanced Actions** to open the Advanced Actions dialog.
- Create a second Advanced Action named `hideCC` that assigns the value 0 to the `cpCmndCC` System Variable and then goes to the next slide.
- Save the script as an Advanced Action.
- On slide 16, in the **Properties** panel of the **Continue** button, bind the `hideCC` Advanced Action to the **On Success** event.
- Save the file and preview the entire Project. In the **Preview** pane, make sure that Closed Captions are turned on at slide 2 and are turned off at the end of slide 16.

This second example illustrates how an Advanced Action can be bound to a student-driven event (the click on a button) instead of a system event.

Using Conditional Actions

The second kind of Advanced Action available is the Conditional Action. A Conditional Action is a bit more complex than a Standard Action in that it is able to evaluate if a condition is true or false and act accordingly.

To illustrate this capability, you will add a new slide in the project after slide 12. On that new slide, you will display a feedback message to the students that is specific to the way they answered the two preceding questions.

Variables, Advanced Actions, and Widgets

Remember that you ask the students two questions in the first part of the movie (the measurement unit they use to measure speed and if they drive on the right or on the left side of the road). If you aggregate the answers of those two questions, you can face three different situations:

Situation	Speed units	Side of road	Score	Meaning
1	Km/h	Right	2	Ok to drive in Belgium
2	MPH	Left	0	Change all your habits to drive in Belgium
3	MPH Km/h	Right Left	1	Change some driving habits to drive in Belgium

To keep track of the answers, you will assign a score to each question. A score of 1 if the student does the same thing as in Belgium and a score of 0 if the student's habits are different from the Belgian ways of driving.

Your Conditional Action will display a feedback message that depends on the score of the student.

Creating the necessary variables

You will begin this exercise by creating yet another user-defined variable using the following steps. You will use it to store the score of the student as he or she progresses through the project and answers the questions:

1. Return to the `drivingInBe.cptx` project under the `Chapter11` folder.
2. Navigate to **Project** | **Variables** to return to the **Variables** dialog.
3. Click on the **Add New** button to create a new variable.
4. In the **Name** field, type `v_num_studentScore`.

`v_num_studentScore` will be the name of the new variable. The `num_` prefix states that this variable will hold numeric data.

5. In the **Value** field, give this variable an initial value of `0`.

The action of giving an initial value to a variable is named **initialization**. In the programmer's jargon, what you are doing in the **Variables** dialog translates to "declare the `v_num_studentScore` variable and initialize it to `0`".

6. Optionally, type a description in the **Description** field.
7. Click on the **Save** button to save the new variable.

Make sure the **Variables** dialog looks like the following screenshot:

8. Click on the **Close** button to close the **Variables** dialog.
9. Don't forget to **Save** the file when done.

Thanks to this new variable, you now have a mechanism in place to track the student's score throughout the entire project.

About naming variables

You already know that the name of a variable must comply with strict naming rules (no space, no special characters, and so on). That being said, any name that complies with these rules is not necessarily right. When naming variables, it is important to stick to **conventions** in addition to complying with the rules, especially when working in a team. If no naming convention exists among the developers of a team, everyone ends up with his own naming rules and habits. In such a case, it is nearly impossible to keep track of the variables and to maintain the projects over time. In this exercise, you used the `num_` prefix to remember that this particular variable stores numerical values. This is one of the possible naming conventions, but any other convention will do! The bottom line is: complying with the technical rules is not enough!

Variables, Advanced Actions, and Widgets

Assigning a score to each possible answer

At the beginning of the project, each student has a score of zero. Technically, you have translated this situation by *initializing* your v_num_studentScore variable to 0. Now the score of each student will evolve depending on the answers given in the project.

There are two places where the score of the student can change:

- When entering slide 6, the score has to increase by one point. Slide 6 is the feedback slide when the student chooses the Km/h answer to the first question.
- When entering slide 11, the score has to be incremented by one again. Slide 11 is the feedback slide when the student answers "On the right side" to the second question.

In the programmer's jargon, increasing the value of a variable is called *incrementing* a variable *by* a value. In this case, you will increment the value of the v_num_studentScore variable by one when entering slide 6 and slide 11 using the following steps:

1. Use the **Filmstrip** panel to go to slide 6 of the project.
2. Make sure that the **Properties** panel shows the properties of the **Slide**.
3. In the **Action** section of the **Properties** panel, open the **On Enter** dropdown.
4. Select the **Increment** action in the list.
5. In the **Increment** drop-down menu, make sure that the v_num_studentScore variable is selected.
6. Type 1 In the **By** field.

The whole action should read: "Increment the v_num_studentScore variable by one when entering slide 6". This is shown in the following screenshot:

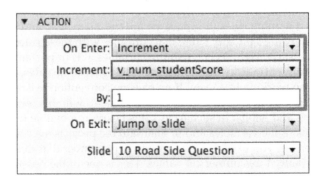

7. Repeat the same sequence of actions when entering slide 11 of the project.

Depending on the student's answers to the questions, the `v_num_studentScore` variable can now have three different values:

- If the student uses *Miles per Hour* and drives on the *left* side of the road, the `v_num_studentScore` variable is never incremented and stays at its initial value of 0

- If the students used *Kilometers per Hour* and drives on the *right* side of the road, the `v_num_studentScore` variable is incremented twice, so its final value is 2

- In the in-between situation, the `v_num_studentScore` variable is incremented only once, so its final value is 1

In the next step of the exercise, you will insert a new slide in the project and prepare three feedback messages to face the three situations described previously.

Giving names to objects

First of all, you will insert a new slide in the project and prepare three standard Text Captions on it using the following steps:

1. Use the **Filmstrip** panel to go to slide 12 of the `drivingInBe.cptx` file.
2. Open the `DIB_feedback.cptx` file under the `Chapter11` folder.
3. Copy the only slide of the `DIB_feedback.cptx` file, and paste it as *slide 13* of the `drivingInBe.cptx` file.

The slide you just copied contains three Text Captions that are situated on top of each other in the center of the slide. In the **Timeline** panel, these three Text Captions are set to appear on stage at the very same time and to stay visible for 6 seconds.

At runtime, only one of these Text Captions will be displayed to the student. The chosen Text Caption will depend on the student's score as described in the preceding table. To make this possible, all three Text Captions must be initially hidden from the stage. Advanced Action will be used to check the score of the student and turn the visibility of the right Text Caption on.

In the next exercise, you will prepare this system by assigning a name to each Text Caption and by turning their visibility off.

4. Go to slide 13, and use the **Timeline** panel to select the topmost Text Caption.

This first Text Caption will be shown when the `v_num_studentScore` variable has a value of 0.

Variables, Advanced Actions, and Widgets

5. Make sure the **Properties** panel shows the properties of the selected Text Caption.
6. At the top of the **Properties** panel, change the **Name** of the Text Caption to `TC_feedback0Points`.

This name will make it much easier for you to pinpoint this particular object while writing the Conditional Action in the next section. The second thing to do is to instruct Captivate to hide this Text Caption by default.

7. Still in the **Properties** panel of this Text Caption, deselect the **Visible in output** checkbox.

Note that this action does not hide the object from the stage in the editing environment of Captivate, but it does hide it from your students. To hide the object from the stage in Captivate, it is necessary to turn off the associated Eye icon in the **Timeline** panel.

8. In the **Timeline** panel, close the Eye icon associated with the **TC_feedback0Points** Text Caption.
9. Use the **Timeline** panel to select the middle Text Caption.
10. In the **Properties** panel, change the **Name** of that Text Caption to `TC_feedback1Point`, and deselect the **Visible in output** checkbox.
11. In the **Timeline** panel, close the Eye icon associated with the **TC_feedback1Point** Text Caption.
12. Select the last Text Caption. Change its name to `TC_feedback2Points`, and deselect its **Visible in Output** checkbox. Also hide it from the stage by closing the associated Eye icon in the **Timeline** panel.

In this exercise, you have changed the names of three Text Captions. The names you give to the objects must comply with the same naming rules as the Variables (no spaces and no special characters). Remember that observing the technical requirements is not enough! It is much better if you also comply with some kind of naming convention. In this exercise, the `TC_` prefix stands for *Text Caption*, the rest is the name of the object in camel case.

At the end of this exercise, the **Timeline** panel of slide 13 should look like the following screenshot:

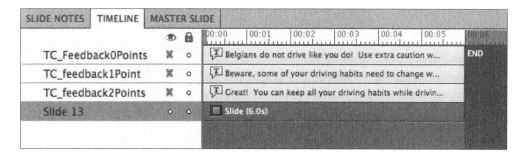

Let's do one last experiment before moving on to the next step.

13. Use the **Filmstrip** panel to go to slide 12.
14. Once on slide 12, use the Preview icon to preview the **Next 5 Slides**.
15. When the preview reaches slide 13, confirm that no Text Caption appears in the **Preview** pane.
16. When done, close the **Preview** pane, and save the file.

The stage is set! The feedback messages are ready, and you have a variable with three possible values to test against. The last piece of the puzzle is to create a Conditional Action that will evaluate the value of the v_num_studentScore variable and decide which of the three feedback messages of slide 13 must be revealed to the student.

Conditionally showing and hiding objects

In this section, you will create a Conditional Advanced Action, which will combine all the pieces of the puzzle together. When it is done, you will bind this action to the **On Enter** event of slide 13 using the following steps:

1. Still in the drivingInBe.cptx file, navigate to **Project | Advanced Actions** to open the **Advanced Actions** dialog.

2. In the top-left corner of the **Advanced Actions** dialog, open the **Action Type** dropdown, and select **Conditional Actions** from the list as shown in the following screenshot:

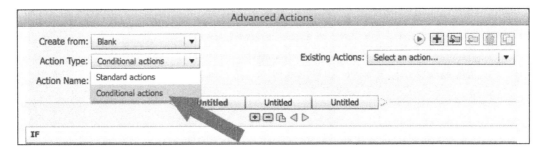

The **Advanced Actions** dialog is updated and shows the interface that you will use to create a Conditional Advanced Action.

3. Still in the top-left corner of the dialog box, type showScoreFeedback in the **Action Name** field.

Remember that the name of an action cannot contain any spaces or special characters.

It is now time to dig into the real stuff and to create the Conditional Advanced Action. You will start by coding the first-case scenario, when the v_num_studentScore variable has a value of 0.

4. At the top of the box, double-click on the blue **Untitled** button, and change the text to **Score 0**.

This step is optional and has no technical influence on how this action will be executed. By adding a title to a branch of a Conditional Action, you just make your job a little bit easier when debugging and maintaining this action in the future.

5. In the **If** part of the box, double-click on the first line of the table to add the first condition.
6. Open the **Variable** dropdown and select the **Variable** option from the list. Then, open the list again to select the v_num_studentScore variable.
7. Open the **Select comparison operator** dropdown, and choose the **is equal to** option from the list of available operators.
8. Open the last dropdown, and choose **Literal** from the list, and then type 0 in the field.

Chapter 11

The whole expression should now read `v_num_studentScore is equal to 0` and a green checkmark should appear in the first column of the table, as shown in the following screenshot:

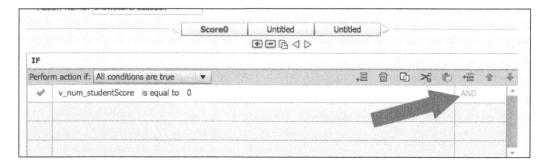

Notice the **AND** word at the end of the table row (see the arrow on the preceding screenshot). It tells you that you can add more conditions that will be united by an `AND` operator. In other words, every individual condition should be true for the entire condition to be true.

9. Open the **Perform actions if** dropdown, and choose the **Any of the conditions true** option from the list.

Note that the **AND** keyword switches to **OR**. In this case, the entire condition is true if any of the individual condition is true.

10. Open the **Perform actions if** dropdown again and choose the **Custom** option from the list.

In this situation, it is up to the developer to choose between **AND** and **OR** at the end of every single condition. This allows you to create very complex conditions. In this exercise, you only have a single condition, so the choice between **AND** and **OR** is not important.

11. Open the **Perform actions if** dropdown one last time, and choose the **All conditions are true** option to return to the default situation.
12. In the **Actions** area of the dialog, double-click on the first row of the table to add a first action.
13. Open the **Select Action** dropdown, and choose **Show** from the list of available actions.
14. Open the **Select Item** dropdown, and choose the **TC_feedback0Points** item from the list.
15. Add a **Continue** action in the second row of the **Actions** area.

[467]

Variables, Advanced Actions, and Widgets

Make sure there is a green checkmark in front of both actions before continuing. Notice how the name you added to the Text Caption in the previous section comes in handy now. Make sure the **Advanced Actions** dialog looks like the following screenshot before continuing:

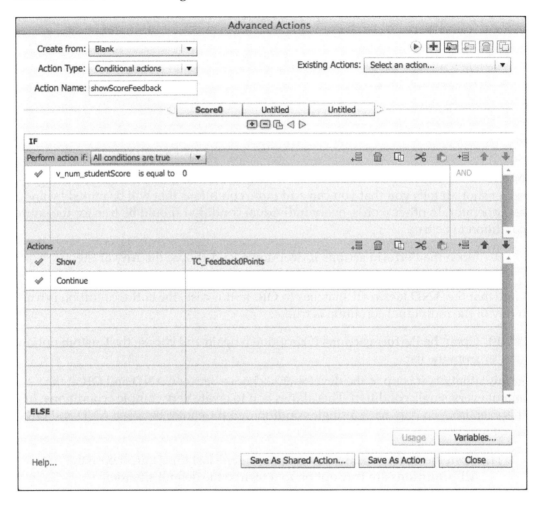

So far, you have coded the first of three scenarios. You will now add a second branch to this Conditional Advanced Action to cope with the second scenario.

16. At the top of the Conditional Action, double-click on the first **Untitled** button. Rename this button `Score 1`.

This opens a second `If... Else` table in the Advanced Actions dialog. In Captivate, such a table is called a **decision**. By default, a Conditional Advanced Action contains three decisions, hence the three buttons at the top of the interface.

17. In the **IF** part of the second decision, double-click on the first line of the table to add a first condition.
18. Open the first dropdown, and choose **Variable** from the list. Open the same dropdown again, and choose the `v_num_studentScore` variable from the list of available variables.
19. In the second drop-down list, choose the **Is equal to** operator.
20. Open the last dropdown, and choose **Literal** from the list, and then type `1` into the field that appears.

The condition should now read `v_num_studentScore is equal to 1` with a green checkmark in the first column. With the condition in place, you can now turn your attention to the bottom part of the dialog where you must set up the corresponding action.

21. Double-click on the first line of the **Actions** area.
22. Open the **Select action** dropdown, and choose the **Show** action from the list.
23. Open the **Select Item** dropdown, and choose the **TC_feedback1Point** item from the list. In the second row of the table, set the second action to **Continue**.

The Conditional Action now accommodates two of the three possible scenarios. To code the last scenario, you will simply add a third decision to the mix.

24. Double-click on the third (**Untitled**) decision, and rename it `Score 2`.
25. In the **IF** panel of the third decision, use the same techniques as discussed in the previous steps of this exercise to code the condition. It should read `v_num_studentScore is equal to 2`.

Variables, Advanced Actions, and Widgets

26. In the **Action** panel, set the first action to **Show TC_feedback2Points** and the second action to **Continue**.

27. Make sure the **Advanced Actions** panel looks like the following screenshot. Notice the three decisions at the top of the dialog:

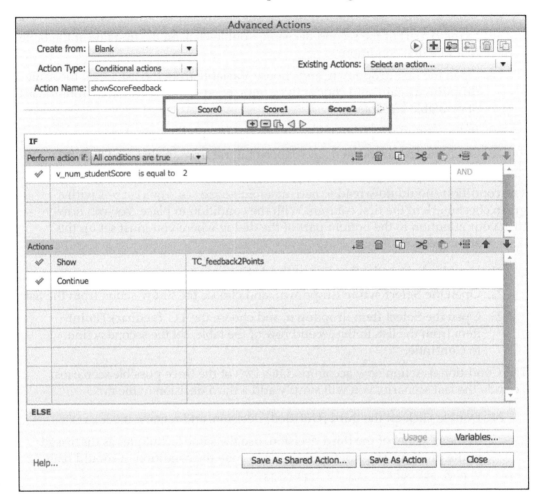

28. At the bottom of the **Advanced Actions** dialog, click on the **Save As Action** button.

29. Acknowledge the successful save of the script, and click on the **Close** button to close the **Advanced Actions** dialog.

The Conditional Advanced Action is now correctly coded, but there is one last step that is missing. Remember that an action must be triggered by an event. In this case, you want the action to run when entering slide 13.

30. Use the **Filmstrip** panel to go to slide 13.
31. In the **Properties** panel of slide 13, open the **On Enter** dropdown.
32. Choose **Execute Advanced Actions** from the drop-down list.
33. Choose the **showScoreFeedback** action in the **Script** dropdown.

You must also change the Action of the **Continue** button of slide 11.

34. Use the **Filmstrip** panel to go to slide 11, and select the **Continue** button.
35. In the **Action** section of the **Properties** panel, change the **Action** to **Jump to slide**. Choose to jump to **slide 13** in the **Slide** dropdown.

For the testing phase, you have to preview the entire project three times in order to test each of the three possible situations. Each time a test is run, you will answer differently to the question and see if the right feedback message shows up on slide 13.

36. Use the Preview icon to preview the entire project. When the preview reaches slide 13, pay close attention to the message that is displayed.
37. Repeat this operation two more times. Make sure that you answer differently to the first two questions each time.

Normally, all three tests should run fine. The message displayed on slide 13 depends on the value of the `v_num_studentScore` variable, which itself depends on the answers of the student.

Using a Conditional Action to implement branching with the Pretest

In this section, you will return to the Encoder Demonstration project to finalize the insertion of the Pretest using the following steps:

1. If needed, open the `encoderDemo_800.cptx` project under the `Chapter11` folder.

Variables, Advanced Actions, and Widgets

The Pretest is composed of three question slides. These question slides are slides 4, 5, and 6 of the project. Slide 7 is the automatically generated **Quiz Results** slide. Remember that because the Pretest questions are not actually part of the Quiz, the **Quiz Results** slide displays a score of 0 regardless of the outcome of the Pretest. That's why you decided to hide slide 7 and to replace it with slides 8 and 9. Earlier in this chapter, you used the cpQuizInfoPretestScorePercentage System Variable to display the student's score on these two slides.

In the next exercise, you will instruct Captivate to display slide 8 if the student has passed the Pretest and slide 9 if the student has failed the Pretest.

2. Use the **Filmstrip** panel to go to slide 6 of the project.

Slide 6 is the last question slide of the Pretest. Since slide 6 is a Question Slide, options are available in the **Quiz Properties** panel.

3. Open the **Quiz Properties** panel of slide 6. By default it is situated on the right-hand side of the screen next to the **Properties** and **Library** panels.
4. In the **Action** section of the **Quiz Properties** panel, click on the **Edit Pretest Action** button.

This opens the **Advanced Actions** dialog box. A Conditional Advanced Action named **CPPretestAction** automatically loads into the dialog box.

If the **CPPretest** action does not load automatically, just make sure that the **Action Type** drop-down menu is set to **Conditional Actions**, and choose **CPPretestAction** in the **Existing Actions** dropdown. This is shown in the following screenshot.

Captivate automatically generated **CPPretestAction** when you inserted the first Pretest Question Slide in the project. This action is automatically triggered at the end of the Pretest. Note that it uses the cpQuizInfoPretestScorePercentage System Variable and compares it to 50. By default, the action is set to **Go to Next Slide** as shown in the following screenshot:

Chapter 11

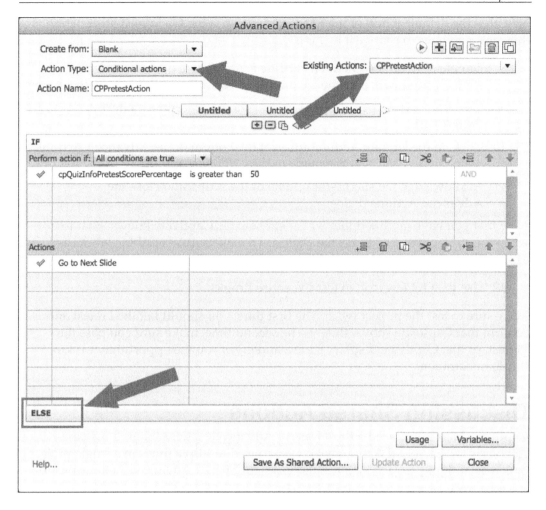

5. Double-click on the **Go to Next Slide** action. Then, open the **Select Action** dropdown, and choose the **Jump To slide** action.

6. Open the **Select Slide** dropdown, and choose to jump to slide **8 Pretest Success**.

The first part of the branching is finished! Captivate knows that it has to display slide 8 if the value of cpQuizInfoPretestScorePercentage is greater than or equal to 50, or, in other words, if the student has passed the Pretest. If the student receives a grade less than 50, he or she fails, and Captivate must jump to slide 9.

7. At the bottom of the **Advanced Actions** dialog, click on **ELSE** (see the red rectangle in the preceding screenshot).

Note that the default action of the **ELSE** clause also is the **Go to next slide** action. In this case, you have to change it to `Jump to slide 9`.

8. Double-click on the **Go to Next Slide** action. Then, open the **Select Action** dropdown, and choose the **Jump To slide** action from the list.
9. Open the **Select Slide** dropdown, and choose to jump to slide **9 Pretest Fail**.
10. Click on the **Update Action** button at the bottom of the **Advanced Actions** dialog to save the changes made to the **CPPretestAction**.
11. Acknowledge the successful update of the script, and close the **Advanced Actions** dialog.

Now that you have modified the `CPPretestAction`, Captivate knows what to do when the student passes or fails the Pretest. To make sure everything works as expected, it is necessary to preview the project.

12. Use the Preview icon to test the entire **Project**.

Make sure to test the project twice. The first time, you should fail the Pretest and confirm that Captivate shows slide 9. The second time, make sure you pass the Pretest, so that Captivate displays slide 8 and gives you the opportunity to skip the demonstration.

Discussing Shared Actions

Captivate 7 has introduced a third kind of Advanced Actions. Shared Advanced Actions is an Advanced Action that can be reused multiple times in a single project or across multiple projects. Typical use cases for Shared Advanced Actions include:

- Using Advanced Actions to turn the visibility of objects on and off. Thanks to Shared Advanced Actions, you could only create two actions, one for showing objects and a second one for hiding objects. Each time you use one of these two actions, you supply the name of the object to hide or show as a parameter of the Shared Action.
- Import the Shared Actions of another project into the current project and use them as templates to create new Advanced Actions.

Shared Advanced Actions is a very powerful new feature of Captivate 7. If you want to know more about it, feel free to consult the official Captivate **Help** page on Shared Actions at `http://helpx.adobe.com/captivate/using/shared-actions.html`. There are also lots of video tutorials on Advanced Actions on the Captivate YouTube channel. See, for example, the following video on how to create Shared Advanced Actions that can be reused across projects `http://www.youtube.com/watch?v=AWC0uPMpY5w`.

This concludes the discussion on Variables and Advanced Actions. Let's quickly summarize what has been covered:

- There are three kinds of Advanced Actions in Captivate: Standard Actions, Conditional Actions, and the all-new Shared Actions.
- A Standard Action is a simple list of instructions executed one by one and in order at runtime.
- A Conditional Action checks if a condition is met before executing an action.
- A Shared Action is an Advanced Action that can be reused multiple times in a project or even across multiple projects.
- When creating a Conditional Action, you can create as many decisions as needed. Each decision is executed one by one by Captivate regardless of the outcome of any preceding decision.
- The Advanced Actions can be used to manipulate System or user-defined Variables as well as to manipulate the objects of the project.
- It is possible to give a name to any objects added in Captivate. This makes it easier to manipulate these objects with Advanced Actions or to use them as parameters of a Shared Advanced Action.
- It is necessary to bind an action to an event in order to instruct Captivate about when an action should be executed.
- There are two kinds of events in Captivate: system events and student-driven events.
- System events are triggered automatically by the project. Examples of system events are the beginning or the end of a slide, the start of the project, and so on.
- Student-driven events are triggered by an action performed by the student. The typical student-driven event is a click on a button, but it can also be a click on a Click Box, the answer to a Question Slide, and so on.
- When inserting a Pretest in a project, Captivate automatically creates the `CPPretestAction` Conditional Advanced Action. This Advanced Action is automatically executed at the end of the Pretest. You can use it to implement branching based on the outcome of the Pretest.

Variables, Advanced Actions, and Widgets

Variables and Advanced Actions is one of the most advanced topics found in Captivate. You've only scratched the surface of this powerful feature in this book. With time and experience, you'll be able to take full advantage of this most powerful tool.

For more on Advanced Actions, make sure you subscribe to the Blog of Lieve Weymeis aka Lilybiri at `http://blog.lilybiri.com/`. She is a world-class specialist of Advanced Actions, and her blog is second to none when it comes to Variables, Advanced Actions, and other advanced tips and tricks on Captivate.

Understanding and using Widgets

According to the help files of Captivate:

> *Widgets are configurable SWF objects created in Flash. Widgets can help provide enhanced interactivity and rich content rapidly.*

To make it short, a Widget is an external `.swf` file that adds an extra feature to the already rich set of tools provided by Captivate. These Widgets are created outside of Captivate with tools such as Adobe Flash Professional or Adobe Flash Builder.

Creating Widgets

Creating Widgets is reserved to developers with a somewhat deep knowledge of Flash, ActionScript, and JavaScript, and it is way beyond the scope of this book. If you have such knowledge and want to start programming your own Captivate Widgets, make sure you subscribe to the blog of Tristan Ward at `http://www.infosemantics.com.au/widgetking/`. You can also read the following tutorials to get you started: `http://blogs.adobe.com/captivate/2009/06/captivate_widgets_tutorial_cre.html` and `http://blogs.adobe.com/captivate/2010/10/flex-based-widgets.html`.

Some Widgets are shipped with Captivate, but the ultimate goal of Widgets is to let anyone create and share their customized Widgets, so most Widgets can be downloaded from the Internet. Some can be downloaded for free, while others are for sale.

Locating Widgets

By default, Captivate looks for the Widgets at [Captivate Install Path]/Gallery/Widgets, but Widgets can be located anywhere on your hard disk.

1. Open Windows Explorer (Win) or the Finder (Mac), and browse to [Captivate Installation]/Gallery/Widgets.

You already used the Gallery folder earlier in the book (see *Chapter 3, Working with Standard Objects*, and *Chapter 6, Working with Audio*). As a reminder, the Gallery folder is a folder that contains various assets that you can use in your projects.

The Widgets folder of the Gallery folder contains lots of .swf files and some .wdgt files. These are the two file extensions used to define Captivate Widgets. Each of the files present in the Widgets folder under Gallery is a *Widget* that you can insert in your Captivate projects.

2. Return to Captivate, and navigate to **Window | Widget** to open the **Widgets** panel.

By default, the **Widgets** panel appears at the bottom-right corner of the screen, below the **Properties** panel.

3. Inspect the list of available Widgets, and compare it with the files situated in the Widgets folder under Gallery.

4. At the very bottom of the **Widgets** panel, click on the first icon named Change Path as shown in the following screenshot:

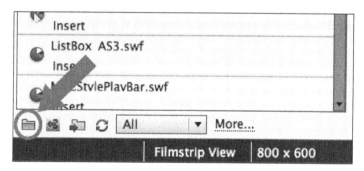

The window that opens lets you choose another folder on our hard disk from which Captivate retrieves the Widgets used to populate the **Widgets** panel. Thanks to this icon, you can store your Widgets anywhere on your computer.

5. Click on the **Cancel** button to close the dialog box without changing the path.

For the following exercises, you will use Widgets that are provided with Captivate, so make sure that the path is set to [Captivate Installation]/Gallery/Widgets.

You may be wondering what the difference is between a Widget and a standard .swf Animation as those you inserted in the project back in *Chapter 3, Working with Standard Objects*. Both are external .swf files, and both are situated in the gallery folder of Captivate. The answer is simple and is what makes Widgets truly awesome. Unlike the standard .swf animations, you can **customize** the widgets right within Captivate.

Modifying Widgets

For the ActionScript and JavaScript developers reading these pages, Adobe provides the source files of these Widgets at [Captivate Installation]/Gallery/Widgets/Source. Feel free to inspect the code and to customize these widgets at will. If you come up with a nice Widget, don't forget to make it available to the community!

Understanding the three types of Widgets

Captivate proposes three types of Widgets:

- **Static Widget**: This is an extra object that you can add to your slides. It has the same basic capabilities as any standard objects of Captivate. It is visible on the **Timeline** panel and can be synchronized with the rest of the objects of the slide.
- **Interactive Widget**: This is an extra interactive object. It has the same basic capabilities as the existing interactive objects of Captivate. That is, it can stop the playhead, interact with the student, and implement branching.
- **Question Widget**: This is an extra question type that you can include in your quizzes. It has the same basic capabilities as any regular Question Slide of Captivate, and its answers can be reported to an LMS using the same techniques as the ones used to report the answers of any other question types of Captivate.

Let's take a second look at the **Widget** panel and explore each type of widget.

1. If needed, return to the drivingInBe.cptx file under the Chapter11 folder.
2. Return to the **Widget** panel situated in the bottom-right area of the screen. If the **Widget** panel is not displayed, navigate to **Window** | **Widget** to make it visible.

At the bottom of the **Widget** panel, notice the **Filter Widgets** drop-down menu. By default, it should be set to **All**, indicating that no filter is active and that all the available Widgets are currently displayed.

3. Open the **Filter Widgets** drop-down menu.

4. Choose the **Static** option as shown in the following screenshot:

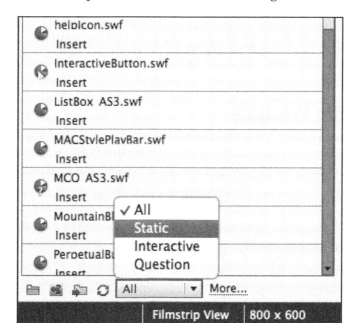

Interactive and Question widgets are filtered out of the list, so only Static Widgets are displayed.

5. Take some time to examine the list of available Static Widgets. Use the preview area at the top of the **Widget** panel to have an idea about how the selected widget looks.
6. At the bottom of the **Widget** panel, open the **Filter Widgets** drop-down menu again, and choose the **Interactive** option.

By default, Captivate 7 ships with three Interactive Widgets. All those widgets are extra button types that can be added to the projects. Remember that Interactive Widgets have the ability to stop the playhead and wait for the click of the student and that they implement branching. Feel free to experiment with these Interactive Widgets by replacing one of the buttons in your project with one of these Interactive Widgets.

7. At the bottom of the **Widget** panel, open the **Filter Widgets** drop-down menu again, and choose the **Question** option.

By default, Captivate 7 proposes only one Question Widget. This particular Question Widget is just another form of Multiple Choice question. It is there for demonstration purposes only and does not offer a significant added value in comparison to the standard Multiple Choice question you used in *Chapter 7, Working with Quizzes*.

8. At the bottom of the **Widget** panel, open the **Filter Widgets** drop-down menu again, and choose **All**.

The **Widget** panel now displays the complete list of all the available Widgets. In the next exercise, you will experiment with Widgets hands-on by inserting Static Widget in your project.

Using Static Widgets

Captivate proposes many objects that you can insert on the slides of your projects. You have studied most of these objects throughout this book, so they have no more secrets for you by now. Static Widgets simply are extra standard objects.

In the next exercise, you will insert a Static Widget in the *Driving in Belgium* project.

1. Return to the `drivingInBe.cptx` file under the `Chapter11` folder.
2. Use the **Filmstrip** panel to go to slide 14.

Slide 14 contains a lot of information that is very important for anyone who wants to drive a car in Belgium. Your students have reported that they have a hard time remembering all this information, so you decided to provide your students with a way to print this slide. This will be easily achieved thanks to one of the Static Widgets of Captivate.

3. Return to the **Widgets** panel, and locate the **print.swf** Widget.
4. Click on the associated **Insert** link to insert the Widget to the current slide.

The Print Widget is inserted on the slide, and the **Widget Properties** dialog pops up in the center of the screen.

The **Widget Properties** dialog lets you customize the Widget being inserted in various ways. Its actual content depends on the Widget being used. It is up to each Widget developer to develop this dialog box and to provide options to customize the Widget. Sometimes, there are very few customizations available, and sometimes, a lot more options are available. Refer to the documentation of each Widget for explanation, support, and troubleshooting. In this case, the options of the Print Widget are pretty much straightforward.

5. Take some time to examine the available options. Don't hesitate to change them at will.
6. When you are satisfied with the options, click on **OK** to validate your choices and insert the Widget.

7. Move the Widget to the upper-right corner of the slide as shown in the following screenshot:

8. With the Widget still selected, return to the **Properties** panel.

Most of the sections of the **Properties** panel are the same as those used for the other standard objects of Captivate. Only the first section of the **Properties** panel is specific to the Widget.

9. Click on the **Widget Properties** button situated in the **Animation** section of the **Properties** panel.

The **Widget Properties** button reopens the **Widget Properties** dialog where you can further customize the Widget. Remember that the content of this box is different for each Widget.

10. Click on **Cancel** to close the **Widget Properties** dialog without doing any changes.
11. Move the Print Widget to the end of the **Timeline** panel.
12. Save the file, and use the Preview icon to test the entire **Project**.

Don't forget to click on the **Print** button when on slide 14 of the preview.

>
> **Inserting a Widget for the whole project**
>
> You might want to insert a Widget, such as the Print Widget, on each and every slide of your project. If so, there is an easy way to do it! Just insert the Widget on the first slide of the project you want to see the Widget on and customize the Widget as previously discussed. When the Widget is ready, use the **Display For** drop-down menu situated in the **Timing** section of the **Properties** panel, and choose **Rest of Project**. The Widget now appears from where you inserted it till the end of the project. Note that this technique is valid for almost every object of Captivate.

Finding Widgets

In addition to the Widgets provided by Captivate, many Widgets can be found on the Internet. Some are for free, and some are for sale. In this section, we would like to introduce some reference sites where great Widgets can be found. This section is not intended to be a comprehensive list of all the greatest Captivate sites, but we feel these references are a good starting point to start your own research.

When you find a Widget that suits your needs, pay attention to the Captivate version for which the Widget is designed.

Adobe Captivate Exchange

The first reference is the Adobe website itself, and more specifically, a section of the site named **Adobe Exchange**. On Adobe Exchange, you'll find many plugins, Widgets, scripts, extensions, and so on, for various Adobe products including Captivate. Adobe Captivate Exchange can be accessed right from within the Captivate interface using the following steps:

1. Return to Captivate, and open the **Widgets** panel if necessary.
2. At the bottom of the **Widgets** panel, click on the second icon to access **Adobe Captivate Exchange**.

This action opens your default web browser and takes you to the Adobe Captivate Exchange website where lots of great assets can be found, including Widgets, sounds, images, and more.

Blogs and websites

There are lots of websites and blogs that discuss the Captivate Widgets. There are also lots of websites where widgets can be found. The following is a short list of what I consider the best online resources on Widgets.

- **Cpguru**: A great website for widgets is www.cpguru.com. Both free and commercial Widgets can be found on this site, and you can even request Michael Lund to develop a custom Widget just for you. Michael also maintains a great Captivate blog on this website.
- **CaptivateDev**: The www.captivatedev.com website is maintained by Jim Leichliter. He provides lots of free and commercial Widgets for Captivate. He also runs his own blog. You certainly want to bookmark this site while working with Captivate.
- **Infosemantic**: This is an Australian company that specializes in developing Widgets for Captivate. Their Widgets can be found on their website http://www.infosemantics.com.au/. The list of their free Captivate Widgets can be found at http://www.infosemantics.com.au/adobe-captivate-widgets/download-free-trial-widgets.

> Infosemantic also is the ultimate stop for those who want to develop Widgets for Captivate. Tristan Ward (aka the Widget King) has released an open source framework for developing Widgets, named the **Widget Factory**. If you feel like developing your own Widgets, you definitely want to take a look at it. More info can be found at https://code.google.com/p/widgetfactory/.

Working with Smart Learning interactions

Smart Learning interactions were introduced in June 2012 as a new feature of Captivate 6. **Smart Learning Interactions** are complex interactive objects with built-in behavior. Smart Learning interactions and Widgets have a lot in common. First, it is possible to download more interactions from the Internet. Second, Smart Learning Interactions can be customized in various ways using a workflow that is very similar to the one used to customize Widgets. The main thing that makes them different is that Smart Learning Interactions are entirely compatible with both Flash and HTML5, which is not the case with most Widgets.

Variables, Advanced Actions, and Widgets

Captivate 7 has added many interesting, new, and improved Smart Learning interactions. In the next sections, you will explore a few of these Smart Learning interactions.

Working with the Accordion interaction

In the next exercise, you will add one more slide to the *Driving In Belgium* project and insert the **Accordions Smart Interaction** into it using the following steps:

1. If needed, return to the `drivingInBe.cptx` file under the `Chapter11` folder.
2. Use the **Filmstrip** panel to go to the first slide of the project.
3. Navigate to **Insert** | **New Slide from** | **Blank** to insert a new slide based on the Blank Master Slide of the Theme.

The new slide is inserted as slide 2 of the project.

4. Add a *Button* to the slide. Use the **MFTC-ButtonContinue** style, and position it at the bottom-right corner of the slide. Make sure its action is **Go to the next slide**.

The stage is set! Your next task is to insert a Smart Learning Interaction on this new slide.

5. Navigate to **Insert** | **Interaction** to open the **Select Interaction** dialog.

The **Select Interaction** dialog shows a list of all the Interactions available in Captivate.

6. Take some time to inspect the available interactions. When done, select the **Accordion** interaction (the first one on the list), and click on **Insert** to insert it onto slide 2. This is shown in the following screenshot:

Chapter 11

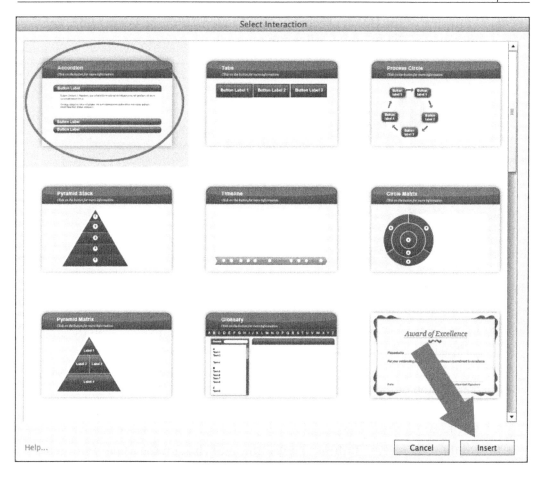

This action inserts the Accordion Smart Interaction onto slide 2 and opens the **Configure Interaction** dialog box. You will use it to customize both the content and the look and feel of the Accordion.

7. Use the left-hand side column of the **Configure Interaction** dialog to choose a Theme of your liking. (In the example of the `final` folder under the `Chapter11` folder, we chose Theme 7.)
8. Navigate to **Custom | Header** on the left-hand side column of the **Configure Interaction** dialog.

Variables, Advanced Actions, and Widgets

9. At the top of the **Header** section under **Custom**, turn the header **Off**. This operation is shown in the following screenshot:

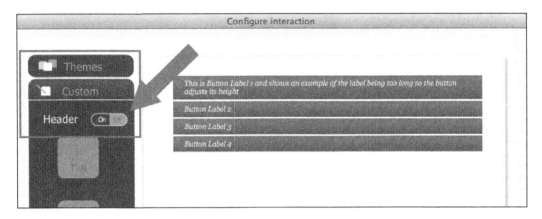

That's it for the look and feel of the interaction. You will now customize the content of the Accordion.

10. In the main area of the **Configure Widget** dialog, double-click on the first button of the Accordion, and change its **Title** to Description.
11. Double-click on the content area of the first Accordion, and type a short description of the project.
12. Change the **Button Label 2** title to Target Audience and the **Button Label 3** title to Length of the project.
13. Double-click on the **Button Label 4** title, and click on the *Minus* button to delete it from the Accordion.

You should now have three panels left in the Accordion Interaction as shown in the following screenshot:

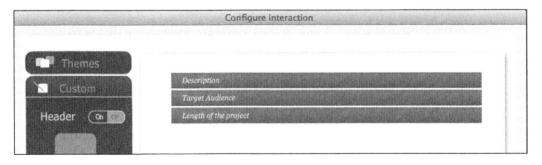

14. Add an appropriate descriptive text in each of the three panels.

15. Don't hesitate to explore the other options available and to further customize your Accordion interaction. When done, click on the **OK** button.
16. Move and resize the Accordion so that it integrates nicely into the slide.
17. If needed, click on the **Widget Properties** button situated in the **Animation** section of the **Properties** panel to reopen the **Configure Interaction** dialog and further customize your Accordion.
18. Use the Preview icon to preview the **Next 5 Slides** in order to test your newly inserted interaction.

Your exploration of the Accordion interaction is now finished. Note that the basic workflow is very similar to the one used for Widgets. Actually, the Smart Learning interactions are a special kind of Widget.

In the next section, you will experiment with one of the new Interactions of Captivate 7.

Working with the YouTube Interaction

The YouTube interaction allows you to insert YouTube videos in your Captivate projects. It is a powerful and easy way to add some great video into your eLearning content without the students having to go to an external link.

In this section, you will return to the Encoder simulation you created earlier to add the **YouTube Smart Learning Interaction** using the following steps:

1. Open the `encoderSim_800.cptx` project under the `Chapter11` folder.
2. Use the **Filmstrip** panel to go to slide 3 of the project.
3. Navigate to **Insert | New Slide From | Blank** to insert a new slide based on the Blank Master Slide of the Theme.
4. Add a **Continue** button to the slide. Use the **MFTC-buttonContinue** style, and position it at the bottom-right corner of the slide. Make sure its action is **Go to the next slide**.
5. Also add a Text Caption to the slide. Type `But first, a small reminder` into the Text Caption. Apply the **MFTC-Title** style to the Text Caption if needed. Move and resize the Text Caption so that it comfortably sits in the upper area of the slide.

The stage is set! You will now add the YouTube interaction in the middle area of the slide. You will use it to display a video file that has been created with Captivate, published as a `.mp4` video, and uploaded to YouTube!

6. Open your default web browser, and navigate to http://www.youtube.com/watch?v=fDExNBOmp1M.

7. Select and copy the URL of the web page as it appears in the address bar of your web browser as shown in the following screenshot:

8. Return to slide 4 of the encoderSim_800.cptx project under the Chapter11 folder.

9. Navigate to **Insert** | **Interactions** to open the **Select Interaction** dialog.

10. Scroll to the end of the list to select the YouTube interaction, and click on the **Insert** button.

This action inserts the YouTube interaction onto Slide 4 and opens the **Configure Interaction** dialog. The main thing to do is to paste the URL of the YouTube video in the **Video URL** field of the **Configure Interaction** dialog.

11. Paste the URL you copied from your web browser in the **Video URL** field of the **Configure Interaction** dialog.

12. Click on the **Test** button to check if the URL is valid.

Clicking on the **Test** button opens your default web browser. If the URL of the video has been correctly entered in the **Configure Interaction** dialog, you should see the YouTube video playing in fullscreen mode in your browser window.

13. Take some time to inspect the remaining properties of the **Configure Interaction** dialog, and adjust them to your liking.

14. When done, click on the **OK** button.

Chapter 11

15. Move and resize the YouTube interaction as needed. When done, slide 4 of the `encoderSim_800.cptx` file should look like the following screenshot:

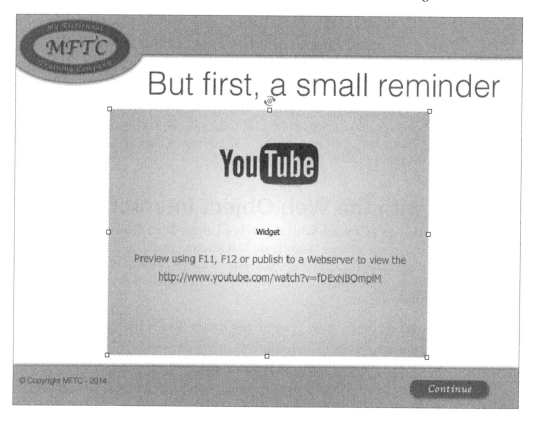

The last thing to do is to test this new interaction. Unfortunately, the YouTube interaction cannot be tested in the usual **Preview** pane of Captivate. To make it work you must see the project in an actual web browser and be connected to the Internet.

16. Click on the Preview icon, and choose to test your project **In a Web Browser**. Alternatively, you can use *F12* (Windows) or *cmd + F12* (Mac) shortcut.

 If the interaction does not work as expected in your web browser, make sure you are using the latest available version of both your browser and the Flash Player. If it still doesn't work, try using another browser for this test.

[489]

Variables, Advanced Actions, and Widgets

When the preview reaches slide 4, make sure the YouTube interaction works as expected. If everything works fine, you should see the YouTube video playing right in the middle of your Captivate slide!

> **Previewing in the web browser**
>
> When previewing the project in a web browser, you actually put yourself in a situation that is very close to the way your students will experience your eLearning content. To make it even more realistic, Captivate 7 embeds an actual web server. You can see the effect of this web server in the URL used to test your Captivate project. The IP address of the web server installed locally on your machine is http://127.0.0.1.

Working with the Web Object interaction

The last interaction you will work with in this book is the **Web Object interaction**. This interaction is a new feature of Captivate 7. It allows you to embed an actual web browser right within your eLearning project. The students can therefore consult a preselected web page right in the middle of their online course! Let's check it out by performing the following steps:

1. Return to the drivingInBe.cptx project under the Chapter11 folder.
2. Use the **Filmstrip** panel to go to slide 18 of the project.

Slide 18 should be the last slide before the Quiz. You will add an extra slide just after slide 18. This slide will display a webpage containing extra information about travelling to Belgium.

3. Navigate to **Insert** | **New Slide From** | **Blank** to insert a new slide based on the Blank Master Slide of the Theme.
4. Add a Button to the slide. Use the **MFTC-buttonContinue** style, and position it at the bottom-right corner of the slide. Make sure its action is **Go to the next slide**.

Now that the slide is ready, let's proceed with the insertion of the Web Object interaction in the middle of this slide.

5. Navigate to **Insert** | **Interactions** to open the **Select Interaction** dialog.
6. Scroll to the end of the list to select the Web Object interaction. When done, click on the **Insert** button.

The Web Object interaction is very similar to the YouTube interaction used in the previous section. All you need to do is to enter the URL of the web page you want to display and configure a few extra options.

7. Enter `http://wikitravel.org/en/Belgium` in the **Address** field.
8. Optionally, click on the Preview icon to see how the interaction will look once inserted on the slide.
9. Take some time to examine the other options of the **Configure Interaction** dialog and adjust them at will. Ensure the **Display In Slide** option is selected as shown in the following screenshot:

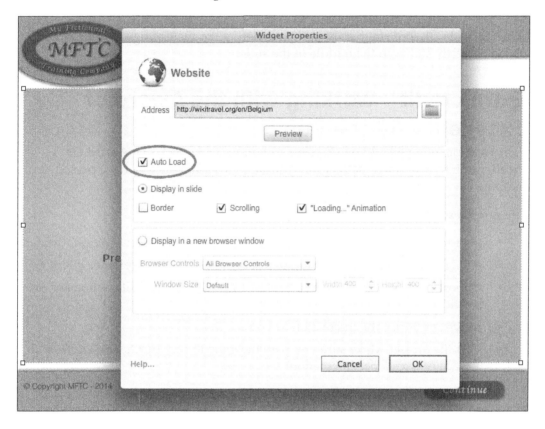

10. Click on the **OK** button to insert the Web Object interaction onto the slide with the selected options.
11. Move and resize the interaction as needed, and save the file.

As with the YouTube interaction, the project needs to be tested in an actual web browser to make the Web Object interaction function correctly.

12. Click on the Preview icon, and choose to test your project **In a Web Browser**. Alternatively, you can use the *F12* (Windows) or *cmd + F12* (Mac) shortcuts.

 If the Interaction does not work as expected in your web browser, make sure you are using the latest available version of both your browser and the Flash Player. If it still doesn't work, try using another browser for this test.

When on slide 19, confirm that the webpage defined in the **Configure Interaction** dialog correctly shows in the middle of the slide.

Extra credit – working with the Award of Excellence interaction

In this section, you will add one last interaction to the project. The **Award Of Excellence** interaction will deliver a certificate to the students that have passed the Quiz.

The general steps are as follows:

- Go to slide 28 of the `drivingInBe.cptx` project under the `Chapter11` folder.
- Navigate to **Insert | Interaction** to insert the **Award of Excellence** interaction.
- Choose one of the predefined Themes, and configure the interaction as you see fit. Most options should be self-explanatory.
- Move and resize the interaction as you see fit.
- Test the project. Make sure you pass the Quiz to see your newly inserted Award of Excellence interaction!

This exercise concludes your exploration of the Smart Learning interactions of Captivate. Keep in mind that you only have used a few interactions in this book. There are a lot more pedagogical and fun opportunities to discover in the other Smart Learning interactions available in Captivate. Don't hesitate to spend some time experimenting with these interactions. There are some great tutorials and videos available on the Internet if you want to have more examples and insights on these features.

> **More on Smart Learning interactions**
>
>
> The following link gets you started with the Smart Learning interactions on Adobe TV available at `http://tv.adobe.com/watch/new-in-adobe-captivate-6/smart-learning-interactions/`.
>
> One of the sneak peeks revealed just before the release of Captivate 6 is available at `http://blogs.adobe.com/captivate/2012/06/adobe-captivate-6-sneak-peek-4-interactions-actors.html`.
>
> A YouTube video on the new interactions of Captivate 7 is available at `http://www.youtube.com/watch?v=zqp4mkpqzT0`.

Summary

Thanks to Advanced Actions and Variables, you have been able to add a whole new level of interactivity to your projects. The good news is that you just briefly approached the tip of the iceberg in this book. The possibilities are virtually endless, and your imagination is the ultimate limit to what can be achieved.

To implement Advanced Actions and Variables, Captivate takes advantage of its Flash roots, and more specifically, of one of the greatest and most powerful tools of the Flash platform: a programming language named ActionScript. When publishing the project to HTML5, Captivate translates these variables and Advanced Actions to JavaScript instead.

Advanced Actions and Variables can be used to create dynamic Text Captions, to turn the visibility of objects on and off, to control the movie, to access information about the movie, and much, much more.

The Flash developers and ActionScript programmers can also contribute to Captivate by creating Widgets. Widgets are extra features that can be added to your Captivate projects. A small selection of Widgets are provided with the standard Captivate installation, but most Widgets can be downloaded from the Internet. If you are an ActionScript developer, don't hesitate to write your own widgets and make them available to the community. The best Widgets are yet to be written.

Finally, Smart Learning interactions work pretty much like the Widgets, but they are entirely compatible with both Flash and HTML5.

With the completion of this chapter comes the end of the book. I hope you have enjoyed reading these pages, and that you have acquired the knowledge you needed to create the next generation of eLearning content with Adobe Captivate.

As for me, I would like to thank you for reading my book. I'm already looking forward to your feedback or to meet you in person during an eLearning or Captivate event somewhere in the world.

Until then, happy Captivating!

Meet the Community

In this section, I would like to introduce you to Josh Cavalier. He had a secret identity in the Captivate community, which for years had been a well-guarded secret. But now, we all know that *Captain Captivate*, the superhero of the Captivate community, is in fact Josh Cavalier! In an exclusive interview, he announced the return of *Captain Captivate* in 2014!

> "I know that I have been laying low as Captain Captivate the last two years, but I have a feeling that the cape is going to be dusted off in 2014."

So watch out for the sign of *Captain Captivate* in 2014, and be ready for some serious Captivate fun!

Josh Cavalier

Josh "Captain Captivate" Cavalier, who founded Lodestone in 1999, is in charge of Lodestone's eLearning consulting services and leads the overall direction and operations of Lodestone's eLearning team. He brings 20 years of eLearning development experience, technology implementation, and vision to his clients. Prior to Lodestone, he was an art director for Handshaw, a leading eLearning services company. He was one of the key resources leading the effort for streamlining Handshaw's eLearning development process and transition from CD ROM delivery to the web. He holds a Bachelor's in Fine Arts from Rochester Institute of Technology.

Contact details

- **Secret identity website:** www.captaincaptivate.com
- **Official website:** www.lodestone.com
- **Twitter:** @joshcav

Index

Symbols

.cptx file format
  disadvantages 368
.mp4 video file
  Captivate project, publishing as 391, 392
  Captivate project, publishing to YouTube 392, 393
.swf file format
  advantages 368
  disadvantages 369

A

Accordions Smart interaction
  working with 484-487
Acrobat.com
  files, uploading to 335
  quiz, taking 335
  using, as alternate reporting method 332, 333
  using, in review process 441
Acrobat.com reporting
  Captivate project, configuring for 333, 334
ActionScript 445
Adobe Audition sound clips
  importing, to Captivate 252, 253
Adobe Captivate Exchange
  widgets, finding in 482
Adobe Captivate Quiz Results Analyzer
  using 336-339
Adobe Captivate Reviewer
  comments, exporting 437
  installing 434
  used, for comments creating 434-436

Adobe Captivate Reviewer AIR application 431
Adobe Flash Professional
  Captivate project, exporting to 424-426
  file extensions 117
Adobe Media Encoder window 47
Adobe Swatch Exchange (ASE) file 178
Advance Automatically feature 414
Advanced Actions
  about 445
  Conditional Actions 459-474
  Shared Actions 474-476
  Standard Action 456-459
  types 455
  working with 455
Advanced Audio Management window
  using 266, 267
Advanced Distributed Learning (ADL)
  URL 320
Advance Slide option 404
AICC
  about 320
  wikipedia, URL 320
Align toolbar
  about 124
  multiple objects, selecting 126, 127
  objects, aligning 128, 129
  objects, distributing 128, 129
AME
  about 42, 122
  preparing, to shoot 42, 43
  sound effects, adding to 240-243
audio
  adding, to objects 240-243
  adding, to slides 247

audio clips
  synchronizing 259
audio files
  importing, library used 253-255
automatic recording modes
  about 54, 55
  Assessment Simulation mode 56
  Custom mode 56
  Training Simulation mode 56
Auto Play option 347
Aviation Industry Computer-based Training Committee. *See* **AICC**
Award of Excellence interaction
  working with 492, 493

B

Background Audio dialog 244
background music
  adding, to project 243-246
Belgium sample application
  driving, experiencing in 30
  quiz, inserting 278, 279
Blank Master Slide
  adding, to project slides 171
Branching
  about 16, 189
  implementing, Conditional Action used 472-474
Branching panel 16
Button object 190, 192
Buttons
  branching with 197-199
  formatting 192-194
  Smart Shapes, using as 195-197
  types 193
  working with 191, 192
Button types
  Image Button 193
  Text Button 193
  Transparent Button 193

C

Calibrate Audio Input dialog 66
Callout type
  modifying, for Text Caption object 83
Camera Sounds click box 57

Caption type
  modifying, for Text Caption object 83
Captivate
  about 12, 73
  automatic recording modes 54-56
  basic concepts 13-16
  Button object 190-199
  Classic workspace, resetting to default appearance 74
  comments, addressing in 439, 440
  controlling, during shooting session 52-54
  custom workspace, creating 23-25
  custom workspace, deleting 25
  custom workspace, renaming 25
  external sound clip, importing to 252
  history 7, 8
  integrating, with PowerPoint 400-415
  interaction level reporting options 321-328
  objects, exploring 77
  obtaining, Captivate perpetual license used 8
  obtaining, Captivate subscription used 9
  obtaining, TCS used 9
  obtaining, ways 8, 9
  panels, adding 20, 21
  panels, moving around 22, 23
  panels, removing 20, 21
  panels, working 17-20
  Photoshop file, importing into 419-424
  project, configuring for Acrobat.com reporting 333, 334
  project-level reporting options 328-330
  recording settings, exploring 57
  reporting, enabling in 321
  review, ending 441
  Rollover objects 199-210
  Round Tripping, between PowerPoint 406-408
  sound clip, editing in 256-259
  Spell Checker, using 342-345
  touring 12
  used, for audio clip recording 247
  used, for content producing 10, 11
  Video Demo preferences 58
Captivate capture engine
  FMR mode 50-52
  inner working 48, 49

Captivate perpetual license
　used, for Captivate obtaining 8
Captivate production process
　about 10
　steps 10, 11
Captivate production process steps
　editing phase 11
　pre-production phase 10
　publishing phase 11
　slides, capturing 10
Captivate project
　application, downsizing during shoot 39
　creating, from PowerPoint
　　　presentation 402-406
　creating, from Template 185-187
　eLearning-enabled project,
　　　publishing 379-388
　exporting, to Adobe Flash
　　　Professional 424-426
　exporting, to XML 418, 419
　goal 43
　localizing, Microsoft Word used 415-418
　other publishing options 395
　other versions, shooting 58-60
　panning feature, using 40
　PowerPoint slide, inserting in 412-414
　publishing 368, 369
　publishing, as .mp4 video file 391, 392
　publishing, as standalone application 390
　publishing, to Flash 371-374
　publishing, to HTML5 375-379
　publishing, to Microsoft Word 393-395
　publishing, to PDF 388, 389
　publishing, to YouTube 392, 393
　rescaling 69, 70
　resizing, after initial shoot 39
　right resolution, choosing for 38-41
　Scalable HTML Content feature,
　　　using 40, 41
　second rushes, previewing 60, 61
　Video Demo project, publishing 369-371
Captivate speech agents
　installing 260
Captivate subscription
　used, for Captivate obtaining 9
Captivate Theme
　about 161
　elements 162-166
Captivate Theme elements
　Master Slides 162-165
　Skin 166
　Styles 165, 166
Captivate, used for audio clip recording
　narration, recording 250, 251
　sound system, setting up 248, 249
CaptivateVersion variable 449
Captivate workspace
　resetting 400
CC Project Settings dialog box 270
characters
　working with 102, 103
Check Spelling window 344
Click Boxes
　about 215
　Failure Caption 216
　Hint Caption 216
　sizing 216
　Success Caption 216
　working with 215-218
Closed Captions
　adding, to slides 267-269
　adding, to video file 271-273
　automatically turning on, Advanced
　　　Actions used 456-458
　turning off, Advanced Actions used 459
　viewing 270, 271
comments
　addressing 437, 438
　collecting 437, 438
　creating, Adobe Captivate Reviewer
　　　used 434-437
　exporting 437
Conditional Actions
　about 455
　names, giving to objects 463-465
　necessary variables, creating 460, 461
　objects, conditionally hiding 465-471
　objects, conditionally showing 465-471
　score, assigning 462, 463
　using 459, 460
　using, to implement branching 471-474
Configure Acrobat.com Settings dialog 333
Configure Interaction dialog 485
Constrain proportions checkbox 315

content
    modifying, of Text Caption object 78, 79
Convert PowerPoint Presentations
        dialog 413
Correct Answers dialog 326

D

decision 469
Drag and Drop Interaction
    used, for branching 228-231
    used, for navigation 228-231
    working with 223-231
Drag and Drop Interaction wizard
    using 224-226
Drag and Drop panel
    using 226, 228

E

effects
    adding, to images 138
    adding, to objects 136
    combining 137, 138
eLearning assets
    downloading 102
eLearning-enabled project
    MultiSco packager, working 382
    publishing 379-382
Embedded presentation 404
Encoder demonstration
    experiencing 26
    Preview icons 26, 27
Encoder demonstration finishing touches
    other project preferences 352, 353
    project accessibility 348-351
    project metadata 348-351
    project preferences, exporting 353, 354
    Skin Editor panel, working with 355-368
    spelling, checking 342-345
    Start and End preferences 346-348
Encoder simulation
    creating 29
    experiencing 28, 29
Equation Editor
    overview 122-124
Experience API (xAPI) 321
Export Comments icon 440

Export Settings dialog 44
external animations
    inserting, in project 117, 118

F

Fade In on First Slide option 347
Failure Caption option 56
files
    uploading, to Acrobat.com 335
Fill-In-The-Blank question
    working with 295, 296
Filmstrip panel 14, 281
Find and Replace feature
    using, in simulation 213-215
Flash
    Captivate project, publishing to 371-373
    Scalable HTML content option, using 374
FMR
    about 50-52
    limitations 52
Format drop-down list 44
format feature, Smart Shape
    objects, grouping 108
    Smart Guides, using 107, 108
format feature, Text Caption object
    Callout types, modifying 83
    Caption type, modifying 83
    characters, formatting 83
    objects, moving 82
    objects, resizing 82
    paragraphs, formatting 83
    Text Effects feature 84-88
Full Motion Recording. *See* FMR
full motion recording, Mouse object
    editing 96-98

G

General Import Format Technology. *See*
        GIFT file
GIFT file
    about 288
    Matching question, importing
        from 289, 290
    Question Slides, importing from 288, 289
    Short Answer question, importing
        from 291, 292

True/False question, importing from 293
Graded question
  about 280
  adding 280-283

H

Hear Keyboard Tap Sounds option 57
Hide Dock Icon checkbox 57
Hide System Tray Icon checkbox 57
Hide Task Icon checkbox 57
Highlight Box object
  about 88
  selecting 89
Hint Caption option 56
Hotspot question
  working with 297, 298
HTML5
  Captivate project, publishing to 375
  project, publishing in 377, 378
  Tracker panel, using 375-377

I

image editing tools
  using 101
image object
  about 98
  image editing tools, using 101
  image, inserting on slide 99
  picture slide, inserting 101
  slide, inserting from project 98
images
  effects, adding to 138
Import from Photoshop feature 419
initialization 460
Insert Questions dialog box 280
Insert Variable dialog 450
Interaction Data checkbox 329
Interaction ID
  about 321
  assigning, to quiz questions 322
Interaction ID field 321
interaction level reporting options
  Drag and Drop interaction, using as Question Slide 323-327
  Interaction IDs, assigning 322
  random Question Slides, reporting 322
  scorable object, using 327, 328
  setting up 321, 322
Interactive Widget 478

K

Keystrokes option 57

L

last slides
  adding, to Templates 184
Learning Management System. *See* **LMS**
Learning Record Store (LRS) 321
library items
  reusing 142, 143
Library panel 14
  library items, reusing 142, 143
  objects, importing from library 143, 144
  unused assets, deleting from 144, 145
  used, for audio files importing 253-255
  working with 140-142
Likert questions
  surveys, creating with 299, 300
Linked checkbox 404, 406
linked PowerPoint presentation
  updating 409-411
LMS
  about 38, 277, 319
  AICC 320
  scores, reporting to 319
  SCORM 320
  SCORM manifest file, creating 331, 332
  Tin Can 321
Loop Audio option 244

M

Macromedia Captivate 7
Main Master Slide
  customizing 168, 169
Maintain Aspect Ratio icon 44
Manifest dialog 332
Master Slide panel 314
Master Slides
  about 162
  adding, to Themes 169, 170
  applying, to project slides 171

blank slide, inserting in themed
    project 164, 165
  resetting 318
  changing 165
  customizing 167
  modifying 172-174
  Placeholders, adding to 170
  slides creation, based on 163, 164
Matching question
  importing, from GIFT file 289, 290
MathMagic 122
Merge With Background feature 416
MFTC-ButtonContinue style 413
MFTC-questionSubmit style 327
Microsoft Word
  Captivate project, publishing to 393-395
  used, for localizing Captivate
    project 415-418
mouse movements
  managing 92-94
Mouse object
  about 92
  formatting 94-96
  full motion recording, editing 96-98
  hiding, steps 211-213
  mouse movements 92-94
**Move New Windows Inside Recording
  Area option 57**
movie
  AME, preparing to shoot 42, 43
  rushes, previewing 48
  scenario, rehearsing 43, 44
  shooting 42, 45
movie, shooting
  actions, recording 47
  assistive devices, access enabling 45
  Captivate, preparing 45, 46
Multiple Choice question
  Partial Scoring, working with 285, 286
  properties, understanding 284, 285
  Question Slides, branching with 286, 287
  Question Slides, finalizing 287
  using 283, 284
multiple objects, Align
  selecting 126, 127

MultiSco packager
  SCORM package, creating from Video
    Demo project 382-385
  single course package, creating 385-388
  working with 382

O

object effects
  touches, finishing 139, 140
objects
  audio, adding to 240-243
  conditionally hiding 466-471
  conditionally showing 465-471
  effects, adding to 136
  hiding, Timeline panel used 130, 131
  importing, from library 143, 144
  locking, Timeline panel used 130, 131
  names, giving to 463-465
  selecting, Timeline panel used 129
  stacking order, modifying with Timeline
    panel 131
objects, Captivate
  Equation Editor 122-124
  external animations, inserting in
    project 117, 118
  Highlight Box 88-91
  image 98
  Mouse 92
  Smart Shapes 104, 105
  Text Animations 111, 112
  Text Caption 77
  video file, inserting 119-122
Object Style manager
  style, creating in 158-160
  style, exporting 155-157
  style, importing 157, 158
  working with 155
object timing
  setting, Timeline panel used 132, 133

P

panels
  adding 20, 21
  moving around 22, 23
  removing 20, 21
  working with 17-20

panning feature
  about 67
  automatic 67-69
  manual 67-69
  using 40
Pan & Zoom feature
  using, in Video Demo projects 233, 234
Partial Score checkbox 286
Partial Scoring
  working with 285
Password Protect Project option 347
PDF
  Captivate project, publishing to 388, 389
Penalty property 312
Photoshop file
  importing, into Captivate 419-422
  Round Trip editing workflow 422-424
picture slide
  inserting 101
Placeholders
  adding, to Master Slides 170
Placeholder Slides
  adding, to Templates 183, 184
Playback Controls page 367
Points property 313
PowerPoint
  Captivate, integrating with 400
  Captivate project, creating from 402-406
  existing presentation, converting to
      Captivate 401
  presentation, viewing in 401
  Round Tripping, between
      Captivate 406-408
PowerPoint slide
  inserting, in Captivate project 412-414
Preferences dialog 330
Preferences window 50, 55
Preloader checkbox 347
Preloader % option 347
Preset drop-down list 44
Pretest question 280
Pretest questions
  about 301
  creating 302, 303
preview
  launching 48

Preview icons
  From this Slide 27
  HTML5 Output in Web Browser 27
  In Web Browser 27
  Next 5 Slides 27
  Play Slide 27
  Project 27
Preview pane 301
Progress Indicator 284
project
  background music, adding to 243-246
  distributing 431-433
project accessibility
  discussing 348-351
Project End Options section
  Action drop-down list 348
  Fade Out on Last Slide 348
Project Expiry Date option 347
Project Info panel 14, 350
Project Information button 364
project-level reporting options
  setting up 328-330
project metadata
  discussing 348-351
Properties panel 14
  new styles, creating 150
  style, resetting 149, 150
  styles, applying 150
  styles, automatically applying 151-155
  styles, modifying 151
  used, for Styles managing 148, 149
  working with 75-77

Q

Question Pool
  about 309
  creating 309, 310
  questions, inserting in 311
  random Question Slides, inserting in
      main project 312-314
Question Pool Manager dialog 310
Question Pool panel 15, 311
Question Slides
  about 277
  adding 294, 295
  creating 279

Fill-In-The-Blank question, working
    with 295, 296
finalizing 287, 288
Hotspot question, working with 297, 298
importing, from GIFT file 288
inserting, in project 280-283
Likert questions surveys, creating 299-301
Matching question, working with 289, 290
Multiple Choice question, using 283-287
Sequence question, working with 298, 299
Short Answer question, working with 291
True/False question, working with 293
Question Slides elements
    quiz buttons, styling 316, 317
    styling 314-318
Question Widget 478
quiz
    inserting, after Driving in Belgium
        project 278, 279
    previewing 301
    taking, Acrobat.com used 335, 336
quiz buttons
    styling 316, 317
Quiz Fail Feedback slide 313
Quiz Passed Feedback slide 313
quiz preferences
    about 304, 305
    Default Labels preferences 308
    quiz passing score, setting 306-309
Quiz Properties panel 14, 312, 440
Quiz Results slide 281, 283
Quiz section 282
Quizzing Workspace 288

R

Random Question slide 312
Rating Scale option 300
Record button 47
Recording section 282
recording settings
    exploring 57
Report Answer checkbox 321
Rescale Project feature 39
Reset Master Slide button 440
resolution
    choosing, for Captivate project 38-41

Restore Defaults button 54
review
    ending 441, 442
review process
    Acrobat.com, using in 441
Review process
    about 430
    Collection Step 431
    Commenting Step 431
    Distribution Step 430
Review Quiz button 284, 301, 305
Rollover Area 200
Rollover Caption
    working with 200, 201
Rollover Image
    working with 204-206
Rollover objects
    about 199
    Rollover Captions, working 200, 201
    Rollover Image 204-206
    Rollover Slidelet 206-210
    Rollover Smart Shapes 201-204
Rollover Slidelet
    formatting 206-208
    inserting, in project 206-208
    objects, inserting in 208-210
    working with 206
Rollover Smart Shapes
    working with 201-204
Round Trip editing workflow
    about 422
    using 423, 424
Round Tripping 406
rushes
    about 37
    previewing 48

S

sample applications
    Belgium sample application 30, 31
    Encoder demonstration 26, 27
    Encoder simulation 28, 29
    Encoder Video Demo 31-33
    exploring 26
sample apps scenario
    discussing 34

Scalable HTML Content feature
  using 40, 41
scenario
  AME, resetting 44
  rehearsing 43, 44
SCO 331, 382, 388
scores
  reporting, to LMS 319
SCORM
  about 320
  wikipedia, URL 320
SCORM manifest file
  creating 331, 332
Select Interaction dialog 484
Send for Shared Review dialog 432
Sequence question
  working with 298, 299
Settings category 282
Sharable Content Object Reference Model. *See* SCORM
Shareable Content Object. *See* SCO
Shared Actions
  about 455, 474-476
  Closed Captions, automatically turning on 456-458
  Closed Captions, turning off 459
  using 456
shooting session
  Captivate, controlling during 52-54
Short Answer question
  importing, from GIFT file 291, 292
Show Mouse Location and Movement option 56
Show Progress checkbox 305
Show Runtime Border checkbox 207
Shuffle Answers checkbox 286
simulation
  Click Boxes, working 215-218
  creating 211
  finalizing 222, 223
  Find and Replace feature, using 213-215
  Mouse object, hiding 211-213
  Text Entry Boxes, working 219-222
Skin Editor floating pane 356
Skin Editor panel
  Borders, working 359-361
  Playback Controls bar, customizing 355-359

  same Skin, applying to other projects 366-368
  Table of Contents, adding 361-366
  working with 355
Skin elements
  Borders 355
  Playback Controls bar 355
  Table of Contents 355
slide
  image object, inserting on 99
Slide Notes panel
  about 21
  working with 260-262
slides
  audio, adding to 247
  Closed Captions, adding to 267-269
  creating, based on Master Slides 163, 164
  duplicating 113, 114
  remaining audio files importing, library used 253-255
Slide Views checkbox 329
Smart Guides
  about 100
  using 107, 108
Smart Learning interactions
  Accordion interaction 484-487
  Award of Excellence interaction 492, 493
  Web Object interaction 490-492
  working with 483
  YouTube interaction 487-490
Smart Shapes
  about 104
  formatting 106, 107
  styling, Swatches panel used 179, 180
  text, adding 109-111
  using, as Buttons 195-197
sound clip
  editing, in Captivate 256-259
sound effects
  adding, to Adobe Media Encoder 240-243
Soundflower system extension 63
speech
  text, converting to 262-264
Speech Management box 262
Speech Management window
  using 264, 265

Spell Checker
  used, for spelling checking 342-345
standalone application
  Captivate project, publishing as 390
Standard Actions 455
Start and End preference page 347
Start and End preferences
  exploring 346-348
Start Queue button 64
Static Widget 478
Static Widgets
  using 480, 481
strange red triangle 134
Styles
  adding, to Theme 174, 175
  applying automatically 151-153
  applying, to existing objects 150
  creating 150
  creating, in Object Style Manager 158-160
  exporting, Object Style manager used 155-157
  importing, Object Style manager used 157, 158
  managing, Properties panel used 148-155
  resetting 149, 150
  saving, in Themes 181
  working with 148
Survey question 280
surveys
  creating, with Likert questions 299-301
Swatches panel 18
  custom Swatches, importing to 178
  used, for Smart Shapes styling 180
  working with 176-178
System Audio
  shooting with 62, 64
System Audio checkbox 63
System Variables
  about 448, 449
  text, dynamically generating 449, 450

T

TCS
  about 9
  used, for Captivate obtaining 9

Technical Communication Suite. *See* **TCS**
Templates
  creating 182, 183
  last slides, adding 184
  new Captivate project, creating from 185-187
  Placeholder Slides, adding 183, 184
  saving 184, 185
  working with 181
text
  adding, inside Smart Shapes 109-111
  converting, to speech 262-264
  dynamically generating, user-defined variables used 454, 455
Text Animations
  about 111
  ending slide, inserting 116
  front slide, inserting 116
  slides, duplicating 113, 114
  Typing object, converting into 114, 115
Text Caption object
  about 77
  adding, in project 81
  content, modifying 78, 79
  creating 80, 81
  formatting 82
  moving 82
  resizing 82
Text Effects feature
  about 84
  experimenting with 84-88
Text Entry Boxes
  used, for values capturing 453
  working, in simulation 219-222
Text Entry Box object 56
Text-to-Speech engine
  about 239
  Captivate speech agents, installing 260
  Slide Notes panel, working with 260-262
  Speech Management window, using 264, 265
  text, converting to speech 262-264
  used, for narration generating 260
Theme Default Skin 357
themed project
  blank slides, inserting in 164, 165

Themes
    creating 167
    elements 162
    Master Slide, adding to 169, 170
    Master Slides, customizing 167-174
    Smart Shapes, styling with Swatches panel 179, 180
    Styles, adding to 174, 175
    Styles, saving in 181
    Swatches panel, working 176-178
    working with 161
Timeline panel 14, 15
    objects, hiding 130, 131
    objects, locking 130, 131
    objects timing, setting 132, 133
    timing, adjusting of slides 134, 135
    used, for modifying stacking order of objects 131
    used, for selecting objects 129
    working with 129
Tin Can
    about 321
    URL 321
TOC button 365
Transitions
    adding, in Video Demo projects 235, 236
True/False question
    importing, from GIFT file 293
Typing object
    converting, into Text Animation 114, 115

U

untiteld_assessment1.cptx 60
untiteld_custom.cptx 61
untiteld_training1.cptx 61
untitled_demo1.cptx 60
unused assets
    deleting, from Library panel 144, 145
user-defined Variables
    about 451
    creating 452
    used, for text dynamically generating 454, 455
    values, capturing with Text Entry Boxes 452, 453

V

Variable content
    name 447
    value 447
Variables
    about 446
    System Variables 447-449
    text, dynamically generating 449, 450
    user-defined Variables 447, 451-455
    working with 447
Video Demo mode
    experiencing 31-33
Video Demo preferences 58
Video Demo project
    publishing 369, 371
    SCORM package, creating from 382-385
Video Demo projects
    Animations in 233-236
    Captivate standard objects, supported in 232
    interactivity in 232
Video Demo projects Animations
    Pan & Zoom feature 233, 234
    Transitions 235, 236
Video Demo recording mode
    about 64
    working 65, 66
video file
    Closed Captions, adding to 271, 272
    inserting 119-122
v_num_studentScore variable 460, 462

W

Web Accessibility Initiative (WAI) 349
Web Object interaction
    working with 490-492
Widgets
    about 446
    finding 482
    finding, in Adobe Captivate Exchange 482
    finding, in blogs 483
    finding, in websites 483
    Interactive Widget 478
    locating 477, 478
    Question Widget 478
    Static Widget 478-481

types 478-480
using 476
workspace
creating, in Captivate 23-25
deleting 25
renaming 25
World Wide Web Consortium (W3C) 349

X

XML
Captivate project, exporting to 418, 419

Y

YouTube
Captivate project, publishing to 392, 393
YouTube Smart Learning interaction
working with 487-490

[PACKT PUBLISHING] Thank you for buying Mastering Adobe Captivate 7

About Packt Publishing

Packt, pronounced 'packed', published its first book "*Mastering phpMyAdmin for Effective MySQL Management*" in April 2004 and subsequently continued to specialize in publishing highly focused books on specific technologies and solutions.

Our books and publications share the experiences of your fellow IT professionals in adapting and customizing today's systems, applications, and frameworks. Our solution based books give you the knowledge and power to customize the software and technologies you're using to get the job done. Packt books are more specific and less general than the IT books you have seen in the past. Our unique business model allows us to bring you more focused information, giving you more of what you need to know, and less of what you don't.

Packt is a modern, yet unique publishing company, which focuses on producing quality, cutting-edge books for communities of developers, administrators, and newbies alike. For more information, please visit our website: www.packtpub.com.

Writing for Packt

We welcome all inquiries from people who are interested in authoring. Book proposals should be sent to author@packtpub.com. If your book idea is still at an early stage and you would like to discuss it first before writing a formal book proposal, contact us; one of our commissioning editors will get in touch with you.

We're not just looking for published authors; if you have strong technical skills but no writing experience, our experienced editors can help you develop a writing career, or simply get some additional reward for your expertise.

Adobe Captivate 7 for Mobile Learning

ISBN: 978-1-84969-955-6   Paperback: 136 pages

Create mobile-friendly and interactive m-learning content with Adobe Captivate 7

1. Explore the various ways to bring your eLearning content to mobile platforms.
2. Create a high definition screencast and upload it to YouTube.
3. Create mobile-friendly and interactive software demonstrations and SCORM-compliant quizzes.

Mastering Adobe Captivate 6

ISBN: 978-1-84969-244-1   Paperback: 476 pages

Create professional SCORM-compliant eLearning content with Adobe Captivate

1. Step by step tutorial to build three projects including a demonstration, a simulation and a random SCORM-compliant quiz featuring all possible question slides.
2. Enhance your projects by adding interactivity, animations, sound and more.
3. Publish your project in a wide variety of formats enabling virtually any desktop and mobile devices to play your e-learning content.

Please check www.PacktPub.com for information on our titles

Mastering Adobe Premiere Pro CS6 Hotshot

ISBN: 978-1-84969-478-0   Paperback: 284 pages

Take your video editing skills to new and exciting levels with eight fantastic projects

1. Discover new workflows and the exciting new features of Premiere Pro CS6.
2. Take your video editing skills to exciting new levels with clear, concise instructions (and supplied footage).
3. Explore powerful time-saving features that other users don't even know about!

Learning Adobe Muse

ISBN: 978-1-84969-314-1   Paperback: 268 pages

Create beautiful websites without writing any code

1. A step-by-step guide to using Adobe's latest design tool to build websites.
2. A thorough coverage of all the features introduced in Adobe Muse.
3. Design tips and advice for new designers.

Please check www.PacktPub.com for information on our titles

CPSIA information can be obtained at www.ICGtesting.com
Printed in the USA
LVOW03s1403190314

378088LV00008B/64/P

Mastering Adobe Premiere Pro CS6 Hotshot

ISBN: 978-1-84969-478-0   Paperback: 284 pages

Take your video editing skills to new and exciting levels with eight fantastic projects

1. Discover new workflows and the exciting new features of Premiere Pro CS6.
2. Take your video editing skills to exciting new levels with clear, concise instructions (and supplied footage).
3. Explore powerful time-saving features that other users don't even know about!

Learning Adobe Muse

ISBN: 978-1-84969-314-1   Paperback: 268 pages

Create beautiful websites without writing any code

1. A step-by-step guide to using Adobe's latest design tool to build websites.
2. A thorough coverage of all the features introduced in Adobe Muse.
3. Design tips and advice for new designers.

Please check **www.PacktPub.com** for information on our titles

CPSIA information can be obtained at www.ICGtesting.com
Printed in the USA
LVOW03s1403190314

378088LV00008B/64/P